Lecture Notes of the Institute
for Computer Sciences, Social Informatics
and Telecommunications Engineering 119

Karl Jonas   Idris A. Rai
Maurice Tchuente (Eds.)

e-Infrastructure and e-Services for Developing Countries

4th International ICST Conference,
AFRICOMM 2012
Yaounde, Cameroon, November 12-14, 2012
Revised Selected Papers

 Springer

Volume Editors

Karl Jonas
Fraunhofer FOKUS RESCON, Schloss Birlinghoven
Sankt Augustin, Germany
E-mail: karl.jonas@fokus.fraunhofer.de

Idris A. Rai
State University of Zanzibar, Tanzania
E-mail: idris.rai@gmail.com

Maurice Tchuente
University Yaoundé 1, Lirima, Cameroon
E-mail: maurice.tchuente@ens-lyon.fr

ISSN 1867-8211　　　　　　　　　e-ISSN 1867-822X
ISBN 978-3-642-41177-9　　　　　　e-ISBN 978-3-642-41178-6
DOI 10.1007/978-3-642-41178-6
Springer Heidelberg New York Dordrecht London

CR Subject Classification (1998): K.4, C.2, H.4, K.6, J.3

Typesetting: Camera-ready by author, data conversion by Scientific Publishing Services, Chennai, India

Printed on acid-free paper

Springer is part of Springer Science+Business Media (www.springer.com)

Preface

Africa is a continent of diversity that is facing dramatic changes in its social, political, and economic environments. Its population is reaching one billion, and in particular young Africans demand their share of social inclusion, educational opportunities, and prosperity.

Information and communication infrastructures provide the basis for access to knowledge worldwide, blurring social and economic differences and opening opportunities that never existed before. E-services enable or enhance health-care, agro-business, higher education, and social participation.

Its history, its geography, its (low) population density, and its culture make Africa different from regions in the world where ICT provides ubiquitous access. Technologies as well as services need to be adapted to local challenges. An example are the submarine cables that are becoming available provide huge capacities at the landing spots but now need to be connected to the inland population. There is no time to waste, because young Africans will not accept the digital divide. The Internet must come to every household, or the young population will leave their home environment in search of a better future.

The challenge is to reduce operational and capital cost to provide affordable connectivity to all. Services must be adapted to local needs, and business concepts must meet local requirements. New ideas must be tested and prove their superiority, they need to be evaluated, discussed, and challenged.

This is where the AFRICOMM Conference comes in. For several years now it has provided an open forum where researchers and politicians can discuss new ideas and new challenges. While some of us see the M-services as the logical next step in ICT evolution (that takes place in Africa first), others see them as an intermediate step based on the fact that low-bandwidth services are required because low-bandwidth networks need to be used. Should applications adapt to frequent network failures, or should networks be improved and become more reliable? Probably both, and small steps toward the all-inclusive ICT future were made at this year's AFRICOMM.

Energy-efficiency has been a challenge in Africa for many years and is now becoming a hype in Europe as well. And, finally, is the (ICT) situation for rural communities in Europe, the USA, or Australia so much different from the situation in rural Africa? While Europeans took advantage of the fact that a monopoly of operators has installed copper networks all over the countries, these networks do not meet the requirements of high bandwidth for all. New ideas are required not only for Africa; perhaps the technological future starts in Africa.

The African continent is, more than ever, in need of cutting-edge and relevant e-infrastructures, e-services, and enabling policies. AFRICOMM was established in 2009 in Mozambique and continued in 2010 in Cape Town and 2011 in

Zanzibar as a series of annual conferences. Its contributions have been published in Springer's *Lecture Notes of the ICST.*

This book contains the proceedings of AFRICOMM 2012, which was held in Cameroon. It includes high-quality research mainly from Africa, but also from Germany, France, Luxembourg, Belgium, Sweden, Australia, and Canada.

November 2012   Karl Jonas

Organization

General Chair

Karl Jonas   Fraunhofer FOKUS, Germany

Technical Program Committee Chair

Idris A. Rai   State University of Zanzibar, Tanzania

Local Chair

Maurice Tchuente   University Yaoundé 1, LIRIMA, Cameroon

Publication Chair

Edward Mutafungwa   Aalto University, Finland

Publicity Chair

Marina Grigorian   Fraunhofer FOKUS, Germany

Workshops and Demos

Dirk Elias   Fraunhofer AICOS, Portugal

Posters and Panels Chair

Hans Schotten   University of Kaiserslautern, Germany

Student Affairs

Thomas Djotio   University Yaoundé 1, LIRIMA, Cameroon

Industrial Participation

Adolfo Villafiorita   Fondazione Bruno Kessler, Italy
                               Darelle Van Greunen, NMMU, South Africa

Conference Coordinator

Ruzanna Najaryan   European Alliance for Innovation, Italy

Table of Contents

e-Services

e-Society

e-Health

e-Security

Student Papers

Towards an Africanised Expression of ICT
(Keynote Speech)

Worksgroup, Macha, Zambia
Nelson Mandela Metropolitan University, Port Elizabeth, South Africa
`gertjan.vanstam@worksgroup.org`

Abstract. This is the text of the keynote address at the Africomm Conference, 12 October 2012, in Yaounde, Cameroon. The keynote postulates that 'ICT challenges in rural Africa and the impact of social aspects are much constrained by a science unaligned with the realities of sub Sahara Africa'. This address explains the mismatch and misalignment of social aspects and priorities and scientific practice in sub-Sahara academia, with specific contributions towards an Africanised expression of ICT. It expands its effects and affects, proposes an overview of antonyms between Western and African science, and provides some directions that can result in adaptation and alignment of ICT to the African reality.

1   Introduction

In the last four weeks, I have had the opportunity to give several addresses on the issue of 'technology and social challenges', with the focus on ICT. Two of these addresses took place in the USA. Their titles were:

- "Observations from rural Africa: An engineer involved in ICTs and critical ethnography in Macha, Zambia", at the first tier University of California, Santa Barbara [1], and
- "Is Technology the Solution to the Worlds Major Social Challenges?" at the Global Humanitarian Technology Conference (GHTC 2012) in Seattle [2].

Both these addresses can be found online.

Today, I am grateful to be able to stand before you, invited to speak on the subject of "ICT challenges in rural Africa and the impact of Social Aspects", and to do so in the heart of the African continent, here in Yaounde, Cameroon.

Before you stands a Caucasian man, who is about to start to talk about Africa. That is a suspicious picture. Whether one picks up a book on Africa, or looks at a video about 'the African reality', it is often a white, male guy telling us what the African world looks like. The Heads of State and Government of the African Union meeting in Khartoum in 2006 drafted the "Charter for African Cultural Renaissance" [3]. It refers to cultural domination during the slave trade and the colonial era and provides guidance on how to edify systems to embody the African and universal values. I just hope that my countenance, which might implicitly link me with our tainted past, does not condition us to Western scientific approaches on issues in Africa. I recognize that such an approach is often detached from the realities on the ground. I agree with the African scholar Adebajo, that Western analysis mostly lacks a proper grasp of the important local, national and regional intricacies of the cases with which they deal [4]. This results in a flawed and sometimes superficial analysis, in which Africa is an exotic backdrop, to draw theoretical generalizations invented in Western laboratories.

As eluded to in my keynote at the Global Humanitarian Technology Conference last month, much of the work in Africa is Western-centric and self-referential. I trust this conference, devoted to the advancement of innovation in the field of ICT in Africa, desires to combine African insights with Western ones, because a combination of both perspectives will enrich analysis, and, I hope, will aid its acceptance.

My perspective is harvested from half an adult life spent living in rural Africa. In 1987, I stayed in Swaziland, and together with my family, 2000-2003 in rural Zimbabwe; then from 2003 till this moment in time, in rural Zambia. I have also travelled much through sub-Saharan Africa, meeting with traditional leaders and rural communities in many places and countries. Since 2010, I have been working full time on research and development, mostly working out and publishing my findings of the last 12 yeasrs from a critical ethnographic perspective.

The conference organizers have requested me to comment on the issues of ICT challenges in rural Africa and the impact of Social Aspects", a hugely complex and often contentious subject. However, what would life be without appreciation of the enormous challenges that we face as humans and humanity? Thus I gladly take the baton, and run with it.

2   Building Up

The issues of Social Aspects are many and complex. While living in Africa, one learns to appreciate the multiple perspectives that exist in this world, perspectives illuminated and empowered by our multiple cultures, traditions, and contexts.

As widely known, when looking to the practices in Africa, most foreign foreheads wear frowns. A whole array of issues come up. Most carry the label 'problems', as there is a tendency to problemise most non-Western issues in Africa. The vocabulary describes situations involving despair, failure and corruption. Sometimes it seems like a world of cliches that fails to recognise the African cultural diversity and unity, factors of equilibrium and strength in African economic systems, conflict resolution and reducing of inequalities and injustice, as they happen in a challenging context.

When reviewing *social aspects*, it is apparent that the darker population in the Third World suffers the worst forms of oppression in the most unjust geopolitical situation of the world. To understand, and analyse African cases, one must properly understand the specific and often intricate local, national and regional dimensions and dynamics of those cases. For instance, my experience is that life in rural Africa is heavily influenced by constraints or contingencies. This is in clear contrast to life in affluent parts of the world, where daily affairs are inspired by opportunities and innovations.

Undoubtedly, social systems that result in *capacity building* provide a way forward. Therefore, to provide for a tangible contribution to this conference, I would like to expand this address to take in leadership development with a focus on science.

Some Facts

As mentioned, I have lived half of my adult life in rural Africa. This leads one to appreciate some often under-rated facts about Africa. For instance, do you know that the combined landmass of the USA, Argentina, India, China, and Western Europe, easily fits into Africa, with room to spare?

And, as an example of the importance of rural areas, do you know that in Zambia 94% of its surface area is designated *rural* [5], 61% of the people live in the rural areas [6], that 83% of 7,576 Zambian schools are in rural areas [7], and that two third of 1,564 Zambian health institutions [8] are in rural areas?

Recently, I made the case that, depending on one's assumptions, the costs of rural internet connectivity has gone up in price 55% since 2004 [1]. At the same time, the average size of a website has gone up 6,800% since 1995. For the rural populations, access to transportation and power is equally troublesome.

African Traditional Characteristics

To build my case, I will briefly touch upon three major African traditional characteristics that are very removed from affluent areas in this world. These are the realities of Orality, Ubuntu and Relatio.

Orality. The society I live in bases its interactions on oral discourse. Community members regard verbal interaction as *instant*. Among others, orality offers the unique ability to assess comprehension and effect instantly. Orality ensures the social cohesion of the African civilization [9]. Orality influences everything. However, there appears to be little research into the possible benefits of using oral characteristics in ICT and research [10]. Findings in primary oral cultures could even be relevant to *the second orality* now gripping the youth in the affluent areas. This second orality emerges through pervasive computing, omnipresent telephones and video cultures.

Ubuntu. Sub-Saharan African culture is based on Ubuntu. The South African scholar, Khoza, explains Ubuntu as an epistemology and humanistic philosophy, a metaphor embodying the significance of group solidarity [11]. The Ubuntu culture is a key to African values, involving collective personhood and collective morality. Tutu writes "[Ubuntu] also means my humanity is caught up, is inextricably bound up, in theirs. We belong in a bundle of life" [12]. He contrasts western philosophy and Ubuntu through: it is not I think therefore I am.

It says rather: I am human because I belong. Despite it being the cultural expression of hundreds of millions of people, literature on Ubuntu is often regarded as idiosyncratic. Practical implications for organisations and ICT, and change theories, have been explored in literature, albeit sparsely. With only a few bookshops in mainstream Africa, books are difficult to access anyway. The study of Ubuntu and ICT appears to be virgin territory.

Of course, when we create and handle ICT, we are performing a political, value-laden act. Westerners design most Information and Communication Technologies. Generally, these technologies do not align with Ubuntu, and therefore serve the values of Western cultures. But when such technology arrives in another cultural setting, what happens? With its implementation we might instil social values that are not in line with local culture. And then it is no wonder that the technology will stand idle or will be discarded when Western people leave. Or, when such technology remains, it will bring about social changes that might be perceived as *imposed* instead of requested.

Relatio. In rural African communities we found (and have published these findings) that two parallel systems exist, each addressing the basic questions of choice and resource management. One is a traditional *rational* Western system, the other a *relational* African system. We came up with a system description which we dubbed *Relatio* [13].

We deduced that the rural community allocates resource in macro-economic terms, by satisfying *relationship equivalents* of banking, markets, and regulation. The majority of micro-economic actions undertaken by those of the Relatio mindset are working towards long-run stability. The African experience, due to the instability of environmental, political, medical, and other factors, has demonstrated the utter unpredictability of the short-run, while one's long-term security is limited only by the aggregate life-span of every member of the community to whom the individual is connected. In practice, the contrasting paradigms result in encouragement of competition in one system, and discouragement of individualism in the other.

The primary mode or dimension of resource allocation in the local context must be fully understood. Without that understanding, ICT development managed exclusively through a Western understanding of economic rationality will make only limited progress. Without an active membership in the Relatio economic model - that is to say, the community at large - the effectiveness of even financially sound projects will be severely limited. We found that without making efforts to display *character* and *actively invest in the social market*, the take-up rates and acceptability of the best researched projects was cut short; without the submission to, and respect for social hierarchy, the most promising developments will be restrained.

3   African Science

Having now introduced social aspects of traditional, African communities and touched upon the challenges that it poses for ICT, let me now focus on science.

To me, science appears as a western-dominated, western-social construct. It is based upon Aristotle's thinking that emerged around 350 BC. The thinking of this remarkable Greek, and his teacher Plato have been influencing western culture since.

Since the scramble for Africa, from 1881 till the first World War, Africa has been forceably exposed to western thinking. European research in Africa was performed to benefit the colonialists or the mother country [14]. Until independence swept through in the 1960's in Zambia for instance, Africans could not attain any high office, including that of a scientist.

After colonialism, the new governments had many issues to attend to, and typically considered support of scientific research unnecessary [14]. The United Nations played a significant role in changing these attitudes toward science and technology. UNESCO has reinforced the importance of science, with dozens of missions to African countries promoting science and technology [14].

The challenges at hand are to understand what an Africanised expression of Technology, or ICT if you wish, would mean. I think the challenge is that science in Africa needs rediscovery/redefinition to engender progress in a way adapted to African societies, a process that I have placed under the banner of "Social Innovation".

Science Realities

The Kenyan scholar, Mazrui, states "A university has to be politically distant from the state; secondly, a university has also to be culturally close to society; and thirdly, a university has to be intellectually linked to wider scholarly and scientific values of the world of learning." [15].

I experience on a daily basis the significant gaps between science and *real life in (rural) Africa*. In general, scientists are poor communicators, allowing politics and business to make selective use of results. And, of course, the role of science and its operations are under pressure from the general access to information provided through the Internet.

As witnessed in practice, and hinted at in the earlier mentioned "Charter for African Cultural Renaissance", within science reigns the hegemony of western scientific thinking with western dominance. Perhaps the West might think that its way of life is superior in all its aspects, and that it must be brought to other parts of the world. Further, the scientific value chain is under western control, through western dominance of scientific journals, peer-review, citations, etc.

However, science does not know how to deal with such social realities as emotions, and fear and greed. Science seems not to know how to deal with religion, and guidance from the Bible, Koran, and/or traditional belief systems. Then also, science seem to falter in the face of ignorance, and the various circumstances of the wielding of power. I quote Erwin Shrodinger, the famous person behind the equations in physics that bear his name: "I'm very astonished that the scientific picture of the real world is very deficient. It gives a lot of factual information, puts all our experiences in a magnificient consistent order, but it is ghastly silent about all and sundry that is real near to our heart, that really matters to us. It cannot tell a word about red and blue, bitter and sweet, physical pain and physical delight, knows nothing of beautiful and ugly, good or bad, God and eternity. Science sometimes pretends to answer questions in these domains, but the answers are very often so silly that we are not inclined to take them seriously" [16].

It appears that science goes through identity crises and must re-invent itself constantly [17]. Certainly in Africa, by focusing on particularisation and its world of experts, science, and thus technology development, it struggles to find its social function. Mittelstrass states that science is losing its existence as a social organism with its educational and research responsibilities, and understanding of moral forms or forms of life [18]. Without moral guidance, and explicit exposure of embedded worldviews, science's research questions can lack orientation. Consequently science is in danger of empowering the production of technology that would make life impossible.

As we all know, the relationship of science and its paymasters can be critical. There is already a fight for fundamental research funding in the Western setting, and universities are notoriously difficult to run. They strive to combine research to provide the inputs, and educational activities to assure the output. Universities are not necessarily regarded as *community*, but they are appearing as *silos*.

All these situations are so much removed from the African communal reality.

4   On the Ground, in Africa

Most of the universities and institutes of *higher learning* I have visited in sub-Saharan Africa were built during colonial times. They model Western examples and are among the key instruments and vehicles of cultural westernisation on the continent [15]. Leadership styles have resulted from western models, as an amazing 98% of leadership theory stems from the USA [19]. During their implementation, it seems that the African background has never been taken seriously, not even as a determining factor for the behaviour of Africans. The local, African community is a much more complex environment than is often assumed.

Western systems were exported to Africa. However, the success of implementing these western examples in Africa has been limited. Additionally, scientific conventions and requirements are met with lack of material resources, and thus exclude Third World scholars from the academic processes [20]. There is no masterplanning to see whether Africa has the resources to keep going with quality: proposed models are often solely based upon examples that work in rich countries.

There is much to do whilst, as traditional African views and their allegiances remain unseen, unknown, or misunderstood in the West. It is the same with African cultural, political, economical, and social contexts. Progress is defined through western eyes and seems to be defined as progress for the West. Khoza, in his book Let Africa Lead, writes "Those of us accustomed to mixing with outsiders are used to hearing a few polite and tentative remarks about the problems of Africa after independence, followed by an embarrassed silence. Aid-givers celebrating their selfless assistance to poor old Africa are wont to lay misgovernment and corruption at our feet, like a corpse at a wedding feast" [11].

Within the traditional African society of the Ubuntu culture, *personal independence* is not necessarily seen as a desirable trait. For instance, the rural African society is much interwoven, and resource limitations make each society a stakeholder, keeping a close eye on the affairs of the other stakeholders, including academics. And I will not even attempt to expand the principle that, in rural areas, one works according to *communal law*.

The list of practical aspects that challenge ICT development in Africa goes on. For instance, there is hardly any funding for science in Africa. Scientists are typically underpaid or sometimes not paid at all. There are no significant 'African research agendas', or any convincing agenda for research at most African universities. If research agendas exist at all, they are most likely to be drafted with or by Western consultants, aligning with foreign development aid support, or are derived from Western universities' support, with its considerable *power distances* [21]. There is a mismatch between the adaption of the kind of studies, and the curricula, and the local challenges and the African background [22].

African societies nowadays feature a complex mix of western and indigenous systems. As an example, although 94% of Zambia's land is rural and under customary governances, there is very little literature dealing with the real facts in rural areas. When literature and studies exist, they mostly deal with the urban areas, which are only 6% of Zambia's land mass. Also, African countries harbour a complex mix of ethnicities. In practice, African governments have a limited span of control, and science must convince many, including traditional leaders and rural communities. For science to have any meaning, it needs its findings to be explained to the whole society. Therefore it is no wonder that foreign-trained African scientists mention that their discipline-based knowledge and training does not fit the problem-based, and people-centered issues that exist in Africa [23].

5   ICT Challenges

Much of my professional experience pivots around ICT in rural Africa. I have learned that ICT provides the conduit for information in the same way as electrotechnics provide the conduit for physical power, and civil engineering provides conduits for transport and water.

Unfortunately, most research in ICT incorporates a quantitative and technological perspective only. Literature biases towards quantifiable responses, and aims at prioritisation of needs, focused on Western topic listings, and conceptualisation of solutions. Work often lacks longterm contextual evidence. In positivistic, technical sciences there seems to be little regard for culture and context. There is no localised science-reporting in most developing countries, and certainly little reporting in the local languages. All this hampers communities from being able to learn about ICT developments in a meaningful way.

My experience is that graduates leave universities:

1. jobless,
2. without the capacity to find solutions for African problems,
3. pressurized by the family that expects their support, since they have helped them to reach that point,
4. 'brain draining' from rural areas to cities or other countries when the opportunity arises.

How technologies like ICT satisfy the basic needs of African society, and how it supports rural development receives little attention. My friend Fred Mweetwa, recently asked the Dean of a Zambian university during a radio interview "Sir, how come that we have Chinese cooking stoves, oil presses, or tools, while we have got the universities in Zambia? What are the results of your work?".

A View of African Reality

As you can see here in Cameroon and elsewhere, Africa is inherently rich so there is much room to search for effective African solutions to build upon these resources [24]. We face many dilemmas, including that of trying to achieve intellectual proximity to global scholarship and a cultural proximity to African society [15].

Colonialism placed a Western system next to an existing indigenous system, disregarding the existing social systems. At this stage, the two systems might both have something to lose, be it knowledge, status, resources or moral values [25]. Currently all entities thrive on their unique paradigms and boundaries, and remarkably, from a western scientific point of view, there might be no urgency to collaborate.

In view of turbulent world events, the way ahead for Africa lies in the involvement of all members of its societies and communities in their own future.

In an effort to provide a view on the dilemmas involved, I and proposing that African and Western scientific expressions differ as antonyms. Here are the antonyms as I have observed them in practice.

Of course, this generic table can be seen as over-generalised, but it highlight the diverse experiences of realities. As explained, the particular dynamics of historical and geographical specifics and the current particular configuration of power, technology and representation, draw from a long western-centric legacy [26]. This legacy goes deep, and is sometimes even mythical.

Inherited from the colonial ethnology and maintained by ignorance and lack of interest, the prejudices about Africa still run rampant ([27] cited in [9]). There remain real questions as to one's value system and attitudes when one builds relationships outside one's own culture.

And with the hegemony of the West, who is there to put such intrusive questions to the *conquerors* [28] [29]?

Table 1. Science Antonyms, as witnessed in practice

African Science	Western Science
Limited Data	Abundant Data
Discursive	Non-discursive
Communities	Institutions
People Focus	Text Focus
Stigmatised	Proud
Foreign language	Own language
Deprived	Funded
Foreign from Greek thinking	Assimilated Greek thinking
Seeking mediation/unity	Seeking critism
Big Picture	Specialisation
Unnoticed	Respected
Not-authoritative	Authoritive
Aims at relationship	Aims at growth
Respects boundaries	No boundaries
Respects teachers	Respects scientists
low quality 1st, 2nd education	high quality 1st, 2nd education

6   The Way Forward

The Health profession has various high grade field research stations in Africa, including some in rural areas. These research centres run research programmes, mostly in collaboration with Western universities and institutes. Although most resources might remain in 'the West' - for instance western universities asking for 60% of the total budget for 'administative purposes', and the support of research salaries in the West - a part of this funding for health research does trickle down and reach the institutes in Africa. The local community does often benefit. There is improved Quality of Living (better health), better policies, and increased funding opportunities (for instance through PEPFAR).

As far as I can see, we do not have the same situation in engineering and ICT research in Africa. There are hardly any field research stations - certainly not in rural areas; there is very limited research participation and there are almost no funding opportunities.

This is an example of the realities on the ground: the Zambian government approved less than one quarter of the University of Zambia's budget submission during 2005-2007, and the *total allocation* of institutes like the Zambian National Technology Center is less than USD 100,000 per year. As another example, this time from my activities, we have been collaborating in research worldwide, but have never received funding for any local operational cost, including that of remuneration, or received anything for our many publications. Only *moral incentives or reasons* motivate research collaboration, written publications, participation in conferences, etc., in a Zambian setting.

Literature shows that equal partnerships and inclusiveness in development of local interventions is a key requirement for long-term sustainability [30]. How does one strike such a balance in ICT Africa? And, how to incorporate human values and culture in our strive for eInfrastructure and eServices for Developing Countries [31]? How to explore a socio-technical approach to technology [32] [33]? It took me many years of living with people in rural Africa to get a 'handle' on the *ethical*, *pragmatic*, and *conceptual* challenges involved in the introduction of ICT in rural Africa.

So, there is room for development of the concepts of science, engineering, and thus ICT, and understanding of what their purposes are, in an African stetting. Necessarily, this needs to start by taking African people and African background seriously, and introducing innovative methodologies, for instance by incorporating orality, Ubuntu and Relatio, to provide theories emerging from African philosophy and culture.

Mazrui [15] suggests, and the African Union echoes, the need for:

1. de-colonising modernity by African universities seeking cultural nearness to African society
2. diversifying the cultural content of modernity, moving the university from a multi-national corporation to a multi-cultural corporation
3. reversing the flow of influence back into Western civilization.

The methods and theories of ethnography, storytelling, transdiciplinarity, Service Learning, Action Research, and others, provide for exciting ways to do this. In national and regional cooperation we can compare notes and research findings, and prioritise research relevant for cooperation. I suggest we must:

1. define the level of quality needed for Africa and develop a road map to achieve that quality in African circumstances
2. discuss the local needs with traditional leaders also
3. focus research to identify opportunities to implement knowledge that is already available in the very different circumstances of African societies
4. find out how to unlock knowledge of other non-western societies for local, African use.

The resulting Africanised expression of ICT will be innovative, introducing new products and services like integrating mobile telephony and community radio, or re-inventing IT platforms to shed its focus on serving individuals by creating truly community-oriented technologies.

7   Conclusions

I conclude that the plural character of the positioning of ICT challenges in Africa stems from two different and often competing paradigms: an African indigenous and a Western paradigm. The paradigms diverge in terms of values, definitions of social aspects and realities, and cultural approaches. At the base of this plurality are inherently different worldviews, which in practice lead to a number of barriers to interaction, and even antagonism.

In my view, these issues can be overcome by focusing on social innovation in the continent of Africa. The current technology hubs that are springing up in Africa are an encouraging development.

Undeniably, ICT provides tools that support people. The challenge is for ICT to be introduced and utilised in the right manner, and with the right timing. The balancing act, in my humble opinion, is an act of reconciling dilemmas [2] when strategy thus derived from reconciliation will facilitate and not denigrate existing and emerging social structures.

In my view, the Worlds social challenges can be solved only in the social realm. It is there that we must find out what is true, what is admirable, and adopt it.

Kenneth Kaunda, the first President of Zambia, once said: Westerners have aggressive problem-solving minds; Africans experience people. His wise observation reveals two complementary priority structures. In the past, emphasis has been placed solely on the development of Africa on Western terms. Now, we must reconcile and begin to experience people.

The process to achieve sustainable progress is an exchange not only of physical capital and currency, but also of values and culture. Development must be conducted in terms of those being developed. This process requires a shift of priority from front-loaded, formula-obsessed, pre-packaged development tactics towards more creative, long-term, flexible programmes that invest genuinely; not merely at a financial or technological level, but on a relationship level as well. In my view it is by integrating and reconciling knowledge of the context and culture with experience and outlook, that the vibrant complexity of human behavior can be released from the shackles of traditional rationality, and appreciated as an unrestrained force of culture, development, and true sustainability.

8   About the Presenter

Gertjan van Stam (Rotterdam, 1965) studied wireless technologies at Hogeschool Utrecht, Netherlands, and worked in Swaziland in 1987. After achieving his degree in telecommunications he took on tasks in various capacities in the incumbent telecommunications operator of the Netherlands. There he participated in practice and strategies for broadcast technologies, standardization platforms, telecommunications network and service operations including mobile networks (paging and GSM), and international business development.

Since 2000 Gertjan and his family have lived in rural Africa, first in Zimbabwe and, from 2003, in Zambia. He works with local talent to engender transdisciplinary practices and holistic theory building. The goal is to identify and inspire local talent and introduce appropriate technologies in order to build the necessary capacity for community-led activities to yield sustainable human development outcomes. His quest is for a logical framework for understanding dynamics of change in rural African communities and engendering leadership capable of inspiring, initiating, implementing, operating, and scaling up of sustainable progress and the use of technology in the local community.

Gertjans activities in Zambia were featured in IEEE The Institute [34], and his career was documented in an award winning IEEE video at tryEngineering' [35]. The activities in Zambia were featured worldwide though BBC Clicks [36]. He is part of IEEEs Ad Hoc Committee for Humanitarian Activities working on Social Innovation, involved with the University of Zambia (Lusaka, Zambia) and SIRDC (Harare, Zimbabwe) and studies at the Nelson Mandela Metropolitan University (Port Elizabeth, South Africa). He authored the book Placemark [37], and publishes articles.

References

1. van Stam, G.: Observations from rural Africa: An engineer involved in ICTs and critical ethnography in Macha, Zambia. In: UCSB Center for Information Technology and Society Lecture Series, Santa Barbara, CA, USA (2012)
2. van Stam, G.: Is Technology the Solution to the World's Major Social Challenges? In: 2012 IEEE Global Humanitarian Technology Conference, Seattle, USA. IEEE (2012)
3. African Union. Charter for African Cultural Renaissance (2010)
4. Adebajo, A.: UN Peacekeeping in Africa. From the Suez Crisis to the Sudan Conflicts. Fanele, Auckland Park (2011)
5. Adams, M.: Land tenure policy and practice in Zambia: issues relating to the development of the agricultural sector. Mokoro Ltd., Oxford (2003)
6. Central Statistics Office Zambia. 2010 Census of Population and Housing Preliminary Report (2011)
7. Government of the Republic of Zambia. Educational Statistical Bulletin. Technical report, Ministry of Education, Lusaka (2005)
8. Government of the Republic of Zambia. Annual Health Statistical Bulletin. Technical report, Ministry of Health, Lusaka (2008)
9. Dobra, A.: The Democratic Impact of ICT in Africa. Africa Spectrum (1), 73–88 (2012)
10. van Stam, G.: Information and Knowledge Transfer in the rural community of Macha, Zambia. The Journal of Community Informatics (in press)
11. Khoza, R.: Let Africa Lead: African Transformational Leadership for 21st century Business. VezuBuntu, South Africa (2005)
12. Tutu, D.: No Future Without Forgiveness. Doubleday, New York (1999)
13. Sheneberger, K., van Stam, G.: Relatio: An Examination of the Relational Dimension of Resource Allocation. Economics and Finance Review 1(4), 26–33 (2011)
14. Heilbron, J.L.: The Oxford Companion to the History of Modern Science. Oxford University Press (2003)
15. Mazrui, A.A.: Towards Re-Africanizing African Universities: Who Killed Intellectualism in the Post Colonial Era? Turkish Journal of International Relations 2(3), 135–163 (2003)
16. Schrödinger, E.: Nature and the Greeks (1954)
17. Mitchell, M.T.: Michael Polanyi, Wilmington, Delaware (2006)
18. Mittelstrass, J.: The Future of the University and the Credibility of Science and Scholarship. Ethical Perspectives 13(2), 171–189 (2006)
19. House, R.J., Aditya, R.N.: The Social Scientific Study of Leadership: Quo Vadis? Journal of Management, 409–473 (1997)

20. Suresh Canagarajah, A.: Material Resources of Periphery Scholars, and the Politics of Knowledge Production. Written Communication (1996)
21. Holm, J.D., Malete, L.: The Asymmetries of University Partnerships between Africa and the Developed World: Our Experience in Botswana. In: Going Global 4 - The British Council's International Education Conference (2010)
22. Ayalew, Y., Renken, J., Mgaya, K.V., Nkgau, T.Z.: Developing a Contextualized Informaton Systems Curriculum for an Emerging Economy. EJISDC 54(2), 1–19 (2012)
23. Gurstein, M.: The Dead Hand of (Western) Academe: Community Informatics in a Less Developed Country Context (2011)
24. Unwin, T.: On the richness of Africa (2008)
25. Langen, E.: Diverging worldviews, diverging worlds? Msc programme, Wageningen University (2010)
26. Dourish, P., Mainwaring, S.D.: Ubicomp's Colonial Impulse. In: UbiComp 2012, Pittsburg, USA (2012)
27. D'Almeida-Topor, H.: L'Afrique. Le Cavalier Bleu, Paris (2006)
28. Morris, I.: Why The West Rules, For Now. Profile Books (2010)
29. Diamond, J.: Guns, Germs, and Steel: The Fates of Human Societies. W. W. Norton & Company (2005)
30. InfoDev. Enhancing the Livelihood of the Rural Poor Through ICT: Tanzania Country Study (2008)
31. Miller, K.W., Larson, D.K.: Agile Software Development: Human Values and Culture. IEEE Technology and Society Magazine (2005)
32. Amadei, B., Wallace, W.A.: Engineering for Humanitarian Development. A Socio-Technical Approach. IEEE Technology and Society Magazine (2009)
33. Kam, M.: Engineering as Liberal Art. In: Scottish Parliament, Edinburgh, August 14 (2012)
34. Karlin, S.: Gertjan van Stam: Macha's Link to the World. IEEE The Institute (2009)
35. IEEE TV. Tryengineering "Careers with Impact": van Stam (2010)
36. BBC Clicks. BBC Clicks - Macha Works (2011)
37. van Stam, G.: Placemark. Gertjan van Stam, Macha (2011)

Testbed for Rural Area Networking –
First Steps towards a Solution

Sami Ruponen and Juha Zidbeck

VTT Technical Research Centre of Finland, Communication Networks,
Vuorimiehentie 3, 02150 Espoo, Finland
{sami.ruponen,juha.zidbeck}@vtt.fi

Abstract. Connecting the unconnected world is a challenging task not only in technological perspective but also economically. Providing a viable solution for a communication network in large rural areas such as parts of Africa or remote Lapland in Northern Finland, surprisingly, share similar challenges. The main criteria for such a network are energy-efficient, robust, and reliable operation even in harsh environment. Important aspects are also low-cost and easy deployment of such a network. Developing a network that would meet all the criteria requires theoretical studies as well as real-world testing and implementations. In this paper, we will present some early results and design highlights of a wireless mesh network testbed deployment that can be used to foster the research work. We also envision it as a base for an actual solution. We introduce some of the concepts and objectives behind the testbed and describe and rationalize the chosen hardware and architecture choices.

Keywords: wireless mesh network, WLAN, energy-efficiency, testbed.

1 Motivations

The Finnish Government has set in its "Broadband to Everyone" policy specific targets for providing 100 Mbps Internet access to 99% of all the permanent residents and offices in Finland by 2015 [1]. But this 100 Mbps network will not reach all the potential users in the remote locations. The remainder will be left for alternative connections such as mobile network with 2G/3G connectivity, if any.

The CIER (Converged Infrastructure for Emerging Regions) project [2] proposes to build wireless mesh networks that are alternative or complementary to the existing systems in order to provide broadband Internet connectivity for the people in the remote areas. Although the initial focus of the project was set to rural Africa, much of the requirements and specifications apply to the remote areas in Finland, which is also the focus of the Finnish part of the project. Such remote areas are Lapland and the archipelago, where many notable applications have been identified.

2 Concept and Objectives

The CIER project aims at designing and implementing energy-efficient, robust, reliable, and affordable heterogeneous wireless mesh networks to connect

K. Jonas, I.A. Rai, and M. Tchuente (Eds.): AFRICOMM 2012, LNICST 119, pp. 14–23, 2013.

geographically very large areas in a challenged environment. When considering different kinds of mesh networks, there are many social, economic, regulatory, and technological risks that might hinder successful business deployments. In order to become successful, the wireless mesh network should provide broadband Internet connectivity to the remote locations for less cost than what is achievable with existing fixed or mobile systems.

Identifying the Nordic Challenges. In Africa, most of the environmental challenges come from the extreme heat, the heavy rains, and of course from the sand. They burden the system in various ways and cause headache to the system designer. In Nordic climate, the challenges are somewhat similar. There are also extreme temperatures present, in this case low temperatures. Also, snow and ice cause lots of trouble.

Nordic environment sets many challenges to different systems. Power production is difficult in the northern locations like above the Polar Circle region. First of all, there is relatively little sunlight throughout most of the year for solar panels. Furthermore, utilization of wind power is out of the question when ice accumulates on the blades of the windmills, not to mention that already the snow makes it challenging to maintain the radio masts functional as shown in Fig. 1.

Fig. 1. Nordic conditions [3]

Towards a Viable Solution. To solve all the technical challenges and prove the viability of a solution in practice, requires an implementation in realistic environment for development and testing purposes. Building such a testbed in outdoor environment to support the research work was well promoted by the start of the CIER project.

Generally, the same testbed can also be utilized in other research areas such as radio coverage estimation, outdoor positioning, and network robustness.

The target was to set up an installation similar to what would actually be used in rural areas. The testbed is mostly located in Otaniemi campus area in Espoo, on the southern coast of Finland. The clear benefits from the urban location are the easiness and cost-efficiency of maintenance and installation of the testbed. Tall buildings support easy access to the roof-top and set up of long-range line-of-sight radio links without using radio masts.

With the aid of the testbed, technical problems or features that are to be solved and supported are: easy deployment and maintenance, energy-awareness and energy-efficiency, and robust and reliable operation.

3   Testbed

One of the design criteria of the testbed is to use hardware that would be robust, readily and commercially available, and low-cost. Naturally, it has to be suitable for outdoor installation and to withstand harsh weather conditions. The following section introduces one such device and its derivative models that meets the criteria and was chosen for the testbed. The analysis excludes intentionally some older models and models with prohibited usage in Finland, and in other European countries due to the radio spectrum regulations.

3.1   Basic Building Blocks – The *Bullet Radios*

A wireless radio device family called Bullet M from Ubiquiti Networks [4] has a very simple design offering just an Ethernet interface and a standard IEEE 802.11 wireless radio with an integrated RF connector. Despite of its simplified appearance, it provides enough features and processing power for a variety of tasks. Besides the Bullet M models, similar devices are available, with different housing and integrated antennas, sharing the same underlying hardware and software. The term *bullet radio* is used throughout the paper to refer to these devices if not specifically mentioned otherwise.

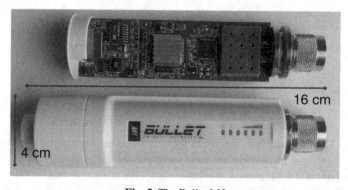

Fig. 2. The Bullet M5

A Bullet M5 model and its main board are shown in Fig. 2. On the left side is the Ethernet connector and on the right side is the Type N RF male connector. It includes a passive Power-over-Ethernet (PoE) capability to supply power for the device. The outer coverage has six LEDs to indicate the power on, network traffic, and the radio signal strength. All the *bullet radios* share the above features excluding the Type N connector on the devices that use integrated antennas.

As seen from the picture, the Bullet M models are very compact sized and the integrated N connector enables direct attachment to the antenna minimizing the cable losses and the overall cabling needs. The physical installation and replacement of the device is straightforward without much risk of damaging it, even for an unskilled person. The weak point of the device is the protective cap for the Ethernet cable (on the left side) and especially its rubber shielding. If it is not carefully fixed, then water and moisture can get inside the device and cause malfunction.

3.2   Inside the *Bullet Radios*

Hardware. The Bullet M5 and other *bullet radios* are built around Atheros AR7240 MIPS 24Kc System-on-Chip running at 400 MHz. They have 32 Mbytes of RAM and 8 Mbytes of flash memory for the operating system and user software. With these specifications there are ample resources for handling network traffic and running advanced applications. The Ethernet interface supports 10 Mbps or 100 Mbps speeds and is equipped with an RJ-45 connector. Additionally, some models have a secondary Ethernet interface supporting PoE output. *Bullet radios* in general accept supply power of up to 24 V dc, but it works also with 12 volts, which is very convenient for battery operated usage.

Bullet radios use either 2.4 GHz or 5 GHz frequency bands, depending on the model, and support the IEEE 802.11n specification. In addition to the standard 20 MHz and 40 MHz channel widths, they support some non-standard channel widths, such as 5, 10, and 30 MHz, giving the option for optimized use of network resources. Some models with integrated antennas also support the multiple-input multiple-output (MIMO) technology.

Software. There are at least two operating systems (OS) available for the *bullet radios*. First is the Ubiquiti's own airOS [5] that is pre-installed into the device, and another is an open-source community driven OpenWrt [6], both running Linux kernel. In fact, the airOS is based on a version of OpenWrt with some proprietary enhancements, such as support for Time Division Multiple Access (TDMA) communication and adjusting the acknowledgement timeout, all targeting for improved throughput and long-range communication. In addition, airOS provides useful built-in functions to aid the antenna alignment, to measure the throughput, and even to use the device as a spectrum analyzer.

Both of the operating systems provide a web interface, and an SSH console access with the basic Linux command line tools. A Software Development Kit (SDK) is available for operating systems enabling users to make modifications or add own functionalities to the system. AirOS SDK is available on request from Ubiquiti Networks [4] and OpenWrt SDK can be freely downloaded from the community website [6].

3.3   Supported Networking Functionalities

The commercial off-the-self (COTS) *bullet radios* support the common networking modes seen in most products on the market: layer 2 bridging, and layer 3 routing. Bullet radios can work as a wireless Access Point (AP), Station, or Repeater with AP functionality. Naturally, more advanced mesh networking requires special routing algorithms and additional software. But as such they provide the base for building up and testing a simple mesh network setup.

Next paragraphs will show how the bullet radios can be used to build up a working mesh network, although a very simple one. Fig. 3 shows a layout of a *bullet radio* working in a transparent Layer 2 bridging mode. Linux kernel provides a logical (software) bridge (*br0*) where the Ethernet (*eth0*) and WLAN (*ath0*) interfaces are connected. In this mode, the forwarding decision is based on the MAC addressing on the Ethernet frames, in this case the destination address. The forwarding functionality, herein the bridging, can be replaced with another one based on different addressing scheme such as IP routing or a more advanced mesh routing functionality.

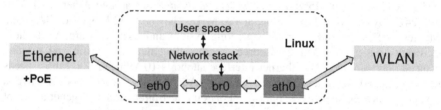

Fig. 3. Bullet radio layout in transparent layer 2 bridging mode

By connecting multiple devices together, on the Ethernet side using a switch, and on the WLAN side using point-to-point (PtP) wireless links, a simple layer 2 mesh network can be created with small effort. In this case, a Spanning Tree Protocol (STP) can be used to build loop free paths from one node to the rest of the nodes in the network.

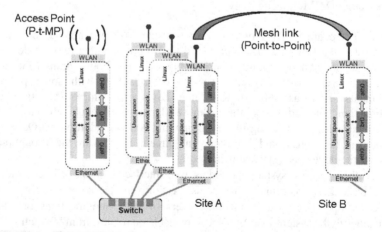

Fig. 4. Mesh network node assembled from bullet radios working in bridge mode

Fig. 4 shows a portion of a mesh network where one site (A) is assembled using four bullet radios, one operating as an access point for client connections and three connecting to other sites. In this scenario, the mesh node and the mesh network can be considered as a carrier providing connectivity for clients connected to the access points.

On each site, the devices are connected to a switch, so that they can communicate between each other. The switch searches for the output port for the destination address from the MAC address table. This information also points the outgoing wireless link. *Bullet radio* then forwards the packet over the wireless link to the other site (B) where similar process continues until the destination is reached.

Traffic coming from the clients can be placed to a separate VLAN, thus isolating it from the management and STP traffic, for added security. Finally, a DHCP server, and a gateway node with an Internet connection can be connected to the switch on one of the sites to provide IP addresses and Internet connectivity to the clients.

For the clients connected to the APs, the network shows as one big switched network. They all belong to the same broadcast domain, also with the *bullet radios*. The drawback of this setup is the fairly large amount of broadcast messages which makes it poorly fitted for larger installations as such. But it still serves the purpose as the first step towards a more advanced mesh network research and experimentation.

The switch in Fig. 4 can be replaced with a unit having more advanced functionalities. In CIER project, one development task focuses on using Fraunhofer's WiBACK [7] platform with *bullet radios*. In this scenario, the WiBACK node provides the routing functionalities, whereas the *bullets* provide the radio part and connections to other nodes.

3.4   Rationale behind the Choices

The following section will present the rationale behind some of the design choices made for the testbed installation. Some of them are due to the regulations, cost issues or even personal decisions. Along the installation and experimentations, some might prove to be less optimal and have to be re-examined.

In Finland, Finnish Communications Regulatory Authority (FICORA) [8] controls the use of radio frequencies and licensing of radio devices. All radio equipments need a radio license to be operated, except the ones exempted from licensing. These radio equipments and their usage is prescribed in "Regulation on collective frequencies for license-exempt radio transmitters and on their use" [9] issued by FICORA. The regulations are aligned with the European Telecommunications Standards Institute (ETSI) [10] regulations and the European Union directives.

In short, the usual WLAN radio devices operating in 2.4 GHz and 5 GHz bands are license-exempt. Table 1 lists the essential part regarding the allowed frequency band and transmission power affecting the usage of such devices.

Table 1. The essential frequency bands with the allowed transmission powers (in Finland)

Frequency (MHz)	Transmission power (EIRP)	Notes
2400 – 2483.5	≤ 100 mW	
5150 – 5250	≤ 200 mW	≤ 10 mW / 1 MHz EIRP (only indoors)
5250 – 5350	≤ 200 mW	≤ 10 mW / 1 MHz EIRP (only indoors)
5470 – 5725	≤ 1 W	≤ 50 mW / 1 MHz EIRP

From the table above, it can be seen that WLAN devices operating in 2.4 GHz band are only allowed to use less than 100 mW equivalent isotropically radiated power (EIRP) measured from the antenna. In 5 GHz band, the two lower sub-bands are only allowed in indoor use. The upper sub-band (5470 – 5725 MHz) allows a maximum of 1 W radiated power. This is clearly much more than would be allowed in 2.4 GHz band thus enabling longer range.

Taking into account that 2.4 GHz band only offers four non-overlapping channels whereas the permitted 5 GHz band has 11 non-overlapping 20 MHz channels, the 5 GHz band offers much better channel allocation. Also, the 5 GHz band seems practically interference free, at least in Finland. One must also take into account the physical characteristics of the higher frequencies: better directivity of the antennas, and the smaller radius of the Fresnel zones, which leads to better line-of-sight clearance requirements. The drawback of higher frequencies is the larger Free Space Path Loss (FSPL), although the higher permitted transmission power can compensate this.

The above reasons have led to a conclusion that the 5 GHz band should be chosen for the mesh links, especially for long-distance links. For the access point use, both have their advantages: 2.4 GHz better supports legacy devices and has better penetration of obstacles, whereas 5 GHz band offers more channels, less interference and bigger transmission power.

It should be noted that devices operating in 5470 – 5725 MHz band must employ Transmission Power Control (TPC) and Dynamic Frequency Selection (DFS) to be capable of detecting and working with other devices operating in the same frequency bands, mainly radars. The maximum transmission power of *bullet radios* is between 300 – 600 mW (depending on the model) and when combined with the antenna gain is in most practical cases more than enough to exceed the maximum radiated power measured from the antenna allowed by the regulations.

4   Testbed Deployment and First Experience

Due to the early phase of the installation process, only few links have been permanently deployed so far. The current ones are mainly used to do some initial tests and verify the viability and operation of the system. Fig. 5 depicts the testbed on maps showing the Southern part of the city of Espoo and the Otaniemi campus. It indicates the current links and node sites, with some additional sites for further installations.

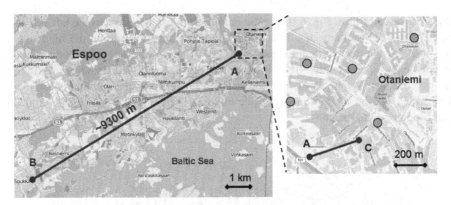

Fig. 5. The testbed location on the map

As stated earlier, the intention is to utilize high places and buildings. Therefore, one key site for the installation was chosen to be a water tower in Otaniemi campus. The top of it is approximately 50 m above the surrounding area and offers a clear view over the whole Southern Espoo and to the neighboring city, Helsinki. The water tower is marked as point A in the map. There is a radio link from the water tower to an apartment house on high ground marked as point B. The range of the radio link between the two sites is 9.3 km. There is also a shorter link from the water tower to one of the office buildings of VTT (point C) that is connected to VTT's research network and to the Internet. In addition, some points are shown on the map that could be used for further deployments.

Power Consumption. For the power consumption measurements, the current drawn by the *bullet radios* at 12 volts was measured using a multimeter. First, the idle state power consumption was measured without any traffic being sent through the WLAN interface. Next, the power consumption was measured using the minimum and maximum available transmission powers while sending a high volume of traffic through the WLAN. The results are shown in Table 2.

Table 2. The power consumption of Bullet M2 and Bullet M5 using 12 V supply voltage

	TX power (dBm)	Current (mA)	Wattage (W)
Bullet M2 (2.4 GHz)	idle / -3 / 28	235 / 315 / 450	2.8 / 3.8 / 5.4
Bullet M5 (5 GHz)	idle / -6 / 25	240 / 440 / 520	2.9 / 5.3 / 6.3

The measured power consumptions were in line with the ones reported by the manufacturer: 6 watts and 7 watts for Bullet M2 and Bullet M5, respectively. A slight increase (0.2 – 0.4 W) in power consumption was seen during the test when the system was performing additional tasks, such as handling the web interface.

Physical Installations. Fig. 6 shows the *bullet radio* installations. On the left side is a NanoStation M5 on the roof of the office building (link AC), and on the right side a Bullet M5 inside the apartment house (link AB). The same *bullet radio* model is used at both ends of each link. Both links are operating in 5 GHz band at maximum allowable transmission power, i.e., the radiated power from the antenna is less than 1 W EIRP. The installation on the office building uses a bracket attached to a metal bar using powerful magnets.

Fig. 6. Bullet radio deployments

Link Quality and Throughput. The initial experiences on the link qualities and throughput seem to be promising. The long-distance link proves to be stable even during heavy rains and fog. The long-distance link (link AB) is using a 40 MHz channel width. The throughput on the link varies between 18 Mbps and 24 Mbps, while the signal strength on the receiving side is reported being approximately - 81dBm. The shorter link (link AC) is using a 20 MHz channel width and MIMO technology (2x2 streams). Its throughput varies between 88 Mbps and 96 Mbps, while the signal strength is approximately -59 dBm. The delay on both links is in the order of few milliseconds including the network stack and packet processing overheads.

For the throughput measurements, a built in test was used that utilizes an *iperf* [11] measurement tool. For the test, a unidirectional UDP stream with maximum sized, i.e., 1514 bytes packets was used. For the delay measurement, a simple *ping* test was used between the adjacent nodes. It should be noted that the devices would allow much higher transmission power, thus enabling higher throughput.

5   Conclusion and Future Work

This paper presented basic building blocks and design choices for a wireless mesh network testbed deployment along with some experiences and discoveries from the initial tests. The first results seem promising and prove that it is indeed realistic to carry on the work. So far, the *bullet radios* have been found to be robust and easy to use, and contain advanced features and enough processing power for sophisticated tasks. More detailed performance measurements along with the interference effects and QoS issues will be conducted later when more links are set up.

The testbed is expected to be expanded during the forthcoming autumn to be able to gather some experience about the operation during winter conditions. Also, a solar power supply is waiting for installation on one of the nodes.

The forthcoming IEEE 802.22 Wireless Regional Area Networks (WRAN) using the Television Whitespaces seem very promising technology, thus in the future we anticipate to use it also as a part of the testbed.

Acknowledgments. The work reported in this paper was partly supported by the Finnish Funding Agency for Technology and Innovation (Tekes) in the framework of the EUREKA/Celtic project Converged Infrastructure for Emerging Regions (CIER).

References

1. Finnish Ministry of Transport and Communications, "Laajakaista kaikille",
   http://www.lvm.fi/laajakaista_kaikille
   (last accessed on October 3, 2012)
2. CIER project information,
   http://www.celtic-initiative.org/Projects/
   Celtic-projects/Call7/CIER/cier-default.asp
3. Celtic CIER project report D2.3.1 "System architecture specifications" (September 2012)
4. Ubiquiti Networks, Inc., http://www.ubnt.com
5. Ubiquiti Networks, Inc., http://www.ubnt.com/airmax#airMaxSoftware
6. Openwrt, https://openwrt.org
7. Fraunhofer, http://net4dc.fokus.fraunhofer.de/content/dam/
   net4dc/en/documents/110913_Whitepaper_Introducing_WiBACK.pdf
   (last accessed on October 3, 2012)
8. Finnish Communications Regulatory Authority (FICORA),
   http://www.viestintavirasto.fi/en/index.html
9. Regulation on collective frequencies for licence-exempt radio transmitters and on their use
   (2011/337/FIN) issued by FICORA (last updated on April 20, 2012),
   http://www.ficora.fi/attachments/englantiav/673vVX0bw/
   FICORA_15AD2012M.pdf (last accessed on October 3, 2012)
10. European Telecommunications Standards Institute, ETSI,
    http://www.etsi.org/WebSite/homepage.aspx
11. Iperf site at SourceForge, http://sourceforge.net/projects/iperf/
    (last accessed on October 3, 2012)

SNS4D: An OnLine Social Network System for Developing Countries

Herve Ahouantchede[1], Fatna Belqasmi[2], and Roch Glitho[1,2]

[1] IMSP-University of Abomey-Calavi, Benin
[2] Concordia University, Canada
herveahouantchede@yahoo.fr,
fbelqasmi@alumni.concordia.ca,
glitho@ece.concordia.ca

Abstract. Online social networks assume a pervasive Internet connection. Unfortunately, Internet connectivity is rather uneven in developing countries. It is sometimes high in selected urban areas but remains generally low in rural areas. On the other hand, cellular network penetration is much higher and more uniform. This paper proposes a social network system for developing countries that enables a pervasive access by offsetting poor Internet connectivity by the rich SMS access provided by cellular networks. It allows all key operations associated with online social networking, using both the Web and SMS. Unlike existing online social networks that offer an SMS access in addition to Web access, it can be quickly deployed by re-using existing social networks. It also offers an SMS interface with a higher level of abstraction for end-users with phones that support J2ME. Furthermore, unlike existing social networks with SMS access, it gives SMS users access to the full set of social network operations. A proof-of-concept prototype has been implemented based on a scenario for an extended family whose members have disparate levels of Internet access.

Keywords: social networking sites, RESTful Web services, OpenSocial API, developing countries.

1 Introduction

Social networks have revolutionized communications – especially how friends and family keep in touch with each other. For a large number of Internet users, social networks have become an integral part of everyday life. The ease of use and the different features they offer make them an unavoidable communication tool. However, their use is limited to areas with a permanent Internet access, which is not the case for developing countries. According to Internet World Statistics [1], the Internet penetration rate rarely reaches 20% in these countries (e.g.: Republic of Benin: 3%, India: 7.8%, Morocco: 19.2%). On the other hand, cellular networks are experiencing an explosive development in these countries. According to the ITU-T, the total number of cellular subscriptions reached 73% in 2010 [2].

K. Jonas, I.A. Rai, and M. Tchuente (Eds.): AFRICOMM 2012, LNICST 119, pp. 24–33, 2013.

This paper proposes a social network system for developing countries (SNS4D) that enables pervasive access by offsetting poor Internet connectivity by the rich SMS access provided by cellular networks. It allows all key operations associated with online social networking (e.g. new account creation and update, sending an invitation to a contact, and sharing news with a list of contacts) using both the Web and SMS. Unlike existing online social networks that offer an SMS access in addition to Web access, the new system can be quickly deployed on top of existing social networks. In this paper we have deployed it on top of a social network built using Apache Shindig, through OpenSocial. OpenSocial is a set of common application programming interfaces (APIs) for Web-based social applications [3]. SNS4D also offers an SMS interface with a higher level of abstraction for end-users with phones that support J2ME.

The SNS4D architecture is composed of two layers: a front-end and a back-end. The front-end layer offers both an SMS and a Web interface to end-users, and uses an open interface to communicate with the back-end. The back-end may consist of an existing social network. We have implemented a proof of concept prototype in which Abdel, a member of a West African extended family, whose members have disparate Internet access, creates and maintains a closed group for his extended family.

The rest of the paper is organized as follows. Section 2 introduces a motivating scenario, presents the requirements, and reviews the related work. Section 3 discusses the proposed SNS4D architecture, including the system's components, interfaces and procedures. Section 4 describes the implemented scenario as well as the proof of concept prototype. The last section concludes the paper.

2   Motivating Scenario and Related Work

The scenario is presented first, followed by the requirements and the related work.

2.1   Motivating Scenario

Abdel comes from a large extended family in West Africa. Aware that his family size kept increasing and wanting everyone to be able to keep in touch, he created a closed group on a social network on behalf of the extended family. He sends out invitations to anyone who shares his surname or with whom he has a direct family relationship. As a manager of the group, he documented his family tree. Each new member identifies himself/herself in that tree or creates his/her own, indicates his/her professional profile and country of residence, and sends an invitation to his/her close family members to join the social network.

Various types of information are exchanged via the network. A member with a job corresponding to the profiles of some members can send these members the text file of the job posting. At each birth in the extended family, the photo of the newborn and his/her name is published in the group. Another example emphasizes family support in the case of a death. In Western Africa, when a person dies, the members of the extended family give a certain amount of money to assist the grieving one. The social network is used to publish the news (with the name and the photo of the deceased) and to negotiate the contribution amount.

Abdel's extended family is composed of members with disparate social positions, and therefore with different Internet access capabilities. Some live in developed countries or in large cities and thus have a permanent Internet connection. Others benefit from a sporadic Internet access but can also communicate via SMS using their operator's cellular network. The third category includes members living in rural areas with exclusive SMS capability and no Internet access. These members can travel to an urban area to check their profiles and participate in the group discussions.

SNS4D, a social network that allows a dual SMS and Web access, could meet the needs of such an extended family.

2.2   Requirements

Taking into account the operations to be performed by the system and the levels of Internet access of the members, the system should fulfill the following requirements. First, as a minimum, it should offer all the key operations associated with online social networking (e.g. a group and account management, the invitation of new members and handling of incoming invitations, publication of new information, commenting on published information, etc.). Second, these operations should be offered via both SMS and the Web. A member may, for instance, publish a birth via the Web or by sending an SMS to the system. The system will then post the information in the social profiles of the members with a permanent Internet connection and send an SMS notification to the others (if they had so requested). The third requirement is that the SMS interface should be made as easy as possible to use (i.e. end-users should not have to type full SMS messages).

The fourth requirement is that the members should be able to send a message (i.e. publish information) to the whole group or only to specific members. The fifth requirement is that the system should reuse existing social networks as its back-end, whenever possible. However, it should remain independent of the social network on which it relies and operate independently of the type of cellular phone used and the cellular network operator. This will facilitate and speed up the system's deployment. The last requirement is that the system should be scalable in terms of the number of members, of groups and the groups' size.

2.3   Related Work

We split the related work into two categories: social networks that support SMS, and all other types of SMS groups. Facebook is in the first category, as it is a social network that supports SMS. Facebook users can receive or publish information on or from their cell phones even when offline. However, as with the other similar social networks, end-users cannot perform all of the social network functionalities via SMS (e.g. they cannot create a group, nor send or accept an invitation via SMS). Furthermore, with these networks, all end-users must use a "raw" SMS, while in our system; end-users with J2ME phones will have access to an interface with a higher level of abstraction.

Within the other category, several SMS-based group services have been proposed, to date, the major ones are Google SMS Channel, SMS GupShup and Mobile Enabled

Social hub. Google SMS Channel allows end-users to create communication channels with the ability to broadcast text messages to a group of people [4, 6]. However, no other social network capabilities are provided (e.g. profile creation and management, sending invitations, sharing videos). Furthermore, the end-user must be connected to the Internet in order to create the channel, communication is only SMS-based and thus limited to the subscribers of cellular networks (i.e. Internet users are not supported).

SMS GupShup allows end-users to create and administer SMS groups using either SMS or the Web [6, 12]. However, the messages are only exchanged via SMS and only the group administrator is allowed to send messages; the other group members are only receivers. In addition, SMS GupShup does not interface with any existing social network and does not support Internet users.

Mobile Enabled Social Hub is another platform that allows end-users to exchange SMS messages [6]. It is entirely based on SMS and it operates independently of the type of cellular phone used and of the operator's subscriber. However, as with the previous two solutions, it does not offer the opportunity for end-users to connect to existing social networks nor use the Internet.

3   Proposed Architecture

The overall architecture is presented first, followed by the main interfaces and procedures.

3.1   Overall Architecture

Figure. 1 depicts the overall architectural building blocks. The architecture is composed of two layers: the front-end and the back-end layers. The front-end layer is decomposed into an access sub-layer and a processing sub-layer. The access sub-layer offers end-users the possibility to access the system via both SMS and the Web, using either the SMS or the Web access modules. Each of these modules includes a request receiving and a response sending module, as well as a request processor that parses the incoming requests, extracts the actions to be executed (e.g. publish new information to a specific group) and calls the appropriate functions on the processing sub-layer. Both modules communicate with the processing sub-layer via a common interface (i.e. the GwF interface). The processing sub-layer implements the logic of the SNS4D services. For example, when a new publication request is received, the request handler will get the target group members, check the access mode for each member (i.e. SMS or Web) by interrogating the user profile management module, and then notify each member using his/her favorite medium. The system maintains an up-to-date profile for each user, stored in a local database.

The processing sub-layer communicates with the back-end layer (e.g. to publish new information to Internet-enabled users) via a Representational state transfer (REST) interface. REST is an architectural style for designing distributed client-server applications [5]. The back-end layer consists of a social network engine, which realizes the social network functionalities. It may be composed of any existing social network that offers an open REST API (e.g. OpenSocial) for application development.

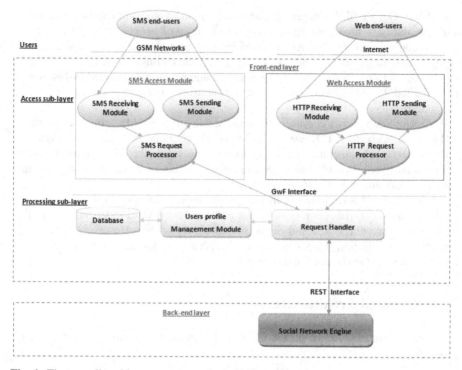

Fig. 1. The overall architecture supports both SMS and Web end-users, and reuses existing social networks as a back-end system to ease the deployment of this new system

3.2   Interfaces

This section is devoted to the front-end layer interfaces. We start with the access sub-layer interfaces, followed by the processing sub-layer interface.

Access Sub-layer Interfaces

This sub-layer offers two types of interfaces, SMS-based and Web-based. They both allow end-users to manage their accounts (e.g. create a new account or update an existing one), their contact lists, their groups (e.g. add or update a group, add friends to a group), accept contact invitations or invitations for joining a group, publish new information, and comment on a received publication.

The Web-based interface is a simple web page. The SMS-based interface, however, requires that the requests and responses be exchanged using a specific format. To publish new information on a specific group, for instance, the end-user sends an SMS such as "pub add groupName message". The first word (i.e. pub) indicates the message type, followed by the operation to be executed, and a list of parameters. The parameters in the example are the group in which the publication should be done, along with the message to be published. The level of abstraction can be raised for end-users with phones that support J2ME. These users are provided with an SMS interface that transforms the collected information from a graphical user interface into a well-formatted SMS message.

To interact with the system via SMS, the end-users send SMS messages from a cell phone registered on their profile. The source cell phone number is used to authenticate the sending end-user.

Processing Sub-layer Interface

This interface provides a set of well-defined APIs to the access modules. These APIs are used to handle both the SMS- and the Web-based end-users' requests and to communicate with the back-end system. To enable a distributed architecture where the front-end sub-layers may reside in separate systems and to minimize the number of interfaces, we chose to offer this interface as REST-based. The interface should remain independent of both the social network engine used and the engine interface.

Following REST design principles, we model the information that needs to be managed (e.g. end-users profiles, groups, publications) into a set of resources. Each resource is identified by a unique Uniform Resource Identifier (URI) and is accessed via a sub-set of HTTP methods. The most common of these methods are GET, POST, PUT, and DELETE, which we use to read, create, update and delete a resource, respectively. The list of resources defined by the GwF interface is shown in Table 1, along with the URI of each resource and the HTTP methods that are supported.

3.3   Procedures

In this section, we discuss two key procedures: the creation of a new end-user account and the publication of new information to a specific group. We chose these two procedures because they clearly illustrate the functioning of the system. The new account creation procedure is presented first, followed by the publication procedure.

New Account Creation Procedure: To create a new account via SMS, the end-user sends an SMS request to the telephone number associated with the SNS4D system. The SMS is intercepted by the SMS access module, which identifies the operation to execute (i.e. account creation) along with its parameters (e.g. end-user name and access mode). The module then calls the appropriate method (i.e. HTTP POST, with the account parameters) on the request handler, via the GwF interface. The request handler uses the user profile management module to create a new profile on the local database, saves the user's phone number, and sets the user access mode as 'SMS'. It also sends a REST request (using OpenSocial API) to the back-end system to create a new account on the back-end social network. When the account is created, the request handler receives a notification that it forwards to the SMS access module. The latter then sends an SMS notification to the end-user.

The same procedure is applied to create a new account via the Web, except that the communication between the end-user and the system is done via the Web and the user access mode is set to 'Web' by default, or to a value given by the end-user. This value might be Web, SMS, or Web&SMS.

Publication Procedure: To publish new information via SMS (via the Web), the end-user sends an SMS (an HTTP request) with the name of the target group and the message to be published. After the SMS (Web) access module has received the request and extracted the pertinent information (i.e. the operation to be executed and its parameter), it sends an HTTP POST request to the request handler. The latter first gets the list of the group members from the back-end system, and then uses the users' profile management module to get the access mode of each member. Next, it sends an SMS notification to all of the SMS-enabled users and publishes the information into the profiles of the Web-enabled ones. A confirmation notification is sent to the publishing end-user, using his/her favorite access medium.

Table 1. GwF resources

Resource	Resource definition	Resource URI Base URI: http://www.pervasiveSNS.com	Supported HTTP methods
User profile	Represents the profile of a specific end-user. Maintains the end-user information such as user name and password, phone number, and the access mode.	/{accountID}	*POST*: create a new user profile *GET*: retrieves information about the user whose 　　　　account ID is given in the URI *PUT*: updates a user's profile information *DELETE*: delete a user's profile
Groups	The groups list of a given end-user	/{accountID}/groups	*GET:* retrieves the list of groups *PUT:* Creates a new group
Group	A specific group of a given end-user	/{accountID}/groups/{GroupID}	*GET:* retrieves the members' list of the group identified by GroupID
Contacts	The list of an end-user's contacts/friends	/{accountID}/contacts	*GET:* Retrieves the contacts list of the end-user whose id is given in the URI
list of publications	A list of the publications posted by a specific end-user	/{accountID}/publications	*POST*: publishes a new posting on a user's profile
individual publication	An individual publication posted by a specific end-user	/{accountID}/publications/{publicationID}	*PUT*: update a published posting *GET*: retrieve the contents of a publication *DELETE*: delete a publication
List of comments	A list of the comments sent by a specific end-user	/{accountID}/publications/{publicationID}/comments	*POST*: post a comment regarding a given publication
Individual comment	An individual comment sent　by a specific end-user	/{accountID}/publications/{publicationID}/comments/{commentID}	*GET:* Retrieve a given comment *PUT*: update a posted comment *DELETE*: delete a posted comment
List of invitations	A list of invitations sent by a specific end-user	/{accountID}/invitations	*POST:* A user sends an invitation to one or more users, given in the request body.
Individual invitation	An individual invitation sent　by a specific end-user	/{accountID}/invitations/{invitationID}	*DELETE*: cancel an invitation whose identifier is given in the request URI

4　Implementation

This section presents the implemented scenario and then discusses the prototype.

4.1　Implemented Scenario

A subset of the scenario described in section 2.1 was implemented as a proof-of-concept prototype. The scenario involves three users, Abdel, Frejus and Christian. Their access modes are SMS, SMS, and SMS&Web, respectively. Figure 2 depicts the scenario sequence diagram.

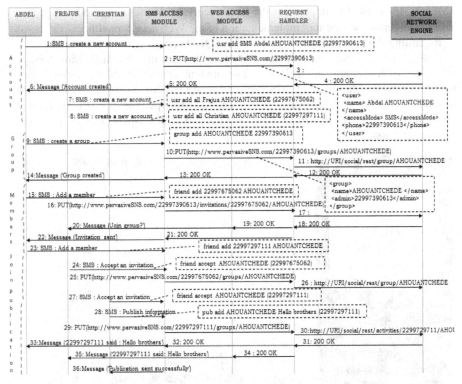

Fig. 2. Sample sequence diagram

First, Abdel creates a new account by sending an SMS request to the system (steps 1 to 6), as do Frejus and Christian. The details for creating the last two accounts are not presented in the figure, since they are similar to the first one. Next, Abdel creates a new family group, again via an SMS request (steps 9 to 14). He then adds Christian and Frejus to the group, which triggers the sending of a notification to both users (steps 15 to 23). Christian and Frejus accept the invitation to join the group (steps 23 to 27) and thereby become members.

In step 28, Christian informs his group mates that he is returning to Benin for a short stay. The information is forwarded to Frejus via the Web and to Abdel via SMS, according to their respective profiles (steps32 to 35); Christian is notified that his information was published successfully (step 36). The three users can now negotiate an eventual meeting by commenting on Christian publication.

4.2   Prototype

The prototype includes the front-end and the back-end layers, as well as a client side J2ME application. To implement the front-end-layer, we use a GSM modem (an Huawei Mobile Broadband E153) attached to the machine running the SMS access module. The SMS messages from the end-users are routed via the end-users' SMS service provider to the number of the SIM card on the GSM modem. The Java library

SMSLib [13] is used to implement the SMS receiving and sending modules. Apache Tomcat server is used for the implementation of the Web access module.

Regarding the processing sub-layer, a MySQL database is used to store the users' profiles. The REST interfaces of the request handler are implemented using Jersey, a reference implementation of JSR-311. The implementation of the back-end layer is based on Apache Shindig [11], which provides an OpenSocial container for the easy hosting of social applications. The standardized OpenSocial API is used to communicate with the back-end system. We have extended OpenSocial API to enable account creation.

(a). J2ME application   (b). Execution screen showing the SMS messages exchanged between the end-users and the system

Fig. 3. The implemented prototype uses Shindig as the back-end system and offers both a Web and an SMS interface. A J2ME application was implemented and tested on Nokia Series 40 phones.

The J2ME application was implemented using Eclipse Pulsar, which is a Java Mobile development environment, and the Nokia suite toolkit [14]. It uses the Wireless Messaging API defined in the Java Specification Requests (JSR)-120 to send SMS messages. The application was deployed and tested on Nokia Series 40 phones.

Figure 3.a illustrates the main menu of the J2ME application, while Figure. 4.b shows the different SMS messages exchanged between the system and the end-users. In the first line, for instance, end-user Abdel AHOUANTCHEDE with phone number 97390613 sends a request to create a new account, stating that his favorite access mode is SMS. In the second line, the system sends a success notification to Abdel.

5   Conclusion

This paper proposes a social network system for developing countries that utilizes the broad reach of SMS and the scarce deployment of the Internet in these countries.

The system can be accessed via both SMS and the Web, and it can be easily deployed on top of existing social networks. A prototype has been implemented on top of a social network hosted on Apache Shindig. A J2ME application was implemented for J2ME-enabled cell phones and was tested on Nokia series 40 phones.

References

1. Internet World Statistics,
   http://www.internetworldstats.com/list4.html
2. http://www.itu.int/ITU-D/ict/material/FactsFigures2010.pdf
3. OpenSocial Specification 2.0.1,
   http://opensocial-resources.googlecode.com/svn/spec/2.0.1/
   OpenSocial-Specification.xml
4. Anandan, V., Mary, V.P., Prashant, S., Jhunjhunwala, A.: SMS based Social Networking over GSM Network for Rural India, IU-ATC project funded by the Department of Science and Technology (DST), Government of India and the UK EPSRC Digital Economy Program
5. Fielding, R.T.: Architectural Styles and the Design of Network-based Software Architectures, these (2000)
6. Vallina-Rodriguez, N., Hui, P., Crowcroft, J.: Has anyone seen my goose? Social Network Services in Developing Regions. In: 2009 International Conference on Computational Science and Engineering (2009)
7. Kolko, B.E., Johnson, E., Rose, E.: Mobile Social Software for the Developing World. In: Schuler, D. (ed.) Online Communities and Social Comput., HCII 2007. LNCS, vol. 4564, pp. 385–394. Springer, Heidelberg (2007)
8. Counts, S., Fisher, K.E.: Mobile Social Networking: An Information Grounds Perspective. In: Proceedings of the 41st Annual Hawaii International Conference on System Sciences (HICSS 2008), p. 153 (2008)
9. Kolko, B.E., Rose, E.J., Johnson, E.J.: Communication as information-seeking: the case for mobile social software for developing regions. In: Proceedings of the 16th International Conference on World Wide Web (2007)
10. Donner, J.: Research Approaches to Mobile Use in the Developing World: A Review of the Literature 24(3), 140–159 (2008)
11. http://shindig.apache.org/
12. http://www.smsgupshup.com/login
13. http://www.smslib.org
14. http://www.developer.nokia.com/

RuKaCS: A Community Services and Proximity Networks Project Framework for Bridging Digital Divide in Rural Cameroon

Thomas Djotio Ndié

National Advanced School of Engineering, LIRIMA, MASECNESS Team Leader
P.O. Box. 8390 Yaoundé, Cameroon
tdjotio@gmail.com

Abstract. In many parts of rural Africa; there is lack of local content in the Internet; lack of community involvement and the need to open the information society to the neighborhood and to overcome obstacles from national monopolis and global Telecoms operators. In this paper, we present RuKaCS, a project initiative where we propose community-based user services on top of an underlying wired or wireless communication infrastructure. We take advantage of proximity to bridge the digital divide in rural Cameroon. The proximity service is a particular type of community user service available within near vicinity and might be built on WIFI technologies. It can concern (but not limited to) proximity marketing, proximity conference, proximity learning. An example of user service is presented: the case of a rural telephony on a wireless mesh network (WMN) in rural Cameroon. The approach we propose to tackle these challenges is oriented community centers of interest, with no need of third party operator, contrary to the traditional wireless services which are generally Telecom Service Provider (TSP) or Internet Service Provider (ISP)-oriented.

Keywords: Community service, community network, virtual network, network sharing, proximity network, wireless mesh network.

1 Introduction

In developing countries like Cameroon, there is real development of the telecommunication services and the Internet. This development results in an unquestionable passion by part of the population mostly concentrated in the big metropolises. A local loop radio (LLR) used by an ISP serves for distributing the Internet to customers in a neighborhood. For a particular (public administration, firm, community, ...) it serves for optimizing services by accomplishing digital economies and by reducing their costs using the VPN technology. These traditional user services are the voice, video and the text. Value-added services provided by wireless macro infrastructures; the TSP and ISP are numerous but are unfortunately advantageous only for some part of the population mainly in cities, having some level of education: e/m-payment, e/m-health, e/m-learning to name only these few examples.

Approximately 3 persons out of 5 in Cameroon own a telephone set, some of whom live in rural areas. Either it is the rural communities which do not have

K. Jonas, I.A. Rai, and M. Tchuente (Eds.): AFRICOMM 2012, LNICST 119, pp. 34–44, 2013.

connectivity or communities with low income that might also live in the cities; they have problems of poverty, accessing to primary health care, education, and more others. There is an incoherent and disorganized use of virtual services because most of the populations are surprised by the speed with which technologies are developed and introduced in the country. It can also be noted that the success of virtual technologies is unfortunately not accompanied by the improvement of the living standard of populations; efforts remain to be made to exploit them for the greater benefit of the underprivileged populations.

The equipments for mobile telephony and wireless technology can provide possibilities for building wireless LAN (WLAN) such as ad hoc networks and WMN. The term wireless here is referred (but not limited) to IEEE 802.11.x (WIFI), IEEE 802.16.x (WiMAX), GSM (Global System for Mobile Communications) and UMTS (Universal Mobile Telecommunications System) [1] [2]. The WMN allows the setting up of community networks at low cost. The range of the signal can go from 100 m for WIFI up to 20 km for WiMAX and even greater with GSM and UMTS with the possibility of relaying. This leads to the following questions: How can we pertinently and efficiently use wireless infrastructure to help the rural populations to improve their health standards, education and proximity security at lower costs? How possible is it to give to our poor populations of the rural areas the possibility of accessing the Internet, voice and video without soliciting the services of a third-party operator? The main conditions for benefiting from such services are like the membership of a community network. More concretely it is a question of giving possibility to people in a close neighborhood and particularly those in rural areas, to access at less cost the same services provided by the ISP/TSP. Indeed, it is the ISP/TSP that is at the center of value-added services in wireless environments at present, which is what brings about strong dependences and generates high costs. This provider-centered approach requires the expenses of subscription besides the communication costs.

Motivations and objectives of our project initiative are quite simple. In many rural areas in Cameroon, community radios are aimed at informing and sensitizing the rural populations in vernacular languages: this is an example of a proximity radio service built on the traditional telecom infrastructure. Today in urban areas, cable TV distributors have succeeded in bringing television to inhabitants at a very accessible cost: approximately FCFA 3000 (€4.5) flat fees per month no matter the number of channels provided. The later is an example of a wired proximity television service. We propose to explore the possibility of implementing community telephony service for rural communities with no connectivity as well as communities with low income that might also be living in cities. Our approach is community-centered with no dependence on a third-party telecom operator. The community network should be set-up by separate (privately owned) entities[1] that are connected to the grid or supplied by solar power cells. The peculiarities of our solution are the following: (1) it is built on wireless mesh networks; (2) it will support roaming within community networks and (3) give the possibility of intuitively switching to third-party telecom operators when necessary. The implementation environment is the rural area in Cameroon.

---

[1] These entities should constitute the community network and provide access and services to mobile phone users (via Bluetooth for proximity services for example or, more likely, wireless LAN access based on WIFI or WiMAX)

The rest of the paper is organized as follow: section 2 gives a brief overview of related work carried out in developing countries. Section 3 presents a possible community-based user service: the community telephony and also outlines the possible framework. The methodological approach and the expected scientific results are addressed in section 4. Section 5 is dedicated to the social implication of our project. We end with section 6 which depicts the local and sub-regional impact, the benefits and the perspectives of the project.

2   Related Works and Projects

It is established that the broadband penetration in developing regions, especially Africa, is very poor compared to developed world. www.infodev.org presents in "The Wireless Internet Opportunity for Developing Countries[2]" interesting case studies on WIFI, WiMAX and related technologies and shows how they can be used to facilitate access to knowledge and information, for example by making use of unlicensed radio spectrum to deliver cheap and fast Internet access and helping countries to leapfrog generations of telecommunications technology and infrastructure and empower their people [7], [8], [9], [10], [11]. Proceedings of the AFRICOMM conference series help to learn new opportunities, "trends, recent research, innovation advances and on-the-field experiences related to e-Infrastructure, e-Governance, e-Business and enabling policy and regulations with a deep focus on developing countries"[3]. The book of wndw.net "Wireless Networking in the Developing World" is an interesting practical guide to plan and build low-cost telecommunications infrastructure in the context of developing countries to [12]. From here http://w2i.com/events/schedule/ event_overview/p/eventId_53/id_195, there are webinar proceedings that help to learn how to exploit broadband to build digital cities and convert the virtual economy into development potential. A case of small and medium sized enterprises in Sub-Saharan Africa is studied. The provided technology is based on the USSD technology on smart phones to deliver information at any time and from any location with a mobile carrier signal [7]. Jonathan Backens & al in [13] and [14] give a proof of concept of rural wireless connectivity problems from a test case in Macha, a rural village of Zambia with special considerations of real world rural mesh network implementation challenges. They provided a proposal and performance analysis of a unique indoor to indoor community based rural WMN using 802.11 equipments. Amos Nungu & al discuss in [19] and [20] a framework for the establishment of sustainable broadband communication in under-served areas with special focus on Africa. The experimentations are carried out in Serengeti, a northern rural Tanzania. It is a self sustained broadband Island with its own network services (domain name, mail, web and VoIP, e-Governance, e-Health and e-Learning) hosted locally. The Testbed in Sankt Augustin and the CARMEN projects are interesting implementations of WMNs on which can be built efficient wireless services [3] platforms. Vinoth Gunasekaran & al in [4] propose a strategic wireless framework to address challenges in three different economic sectors of a developing country: (a) metro economy, which is

---

[2] www.infodev.org/en/Document.24.PDF
[3] http://www.africommconference.org/index.shtml

well-urbanized and integrated with the global economy; (b) sub-urban economy, which has niche economic or development activities compared to (a); and (c) the rural economy, characterized by informal economic activity and poverty. They have based their studies on Broadband; Wi-Fi; WiMAX wireless technologies. The Fraunhofer FOKUS NET4DC project (http://net4dc.fokus.fraunhofer.de/) aims at establishing reliable communication infrastructures to connect the unconnected regions with target areas in Africa, Asia and South America, by using wireless wide-area communication.

No matter the results obtained, there are still problems to challenge. David Johnson & al in [5] pose the problem of routing loops which are created in a WMN due to the asymmetrical links when one does not use an adequate routing protocol like OLSR. As alternative, the authors propose BATMAN, a routing protocol based on a pragmatic approach for routes learning in a mesh network. Another alternative in terms of a real world case experimentation is Roofnet [6], an urban test case 802.11b/g mesh network which aims at challenging routing problems in the field such as link-level measurements of 802.11, finding high-throughput routes in the face of lossy links and link adaptation. The Fraunhofer WiBAC project is an alternative to DiffServ of providing QoS mechanisms to differentiate between streams in a network infrastructure. The implementation of our community wireless telephony network will require the use of WMN.

We learn then that there are currently mesh deployments being implemented worldwide [14], [15], [16]. Many researchers target their challenge instead on the substantial need for rural wireless test case analysis [12]. Most of the solutions being offered remain limited to network infrastructure mainly for providing Internet service to the community instead of providing community wide availability of user services. Some accompany their architecture with their business models [17] because costs are important key element to consider. To the best of our knowledge, the aspects of user services still have interesting research opportunities to explore, particularly community-based user services. At a large scale, such environments to our knowledge do not exist, at least in the context of the developing countries mostly surprised by stakes of virtual technologies. In many parts of rural Africa there is a lack of local content in the Internet, there is a lack of people's involvement. There is a need to open the information society to the neighborhood and to overcome obstacles from national monopolis and global Telecom operators. Proximity networks refer to networks where the physical proximity of a user to a network immediately creates a local service environment. It promotes an integration of user devices into a networked services environment. Proximity also takes advantage of local trust, enabling completely new relational and economic concepts.

3   Presentation of the Project: Community-Based User Services

In this section, we start by defining concepts and presenting the community telephony service on a rural WMN. The technical architectures are proposed. We also suggest a global functional framework which will be able to accommodate our services.

3.1   Definition of Concepts: User Services, Community-Based User Services

By user service, we mean any type of service which requires the wireless or wired communication infrastructure to be exploited by end users. It includes but not limited to: (m/e)-Learning, (m/e)-government, (m/e)-administration, (e/m)-health, (e/m)-training, (e/m)-commerce, (e/m)-payment. We will particularly focus on wireless user services which can possibly be built on top of wired network. The community service refers to all type of user services that can be exploited in a community network at the range of IEEE 802.16.x, GSM or UMTS wireless technologies. More generally, the community-based user services include (but not limited to) community radio, community telephony, payment services, health services, learning services, accessible within a virtual community built thanks to a middle or wide range wireless technology. In a community network, people share the same center of interests and can dynamically be self-organized. The proximity service is a restricted community service available within near vicinity at the range of IEEE 802.11.x wireless technology. In proximity networks, a user can immediately and automatically access a network service available in a close neighborhood. It helps to exploit every day applications due to ubiquitous communications.

3.2   Example of Community Service: Community Telephony

The community telephony is about deploying an autonomous rural telecom provider (RTPr) to provide the rural population with the telephony service. The network infrastructure is a WMN coupled with WIFI and WIMAX [2] or GSM. A WMN is a communications network characterized by a "dedicated static or quasi-static wireless routers which carry out the function of routing packets through the network, and client devices, which have no routing functionality, connecting to the wireless routers" [5]. Some good examples of WMNs are broadband municipal wireless networks. A look is taken at how to switch a call from such an infrastructure to the national backbone according to pre-specified agreements (contracts, license sharing, costs,...). The environment of experimentation is a rural area in Cameroon.

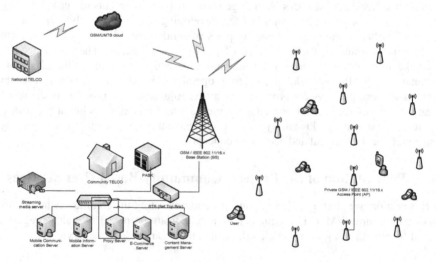

Fig. 1. Proposed architecture of the community telecommunication

The architecture illustrated figure 1 is an example of WIFI/WiMAX/GSM wireless local loop (WLL). The community Telecom provider (CTPr) will provide the rural community with (1) a switching service point (SSP) from the core technology composed of WIFI, WiMAX and GSM; (2) the support of wireless technology and available applications developed; (3) the Control service point (SCP) that will give for example end user identification, authentication and accounting; (4) the Data service access (DSA) and (5) a wireless service centre control (WSCS) which consist of user services as described earlier.

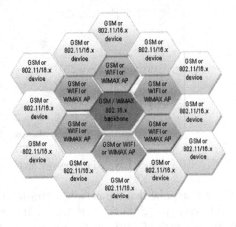

The figure 2 depicts the repartition of IEEE 802.11/16.x and/or GSM devices. A IEEE 802.16.x or GSM base station (WBS) will constitute the wireless community service backbone. It is surrounded by IEEE 802.11/16.x and private GSM APs by which the end users will get access to the community services.

Fig. 2. IEEE 802.(11/16).x / GSM signal coverage

QoS mechanisms and roaming remain great challenges. The need of transmitting voice and video over the same link implies taking into account some QoS mechanisms to differentiate between streams.

3.3   An Outline of a Community-Based User Services Framework

To further implement, test and run the user services we identified and described earlier, we need to situate our problem within a logical framework. We suggest a layered framework called *WSF4DC (Wireless Service Framework for Developing Countries)*; illustrated by the figure 3 which can permit the development and the hosting of user services. The WSF4DC provides means of creating and managing the whole of user services hosted by server accessible via a wireless network infrastructure from a mobile terminal of variable configuration going from the bottom-of-the-range to the high-end. It includes but not limited to: mobile phones, laptop, GSM/UMTS terminals and IEEE 802.(11/16).x-based equipment. The figure 3 depicts the three abstract layers of the proposed framework. Each layer consists of components or modules which interact together by means of interfaces. We briefly present hereafter the layers of our framework from bottom to top.

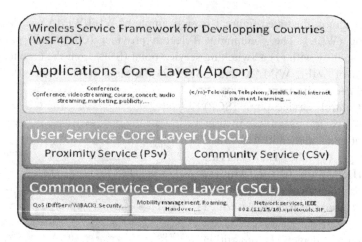

Fig. 3. Layered framework architecture of wireless services

We will assume that the network infrastructure (low-level connectivity as well as network services such as privacy and mobility management) is available. This implies that we will instead work on the service layer with no regard for the transmission technology. At the Common Service Core Layer (CSCL) are managed network services problems like QoS, security, mobility management, handover, roaming, and network protocols. The User Service Core Layer (USCL) constitutes the basis of our work. It includes two sub layers: the proximity service layer (PSv) and the community service layer (CSv). The Application Core Layer (ApCor) is that which will be implemented by the various user services. The WSF4DC is the container of all the above mentioned components. It must be (1) **open**, capable of allowing the development, addition, integration and subtraction of new services; (2) **modular**, interaction between layers and components will instead focus on the interfaces' implementation; (3) **secured or manageable**, it must allow the tracking and the monitoring of intrusions, errors and fault notification to ensure the relevance and the effectiveness of the service provided.

4   Methodological Approach and Scientific Outcomes

4.1   The Design and Implementation Approach

When trying to improve something, it is always very important to start by seriously surveying the field to learn from the succeeded and failed real-world case studies and implementations of the past. That is why the study of communication networks, service concepts, community-based approaches and their deployments [5], [6], [12], [15] is needed; with a special focus to community communication service. A concrete implementation as a proof-of concept in rural Cameroon will help to validate our model. The prospection for partnerships with some research labs or teams working on the same challenges in the field is also important to share experiences.

4.2   The Scientific Outcomes

Some key aspects to be considered in any large wireless communication infrastructure are mobility management (handover, roaming), security, privacy, and charging/accounting just to name a few. Mobility management problems are currently under investigation in our Labs. The routing protocol concerns in WMNs need to be clearly study. Some routing protocols like OLSR creates routing loops due to asymmetrical links. BATMAN or Roofnet routing protocols can be used as shortcomings of OLSR to implement WMNs and especially when nodes grow in number. On the forensics point of vue; who makes sure that services are secure, that some users don't prevent others or sniff their traffic?

Other critical points are QoS mechanisms to differentiate between streams: DiffServ or WiBACK. They pose serious constraints for the implementation and operation of community communication service to operate among and over community networks; particularly when trying to connect to the rest of the world and, mainly to allow a community network to interconnect to other national network operators in the case of providing international access to the Internet and voice services. One or multiple operators can use the community network and offer their services. This leads to the situation of network sharing and virtual networking. At the same time we want to allow people to have free local calls and services. This is called a "local break-out" where some operator's service infrastructures can be bypassed.

4.3   Key Cost Elements and Technical Features

The installation of a wireless network depends on several factors namely: the geographical situation and the administrative level of the area, the networks and other infrastructures (such as electricity) present in the area, the financial means and the type of technologies to be used. The main problem to which we are confronted is the following: how to build up a reliable wireless services framework for rural with affordable costs? Indeed, many questions remain unanswered such as how to assure competition among traditional service providers? What about cost, business cases? Who will provide the community network infrastructure and how much would it cost? What about communication into/out of the community network? Who serves, who pays Internet connectivity? Who provides long-distance links to the rural areas?

Key cost elements include the cost for renting and setting up the host location (the community services centre), the cost of acquisition and installation of the servers for providing user services (streaming media, mobile communication and information, proxy service, content management, SIP proxy...) and the community network equipment (WiMAX/WIFI/GSM/UMTS base stations (BS), access points (AP), and subscriber units (SU), PABX/IPPBX, Set Top Box(STB)). Having an adequate and reliable energy supply remains a fundamental concern for the deployment of community services in rural areas of developing countries. Additional cost elements here include (1) the cost of battery backups for the protection of servers from power outage, and (2) the cost of standby power generators, their installation or alternatively, the cost of renewable energy like solar / wind energy system and a battery bank in addition to the connection to the national electricity grid [21], [22]. Other costs may include that of connecting to the national fiber optic or a third party wireless broadband backbone (as an option), consumables, cost of training and overheads. Overheads might include the infrastructure's deployment constraints and the agreement cost involved in setting up conventions with the national Telecom operators and/or other WLAN operators

In addition to outline these key cost elements, technical aspects need to be addressed: what technologies to acquire with respect to the local environments and climate constraints? What type of software to build or acquire? Some Linux-based systems open source include (but not limited to) Linux Router Project, FreeBSD-based router, Vyatta (http://www.vyatta.com/) … , MicroTik wireless router software (http://www.mikrotik.com) that supports several wireless technologies with management possibilities via telnet, ssh and http. In [22] and [23], the authors advocate the use of open source software routers, selected standard hardware and renewable energy solutions. They build and experiment in Serengeti in Tanzania, a fascinating low cost, low power, high performance routers to be used in community networks based on Linux/Bifrost distribution.

5   Local Applications or Social Implications of Our Project

One of the greatest challenges of the information age is to reverse the top-down approach of the Internet to provide instead at real time original content from rural areas. Today, we have to go inside the rural areas, collect the information, treat and publish them sometimes with a very long delay. The proximity services are characteristic of the African society where people organize themselves in united or interdependent communities. These communities exist in the form of meetings, groups, tontines (financial operations) and assistance of any kind. Our project will contribute to create economic opportunities for many individuals and to reinforce the social networks in the rural areas.

The individuals in the communities become actors, contributors and authors of original content. The information from now on comes from the village, from the community towards the center. This is the down-top approach contrary to the Internet. The popularization of the rural know-how (for example traditional medicine) becomes really concurrent with the modern know-how (for example the modern medicine). As in the field of health, it will be possible to carryout tele-diagnoses. It is also going to help in the popularization of cultures and traditional values by allowing the documentation and the diffusion of the good practices gathered from successful local innovations which had an impact on the rural means of subsistence, and that can be reproduced elsewhere. Contents can even be provided in the local languages. Parents will become teachers of the local traditions and cultures. In the case of agriculture and breeding, it can help to create a virtual market, to support trade follow-up and the popularization of financials' information. It can favour quick access to the market and ground data in real-time, it can also facilitate online advices to make consequent decisions. It can favour proximity training or simply onsite training: mutually interdependent people within the community can come together spontaneously and, assistance to the needy is possible. Access to user services will be done at a very competitive cost compare to the actual ISP/TSP top-down approach, and can contribute to boost the rural entrepreneurship.

The provision of a Community telephone call centre through which authorities can access by satellite in real-time following an alarm, can contribute to fight against (a) organized crime; (b) attacks and kidnapping of people; (c) formal education in backward country. This will concern particularly distant regions with serious access difficulties such as East-Cameroon, cross-border zones as well as other areas where these crimes are very common.

6   Conclusion and Future Works

In this paper, we started by giving the context, describing the problems, and outlining motivations and objectives of our project initiative. We gave a brief overview of related works in the context of developing countries in section 2. In section 3, we respectively gave some definitions around the concepts of user wireless services; introduced the community telephony as one possible example of community-based user service; and outlined a framework that can host and manage this user service. We continued in section 4 by exposing the methodological approach we will adopt, the expected scientific results and some key elements that will help to build an in-depth costs' analysis. In section 5, we presented the local applications and social implications of our framework.

The main feature of user services to be developed for wireless networks will be their capacity to contribute to catch up with the developing countries on the digital divide. In the case of Cameroon, it will strongly contribute to the success of the government's policy which aims at becoming an emerging economy by the year 2035. It will constitute the innovation in the rural telecom.

Currently, some research studies are undertaken on the topic and some results like handover and roaming solutions, proximity telephony on the university campus based on Bluetooth, will be tested in the near future.

References

1. Shoemake, M.B.: Wi-Fi (IEEE 802.11b) and Bluetooth Coexistence Issues. White paper, Texas Instruments (2001)
2. Labiod, H., Afifi, H., De Santis, C.: Wi-Fi, Bluetooth, Zigbee and Wimax. Springer, Berlin (2007), doi:10.1007/978-1-4020-5397-9
3. Fraunhofer FOKUS: Connecting the Unconnected Internet Access for Five Billion People (2010), http://www.net4dc.org
4. Gunasekaran, V., Harmantzis, F.C.: Emerging wireless technologies for developing countries. Technology in Society 29, 23–42 (2007)
5. Johnson, D., Ntlatlapa, N., Aichele, C.: A simple pragmatic approach to mesh routing using BATMAN, http://wirelessafrica.meraka.org.za, http://wirelessafrica.meraka.org.za/wiki/images/9/98/Batman_ifip.pdf
6. Wikipedia, the free encyclopedia, Roofnet, http://en.wikipedia.org/wiki/Roofnet
7. World Times, Inc.: The Wireless Internet Opportunity for Developing Countries, Wireless Internet Institute (2003), http://www.w2i.org

8. McNamara, K.: Building Local Capacity for ICT Policy and Regulation: A Needs Assessment and Gap Analysis for Africa, the Caribbean, and the Pacific, infoDev, Working Paper No. 16 (January 2008),
http://www.infodev.org/publications

9. Fourie, L.: Enhancing the Livelihoods of the Rural Poor Through Ict: A Knowledge Map South Africa Country Report infoDev, Working Paper No. 13 (June 2008), edited by Kerry McNamara (infoDev), http://www.infodev.org/publications

10. InfoDev Improving Health, Connecting People: The Role of ICTs in the Health Sector of Developing Countries, Working Paper No. 1 (2007),
http://www.infodev.org/publications

11. Lehdonvirta, V., Ernkvist, M.: Converting The Virtual Economy Into Development Potential (April 2011), http://www.infodev.org/publications

12. WNDW project: Wireless Networking in the Developing World 2nd Ed. A practical guide to planning and building low-cost telecommunications infrastructure (December 2007),
http://wndw.net/,
http://wndw.net/pdf/wndw2-en/wndw2-ebook.pdf

13. Backens, J., Mweemba, G., van Stam, G.: A Rural Implementation of a 52 Node Mixed Wireless Mesh Network in Macha, Zambia,
http://www.share4dev.info/kb/documents/4774.pdf

14. Backens, J., Song, M., Engels, L.: Rural Wireless Mesh Networking in Africa: an Experiential Study, http://www.share4dev.info/kb/documents/4780.pdf

15. Wang, X., (XXXXXXXX): Video Streaming over Bluetooth: A Survey Institute for Infocomm Research (I2R) / School of Computing, NUS

16. Seibel, R., Klann, N.-H., Waage, T., Hogrefe, D.: Wireless Mesh Networks for Infrastructure Deficient Areas. In: Pont, A., Pujolle, G., Raghavan, S.V. (eds.) WCITD 2010. IFIP AICT, vol. 327, pp. 26–38. Springer, Heidelberg (2010)

17. Gomes, C.F., Gomes, F.C., Fernandez, M.P.: Infrastructure and Business Model for Universal Broadband Access in Developing Regions: The Ceara State Digital Belt. In: Pont, A., Pujolle, G., Raghavan, S.V. (eds.) WCITD 2010. IFIP AICT, vol. 327, pp. 51–59. Springer, Heidelberg (2010)

18. Nungu, A., Brown, T., Pehrson, B.: Business Model for Developing World Municipal, Broadband Network - A Case Study. In: GIIS 2011, pp. 1–7. IEEE (2011)

19. Nungu, A., Pehrson, B.: Towards Sustainable Broadband Communication in Rural Areas. In: Szabó, R., Zhu, H., Imre, S., Chaparadza, R. (eds.) AccessNets 2010. LNICST, vol. 63, pp. 168–175. Springer, Heidelberg (2011)

20. Nungu, A., Brown, T., Pehrson, B.: Challenges in Sustaining Municipal Broadband Networks in the Developing World. In: Yonazi, J.J., Sedoyeka, E., Ariwa, E., El-Qawasmeh, E. (eds.) ICeND 2011. CCIS, vol. 171, pp. 26–40. Springer, Heidelberg (2011)

21. Nungu, A., Brown, T., Pehrson, B.: On Powering Communication Networks in Developing Regions, pp. 383–390. IEEE (2011)

22. Nungu, A., Olsson, R., Pehrson, B.: On the Design of Inclusive Ubiquitous Access. In: ICUFN 2011, pp. 346–352. IEEE (2011)

23. Nungu, A., Olsson, R., Pehrson, B.: Short Paper - On the Design of Affordable and Green High-Performance Routers for Community Networks. In: NSDR 2010. ACM (2010)

Achievable Capacity Design for Irregular and Clustered High Performance Mesh Networks

Thomas Otieno Olwal[1] and Moshe Timothy Masonta[1,2]

[1] Council for Scientific and Industrial Research (CSIR), Meraka Institute,
P.O. Box 395, Pretoria, 0001, South Africa
{tolwal,mmasonta}@csir.co.za
[2] Department of Electrical Engineering, Tshwane University of Technology,
Private Bag X680, Pretoria, 0001, South Africa

Abstract. This study has presented the End to End (E2E) upper bound capacity limits for high performance mesh nodes that can be deployed in rural and remote areas. The achievable capacity limits for both irregular and clustered placements of nodes have been analytically derived. Numerical results based on the data sheets of IEEE 802.11a/n standards reveal the efficacy of such designs to typical rural networks such as the Peebles valley mesh in rural South Africa.

Keywords: Achievable capacity, clustered & irregular placement, HPN.

1 Introduction

The next generation fixed wireless broadband networks have increasingly been deployed as mesh networks in order to provide and extend access to the internet. These networks are characterized by the use of multiple orthogonal channels available within the industrial, scientific and medical (ISM) licensed-free frequency bands. Nodes in the network have the ability to simultaneously communicate with many neighbors or stream different versions of the same data/information using multiple radio devices over orthogonal channels thereby improving effective "online" channel utilization [1]. The ability to perform full duplex communication by individual multi-radio nodes without causing network interference has also been achieved through decentralized transmission power control schemes in [2], [3]. That is, one radio interface can be used for receiving packets and the other radio interfaces on seperate non overlapping channels are used for transmitting packets. Many such networks emerging from standards such as IEEE 802.11 a/b/g/n and 802.16 are already in use, ranging from prototype test-beds [4] to complete solutions [5].

The increasing question is how the end to end (E2E) theoretical capacity of such multi-radio network scales with the node density, irregularity of node placement and link obstructions [6]. In their seminal work, Gupta and Kumar [7] determined the capacity of single radio single channel networks. Their findings have been later extended to derive the capacity bounds of a high performance network [8]. In addition, the link throughput performance parameters in IEEE

K. Jonas, I.A. Rai, and M. Tchuente (Eds.): AFRICOMM 2012, LNICST 119, pp. 45–54, 2013.
© Institute for Computer Sciences, Social Informatics and Telecommunications Engineering 2013

802.11 networks have also been discussed in [9]. However, the considered network architectures have so far been presented with a number of impractical assumptions. The first assumption asserts that the location of nodes and traffic patterns can be controlled in arbitrary networks. The second assumption claims that channel fading can be excluded in the capacity analysis such that each frequency channel can support a fixed data rate. Lastly, nodes are randomly located on the surface of a torus of unit area to avoid technicalities arising out of edge effects. However, in realistic networks, location of nodes is determined by the irregularity of the terrain, the presence of tree foliage [6], and needs and locations of terminal users [10]. Moreover, typical rural based wireless networks can be described by (i) long single hop links, (ii) limited and unreliable energy sources, and (iii) clustered distribution of Internet users [11]. The main problem constitutes the need to increase capacity of community owned existing wireless broadband networks so that multimedia services can be delivered to remote and rural areas without losing connectivity [2].

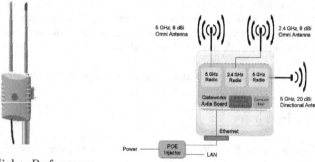

Fig. 1. High Performance Node (HPN)^{TM} [10]

Fig. 2. Block Diagram of HPN^{TM} [10]

In response to this need, high performance nodes (HPNs)^{TM} for community-owned wireless mesh networks, have been implemented in most parts of rural South Africa [12]. The innovation as shown in **Figure 1** has been developed by the CSIR Meraka Institute and it provides high throughput in mesh networks. The HPN^{TM} is an IEEE 802.11 based multi-interface node made up of three interfaces or radio devices and controlled by an embedded microcontroller technology [10]. To ensure high speed performance, the innovation has the first radio interface card attached to a 5 GHz directional antenna for backhaul mesh routing; the second interface card is connected to a 5 GHz omni-directional antenna for backhaul mesh connectivity and access. The third radio interface card is attached to a 2.4 GHz omni-directional antenna for mesh client access network. As shown in **Figure 2**, the HPN block diagram has a weather proof Unshielded Twisted Pair (UTP) connector at the bottom of the node that provides Power-Over-Ethernet (PoE) and Ethernet connectivity to the HPN. To attach the HPN to a pole or a suitable structure, a mounting bracket is fixed at the back of the router for other operational details [10]. The HPNs are often installed on roof tops, street poles and buildings of villages, local schools, clinics, museums and agricultural farmlands.

In this study, the focus will be the design of E2E capacity limit of the terminal backhaul connectivity of the HPNs. The terminal backhaul connectivity offers aggregated traffic volumes of all flows within the network. The traffic flows traverse long links between any two HPNs and are faced with severe climatic and topographical conditions [11], [12]. Thus, E2E upper bound capacity limits for irregular and clustered placement of HPNs are analytically found to be as follows:

$$O\left(Rn\sqrt{\tfrac{mc}{\delta p}}\right) \text{ and } O\left(Rn\sqrt{mc[\tfrac{n_1}{\delta_1} + \tfrac{n_2}{\delta_2}]}\right).$$

Here, R is the rate of a single link in bits/s computed by taking into account multipath effects and the built-in structure of the innovative HPNs, n is the number of HPNs, m is the number of radio interface cards per each HPN, c is the number of frequency channels that do not cause interference in duplex communication, $0 < p < 1$ is the rate of the regularity (probability) of the placement of HPNs, and is the HPN distribution density that is varied over a fixed deployment area. In clustered placements, δ_1 and n_1 are the intra-cluster density and number of HPNs, respectively. On the other hand δ_2 and n_2 are similar values for the inter-cluster.

The rest of the paper is organized as follows. In Section 2, design of upper bounds E2E capacity limits for HPN networks is provided. Section 3 furnishes numerical capacity limits and related discussions for real networks in a given rural area size. The paper is concluded in Section 4, with highlights of the main contributions of this study, and future research and development (R&D) perspectives.

2   Achievable Capacity of HPN Wireless Mesh

In order to design the achievable capacity bound for the HPN (the dual channel dual radio) based mesh network we consider a typical static wireless mesh network. Suppose the network is assumed to consist of varying n number of HPNs within a fixed area of deployment region (i.e., 5 Km by 5 Km). Also to generalize our derivations and only apply specific cases later with numerical examples, we employ the approach presented by [8] in order to investigate the impact of number of channels and interfaces on the capacity of multi-channel wireless networks. In our derivations, the term "channel" will refer to a part of frequency spectrum with some specified bandwidth and the term "radio" will mean the network interface card. Let us assume that the HPNs based mesh network has channels and every node is equipped with m interfaces so that the relation between the number of interface cards and channels is $2 \leq m \leq c$. Each interface card can only transmit and receive data on any one channel at a given time. It is a half-duplex. Thus, the mesh network of m interfaces per node, and c channels will be noted as m, c-network. Suppose each channel can support a multi-path dependent data rate of $R = R_{multipath}$, independent of number of non-overlapping channels of the network. Then, the total data rate possible by using all c non-overlapping channels is Rc. The number of non-overlapping channels can be increased by utilizing extra frequency spectrum of the standard technologies [13].

2.1   Capacity Limit for Irregular Placement

Consider Figure 3 that shows irregular placements of HPNs in a fixed area. In rural areas, the inter node distance is large and the topography of landscape affects node placements. To avoid interference, it is assumed that no any two HPNs are placed within a radius less than 400 m at the edge and less than 700 m toward the centre of the deployment area. However, between any two HPNs the largest separation distance is allowed as much possible as the size of the area can accommodate. Thus, a capacity theorem can be formulated.

Theorem 1: The E2E upper bound on capacity of a statically assigned channel network of type m, c-arbitrary and irregular placement of HPNs is found to be, $\lambda n \bar{L} = O\left(Rn\sqrt{\frac{mc}{\delta p}}\right)$ bit-meters/sec when $\frac{c}{m} = O(n)$.

Proof: Let us consider that in irregular and static networks, the node density varies over space (i.e., an area) but stays constant over time. Suppose the regularity rate (probability) of HPN placements is denoted as $0 < p < 1$, then the area A is defined as $A = n/\delta p$. Thus, the capacity of the network is assumed to be inversely proportional to the δp factor for an irregular placement.

Define the capacity of each channel, R as $R = kA = kn/\delta p$ for some constant k (in bits/s/square meters). Suppose each source HPN can generate packets depending on the application at a rate of λ bits/sec and the mean separation distance between the source and destination HPN pairs is $\bar{L}$ meters (via multiple hops), then the E2E network capacity of the network is given by [7]:

$$\lambda n \bar{L}, \quad bit - meters/sec. \tag{1}$$

The expression in (1) does not take into account the number of frequency channels, interference, path loss effects and number of interface cards. Relating this high level network capacity with the actual number of hops between the source and destination nodes requires that the overall bits transported in the network be evaluated as follows. Suppose bit b , $1 \leq b \leq \lambda n$ (bits/sec), traverses $h(b)$ hops on the path from its source to its destination, where the hth hop traverses a distance of r_b^h, then the overall bits transported in the network in every second is summed. This summation must be at least that in (1):

$$\lambda n \bar{L} \leq \sum_{b=1}^{\lambda n} \sum_{h=1}^{h(b)} r_b^h, \quad bit - meters/sec. \tag{2}$$

The inequality in (2) holds since the mean length of the line joining the source and destination, is equal to at most the distance traversed by a bit from its sources to its destination [8]. Additionally, HPNs have m interfaces per node and with achievable data rate of R possible per channel. Then, the total bits per second that can be transmitted by all interfaces in the network and all channels is at most $\frac{Rnmc}{2}$ (transporting one bit across one hop requires two interfaces, one each at the transmitting and the receiving nodes). Let $X = \sum_{b=1}^{\lambda n} X(b)$ as the number of bits transmitted by all nodes in a second (including bits forwarded). Then, the relation between the rate of a single channel link, the number of interface cards creating single links, the number of nodes in the network, and the total number of hops traversed by all bits in every second is given by,

$$X \leq \frac{Rmn}{2}, \;\; bits/sec \tag{3}$$

It should be noted that under the interference protocol model [8], a transmission over a hop of length r in a path loss link is successful only if there can be no active transmitter within a distance of $(1 + \triangle)r$. In IEEE 802.11a/b/g/n standards, the medium access control (MAC) layer protocols execute carrier sense multiple access with collision avoidance (CSMA/CA) mechanism which ensures that this condition is always satisfied. To illustrate this concept further, suppose node A is transmitting a bit to node B, while node C on one side of node B, is simultaneously transmitting a bit to node D furthest from node A and both the sessions are over a common frequency channel, W. Then, using the interference protocol model and the geometry sufficient for successful reception, node E which is between nodes B and C, cannot transmit at the same time with nodes A and C [6]. That is,

$$d(C, B) \geq (1 + \triangle)d(A, B) \quad and \quad d(A, D) \geq (1 + \triangle)d(C, D). \tag{4}$$

Adding the two inequalities together, and applying the triangle inequality to (4), we can obtain the inequality in (5),

$$d(B, D) \geq \frac{\triangle}{2}(d(A, B) + d(C, D)). \tag{5}$$

Therefore, in collision avoidance (CSMA/CA) principle, expression (5) can be viewed as each hop covering a disk of radius $\frac{\triangle}{2}$ times the length of the hop around each receiver. Then, the separation distance between receiver B and transmitter C is at least $(AB + \triangle AB)$ and that of transmitter A and receiver D is at least $(CD + \triangle CD)$. Thus, the summation over all channels (which can potentially transport R_c bits per second) will yield the constraint formulated as:

$$\sum_{b=1}^{\lambda n} \sum_{h=1}^{h(b)} (r_b^h)^2 \leq AR_c \Rightarrow \sum_{b=1}^{\lambda n} \sum_{h=1}^{h(b)} \frac{1}{X}(r_b^h)^2 \leq \frac{4AR_c}{\pi \triangle^2 X}. \tag{6}$$

Using the convex inequality rule [6] the left hand side in (6) is rewritten as,

$$\left(\sum_{b=1}^{\lambda n} \sum_{h=1}^{h(b)} \frac{1}{X} r_b^h \right)^2 \leq \sum_{b=1}^{\lambda n} \sum_{h=1}^{h(b)} \frac{1}{X}(r_b^h)^2. \tag{7}$$

Therefore, from (6) and (7) one gets,

$$\sum_{b=1}^{\lambda n} \sum_{h=1}^{h(b)} r_b^h \leq \sqrt{\frac{4AR_cX}{\pi\triangle^2}}. \tag{8}$$

From (8), it can be found that:

$$\sum_{b=1}^{hn} \sum_{h=1}^{h(b)} \frac{1}{X} r_b^h \leq \sqrt{\frac{4ARR_{nmc}}{2\pi\triangle^2}} \Rightarrow \sum_{b=1}^{hn} \sum_{h=1}^{h(b)} r_b^h = \lambda n\bar{L}. \tag{9}$$

So that,

$$\lambda n\bar{L} \leq R\sqrt{\frac{2Anmc}{\pi\triangle^2}} = Rn\sqrt{\frac{2mc}{\delta p\pi\triangle^2}} \Rightarrow \lambda n\bar{L} = O\left(Rn\sqrt{\frac{mc}{\delta p}}\right), \quad bit-meters/s. \tag{10}$$

2.2   Capacity Limit for Clustered Placement in Real Network

Suppose that n nodes are arbitrarily located in a cluster fashion on a square of a fixed area with a guaranteed line of sight (LOS) is guaranteed between any two neighbouring nodes shown in Figure 4. Thus, within a cluster a minimum separation distance of 700 m is considered, while any largest separation distance possible is considered between clusters. Thus, the following theorem on capacity limit can be formulated.

Theorem 2: The E2E upper bound on capacity of statically a signed channel network of type m, c-arbitrary clustered placement of nodes when $\frac{c}{m} = O(n)$ is given as $\lambda n\bar{L} = O\left(R\sqrt{nmc(\frac{n_1}{\delta_1} + \frac{n_2}{\delta_2})}\right)$ in bit-meters/sec, where R is the $min(R1, R2)$ for intra and inter cluster rates, n_1 are number of nodes in a regular cluster and n_2 are number of clusters in the network.

Proof: We assume a *clustered placement* of the mesh network as *a special case of regular or uniform HPNs placement* [6]. However, in this case the node densities are: $\delta_1 = n_1/A_1$ as the density of nodes within a cluster consisting of n_1 nodes in A_1 of an area and as the density of clusters consisting of n_2 clusters in A_2 of an area. This assumption is reasonable since HPNs within a cluster form different densities from those between clusters. Thus, the application layer generates the E2E capacity that depends on the number of nodes denoted as $\lambda n\bar{L}$ bit-meters/s. Suppose bit b, $1 \leq b \leq \lambda n$ (bits/sec), traverses $h(b)$ hops on the path from its source to its destination, where the hth hop traverses a distance of $r_b^h = r_b^h(\delta_1) + r_b^h(\delta_2)$. That is, the intra-cluster and inter-cluster components of hop distance. Then, one obtains network capacity by summing over all bits in the network as have provided in (2). Therefore, using similar arguments, steps (3), (7) through (10) as provided in the *Proof of Theorem 1*, the interference constraint protocol holds for any networks [6]. Consequently, the derived E2E capacity limit will be upper bound according to:

$$\lambda n \bar{L} \leq R \sqrt{\frac{2nmc}{\pi \triangle^2} \left(\frac{n_1}{\delta_1} + \frac{n_2}{\delta_2} \right)}, \ \ bit-meters/sec \tag{11}$$

So that the asymptotic E2E upper bound capacity limit for a clustered placement of an HPN network is given by:

$$\lambda n \bar{L} = O \left(R \sqrt{nmc \left(\frac{n_1}{\delta_1} + \frac{n_2}{\delta_2} \right)} \right), \ \ bit-meter/sec \tag{12}$$

In all derivations, R is a dependent variable that varies with the number of multiple paths, number of antennas and antenna gains [6], [15]. The link rate is calculated using models derived in [6].

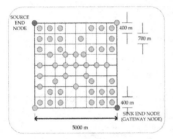

Fig. 3. Irregular placement

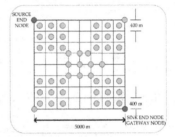

Fig. 4. Clustered placement

3 Numerical Examples

3.1 Conditions and Results of E2E Achievable Capacity

Results in Tables 1, 2 and 3 are obtained based on the datasheets of IEEE 802.11a/n standards [13]. Table 1 records the effects of irregular placement on the E2E capacity limits of IEEE 802.11a HPNs. Tables 2 and 3 show the E2E numerical values of achievable capacity computed right from the Ethernet at one end of the network to Ethernet at the other end of the network. The results assume that the interfaces, $m = 2$, the channels $c = 2$, the deployment area $A = 5000m \times 5000m$, and the bandwidth $W = 20MHz$ at carrier frequencies $c1 = 5.260$GHz, tuned to an 8 dBi omni-antenna and $c2 = 5.725$GHz, tuned to a 20 dBi directional antenna. The OFDM sub channels $= 48$, the effective antennae gain $= 28$ dBi and hilly path loss exponent $= 3$ are assumed. Suppose that CSMA/CA protocol is employed in order to identify node pairs that can simultaneously transmit [1]. Also, let $\triangle = 10\%$ defines a fraction of one hop distance which is sufficient to prevent neighboring nodes from transmitting on the same sub channel at the same time. If an optimized link state routing (OLSR) protocol that proactively maintains fresh lists of destinations and their routes is also

Table 1. Placement Irregulaity versus E2E capacity of IEEE802.11a HPNs

p	0.1	0.2	0.3	0.4	0.5	0.6	0.7	0.8	0.9	1
E2E capacity (Mbps)	2.9480	2.0845	1.7020	1.4740	1.3184	1.2085	1.1142	1.0423	0.9827	0.9322

Table 2. Numerical values of E2E capacity in IEEE 802.11a of HPNs

HPNs placement in a 5 km x 5 km area	No. of HPNs	Achievable link capacity (Mbps)	E2E achievable capacity (Mbps)
Regular at p = 100%	10	R(2100 m) = 281.12	0.5192
	50	R(700 m) = 376.22	0.9322
Irregular at p = 90%	10	R(2100 m) = 281.12	0.5473
	50	R(700 m) = 376.22	0.9827
Clustered	10	R_1(700 m) = 376.22 R_2(4200 m)= 221.13 R = min (R_1, R_2)	0.4202
	50	R_1(700 m) = 376.22 R_2(1400 m)= 316.22 R = min (R_1, R_2)	0.5374

Table 3. Numerical values of E2E capacity in IEEE 802.11n of HPNs

HPNs placement in a 5 km x 5 km area	No. of HPNs	Achievable link capacity (Mbps)	E2E achievable capacity (Mbps)
Regular at p = 100%	10	R(2100 m) = 722.24	1.3339
	50	R(700 m) = 912.44	2.2609
Irregular at p = 90%	10	R(2100 m) = 722.24	1.4061
	50	R(700 m) = 912.44	2.3832
Clustered	10	R_1(700 m) = 912.44 R_2(4200 m)= 602.24 R = min (R_1, R_2)	1.1443
	50	R_1(700 m) = 912.44 R_2(1400 m)= 792.44 R = min (R_1, R_2)	2.0201

considered [14]. Then, routing tables are periodically distributed in the network. The OLSR ensures that a route to a particular destination is immediately available. The expected transmission count (ETX) metric to calculate the expected number of retransmissions that are required for a packet to travel to and from a destination can be adopted [14]. Using ETX information, the E2E capacity designs can be validated practically. In particular, consider the following cases: irregular pattern when $n = 10$ and when $n = 50$. Assume that the average distance of source-destination pair is 6505 m. The value enables the computation of achievable capacity over direct LOS path (i.e. without multi-hops) between the source and destination nodes. For irregular placements, the rate (probability) p is constrained by $0 < p < 1$. The choice of p depicts the degree of irregularity, with smaller values of p depicting more irregular placement.

3.2   Discussions on E2E Achievable Capacity

From Table 1, the average node density is inversely proportional to the E2E capacity according to *Theorem 1*. Thus, a lower average density in an irregular node placement for the same number of nodes will yield a higher E2E capacity if and only if the area of deployment is fixed or decreased. Using similar argument, when values of p is decreased (i.e., 0.8, 0.7, 0.6, etc.), the average δ decreases proportionately and if the area of deployment is fixed or reduced then for the same number of nodes, the capacity will increase. From Tables 2 and 3, in a fixed area of 5 km by 5 km, the E2E achievable capacity evaluated shows that there is lower capacity when number of HPNs is ten than when the number is 50 for both irregular and clustered placements. The reason is that a series of long links created between any two immediate nodes degrades the achievable E2E capacity, due to long link attenuations. For instance, at ten HPNs in the fixed sized network, the hop distances are much larger than the case for 50 HPNs. In each hop, the propagating signal is attenuated by the terrain irregularity, foliage and wireless medium conductivity. The implication is that signal traversing longer hop distances are faced with higher attenuation resulting in lower E2E capacity than signal propagating over shorter hops. Although effects of forwarding delays exacerbate throughput, delays due to lossy links degrades the capacity more. Considering the same number of nodes and fixed area of deployment, the inter hop distances defining the position of the nodes will be much smaller by 10% than in the case of regular HPN placements when $p = 100\%$. However, shorter hops imply higher capacity if and only if there is limited interference and forwarding delays. Moreover, increasing or keeping constant the number of nodes placed in a fixed area automatically increases or keeps constant the average node density. It was also noted that network throughput dropped significantly from source HPN to the destination HPN or the gateway. In particular, the drop was by about 99% across 3 long distance hops and by about 99% across 3 long distance hops considering irregularly and clustered HPNs from Tables 2 and 3, respectively. The explanation is that, the channel gain drops with increase in propagation distance, and there are also overhead losses associated with MAC and the multi-hop routing such that the number of packets sent is not always equal to the number of packets received successfully, even in free space medium. Despite this observation, HPNs derived from IEEE 802.11n radios have a better E2E capacity achievable mainly due to the MIMO technologies that are capable of combating multi-path fading [15].

4   Conclusions

The HPNs^{TM} architecture makes use of omni-directional antennas to maintain mesh connectivity, while directional antennas support information relay over long distances with high power gains. It was confirmed analytically and numerically that increasing the number of interfaces per HPN with carefully configured antennas and non overlapping frequency channels in the network does increase the achievable E2E capacity in any arbitral network placement. For overlapping channels, the capacity depends on the dynamic channel assignment and transmit power control which is in the future work. One of the contributions of this study was the design of capacity for the innovation constructed to improve performance of the commercially available WLAN devices. Other possible explorations of increasing capacity of community networks such as Peebles valley mesh in South Africa [6] include the utilization of unused TV frequency spectrum. The low frequencies of the TV spectrum foster high capacity signal transmissions over long distances in rural terrains. Thus, cognitive and energy foraging radio techniques are promising tools toward spectrum and energy efficient network management for the next billion internet users.

References

1. Kodialam, M., Nandagopal, T.: Characterizing the capacity region in multi-radio multi-channel wireless mesh networks. In: MobiCom 2005, Cologne, Germany (2005)
2. Olwal, T.O.: Decentralised dynamic power control for wireless backbone mesh networks, PhD Thesis, University of Paris-EST and TUT (2010)
3. Olwal, T.O., et al.: Optimal control of transmission power management in wireless backbone meshes networks. In: Funabiki, N. (ed.) Wireless Mesh Networks, pp. 3–28. InTech, Croatia (2011)
4. Eriksson, J., Agarwal, S., Bahl, P., Padhye, J.: Feasibility study of mesh networks for all-wireless offices. In: Proc. of MobiSys 2006, Sweden, pp. 69–82 (2006)
5. Mesh Dynamics Inc.: Wireless mesh networks that scale like switch stacks (2010), http://www.meshdynamics.com
6. Olwal, T.O., et al.: Achievable capacity limit of high performance nodes for wireless mesh networks. In: Krendzel (ed.) Wireless Mesh Networks, pp. 1–28. InTech (2012)
7. Gupta, P., Kumar, P.R.: The capacity of wireless networks. IEEE Transactions on 4 Information Theory 46(2), 388–404 (2000)
8. Kyasanur, P., Vaidya, N.H.: Capacity of multi-channel wireless networks: impact of number of channels and interfaces, Technical Report, Dep. of Comp. Science, Univ. of Illinois, Urban-Champaign (2005)
9. Berthilson, L., Pascual, A.E.: Link performance parameters in IEEE 802.11: How to increase the throughput of a wireless long distance link, White paper (2007)
10. Makitla, I., Makan, A., Roux, K.: Broadband provision to underprivileged rural communities. In: Proc. of CSIR 3rd Biennial Conference (2010)
11. Ishmael, J., Bury, S., Pezaros, D., Race, N.: Deployment rural community wireless mesh networks. IEEE Internet Computing (2), 22–29 (2008)
12. Roux, R., et al.: Broadband for all (BB4all)^{TM}. CSIR Science Scope Magazine 3(3), 16–17 (2009)
13. Cisco Systems Inc.: Channels and maximum power settings for Cisco Aironet lightweight access points, pp. 1-130, No: OL-11321-08 (2011)
14. Johnson, D.L., Roux, K.: Building rural wireless networks: lesions learnt and future directions. In: Proc. of ACM Workshop on Wireless Networks and Systems for Developing Regions, San Francisco, USA, pp. 17–22 (2008)
15. Franceschetti, M., et al.: The capacity of wireless networks: information-theoretic and physical limits. IEEE Trans. on Inf. Theory. 55(8), 3413–3424 (2009)

VHF Spectrum Monitoring
Using Meraka Cognitive Radio Platform

Adebayo I. Aderonmu[1], Rotimi H. Adegnandjou[1],
Moshe Timothy Masonta[1,2], and Mjumo Mzyece[1]

[1] Dept. of Electrical Engineering, Tshwane University of Technology, Pretoria, South Africa
[2] CSIR– Meraka Institute, P.O. Box 395, Pretoria, South Africa
bayoo4real2000@yahoo.com, haroldrotimi@yahoo.fr,
mmasonta@csir.co.za, mzyecem@tut.ac.za

Abstract. The radio frequency (RF) spectrum is a natural resource used by wireless network operators to provide radio communications and transmission systems. The scarcity of RF spectrum has led to the development of dynamic spectrum access techniques to achieve more efficient spectrum utilisation. A number of related questions arise, including: How much of the RF spectrum is currently available? How much of it can be used opportunistically and dynamically without interfering with licensed or primary users (PUs)? In this paper, we present work being conducted in South Africa on the application of software defined radio (SDR) to dynamic RF spectrum usage. Specifically, we discuss the Meraka Cognitive Radio Platform (MCRP) which is based on Universal Serial Radio Peripheral version 2 (USRP2) hardware and GNU radio software. We also discuss the implementation and operation of the spectrum monitoring sub-system in MCRP. Lastly, the results of the measurements which were conducted using the MCRP are presented.

Keywords: cognitive radio, GNU radio, spectrum management, universal software radio peripheral, graphical user interface.

1   Introduction

Wireless communications has become the effective standard for our growing and diverse demands. For communication purposes, many wireless technologies make use of the radio frequency (RF) spectrum. Hence, the RF spectrum is regarded as a valuable and highly priced resource that needs to be controlled wisely and in the most efficient way in order to allow room for future innovations. The RF spectrum refers to the range of frequencies from 3 KHz to 300 GHz. Accordingly, a new communication paradigm to exploit the existing wireless spectrum opportunistically is considered necessary in order to overcome the limited available spectrum and inefficiency in spectrum utilisation [1].

To enable opportunistic access to the RF spectrum and the efficient sharing of allocated bands, more flexible spectrum management techniques are required, such as opportunistic spectrum sharing, where secondary users (SUs) are allowed to operate

K. Jonas, I.A. Rai, and M. Tchuente (Eds.): AFRICOMM 2012, LNICST 119, pp. 55–64, 2013.

frequency bands without the permission of primary users (PUs) provided that it does not introduce harmful interference with PUs. For this reason, cognitive radio (CR) is being intensively investigated by the research community, major industry communication regulators and standardisation bodies as key enabling technology [2].

CR [3] is defined by the Federal Communications Commission (FCC) as "an intelligent wireless communication system capable of changing its transceiver parameters based on interaction with the environment in which it operates". A cognitive radio network imposes distinctive challenges owing to the fact that there is high fluctuation in the available spectrum over time. Thus, the various CR nodes offer different available channels at different times. As a result, some challenges are introduced, such as: (1) spectrum sensing, which needs to be done correctly and frequently; (2) the availability of routes between nodes that recognize different channels and multi-hop routing; (3) spectrum decision and sharing in a distributed setting without a central coordinator; and (4) coordination among the nodes with or without the availability of a common control channel.

Most countries have regulatory agencies that regulate the radio spectrum by means of renewable licences. However, the RF spectrum monitoring systems (equipment) used by regulators are specialised and very expensive. Consequently, in order to allow the RF spectrum to be researched and studied, there is a need to develop low-cost test beds or prototypes for spectrum monitoring. These prototypes could then be used mainly by students, but also by the wireless industry to make the spectrum usage and occupancy process more efficient and ready to accommodate existing and innovative radio-communication systems.

The advancement of radio technology to SDR has made the development of radio systems easier and more affordable. SDR refers to radios in which some or all the physical layer functions are software defined [4].

In [1], Rashid et al. found that spectrum utilisation can be significantly improved by adopting SDR technology. Such radios are able to sense the spectral environment and use this information opportunistically to provide wireless links that meet the users' communications requirements optimally. These researchers investigated sensing performance implemented on a real-time testbed of GNU radio and USRP SDR communication platform operating at 2.48 GHz with a bandwidth of 4 MHz.

In [5], Yucek and Arslan present a survey of spectrum sensing methodologies. Various aspects of the spectrum sensing problem are studied from a CR perspective and a multidimensional spectrum sensing concept is introduced. The challenges associated with spectrum sensing are discussed and enabling spectrum sensing methods are reviewed. The paper explains the concept of cooperative sensing and its various forms. External sensing algorithms and other alternative sensing methods are also discussed. Finally, the sensing features of some current wireless standards are given.

In this paper, active spectrum scans are used to show that it is possible to monitor the frequency occupancy within the VHF band. As a real-time monitoring tool, the graphical user interface (GUI) has been proven to be capable of scanning spectrums. These spectrum scans were conducted in Pretoria.

The rest of this paper is organised as follows: Section 2 discusses how SDR is adopted in RF spectrum usage and Section 3 describes the platform used to collect the frequency scans and monitor them using a GUI. The results of our measurements are discussed in Section 4. Section 5 concludes the paper.

2   Overview of Software Defined Radio (SDR)

2.1   Software Defined Radio

The Wireless Innovation Forum defines SDR as a radio in which some or all the physical layer functions are software defined [4]. At the baseline, software radios can do pretty much anything a traditional radio can do. In this case, software pieces, and not hardware components, treat the signals to extract the information.

SDR has the ability to tune into any frequency band and receive different modulations across a large frequency spectrum by means of programmable hardware, which is controlled by software. A typical SDR is expected to perform significant amounts of signal processing in a general purpose computer. The principle behind SDR is that all the modulation and demodulation is done with software instead of using hardware circuitry.

The benefit of SDR is that, instead of having to build extra hardware to handle different types of radio signal, you merely have to write an appropriate software program. A computer [6] can then be used to switch from an amplitude modulation (AM) radio to a high definition television (HDTV) or FM radio, depending on the software loaded. The advantage of this approach is that the equipment is more versatile and cost-effective compared to traditional radios.

2.2   Software Defined Radio Design Overview

The diagram in Figure 1 shows how the signal flows through the system. The SDR used for this project is made of GNU radio [7] and USRP2 [8]. GNU radio and the USRP2 are the software and hardware parts, respectively, of a complete low-cost SDR platform that has gained widespread use [9]. The USRP is a product developed by Ettus Research [8], and follows a basic design with a motherboard containing ADC/DAC, an FPGA performing sampling rate conversion, a host interface, and a plug-in daughterboard containing frequency-specific RF front ends. The antenna picks up the signals from the air and feeds them into the USRP2. From the USRP2, the signals are transmitted to the personal computer (PC). For a receiving scenario, the real-time signal is fetched by the RF transceiver via the antenna; it is subsequently converted from RF to an intermediate frequency (IF). Then the signal is passed to an analogue-to-digital converter (ADC). The USRP2 contains a 14-bit ADC converter. After digitisation, the ADC passes the resultant data to the field programmable gate array (FPGA). In the FPGA, the signal is converted from IF to baseband and the signal samples are decimated so that the data rate can be adapted by the performance of the transmission interface (Gigabit Ethernet) and the computers computing capability.

Finally, the FPGA transfers the processed data to the Gigabit Ethernet controller, which passes it over to the computer. For real-time monitoring, the spectrum at a certain centre frequency is displayed over a GUI window. For non-real-time monitoring the code in GNU radio processes the captured data and outputs to a file readable by MATLAB if post-processing is needed. However, post-processing is beyond the scope of this paper.

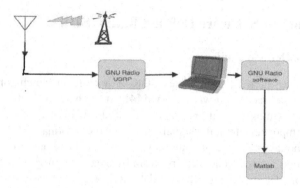

Fig. 1. SDR architecture [6]

3   Cognitive Radio Platform and Measurement

In this section we give a brief description of the Meraka Cognitive Radio Platform (MCRP) and then discuss the setup used for spectrum scanning in a real-time environment, which was carried out in Meraka Innovation Laboratory.

3.1   Meraka Cognitive Radio Platform (MCRP)

The MCRP [10] is shown in Figure 2. The platform consists of four CR nodes, and each node is connected to the internet using the Ethernet cable. A single node is built up of three major hardware components, as shown in Figure 3: a high speed computer (powered by 2.60 GHz Dual Core Intel Pentium Processor, 2 GB memory and 500 GB hard-drive), version two of the Universal Software Radio Peripheral or USRP2 package (with a single WBX daughter-board) and high gain VHF/UHF antenna (Ellies aerial VHF/UHF Combo with 15 elements). The USRP2 is a flexible SDR device developed by Ettus Research LLC, which allows for the creation of a CR node.

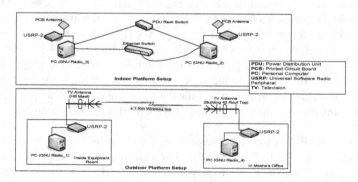

Fig. 2. The Meraka Cognitive Radio Platform [10]

3.2   Detailed Explanation of the MCRP

The USRP2 is composed of a motherboard that performs some baseband processing and of daughter-boards that carry out the RF front-end part of the radio. Various plug-on daughter-boards allow the USRP to be used on different RF bands. In our lab, WBX daughter-boards with the transceiver of 50 MHz to 2.2 GHz frequency range are used. SDR is a radio communication system in which components that would have typically been implemented with hardware are implemented using software.

While traditional hardware- based radio devices limit cross-functionality and can only be modified through physical intervention, SDR can receive and transmit widely different radio protocols based solely on the software updates. The CR can be viewed as an SDR that is intelligent and aware of its external operating environment. Each computer hosts the GNU Radio software. GNU Radio is a free software development tool-kit that provides the signal processing runtime and processing blocks to implement software radios using external RF hardware (such as USRP) and commodity processors. GNU Radio has a large and steadily growing worldwide community of developers and users that have contributed to a substantial code base.

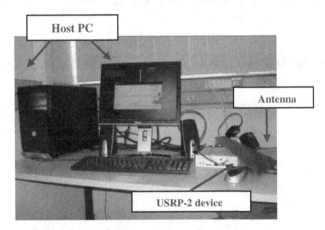

Fig. 3. GNU radio-based SDR components

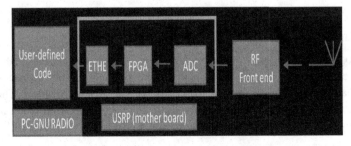

Fig. 4. Hardware block diagram [6]

4   VHF Measurements and Results

The aim of our measurement is to scan the very high frequency (VHF) spectrum band, from 30 MHz to 300 MHz. A GNU Radio program is used to collect the raw data from the USRP2 and store them in a data file (.dat). The frequency scans were conducted in the innovation laboratory in real time at the Council for Scientific and Industrial Research (CSIR). Multiple consecutive VHF scans were done using approximately 700 kHz bandwidth and Fast Fourier Transform (FFT) size of 1024. The data (.dat file) is accessed by MATLAB for post-processing (see Figures 8–9).

The results of the spectrum scans were also displayed in real time over a GUI developed for convenience (see Figures 5–7). The interface takes the desired centre frequency and other parameters and gives the command to the USRP2 through GNU Radio.

From the plots, it can be seen that some of the channels appear to be busy, while some are not. For instance Figure 5 is the result of the frequency scans at 50 MHz centre frequency. The gain is set at 15 dB to amplify the signal, while the channel is unoccupied. This simply means that a specific channel in the radio frequency spectrum is available for use.

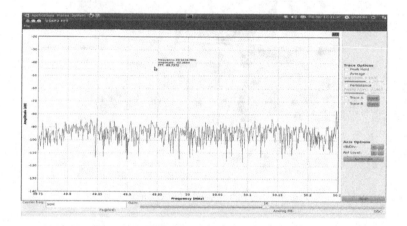

Fig. 5. Centre frequency for 50 MHz

Figure 6 shows the results of the monitored very high frequency (VHF) at 100 MHz centred frequency. It can be seen that there is huge activity going on in the spectrum band. The gain is also set to 15 dB for signal amplification. This result simply means that a special channel in the radio frequency spectrum is not available for use. Any attempt at using that frequency for transmission purposes will result in interference.

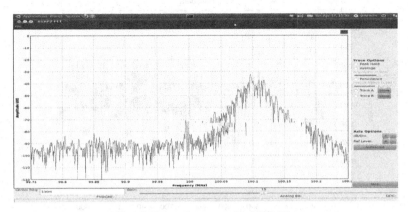

Fig. 6. Centre frequency for 100 MHz

Figure 7 shows the monitored VHF at centre frequency 189.2 MHz. The gain is set at 20 dB. It can be seen that there is some activity going on; therefore, in the radio frequency spectrum this channel is not available for use. Any attempt at using the frequency or any neighbouring channels will result in interference.

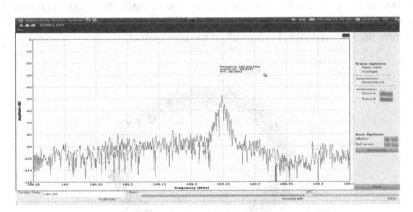

Fig. 7. Centre frequency for 189.3 MHz

Figure 8 below shows the MATLAB plot of the RF spectrum which was captured in a non-real time environment and post-processed using the MCRP. The raw data were captured at a centre frequency of 100 MHZ and plotted over 2000 samples, appended in a (.dat) file. A MATLAB program was used to access and plot the raw data file. Thus, the magnitude, in decibels (dB) was plotted against time (in seconds). This graph helps to verify the utilisation of monitored RF spectrum bands in a real-time environment.

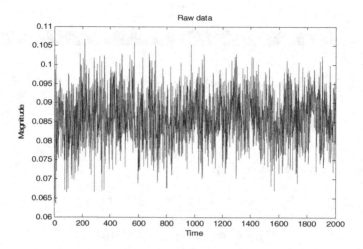

Fig. 8. Raw data captured at 100 MHz plotted over 2000 samples

Figure 9 below shows the scattered plot of the same data captured at 100 MHz using a spectrum analyser. We obtain the constellation diagram by sampling both the I and the Q channels at the same instant and then plotting the I component against the Q component of the signal on an x–y diagram. Accordingly, the x-axis represents the in-phase carrier and the y-axis represents the quadrature carrier. The exceedingly high offset from the received signal is a result of the noise effect.

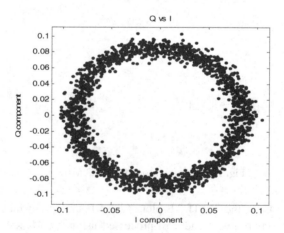

Fig. 9. Signal constellation plot

The results show that it was possible to monitor the frequency occupancy within the VHF band. It can be seen in Figure 5 that at 50 MHz, there was no ongoing activity, which means that the specific channel is available for use and attempts to use it for transmission or any other radio usage will not result in interference. The monitoring was also conducted in real time at 189.3 MHz and 100 MHz. The monitoring was also conducted in real time at 189.3 MHz and 100 MHz, with the strongest signal being noticed at 100 MHz. Thus, we post-processed the data captured at 100 MHz in non-real time. The GUI was the real-time monitoring part of the project and it has been proven that the monitoring tool proposed in this project is capable of spectrum scanning. The MATLAB post-processing, which took place in non-real time, was intended to provide information on the spectrum usage at a certain frequency for someone who was not present during the real-time monitoring.

With these results, the monitoring tool proposed in this project can well be used to avoid interference in the VHF part of the spectrum between RF users.

5   Conclusions

In this paper, we presented an overview of SDR, its design implementation and the way the RF spectrum can be monitored via GUI using MCRP. A detailed description of the platform was given. We have also shown that, through active spectrum scans, it is possible to monitor the frequency occupancy within the VHF band. As a real-time monitoring tool, the GUI has been proven to be capable of performing spectrum scanning and can be used to avoid interference between RF users. Illegal transmissions can also be detected within the VHF band and the tool can therefore be used to support the work of ICT regulatory services. In further work, this sub-system could also be extended by improving the integration and inter-operation of its components and by incorporating security features.

References

[1]   Rashid, R.A., Sarijari, M.A., Fisal, N., Yusof, S., Mahalin, N.H.: Spectrum Sensing Measurement using GNU Radio and USRP Software Radio Platform. In: Proc. of The Seventh International Conference on Wireless and Mobile Communications 2011, pp. 237–242 (2011)

[2]   Mitola III, J., Maguire Jr., G.Q.: Cognitive radio: making software radios more personal. IEEE Personal Communications 6(4) (1999)

[3]   Federal Communications Commission (FCC): Facilitating opportunities for flexible, efficient and reliable spectrum use employing cognitive radio technologies: Notice of proposed rulemaking and order. ET Docket 03–108 & 03-322 (2003)

[4]   Wireless Innovation Forum (was SDR Forum), What is software defined radio, http://www.wirelessinnovation.org/page/whatisSDR

[5]   Yucek, T., Arslan, H.: A Survey of Spectrum Sensing Algorithms for Cognitive Radio Applications. IEEE Communications Surveys & Tutorials 11(1), 116–130 (2009)

[6]   Manicka, N.: GNU radio test bed. M.S. thesis. Dept. Computer Science and Electrical, University of Delaware (Spring 2007)

[7]   Ettus Research website, USRP, http://www.ettus.com/
      (accessed: April 01, 2012)

[8]   GNU Radio website, http://gnuradio.org/redmine/
      (accessed: April 01, 2012)

[9]   Newman, T.R., Bose, T.: A cognitive radio network testbed for wireless communication
      and signal processing education. In: Proc. DSP Workshop and Signal Processing
      Education Workshop, Marco Island, FL, USA, pp. 757–761 (January 2009)

[10] Masonta, M.T., Johnson, D., Mzyece, M.: The White Space Opportunity in Southern
      Africa: Measurements with Meraka Cognitive Radio Platform. In: Popescu-Zeletin, R.,
      Jonas, K., Rai, I.A., Glitho, R., Villafiorita, A. (eds.) AFRICOMM 2011, Part I.
      LNCST, vol. 92, pp. 64–73. Springer, Heidelberg (2012)

Open BTS, a GSM Experiment in Rural Zambia

Jacqueline Mpala[1] and Gertjan van Stam[2]

[1] University of Zambia, Lusaka, Zambia
jacqmpala@yahoo.com
[2] Nelson Mandela Metropolitan University, Port Elizabeth, South Africa
gertjan.vanstam@worksgroup.org

Abstract. This paper presents an OpenBTS implementation case study in rural Zambia. The work focused on applied research and development of a cost effective telecommunication system to provide mobile communications in a rural village. The system aimed to test appropriate technologies involving limited hardware needs, incurring low capital expenditure, and with limit operational costs. The practical experience revealed that nontechnical aspects like logistics of equipment availability, internet bandwidth constraints, and interaction with the frequency regulator are the main implementation constraints.

Keywords: openBTS, Zambia, low-cost communication, rural area networks, mobile telephony.

1 Introduction

Access to information is a basic human right. Article 20(1) of the Zambian constitution states that a person shall not be hindered in the enjoyment of his freedom of expression which includes freedom to receive ideas and information [1].

In Zambia, the market for Information and Communication Technologies (ICT) and services grows significantly. A survey depicts mobile communication growing from 464,000 in 2004 to 4.4 million users in 2009 [2]. The liberalization of the ICT sector in Zambia facilitates this increase in usage of ICT [3]. Growth in ICT access facilitates economic growth in Zambia [4].

Liberalization of the telecommunications market results in increased competition. This contributes to lower access and user costs [2]. The International Telecommunications Union (ITU) mentions Zambia among the top ten countries with decreasing costs for ICT. However, in Zambia, real costs of ICT are still among the highest in the world [5].

Although there are large differences in terms of urbanization in Africa, on average in developing countries the vast majority of people (approximately 70% to 85% of the labor force) live in rural areas. 93.9% of Zambia's surface is customary, rural land [6] and 61.2% of Zambia's population lives in rural areas [7].

It is essential for rural areas to develop, so new opportunities emerge and innovations occur [8]. Opportunities and innovations provide for increase in productivity and for the populace to enjoy an improved quality of life. Chief Chikanta

K. Jonas, I.A. Rai, and M. Tchuente (Eds.): AFRICOMM 2012, LNICST 119, pp. 65–73, 2013.
© Institute for Computer Sciences, Social Informatics and Telecommunications Engineering 2013

and Mweetwa mention that rural areas face significant resource challenges in the form of poor network coverage, limited transport, electricity, and water supply. They deem a disparity in access undesirable, as it demonstrates that people of different communities have unequal opportunities to benefit from technology in their daily lives.

The ICT sector in Zambia lacks sufficient people with adequate ICT skills. Zambia needs people with such skills to drive the nations envisioned progress towards a knowledge economy by 2030 [9][4]. Habeenzu cites a survey on ICT industry skills that reports the figure of 300 people with graduate qualifications in ICTs in Zambia in 2008. He contributes the low number of skilled persons to the lack of adequate formal ICT training facilities at tertiary education level in Zambia. Low numbers of engineers are a common occurrence in developing countries [10].

Though there has been a considerable reduction in the cost of access to mobile phones, other factors such as geographical challenges, lack of supporting infrastructures, and limited abilities to recognize opportunities play a role in the availability of mobile services in rural areas. The World Bank observes that mobile network operators find it commercially infeasible to operate in rural areas [11].

Zambian rural areas are usually not connected to the electricity grid. They encapsulate sparsely populated areas and poor road infrastructure. Rural areas have always lagged in development, including limited availability of ICT. Deploying traditional GSM networks in rural areas is inefficient as villages are much dispersed, typically separated by kilometers of uninhabited areas.

In developing nations, more people own mobile phones than personal computers. In 2011, the National Geographic magazine reports that the world's 1 billion poorest own 22 mobile phones per 100 people, but only have 1.2 computers per 100 people [12]. The yearly income of people at 'the bottom of the pyramid' is USD 1,000 or less, and most reside in Africa. Lower-middle income populations, which account for 4 billion people, earning between USD 1,000 and 4,000 per year, living mostly in India, China, Southeast Asia, and parts of Africa, own 47 mobile phones per 100 people and have 4.3 personal computers per 100 people.

Coming from this setting, this paper about an OpenBTS study in rural Zambia, presents an overview of the specific, Zambian environment (section 2), related work (section 3), and a description of the works and the findings (section 4 and 5). A discussion of this first practical implementation experiment fills section 6, and the conclusions feature in section 7.

2   Environment

The OpenBTS case study is part of the collaboration per Memorandum of Understanding, by the University of Zambia and LinkNet. LinkNet is a rural based, co-operative organization that provides internet connectivity in rural areas of Zambia [13]. LinkNet is an operational unit of Macha Works. Macha Works' vision is to inspire people in rural communities to reach their collective and individual potential. The co-operation of UNZA and LinkNet facilitate enhancing educational and learning facilities with a focus on rural areas. It aligns with national key objectives in human capacity building, research and development, and innovation in Zambia's ICT sector [14]. LinkNet's network operations center is in the rural community of Macha, in the Southern Province of Zambia.

Macha Works facilitates community driven projects, including internet connectivity, in seven villages in Zambia. These sites are Chilonga (Northern Province), Chitokoloki, Kalene, and Mukinge (North Western Province), Minga (Eastern Province), and Chikanta and Macha (Southern Province). In each site, LinkNet packages ICT functionalities using a Linknet Resource Container (LRC) base. A LRC is a locally-refurbished shipping container. It hosts a VSAT outdoor unit for satellite connection to the Internet, an uninterrupted power supply (UPS), a network server and gateway, user-PCs, and wireless area network connections. It provides a secure area with PCs for training and community purposes. Solar panels supply power to two LRCs (Chikanta and Chitokoloki), while the other LRCs connect with the national electricity grid.

In 2011, mobile phone, GSM, coverage is adequate at 4 out of 7 LinkNet locations in Zambia. Two locations have limited GSM coverage, where one has to search for 'catching a signal' from a distant transmitting point. Up to the beginning of 2012, Chikanta, a village located 100 kilometer northeast of Kalomo did not have GSM coverage. The nearest GSM tower stands at a distance of 40 kilometers.

Macha Hospital's catchment area involves operations of 12 rural health centers. In turn, each rural health center caters for a number of rural health posts in its own area. Not all these health centers have mobile coverage, and fewer of the health posts are within the range of a mobile signal. Even with patchy, limited coverage, the use of GSM is advantageous for health interventions. For instance, Macha Research Trust reports on the use of SMS to send weekly information of rapid malaria tests used, and number of positive diagnoses to Macha [15].

3   Related Work

The OpenBTS is a UNIX/Linux based, free and open source software (FOSS) that configures Software Defined Radios as an independent GSM access point. The system allows GSM handsets to connect, and facilitate call set-up. OpenBTS integrates the GSM-network functionalities of traditional, high cost Base Tranceiver Station (BTS), Base Switching Center (BSC) and Mobile Switching Center (MSC) into one low cost platform. Calls route through an Internet Protocol (IP) data network with an Asterisk Private Branch Exchange (PBX), using Voice-over-IP (VoIP) through Session Initiation Protocol (SIP), instead of call traffic through a GSM switch (the MSC).

OpenBTS necessitates software radio hardware known as Universal Software Radio Peripheral (USRP). The cost of a USRP is about USD 700. With generic GSM to SIP conversion behind the air interface, OpenBTS interfaces with standard IP components. The USRP presents a GSM air interface (Um) to standard GSM handset and uses the Asterisk software PBX to connect calls [16]. The combination of the global-standard GSM air interface with low-cost VoIP backhaul forms the basis of the cellular network, with deployment and operational costs at substantially lower level than existing technologies in many applications, including rural cellular deployments and private cellular networks in remote areas [16], [17].

During 2011, Anand et al. did OpenBTS experiments in a USA based laboratory environment. These experiments focused on preparation of further OpenBTS research for rural deployment, in collaboration with LinkNet/UNZA [18]. In their paper, Anand et al expand on the rationale for OpenBTS, and describe the technical performance that can be expected in a mixed traffic environment, using traffic patterns observed in Macha. Other work mentions the Village Base Station as a generic concept [19], or providing input for financial business planning [20]. Kretchmer et al. evaluated the Quality of Service of OpenBTS mobile calls across a multi-hop wireless testbed that carries typical Internet traffic [21].

4   Study Design

The case study focused on an actual implementation of OpenBTS in rural Africa. The aim of the study was to deploy and review such implementation by monitoring its deployment and usability by establishing real communication of mobile phones with each other and the outside world. The study aimed to provide a basis for replication of OpenBTS tests, by running experiments in the rural area of Chikanta, in Zambia's Southern Province.

The implementation involves a small base transceiver station utilizing OpenBTS software. This Linux-based software application configures the universal software radio peripheral (USRP) to present a GSM air interface to standard GSM phones and interfaces with the Asterisk Voice over Internet Protocol Private Branch exchange (VoIP PBX) to connect calls. OpenBTS implementations can connect with each other and to the internet via standard IP technologies and backhaul, like Wifi or Wimax. Such implementation differs substantially from conventional GSM BTS implementations. A standard BTS routes calls via a MSC and its dedicated back-bone network. The project did not address billing system integration.

The research focused on a deployment, with prime investigation done in a rural Zambian community by Zambian researchers. This is the first exercise in rural Zambia as far as we know.

For practical support, the research linked up with computer science students in Germany. They work on a project to combine a low cost GSM base station with a Wi-Fi mesh network. Relationships also exist with computer science students in the USA.

Practical deployment of the implementation took place between October 2010 and July 2011. It involved practical implementation of a low power, OpenBTS implementation, aimed at establishing and testing calls using mobile phones in Zambia. Notes on the project execution and experiences provide information on challenges posed by many forms of constraints.

5 Findings

The activities succeeded in establishing calls between and from mobile telephones in Zambia. However, to achieve this, a whole range of physiological, legal, and practical challenges had to be overcome.

Equipment required by OpenBTS is not for sale in Zambia. International purchase of equipment was challenging since most suppliers requested payment by credit cards. Credit cards are not available in Zambia. At the time of the research, VISA debit cards were entering the urban Zambian market for the first time. However, none of the research team members possessed a debit card or an (international) credit card. International collaborators intervened. They purchased the equipment abroad and facilitated processing of the payment to the supplier. Final payment involved a cash transfer from the project to the collaborator.

Logistics in transport and importing of equipment raised significant hurdles. After much trial and error, a LinkNet research partner in Germany stepped in. They sourced the test equipment and brought it in person from Germany to a conference in South Africa. From there, the equipment was flown to Zambia.

Rural villages are far apart, and the roads are dangerous. The project team travelled frequently between urban and rural areas for discussions with the community and regulator and to deliver progress reports to various institutes involved, and for actual testing. At one of these journeys, while returning from project demonstrations and community-capacity building activities in Chikanta, the author and IEEE colleagues had a road traffic accident, after hitting a bump on a gravel road. Several people needed medical attention in the rural hospital, and one car was destroyed.

The research partner in Germany preconfigured the equipment. Upon arrival, it worked for tests establishing local calls. The test system consisted of a low power PC and an USRP. On site, the addition of an additional harddrive added more capacity to the system. This increase in capacity facilitated the expansion of functionalities. Configuring the increased capacity of the equipment took much unexpected effort. Core software and various driver upgrades for the USRP and Asterisk had to be downloaded from project sites on the internet. This requires broadband internet connectivity. Although the rural project site in Macha is relatively well connected by Zambian standards (Committed Information Rate 256 kbs, bursting up to 1028 kbs, discounted cost USD 1,400 per month), uninterrupted facilitation of the large file downloads provided became an immense challenge. The sheer number of files that needed to be downloaded, issues of shared bandwidth use, frequent electricity outings, and international satellite bandwidth interruptions contributed to the challenges. Downloads took place during the nights and at weekends, trying to limit the effect of the download on operational use of the network in Macha. It took several weeks to complete all downloads.

After concluding the initial configurations, the test frequencies were set. The Zambia Information and Communications Technology Authority (ZICTA), regulates the utilization of radio transmissions. This institute was established through the Information and Communications Act in 2009 [22]. Its mandate includes service and supplier's licenses, provision of radio services, settings and allocation of frequency spectrum, numbers and electronic addresses, and interconnection. ZICTA is also the implementer of universal service programs. Gaining permission from ZICTA took many meetings and much travel from the rural area (test site in Macha) to the urban area (ZICTA offices in Lusaka). As all concepts involved in the project were new to Zambia, contents of the meetings involved detailed sensitization and explanation of underlying engineering concepts, explanation and providing proof of the research and development nature of the activities, and brainstorming sessions as how to facilitate and proceed.

OpenBTS operates in the GSM frequency bands. Zambia does not have a legal framework for test frequencies for research in ICT. Unlike, US' regulator FCC granting experimental licences for radiated power levels lower than 8 Watt, there is no regulation regarding the allotment of test frequencies for pilots in Zambia. The commercial nature of GSM frequencies rendered ZICTA apprehensive of allocating frequencies for the OpenBTS tests. After many meetings, ZICTA allocated the project temporarily frequencies in the extended GSM-900 range.

To assure close supervision of the use of tests, ZICTA requested activities to take place under their scrutiny on site at ZICTA's premises in Zambia's capital city Lusaka. As a consequence, equipment travelled thousands of kilometers within Zambia. Internet access at ZICTA's offices is limited. Actual tests were difficult to perform due to limited access and bandwidth there.

Within the OpenBTS coverage area, calls can be made even when the internet link is not available. For calls to other networks there is the necessity for a (relatively) solid internet connection, which was available in Macha, but not at ZICTA offices in Lusaka.

The quality of calls were highly dependent on the speed of the internet connection. The OpenBTS set-up in rural Macha varied, depending on congestion and latency of the VSAT connection. Especially in the highly congested lines at ZICTA, delays became great and hampered conversations. Tests showed that a number of no-brand handsets sold 'on the streets' in Zambia are incompatible with the system.

Calls from within the OpenBTS can be routed via VoIP service providers. When using a VoIP gateway, payment for such services necessitates international payments mostly involving credit cards, or otherwise by international transfer, both of which proved a hurdle for use. As mentioned, credit cards do not exist in Zambia. Facility Management centers regularly block network or service access for African IP addresses. Also, use of debit or credit card from African IP addresses regularly fail, due to settings that restrict services provided to African IP numbers. Depending on the availability of suitable international internet connectivity, it proved feasible to establish high quality connections with western based VoIP or Public Switched Telephony Network (PSTN) users. However, routing calls from Zambia to Zambia, using existing VoIP providers, are expensive and offer low quality. No VoIP-to-PSTN gateway service provider exists in Zambia.

6 Discussion

The project was the first practical implementation experiment with OpenBTS in Zambia. Practicalities involving sourcing of equipment, downloading of software, and gaining permission to use radio frequencies, took months to complete. These practical challenges were intertwined with many logistical issues and travel hazards. These non-technical project aspects took most of the research efforts (cf [23]).

A pre-requisite for the acquisition of test frequencies was a close relationship with the regulator. Further, there is a need for healthy relationships with the community for the implementation of test deployments. Constant communication with the wider community in a culturally acceptable manner is another pre-requisite. Building such relationships took much effort and financial resources, and many days of travelling.

Although the project was able to establish GSM calls, the quality of the internet backbone proved to be of prime importance for a feasible deployment of OpenBTS. Trunk calls use routings over the IP/internet network. Adding more traffic on an already congested, limited bandwidth internet link in rural areas degrades the performance of the system. When international internet capacity was sufficient, the establishment of connections with western receipients proved achievable. However, reaching a Zambian telephone recipient proved difficult, involving challenging financial interactions, high costs and low quality connections.

Use of OpenBTS showed to have considerable limitations:

1. the system does not support data transmission, i.e. does not support GPRS;
2. the system does not necessarily operate with all phones that sell in the Zambian market;
3. OpenBTS did not support roaming, and there is no handover of calls between base stations (an issue currently being addressed).

7 Conclusion and Future Work

OpenBTS is a viable and low cost system to build a local rural cellular GSM network. It can be used in sites when enough internet bandwidth is available. Local calls can be made even if an internet link is not available.

Though OpenBTS comes with clear limitations, it shows promising potential for rural mobile telecommunication. It provides a solution where low-cost, basic communication functions suffice. The case study provides insight into non-engineering aspects that influence implementing an OpenBTS testbed in rural Zambia.

Universal Service Funds aim at encouraging service providers to invest in rural areas. OpenBTS is an innovation that could be implemented in rural areas as a stand-alone system.

Under the banner VillageCell [18], and based upon the relationships established, and experiences gained by this project, future work envisions deriving a simple and easy system architecture for localized cell phone communication software involving defined radios (SDRs) and open-source solutions (OpenBTS and Asterisk) to further explore the opportunities for low-cost alternatives to high-end cell phone networks. Propsals for implementation of OpenBTS for rural communications are being submitted for universal access funding by ZICTA.

Acknowledgement. Authors acknowledge the input and feedback of Mr. A.C. Nalubamba (Zambia), LinkNet staff at Macha for facilitation and Linux training, and Peter Hasse (Fraunhofer FOKUS, Germany) for much practical help. Further gratitude to Tim Patton (UK) for unpacking OpenBTS, Hanna Weijers (NL), Karl Jonas (Germany), and David Johnson (USA) for scientific support and logistics, and Mr. M. Phiri, IEEE Zambia, for all assistance rendered. We thank the reviewer for valuable comments and suggestions.

IEEE's Engineering Projects in Community Service (EPICS) provided seed funding for this project.

References

1. Government of the Republic of Zambia. The Constitution of the Republic of Zambia (1996) as amended by Act No. 18 of 1996 (1996)
2. Montez, D.: Mobile Communications in Zambia A demand-side analysis based on the AudienceScapes Survey, including insights on mobile money use. InterMedia Survey Institute, Washingtion, DC (October 2010)
3. Ministry of Commerce Trade and Industry. Investment Policy Review of Zambia. Advancing investment policy reform. Government of the Republic of Zambia, Lusaka (2011)
4. Government of the Republic of Zambia. ICT Policy Zambia (2005)
5. ITU-D. Measuring the Information Society. ITU, Geneva (2011)
6. Adams, M.: Land tenure policy and practice in Zambia: issues relating to the development of the agricultural sector. Mokoro Ltd., Oxford (2003)
7. Central Statistics Office Zambia. 2010 Census of Population and Housing Preliminary Report (2011)
8. His Royal Highness Chief Chikanta and Fred Mweetwa. The Need for Information and Communications Technologies. LinkNet (2007)
9. Habeenzu, S.: Zambia ICT Sector Performance Review 2009/2010 vol. 2. Research ICT Africa (2010)
10. UNESCO. Engineering: Issues Challenges and Opportunities for Development. UNESCO Publishing, Paris (2010)
11. World Bank. Information and Communications for Development 2012: Maximizing Mobile. World Bank, Washington, DC (2012)
12. Duffy, J.: 7 Billion People: Who Owns the Computers and Cell Phones? PC Magazine (2011)
13. Matthee, K., Mweemba, G., Pais, A., van Stam, G., Rijken, M.: Bringing Internet connectivity to rural Zambia using a collaborative approach. In: ICTD 2007. IEEE (2007)
14. Government of the Republic of Zambia. National Policy on Science and Technology (1996)
15. Kamanga, A., Moono, P., Stresman, G., Mharakurwa, S., Shiff, C.: Rural health centres, communities and malaria case detection in Zambia using mobile telephones: a means to detect potential reservoirs of infection in unstable transmission conditions. Malaria Journal 9(96) (2010)

16. Burgess, D.A., Samra, H.S.: The Open BTS Project (2008)
17. OpenBTS. The OpenBTS Project
18. Anand, A., Johnson, D.L., Belding, E.M.: VillageCell: Cost Effective Cellular Connectivity in Rural Areas Categories and Subject Descriptors. In: ICTD 2012 (2012)
19. Heimerl, K., Brewer, E.: The Village Base Station. In: Proceedings of the 4th ACM Workshop on Networked Systems for Developing Regions Systems, NSDR 2010, pp. 5–6 (2010)
20. Rey-Moreno, C., Roro, Z., Siya, M.J., Simo-Reigadas, J., Bidwell, N.J., Tucker, W.D.: Towards a Sustainable Business Model for Rural Telephony. In: III International Conference on Research in ICT for Human Development (JITIC4DH), Cuzco (2012)
21. Kretschmer, M., Hasse, P., Niephaus, C., Horstmann, T., Jonas, K.: Connecting Mobile Phones via Carrier-Grade Meshed Wireless Back-Haul Networks. In: Popescu-Zeletin, R., Rai, I.A., Jonas, K., Villafiorita, A. (eds.) AFRICOM 2010. LNICST, vol. 64, pp. 1–10. Springer, Heidelberg (2011)
22. Government of the Republic of Zambia. The Information and Communication Technologies, Act No. 15 of 2009 (2009)
23. Brewer, E., Demmer, M., Ho, M., Honicky, R.J., Pal, J., Plauche, M., Surana, S.: The Challenges of Technology Research for Developing Regions. IEEE Pervasive Computing 5(2), 15–23 (2006)

Performance Evaluation of RSSI Based Distance Measurement for Localization in Wireless Sensor Networks

Omotayo Adewumi[*], Karim Djouani, and Anish Kurien

Tshwane University of Technology, F'SATI/Department of Electrical Engineering,
Private Bag X680, Pretoria 0001, South Africa
{adewumiog,djouanik,kurienam}@tut.ac.za

Abstract. Research has shown that the awareness of positions of wireless sensor nodes is a desirable feature for many applications in Wireless Sensor Networks (WSN). The key in ranging and localization technologies in WSNs is the relationship between the Received Signal Strength Indication (RSSI) values and distance. The RSSI of radio channels provides a feasible way of estimating the distance between nodes because the use of it does not require any additional hardware but simply a radio transceiver compared to other range based models. In this paper, an RSSI model that estimates the distance between sensor nodes in WSNs is presented. The performance of this model is evaluated and analyzed in a real system deployment in an indoor environment by performing an empirical measurement using Crossbow IRIS wireless sensor motes. It is shown that the results of this evaluation can contribute towards obtaining accurate locations of wireless sensor nodes.

Keywords: WSN, RSSI, Distance, Localization.

1 Introduction

Research on WSN (Wireless Sensor Networks) has attracted a lot of interest in recent times, and this interest is growing because WSNs promise to be an enabling technology of the future owing to the fact that processors, sensors and wireless radios are becoming extremely small and inexpensive. In the near future, the world we live in will be populated by objects that are globally networked such that physical environments are enriched by computational power. A WSN is a network consisting of a large number of wireless radio nodes equipped with sensing devices and are densely distributed for specific applications. Each node is equipped with a transceiver to communicate with another node within its communication radio range. The requirements for WSN differ when compared to traditional ad-hoc networks. For instance, the quality of service (QOS) requirements of an ad-hoc network does not apply to WSN; moreover WSN has to be fault tolerant such that the connectivity of

---

[*] Corresponding author.

K. Jonas, I.A. Rai, and M. Tchuente (Eds.): AFRICOMM 2012, LNICST 119, pp. 74–83, 2013.

the wireless sensor nodes has to be robust against failure [1]. Deployed for a specific application with known lifetime, they must be able to support a large number of nodes (Scalability) and must either be able to support a vast number or small number of nodes per unit area.

Typical sensors incorporated into wireless sensor nodes are light sensors, sound sensors, ultrasound sensors, accelerometers, temperature sensors, pressure sensors, humidity, and touch sensors to name a few. Some of the applications of WSN include disaster and relief operations, biodiversity mapping for wildlife observation, intelligent building and bridges, military operations and health where motes may be deployed to collect vital information such as pulse and heart beat rate. Some WSN applications are seen underground for monitoring earthquake, soccer fields, locating people in a collapsed building, under water applications which are implemented for ocean sampling networks, disaster prevention, assisted navigation, pollution monitoring specifically for chemical and biological spillage and distributed tactical surveillance [1], [5].

In many applications of WSN, sensed information only becomes useful when it is accompanied by the location of the area and accurate distances of where such information is been sensed. Hence, sensor nodes need to know the distance between one another in order to calculate their positions [2], [3]. There are many techniques for determining distance between sensor nodes. Physically, the Time of Signal (Acoustic or RF) Arrival (TOA) calculates the distance by use of signal propagation velocity and propagation time, Angle of Arrival (AOA) is measured by getting the signal direction sent by the adjacent node through the combination of array antenna and multiple receivers, while Received Power of Signal (RSSI) measures received power by receiving node, calculates propagation loss, transform propagation loss to distance by theoretical or empirical signal path loss mode, without any additional hardware so as to reduce input cost [4], [5], [6].

In this paper, a model that estimates the RSSI signal propagation for WSN to estimate the distance of deployed sensor nodes is considered. The model is compared to TOA and AOA which works effectively in outdoor environments but suffers from the limitations of multiple reflections of radio frequency (RF) and sound signals in indoor environments [7]. The RSSI signal propagation model is currently of three types; Free Space propagation model, Two-ray ground Model and Log Normal Shadowing Model (LNSM) [8], [9], [10], [11]. The first two models have special requirements for the application environment while the third model is a more general signal propagation model.

The remainder of this paper is organized as follows; in Section 2, the RSSI model is defined together with a theoretical and empirical description. In section 3, the experimental setups and a brief description of the crossbow motes is explained while in section 4, the experimental analysis together with the implementation is enlightened. The results are presented and explained in section 5. Finally in section 6, conclusions with a short summary of the results and future research directions are provided.

2   RSSI-Distance Measurement Model

RSSI, which is a standard feature in most wireless radios, has attracted a lot of attention in recent literature. RSSI is defined as the voltage measured by a receiver's received signal strength indicator (RSSI) circuit. Often, it is equivalently reported as measured power, i.e., the squared magnitude of the signal strength. It eliminates the need for additional hardware in small wireless devices and exhibits favorable properties with respect to power consumption, size and cost. Given a model of radio signal propagation in a building or other environment, RSSI can be used to estimate the distance from a transmitter to a receiver in order to estimate the positions of the sensor nodes. However, this approach requires detailed models of radio frequency (RF) propagation and does not account for variations in receiver sensitivity and orientation [11].

Wireless sensors communicate with neighboring sensors. As a result, the RSSI of RF signals can be measured by each receiver during normal data communication without presenting additional bandwidth or energy requirements. RSSI measurements are relatively inexpensive and simple to implement in hardware. In distance prediction based methods, RSSI data are directly mapped to distances through a signal propagation model. In the case of outdoor deployments, where there are no obstacles, a single signal propagation model is in all the profiling data required. In the case of indoor deployments the same applies. However, the signal propagation model might be different across different buildings with different furniture and wall arrangements in this case [11], [12], [13].

Given an underlying signal propagation model, RSSI data can be mapped to specific distances. This distance is used directly in order to perform localization. The accuracy of the distance prediction based methods depends heavily on the accuracy of the signal propagation model used for translating RSSI values to distances [13].

2.1   Basis of RSSI Model

The principle of RSSI ranging techniques describes the relationship between the received power, transmitted power of wireless signals and the distance among wireless sensor nodes. This relation is shown in equation (1). P_r is the received power of wireless signals. P_t is the transmitted power of wireless signals, d is the distance between the sending nodes and the receiving nodes, n is the transmission factor whose values depend on the environment of propagation (indoor and outdoor) [12].

$$P_r = P_t \times (1/d)^n . \tag{1}$$

P_t, the transmitted power of nodes given, the received power in dBm is then given as

$$P_r(dBm) = A - 10 \times n \times \log d . \tag{2}$$

In equation (2), it is clearly shown that the values of parameter A and parameter n determine the relationship between the strength of received signals and the distance of signal transmission [12].

2.2 RSSI Based Ranging Theoretical Model

As stated in [8], [9], [10], [11], RSSI propagation models in wireless sensor networks include the free space model, two ray ground model and log-normal shadowing model. The free space propagation model is used to predict received signal strength when the transmitter and receiver have a clear unobstructed line of sight path between them. As with most large scale radio wave propagation models, the free space model predicts that received power decays as a function of the Transmitter-Receiver separation distance. The free space power received by a receiver antenna separated from a radiating transmitter antenna by a distance d, and is given by the Friis free space equation below;

$$P_r(d) = (P_t \times G_t \times G_r \times \lambda^2) / (4\pi)^2 \times d^2 \times L . \tag{3}$$

where P_t is the transmitted power, $P_r(d)$ is the received power which is a function of the transmitter to receiver separation, G_t is the transmitter antenna gain, G_r is the receiver antenna gain, d is the transmitter to receiver separation distance in meters, L is the system loss factor not related to propagation (L is greater or equal to 1) and λ is the wavelength in meters.

The two ray ground model is the case when the single direct path between the transmitter and the receiver is the only physical means of propagation of the radio signal. The two-ray ground model considers two propagation paths; the directed path and a ground reflected propagation between the transmitter and the receiver.

$$P_r(d) = (P_t \times G_t \times G_r \times (h_t^2 h_r^2)) / d^4 . \tag{4}$$

In the two-ray ground propagation model, the received power at distance d is given in the equation (4) above where h_t is the transmitter antenna height and h_r is the receiver antenna height.

Log-normal shadowing model is a general propagation model. It is suitable for indoor and outdoor environments. This model provides a number of parameters which can be configured according to different environment. The formula is given in equation (5).

$$PL(dB) = PL(d_0) + 10 \times n \times (\log d / d_0) + X_\sigma . \tag{5}$$

In equation (5) d_0 is the near-earth reference distance which depends on the experiential value. n is the path-loss index which depends on specific propagation environment and its value will become larger when there are obstacles. X_σ is the zero mean Gaussian random variable. The Log-normal shadow model is most suitable for wireless sensor networks applications and is the main focus of this paper because of its universal nature and the ability of being configured according to environments.

2.3 RSSI Based Ranging Empirical Model

Received signal strength techniques measures the power of the signal at the receiver based on the known transmit power. The respective propagation loss can be calculated. Theoretical and empirical models are used to translate this loss into a distance estimate. This method has been used mainly for RF signals. The relationship between RSS values and distances are derived as follows by [15].

The received signal power is inversely related to distance as;

$$P \alpha 1 / D^n . \tag{6}$$

$$RSS \alpha 10 \times \log(1 / D)^n . \tag{7}$$

$$RSS = -10 \times n \times \log(D) + C . \tag{8}$$

D is the distance of deployed sensor and n is the path-loss exponent factor. From equation (8), it is clear that RSS has a linear relationship with the logarithm of distance. C is considered to be a fixed constant. In more compact form, RSS can be represented as:

$$RSS = -m \times \log(D) + C . \tag{9}$$

Here m is the slope of linear equation between RSS and $\log(D)$. From equation (8 & 9), the path-loss exponent factor is given as:

$$n = m / 10 . \tag{10}$$

3   Experimental Setup

IRIS Motes are the motes used for our experimentation and they form part of the latest generation of Motes from Crossbow Technology, XM2110 (2400 MHz to 2483.5 MHz band). The radio used by the IRIS is an IEEE 802.15.4 compliant RF transceiver designed for low-power and low-voltage wireless applications. It uses Atmel's AT86RF230 radio that employs O-QPSK (Offset Quadrature Phase Shift Keying) with half sine pulse shaping. The 802.15.4 radio includes a DSSS (Digital Direct Sequence Spread Spectrum) baseband modem providing a spreading gain of 9 dB and an effective data rate of 250 kbps [17].

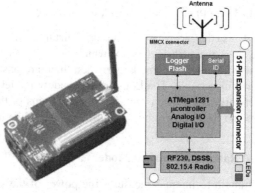

Fig. 1. Figure taken from [17], *XM2110 IRIS* mote with standard antenna and its respective block diagram

Table 1. This table from [17] summarizes the details regarding IRIS XM2110 Crossbow mote

Mote Hardware Platform	Platform Types	IRIS XM2110
MCU	Chip	AT Mega 1281
	Type	7.37 MHZ, 8Bit
	Program Memory(KB)	128
	SRAM(KB)	8
Sensor Board Interface	Type	51 Pin
	10Bit ADC	7, 0V to 3V Input
	UART	2
RF Transceiver (Radio)	Chip	RF 230
	Radio Frequency(MHZ)	2400
	Max Data Rate (Kbits/sec)	250
	Antenna Connector	MMCX
Default Power Source	Type	AA, 2^x
	Typical Capacity(mA-hr)	2000

4   Experimental Analysis

The experiment was carried out in an indoor environment. The IRIS sensor nodes were programmed before performing any forms of measurements. The base node was connected to the laptop via an MIB520 interface board through a USB cable and which acts as the gateway. Application software called mote-view which acts as an interface between the user and the deployed wireless sensors was also installed on the laptop. It provides the tools to simplify deployment and monitoring. It also makes it easy to connect to a database to analyze and to graph sensor readings.

The indoor experimentation was done in the computer laboratory of the institution in which there are forms of obstruction due to the fact that there are computer systems, furniture's and movement of student in the territory. The effects of the antenna orientation of the sensor nodes were taking into consideration so that all the sensor nodes are resting on their bases with antenna pointing vertically upwards.

Hence, in order to avoid these errors and to provide ideal environment for the measurements, measurements were taken in such a way that no other device working in the range of 2.4GHz were present in the vicinity of experimental location and it was ensured that the deployed sensor nodes are in line of sight with the base node and no obstacles were present between them. The RSSI readings were taken at a fixed distances at different time intervals in order to take into consideration the effect of shadowing due to the fact that RF channels vary with time.

5   Simulation Result

The result of the indoor experimentation is shown in the figure (2). The RSSI readings were taken from I meter to 7 meters in distance. The figure shows the plot of the RSSI values in dBm recorded at different time interval of each distance.

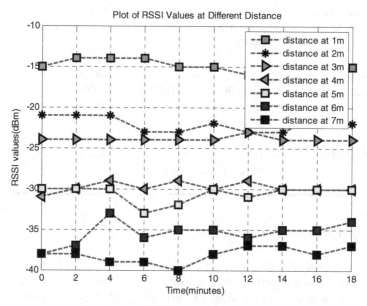

Fig. 2. Plot of RSSI values at each distance

Table 2. The table below shows the mean, variance and the standard deviation of the RSSI values in an indoor environment

Distance(m)	Mean of RSSI Values(dBm)	Variance of RSSI Values	Standard Deviation of RSSI Values
1	-14.9	0.5444	0.7378
2	-22	0.8888	0.9428
3	-23.9	0.1000	0.3162
4	-29.8	0.4000	0.6324
5	-30.6	1.1555	1.0749
6	-35.4	2.0444	1.4298
7	-38.1	0.9888	0.9944

The corresponding plots of the mean of the measured RSSI values are shown in the figure below:

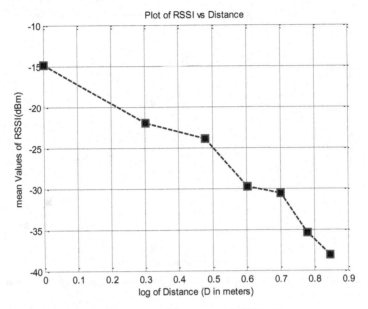

Fig. 3. Plot of mean of the measured RSSI values

Since the measured RSSI values vary randomly with time, the mean values were considered for calculating the distances of the deployed sensor nodes. In order to describe the functionality of the measured RSSI values, an illustration which represents as exactly as possible the distances for measured RSSI values is needed.

So therefore in our experiment, we recognized that the data can be best described by a linear function. The experiment for generating the calibration equation relating to the RSSI to distance was conducted. The plot in figure (4) shown below was used for the calibration. The calibration equation and curve were fitted with MATLAB's basic fitting tools. It shows a linear curve fit between RSSI(dBm) and the log10(Distance).

The linear curve fitting in figure (4) gives the following relationship between mean RSSI(dBm) and the distance in an indoor environment which is shown below.

$$y = -27x - 14 . \tag{11}$$

Where y represent RSSI(dBm) and x represent log(D), where D is the distance.

$$D = 10^{((y +14)/ -27)}. \tag{12}$$

From equation (12), the path-loss exponent factor has been found to be 2.7 for indoor environment in which we have conducted the experiment.

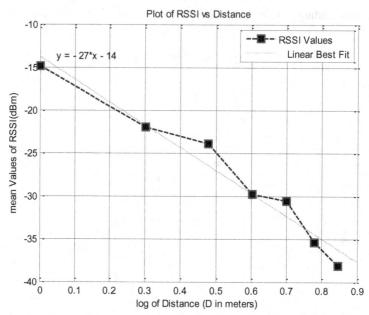

Fig. 4. Calibration curve of the linear regression based on the mean of the measured RSSI values

From the table below the estimated distance was obtained using the equation (12) which was derived from the calibration. The distance error is the diference between the actual distance and the estimated distance.

The mean error estimated from the distance error measurement in the table (3) is: Mean Error = 0.4029 m.

Table 3. The table below shows the estimated error in distance measurement of each node deployed at different locations

Actual distance of Deployed node (m)	Measured RSSI Values (dBm)	Estimated Distance (m)	Distance Error (m)
1	-14.9	1.0798	0.0798
2	-22	1.9783	0.0217
3	-23.9	2.3263	0.6737
4	-29.8	3.8476	0.1524
5	-30.6	4.1192	0.8808
6	-35.4	6.2029	0.2029
7	-38.1	7.8089	0.8089

Table (3) shows the results for the distance estimations of the deployed sensor nodes. The calibration method provides distance estimation error of 0.4029m. this result is encouraging compared to measures that can be found in the literature.

6   Conclusion

In this paper, we presented the performance evaluation of RSSI based model in an indoor environment. The study was conducted by using empirical measurements using IRIS motes for distance estimation. Based on the results obtained which gives us distance estimation error less than 0.5m, we concluded that the results is very encouraging and could be used for approximation algorithms under ideal condition to perform localization in WSN. Currently, research work is in progress in developing an accurate algorithm to perform localization of wireless sensor nodes in a given environment.

References

1. Akyildiz, I.F., Su, W., Sankarasubramamiam, Y., Cayirci, E.: Wireless Sensor Networks: A Survey. Elsivier Science B.V Journal of Computer Networks, 393–422 (2002)
2. Jamal, N.A., Ahmed, E.K.: Routing Techniques in Wireless Sensor Networks: A Survey. IEE Wireless Communication Magazine (2005)
3. Adel, G.A.E., Hussein, A.E., Salwa, E.R., Magdy, M.I.: An Energy Aware WSN Geographic Routing Protocol. Universal Journal of Computer Science and Engineering Technology, 105–111 (2010)
4. Amitangshu, P.: Localization Algorithm in Wireless Sensor Networks: Current Approaches and Future Challenges. Network Protocol and Algorithm (2010) 1943-3581
5. Dong, B., Mahdy, A.M.: Underwater Wireless Sensor Networks: Efficient Schemes using SemiDefinite Programming. International Journal on Advances in Networks and Services, 186–195 (2010)
6. He, T., Huang, C., Blum, B.M., Stankovic, J.A., Abidelzaher, T.: Range-Free Localization Schemes For Large Scale Sensor Networks. In: Mobicom 2003, pp. 81–95 (2003)
7. Mohit, S., Puneet, G., Bijendra, N.J.: Experimental Analysis of RSSI-Based Location Estimation in Wireless Sensor Networks
8. Giacomin, J.C., Correta, L.N.A., Heimfarth, T., Pereira, G.M., Silva, V.F., De Santa, J.L.P.: Radio Channel Model of Wireless Sensor Networks Operating in 2.4GHZ ISM Band
9. Willis, S., Kikkert, C.J.: Radio Propagation Model for Long Range Wireless Sensor Networks. IEEE (2007)
10. Sommer, C., Dressler, F.: Using the Right Two-Ray Model? A Measurement Based Evaluation of PHY Models in VANETS
11. Benkic, K., Malajner, M., Planinsic, P., Cucej, Z.: Using RSSI Value for Distance Estimation in Wireless Sensor Networks Based on Zigbee
12. Xu, J., Liu, W., Lang, F., Zhang, Y., Wang, C.: Distance Measurement Model Based on RSSI in WSN. Wireless Sensor Network, 606–611 (2010)
13. Tadakamadla, S.: Indoor Local Positioning System for Zigbee, Based on RSSI. An Msc Thesis Report, Mid Sweden University (2006)
14. Malajner, M., Benkic, K., Planinsic, P., Cucej, Z.: The Accuracy of Propagation Models for Distance Measurement Between WSN Nodes. IEEE (2009)
15. Kumar, P., Reddy, L., Varma, S.: Distance Measurement and Error Estimation Scheme for RSSI Based Localization in Wireless Sensor Networks. IEEE (2009)
16. Awad, A., Frunzke, T., Dressler, F.: Adaptive Distance Estimation and Localization in WSN using RSSI Measures
17. Crossbow: MPR-MIB Users' Manual: Revision A (2007)

Link Calibration in QoS-Aware Wireless Back-Haul Networks for Rural Areas

Christian Niephaus[1], Mathias Kretschmer[1], Karl Jonas[1], Markus Kessel[2], and Michael Rademacher[1]

[1] Fraunhofer FOKUS, Sankt Augustin, Germany
{christian.niephaus,mathias.kretschmer,karl.jonas,
michael.rademacher}@fokus.fraunhofer.de
[2] Bonn-Rhine-Sieg University of Applied Sciences, Sankt Augustin, Germany
markus.kessel@inf.h-brs.de

Abstract. Rural areas all over the world often lacking affordable broadband Internet connectivity. High CAPEX and especially OPEX due to vast and sparsely populated areas often present an uneconomical environment for deploying traditional wireless carrier equipment. Particularly in emerging and developing countries the lack of well-trained personnel requires inherent self-managed networks. To address these issues, we have developed a carrier-grade heterogeneous Back-haul architecture which may be deployed to extend, complement or even replace traditional operator equipment. Our Wireless Back-Haul (WiBACK) network technology extends the Back-haul coverage by building on cost-effective equipment and provides highly automated self-management features still allowing for effective QoS-provisioning. Due to the limited capacity of Wireless Networks compared to cable or fiber networks, it is important to optimally utilize the wireless links and, hence, to configure them properly to match the characteristics of the wireless channel. This *link calibration* includes selecting the best-suited Modulation and Coding Scheme (MCS), Transmission (TX)-power and other MAC parameters such as the acknowledgment timeout. In this paper, we present our WiBACK architecture and its suitability for deployments in rural regions. Moreover, we propose a link calibration algorithm for IEEE 802.11 links and its crucial architectural role.

Keywords: Wireless Backhaul Network, QoS, MPLS, IEEE 802.21, self-configuration, self-management, link calibration.

1 Introduction

In recent years Wireless Mesh Networks (WMNs) have matured tremendously and attracted both researchers and commercial operators equally. Self-configuration and self-management as well as resilience and fault-tolerance potentially leading to lower maintenance and operational cost are seen as major advantages

K. Jonas, I.A. Rai, and M. Tchuente (Eds.): AFRICOMM 2012, LNICST 119, pp. 84–93, 2013.
© Institute for Computer Sciences, Social Informatics and Telecommunications Engineering 2013

of meshed wireless Back-haul networks compared to traditional fixed wireless operator Back-haul technologies. In particular, since cost-effective packet-switched equipment, such as IEEE 802.11[1] or 802.16[2] can be used. Mainly due to these reasons and the associated lower CAPEX and OPEX, meshed wireless Back-haul networks are often seen as a potential solution to connect rural areas without broadband or even without any kind of communication infrastructure, and hence to bridge the "digital divide".

Many rural regions share similar idiosyncratic properties when it comes to Information Communication Technology (ICT) deployments in these environments. While traditional wired connectivity is widely available in large and densely populated cities, it becomes prohibitively more expensive to connect the more rural parts of a country with broadband technology. The same reasoning applies to microwave connections - the costs of setting up a microwave Back-haul infrastructure for relatively few people frequently outweigh the prospective returns to be generated by the targeted group. In particular in emerging and developing regions this holds true due to the limited financial capabilities of target customers.

However, potential wireless Back-haul networks solutions must still fulfill strict requirements in terms of Quality of Service (QoS), availability and predictability even in high load situations in order to be considered as an alternative or extension for an operator Back-haul network. They are required to support the triple-play services today's customers expect. Besides that, the required low OPEX and CAPEX makes self-configuration and self-management functionality vital for each deployed network infrastructure. To address those issues we have developed the heterogeneous multi-radio and multi-channel WiBACK architecture which allows for fast and cost-efficient deployments particularly suited for rural areas while still providing carrier-grade services.

The scope of the WiBACK architecture is to provide or extend existing Back-haul capacity which might range from single-hop long distance wireless connectivity to multi-hop connectivity with up to ten hops. To support cost-effective solutions to cover rural areas [3], WiBACK exploits off-the-shelf components such as IEEE 802.11 radios to form long distance point-to-point links interconnected with multi-radio nodes utilizing multiple orthogonal channels. Analogue to technologies operating in licensed bands, such IEEE 802.11-based backhaul links require to be properly calibrated in terms of the used MCS, TX-power and MAC timing. In case of IEEE 802.11 links, particularly the latter is important to ensure the longer transmission times on long-distance links are not falsely interpreted as a transmission error by the radio device due to a delayed received acknowledgment.

The remaining of the paper is structured as follows: We first discuss the relevant aspects of the WiBACK architecture and propose a link calibration algorithm for IEEE 802.11 in Section 2 and Section 3, respectively. Following that we will validate the design and present evaluation results. Concluding we will summarize our contribution and give an outlook on future work.

2   WiBACK Architecture

Even though mainly on IEEE 802.11 WLAN is relied upon in the targeted deployment scenarios due to cost-efficiency, the multi-radio, multi-channel Wi-BACK architecture is designed to operate with heterogeneous technologies in order to allow for easily incorporating new emerging technologies and being adoptable for different use-cases.

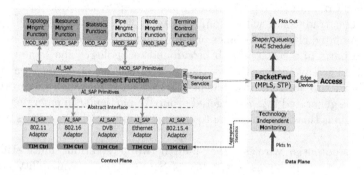

Fig. 1. The WiBACK architecture - MPLS-based Data plane and IEEE 802.21-inspired Control Plane

WiBACK is inspired by the work of the EU FP7 CARrier grade wireless MEsh Network (CARMEN) [4] project and is based on a centrally managed cross-layer concept. Figure 1 depicts the general WiBACK architecture. The control plane is heavily inspired by the IEEE 802.21 standard [5]. Although the purpose of this standard is to facilitate seamless handover between heterogeneous technologies the concepts of media abstraction can be easily extended for other purposes as well. As depicted in Figure 1, the central component of the control plane is the Interface Management Function (IMF) which adopts and extends the functionality of the IEEE 802.21 Media Independent Handover Function (MIHF). It provides a uniform and technology agnostic interface to higher layers by providing a common set of primitives. The MAC adapters located logically below the IMF are responsible for mapping this set of primitives onto technology specific features and mechanisms. The higher layer modules on top of the IMF together provide the functionality of a traditional routing protocol and beyond, such as topology discovery, route calculation, monitoring or mobility services. These modules utilize the generic interface of the IMF via the *MOD_SAP* and the *AI_SAP*. The first is used for communicating with the IMF whereas the latter provides primitives to control and manage the radio interfaces. Besides the media abstraction mechanisms WiBACK also utilizes the messaging service defined by IEEE 802.21 in order to provide a media independent messaging mechanism which allows for exchanging commands and events locally and remotely, either between modules or between modules and MAC adaptors.

The control plane is based on a centralized management approach, where so-called *Controller* nodes manage a set of *Slave* nodes in their administrative area. Dedicated management entities maintain the resource allocation and routing state of their network areas following the concept of a centralized stateful Path Computation Element (PCE) [6]. Multiple *Controller* nodes might be operational within each administrative area in a primary/backup configuration in order to prevent a failed *Controller* from rendering a whole area nonoperational. Contrary to the rather distributed routing protocols such as Open Shortest Path First (OSPF) [7] or Optimised Link State Routing (OLSR) [8] or the Layer 2 multi-hop communication protocols such as IEEE 802.11s, the centralized approach offers the opportunity to perform network wide optimizations when allocating radio resources or when assigning the overall network capacity to best match payload demands. Compared to, for example, Open Shortest Path First - Traffic Engineering (OSPF-TE) [9], only the centralized WiBACK *Master* nodes need to be kept up-to-date regarding the link states and resource allocation in the network, while in typical distributed link state protocols all nodes are required to maintain a consistent state in order to make coherent Traffic Engineering (TE) routing decisions. This is especially crucial for wireless links in unlicensed spectrum which often exhibit rather volatile conditions compared to wired networks. Hence, the state of distributed protocols may often be inconsistent or not even converge at all, see [10].

To support the centralized approach, WiBACK builds upon Multi Protocol Label Switching (MPLS) and operates on so-called *pipes* which are MPLS Label-Switched Paths (LSPs) with dedicated per-hop resource allocation. *Pipes* are used as aggregates enforcing resource isolation as well as fairness among traffic classes or *pipes* of the same traffic class.

Management Pipes are setup between a *Controller* and each of its *Slaves* in order to establish a communication path for the Command, Event and Information messages exchanged among the control plane entities. On the data plane *Data Pipes* can be established among any two arbitrary WiBACK nodes. Using the MPLS Fast Reroute (FRR) feature, if alternative paths are available in the network, WiBACK pipes can be protected against link failure or during periods of spectrum reallocations where links on the primary path may temporarily be down due to channel re-assignments. Monitoring is a crucial task at each WiBACK node to assess the state of each link in the network and to allow for timely reactions to link degradations or failures. The Monitoring component performs fast per-packet link and LSP measurement within the data plane and periodically pushes the accumulated measurement results towards the *Statistics Function* for further processing. The use of MPLS allows WiBACK to support TE processes, to ensure QoS assurances are met or to enforce fairness among nodes.

In particular Voice-over-IP (VoIP) can introduce a high load on capacity-constrained collision-sensitive wireless links due to the small packet size [11]. To address this issue our Wireless Back-Haul (WiBACK) architecture provides a Topology Management Function (TMF) to optimize the usage of scarce radio spectrum resources as well as a Resource Management Function (RMF) which optimizes the allocation of the available link and overall network capacity to best accommodate user QoS-traffic demands while reacting quickly to link status fluctuations reported by the monitoring component on a per-link and per-LSP basis.

A WiBACK network is managed on two time scales. On a slower time scale, the centralized Topology Management Function (TMF) manages identifiers, nodes, radio interfaces and spectrum resources, while at a faster time scale the Resource Management Function (RMF) assigns the available capacity to resource requests for user payload among WiBACK nodes while reacting to capacity changes due to link status fluctuations. The RMF operates on a set of logical links which is a subset of all physical links managed my the TMF. Both TMF and RMF rely on the Pipe Management Function (PMF) to push pipe state into the network, to modify existing pipe resource allocations or tear down pipes.

2.1   Topology Management Function

TMF implements a ring-based approach where a *Controller* node first brings up its own radio interfaces and determines the optimal radio configuration. This is computed based on the capabilities of the radio interfaces and the ambient spectrum usage assessed by passive channel utilization analysis. Once this process is complete, the *Controller* starts sending WiBACK beacons on all its active interfaces to inform adjacent *Slave* nodes about its availability.

Slave nodes determine their configuration during the bootstrap phase and then switch into the *beacon scan* mode in which they periodically scan all administratively permitted channels for WiBACK beacons sent by a *Controller* node or already associates *Slave* nodes. Once they detect WiBACK beacons they will attempt to associate with the sending node. If multiple WiBACK beacons have been detected, they will be sorted by *Signal Quality* and *hop distance*, and associations will be attempted starting with the highest rated sender.

The current optimization criteria are to establish point-to-point links where possible and to select the least occupied channels while ensuring a minimum node-local channel separation in order to minimize interferences, see Figure 2. Once the assignments of frequencies and channel bandwidth have been finished the *Link Calibration* is started, so that the link capacity can be derived.

2.2   Resource Management Function

Upon association of a new *Slaves* TMF computes the optimal channel configuration out of all possible physical links among the adjacent WiBACK nodes and their radio interfaces. Then TMF pushes the set of *ASSIGNED* links to RMF for capacity allocations of *data pipes* within the WiBACK network.

The RMF implementation is based on the concept of a centralized stateful PCE where the relevant messages of the Path Computation Element Protocol (PCEP) are mapped onto Media Independent Handover (MIH)-style primitives.

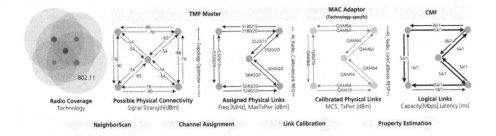

Fig. 2. TMF detects physical connectivity among nodes, choses the optimal links and assigns orthogonal channels, where possible. Then TMF calls AI_Radio_CalibrateLink to determine the optimal radio configuration. Upon successful completion, the response message returns the resulting logical link properties and the parameters of the resource model. This information forms the basis of CMF's capacity management.

For each link, the stateful RMF keeps track of the available resources as well as the currently allocated resources. In order to maintain an up-to-date view of the overall resource state of the links under its control, RMF subscribes to LINK_STATUS_CHANGED events and possible additional *pipe* related events to allow a more fine-grained reaction depending on the QoS requirements of the affected *pipe*, see [12] for a more detailed discussion.

3   Link Calibration for IEEE 802.11 WLAN links

The IEEE 802.11 link calibration algorithm introduced in this paper aims at configuring a stable and reliable link among two arbitrary nodes by determining the optimal MCS, i.e. physical data rate, the TX-power and the distance settings. The latter is used to adopt the Acknowledgment time-out to the signal propagation delay. Figure 3 presents the basic flow of the link calibration algorithm: First, both interfaces between which the link should be calibrated, are configures to the most robust MCS, i.e. 6mbps physical data rate, the highest possible TX-power and largest possible distance in order to ensure communication among the nodes. Afterwards a sufficient amount of probing packets is sent and the retransmission fraction rTx is calculated. If rTx is smaller than a certain limit $rTxMax$ the next modulation which is less robust but provides a higher data rate is chosen and the test is repeated. Initially, $rTxMax$ is set to 1% in order to provide stable and reliable links. These steps are repeated until $rTxMax$ is greater or equal than rTx or the modulation which provides the highest data rate has been reached. This completes the first phase of the algorithm. In the second phase the algorithms aims at reducing the TX-power to the lowest value which allows for a stable communication when using the previously selected Mobile-services Switching Centre (MSC), in order to avoid interferences with other nodes or other systems. For this purpose, again a sufficient amount of probing packets are sent and rTx is calculated and compared with $rTxMax$.

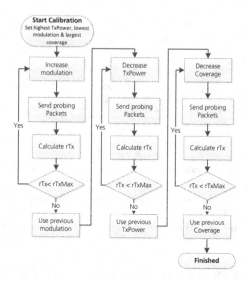

Fig. 3. Flowchart describing the proposed link calibration algorithm for IEEE 802.11

Until rTx is smaller than $rTxMax$ or the minimum TX-power has been reached, TX-the power is decreased in steps of 1dBm. Once rTx is equal or greater than $rTxMax$ the previous TX-power value is chosen and the second phase of the algorithm has finished. Finally, in the last phase the proper distance setting is determined using the same procedure.

4 Validation

In order to evaluate our link calibration algorithm, we have used in outdoor long-distance testbed, which is equipped with high-power Ubiquity XR5 Atheros based WLAN cards operating in the 5GHz spectrum, directional antennae and running a recent Linux Kernel. The antennae are aligned to form point-to-point links. The maximum retransmission limit of the WLAN interfaces was set to one and both WLAN interfaces were tuned on the same frequency so that they can communicate with each other. In the following tests, traffic generated on one of the nodes by the *mgen* traffic generator has been sent to the other node. The amount of traffic is slowly increasing until the link is saturated and even overloaded.

The first measurements have been performed without our link calibration algorithm to have proper reference values. Figure 4 depicts the unidirectional throughput and latency measurement results of a typical IEEE 802.11a link. In the default configuration, shown in the first graph of the figure, the TX-power was set to maximum, and the rate adaptation algorithm *Minstrel*, as implemented in the recent Linux 3.2.7 kernel, was used to determine the MCS. As can be observed, the rate adaptation algorithm constantly attempts to increase

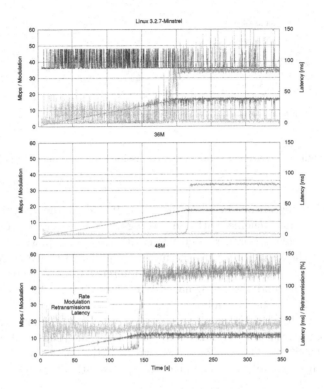

Fig. 4. Throughput, latency and MCS of unidirectional *mgen* flows transmitted over a low-interference IEEE 802.11a link with different MCS configurations at auto/maximum power level

the data rate to 48mbps and keeps falling back to 36mbps. The result is a very jittery throughput and especially the latency measurements exhibit a strong volatility which renders such a link unusable to support low-latency in a multi-hop scenario for, i.e. VoIP traffic. The second graph presents the results with the MCS manually fixed at data rate of 36mbps resulting in almost no jitter and a very low latency up to the point where the link was saturated. Obviously, at this point, the latency jumps to a high value, which here depends on the transmit-queue size used by the *mgen* traffic generator. The third graph in this Figure depicts the results of the same scenario, but with the MCS manually fixed at data rate of 48mbps. As can be seen, throughput and latency experience less jitter compared to the first graph. It should also be noted, that the actual throughput achieved at 36mbps MCS is higher than at 48mbps MCS. This is due to a high ratio of retransmitted frames (as depicted by the yellow graph) at 48mbps compared to 36mbps.

In order to evaluate the robustness of our link calibration algorithm, we have executed 1000 runs on the same link. As discussed above, the optimal MCS setting seems to be 36mbps, while the TX-power was set to auto/max.

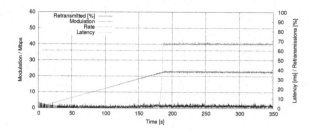

Fig. 5. Throughput, Latency and Retransmission measurement results of the calibrated link

The calibration algorithm has determined in 98,9% of the measurements a 36mbps modulation scheme with an averaging TX-power of 21.11 ±0.79. This shows a stable calibration algorithm with slight TX-power fluctuations, which may be the result of a variance in the amplifier of the WLAN cards. A manual verification revealed that the actual difference in output power between the 21dBm setting and the auto/max setting was only ±1dBm for the used Atheros-based IEEE 802.11a radio.

In order to verify that this configuration results in a stable link, we have run the above *mgen* flow test again, using the configuration determined by our link calibration algorithm. The results are shown in Figure 5. As can be seen, the link performance is stable with low jitter and a low ratio of retransmission.

5   Conclusion and Future Work

We have presented WiBACK architecture and out link calibration algorithm, which is crucial to efficiently utilize the resource-constrained wireless links. Moreover, we have shown that the link calibration algorithm is able to reliably determine the optimal radio configuration settings in a IEEE 802.11 WLAN point-to-point link. Future work will adapted the link calibration algorithm to also handle 802.11n links, including the optimization of the packet aggregation configuration.

Acknowledgment. This work has been funded by the Federal Ministry of Education and Research of the Federal Republic of Germany (Förderkennzeichen 01 BU 1116, SolarMesh - Energieeffizientes, autonomes großflächiges Sprach- und Datenfunknetz mit flacher IP- Architektur). The authors alone are responsible for the content of this paper.

References

1. IEEE standard for information technology–telecommunications and information exchange between systems local and metropolitan area networks–specific requirements part 11: Wireless lan medium access control (mac) and physical layer (phy) specifications. IEEE Std 802.11-2012 (Revision of IEEE Std 802.11-2007), pp. 1–2793, 29 (2012)

2. Issa, O., Li, W., Liu, H.: Performance evaluation of tv over broadband wireless access networks. IEEE Transactions on Broadcasting 56(2), 201–210 (2010)
3. Henkel, D., Englander, S., Kretschmer, M., Niephaus, C.: Connecting the unconnected - economic constraints and technical requirements towards a back-haul network for rural areas. In: 2011 IEEE GLOBECOM Workshops (GC Wkshps), pp. 1039–1044 (December 2011)
4. Banchs, A., Bayer, N., Chieng, D., de la Oliva, A., Gloss, B., Kretschmer, M., Murphy, S., Natkaniec, M., Zdarsky, F.: Carmen: Delivering carrier grade services over wireless mesh networks. In: Proc. IEEE 19th International Symposium on Personal, Indoor and Mobile Radio Communications, PIMRC 2008, September 15-18, pp. 1–6 (2008)
5. IEEE standard for local and metropolitan area networks- part 21: Media independent handover. IEEE Std 802.21-2008, pp. c1–301 (January 2009)
6. Farrel, A., Vasseur, J.-P., Ash, J.: A Path Computation Element (PCE)-Based Architecture. RFC 4655 (Informational) (August 2006)
7. Moy, J.: OSPF Version 2. RFC 2328 (Standard) (April 1998); Updated by RFC 5709
8. Clausen, T., Jacquet, P.: Optimized Link State Routing Protocol (OLSR). RFC 3626 (Experimental) (October 2003)
9. Katz, D., Kompella, K., Yeung, D.: Traffic Engineering (TE) Extensions to OSPF Version 2. RFC 3630 (Proposed Standard) (September 2003); Updated by RFCs 4203, 5786
10. Bernardos, C.J., Fitzpatrick, J., Kuo, F.-C., Kretschmer, M., Lessmann, J., Niephaus, C., de la Oliva, A., Robitzsch, S., Zdarsky, F.: Carrier-grade wireless mesh networks: D3.4-unicast and multicast routing specification and analysis (December 2009), http://www.ict-carmen.eu/wp-uploads/2009/D3.4.pdf
11. del Prado Pavon, J., Shankar, S.: Impact of frame size, number of stations and mobility on the throughput performance of IEEE 802.11e. In: 2004 IEEE Wireless Communications and Networking Conference, WCNC, vol. 2, pp. 789–795 (March 2004)
12. Kretschmer, M., Niephaus, C., Ghinea, G.: QoS-aware flow monitoring and event creation in heterogeneous MPLS-based wireless mesh networks supporting unidirectional links. In: 9th IEEE Malaysia International Conference on Communications, Kuala Lumpur, Malaysia (2009)

IPv4 to IPv6 Transition Strategies for Enterprise Networks in Developing Countries

Julianne S. Sansa-Otim and Anthony Mile

Dept. Networks, School of Computing and Informatics,
Makerere University, Kampala, Uganda
sansa@cit.mak.ac.ug, mileanthony@yahoo.com

Abstract. Internet Protocol version 4 (IPv4) addresses have been reported to be nearing exhaustion and the next generation Internet Protocol version 6 (IPv6) is gradually being deployed in the Internet. IPv6 provides a much larger address space, better address design and greater security, among other benefits. IPv6 deployment requires thorough and careful preparation to minimize network disruption and ensure that the benefits of IPv6 are obtained. The migration from IPv4 to IPv6 cannot be achieved in a short period thus the two protocols will co-exist for some time. Unfortunately, these two protocols are incompatible; hence for them to co-exist, various IPv4-to-IPv6 transition mechanisms have been developed. In this paper, we analyse the different site-to-site tunneling mechanisms through a theoretical and experimental evaluation to study their appropriateness in IPv6 deployment for enterprise networks in developing countries. Using five performance metrics, namely: end-to-end delay, jitter, throughput, packet loss and CPU utilization, our experimental results indicate that Configured Tunneling performs better than the other tunneling mechanisms. This study is of importance to those enterprise networks which want to implement IPv6 and are concerned about which transition mechanisms to embrace depending on the performance requirements.

Keywords: IPv4-IPv6 translation, GRE tunneling, 6to4 tunneling, Configured tunneling.

1 Introduction

The Internet has continued to grow using multiple vendor equipment across all world geographical areas because of its well defined architectural standard, the TCP/IP protocol suite. Internet Protocol (IP) is one of the protocols within TCP/IP protocol suite and its current operational version in the Internet is IPv4. The IPv4 address space has been reported to be depleted in the Internet Assigned Numbers Authority (IANA) registry in February 2011 [1], while just few are remaining within the regional Internet registries, Afrinic depletion is expected by October 2014 while Apnic is already exhausted[1]. This is projected to affect the growth of the Internet greatly. The Internet Engineer Task

K. Jonas, I.A. Rai, and M. Tchuente (Eds.): AFRICOMM 2012, LNICST 119, pp. 94–104, 2013.
© Institute for Computer Sciences, Social Informatics and Telecommunications Engineering 2013

Force (IETF) considered this issue and proposed a new version of Internet Protocol namely Internet Protocol Version 6 (IPv6). IPv6 is the solution to the massive growth of the Internet due to its huge address space. IPv6 addressing contains 128 bits binary value that provides 2^{128} addresses. This means that there must be a transition and that the current IPv4 should start migrating to IPv6. According to Sailan et al [2], IPv6 network penetration is still low but it is expected to grow. IPv6 is not backward compatible with IPv4. There are also performance differences between the IPv4 and IPv6 based architectures. This means that there are compatibility and interoperability issues relating to IPv4 and IPv6 during the migration period. The transition between IPv4 internet and IPv6 is a long process as they are two completely separate protocols and it is impossible to switch the entire internet over to IPv6 over night. IPv6 is not backward compatible with IPv4 and IPv4 hosts and routers will not be able to deal directly with IPv6 traffic and vice-versa. Because the IPv4 and IPv6 will co-exist for a long time, this requires the transition and inter-operation mechanisms[3]. The Next Generation Transition (NGtrans)[4] proposed three main transition mechanisms which allow IPv4 to be able to coexist with IPv6 during the migration period. These included dual stack, tunneling and translation mechanisms. Whereas there has been several mechanisms of tunneling, the main actively used tunneling mechanisms are 6to4, configured, and GRE tunneling, for site to site tunneling while ISATAP and tunnel brokers like Teredo for host tunneling.

The rest of this paper is organised as follows: Section 2 is the background to the study. Section 3 describes the experimental testbed while the experimental results are reported in Section 4. Conclusions and future works are finally given Section 5.

2 Background

This section describes the IPv6 implementation requirements of enterprise networks in developing countries as well as the theoretical underpinnings of the IPv4-to-IPv6 transition mechanisms.

2.1 Enterprise Network

An enterprise network is a network that has a clear interface with its ISP (generally by using a router or firewall) and provides internal and/or external services.Within the context of an enterprise network, the word IP addressing always brings Network Address Translation (NAT) to mind. Nearly all enterprise networks implement NAT for their IPv4 internet access, placing a clear border between the companys internal network and the internet. IPv4 NAT scales well in enterprises, as it provides enough addresses for practically any known enterprise size implementation. This NATv4 principle violates the end-to-end principle, which has been addressed in the new IPv6. Since NAT implies that there are sufficient IPv4 addresses for any enterprise network, one may wonder whether IPv6 is needed at all. The basic reason for the transition is that the users within your enterprise network may need to access content that will only be available in IPv6. Also the external services provided by your enterprise network should be reachable over IPv6, as potentially some external clients only have IPv6 addresses.

In developing countries, these enterprise networks have one or more common characteristics, which include low budgetary costs, lack of skilled IT support personnel, inadequate and unreliable bandwidth, low complexity and unguaranteed QoS [8]. To achieve a successful IPv6 implementation at enterprise level, a preliminary study must be performed to evaluate required skills, deployment strategy as well as prepare a preliminary project. Planning IPv6 implementation for enterprise networks should involve planning the implementation of various aspects such as: deployment strategy, devices, addressing, routing and security.

2.2 IPv4 to IPv6 Transition Mechanisms

IPv4 and IPv6 are expected to coexist for many years to come. A wide range of techniques have been defined to make the coexistence possible and provide an easy transition [7]. These techniques have been mainly categorized into three:

- Dual-stack techniques, which allows IPv4 and IPv6 to coexist in the same devices and networks.
- Tunneling techniques, which allow the transport of IPv6 traffic over the existing IPv4 infrastructure.
- Translation techniques, which allow IPv6-only nodes to communicate with IPv4-only nodes.

These mechanisms can and are likely to be used in combination with one another. The transition to IPv6 can be done step by step, starting with a single host or subnet. You can migrate the whole corporate network, or parts of it, while your ISP still runs only IPv4. Or your ISP can upgrade to IPv6 while your corporate network still runs IPv4. In this section, we present a summary comparison of the different transition mechanisms and as well review literature related to the tunneling transition mechanisms.

Tunneling: In this transition technique, the IPv6 traffic is carried using the existing IPv4 network by encapsulating IPv6 packets in the IPv4 header. At the tunnel end node, the packet is de-capsulated and the IPv4 packet header is stripped. Then the original IPv6 packet is routed to its final IPv6 destination. The start and end nodes of the tunnel are IPv4/IPv6 Dual Stack-enabled.

The main difference between the various tunneling mechanisms is the way that the source and destination of the tunnel are determined. Tunneling is broadly categorised into two: i) the site-to-site tunneling (suitable for enterprise network IPv6 implementation e.g. Configured, 6to4 and GRE tunneling); and ii) the host tunneling (suitable for single host IPv6 implementation e.g. ISATAP tunneling and tunnel brokers) [9].

Configured Tunneling: In this mechanism, both tunnel end-points are manually configured, one at one site and the other at the opposite remote site. This tunneling mechanism builds a permanent virtual link between two IPv6 networks that are connected over an IPv4 backbone. It is a point-to-point static tunnel. The start and end points of the tunnel have IPv4-routable addresses and an IPv6 address is configured on the tunnel interface. These tunnels are generally not scalable, because they have to be manually configured. The primary use is for stable connections that require regular secure communication between two edge routers or between an end system and an edge router, or for connection to remote IPv6 networks.

IPv6 to IPv4 (6to4) Tunneling: This is an address assignment and router-to-router automatic tunneling technology that provides unicast IPv6 connectivity between IPv6 sites and hosts across the IPv4 internet. In this tunneling, the destination is not explicitly configured and is obtained dynamically from the IPv4 address embedded in the destination IPv6 address of the packet. The 6to4 uses the global address prefix 2002:wwwxx:yyzz::/48. The wwwxx:yyzz is the colon-hexadecimal representation of a public IPv4 address (w.x.y.z) assigned to a site or host. This tunneling mechanism, unlike the Configured tunnel, is a point-to-multipoint mechanism.

6to4 tunneling was introduced in an attempt to reduce the configuration complexity of the configured tunneling, its performance introduced major limitations in that:

- It introduces vulnerabilities into the network in that 6to4 routers must accept packets from ALL 6to4 relay routers and it is not possible to know if the relay router is "Trusted" or even existent. As well a 6to4 relay routers have to accept packets from 6to4 routers and native IPv6 hosts without any checks
- It also introduces threats like DOS/DDoS to the network. It is also prone to service theft which can be unauthorized usage of relay router services
- It lacks scalability for smaller sites,
- The encapsulation adds an additional load to the network and the complexity of the IPv6 and IPv4 addresses in the routing tables.
- It supports only static and BGP4 routing protocols, making it of limited use in enterprise networks which run other routing protocols like OSPF, EIGRP, RIP among others.

Generic Route Encapsulation (GRE) Tunneling: The IPv6 over IPv4 GRE tunnel uses the standard GRE tunneling technique that is designed to provide the services necessary to implement any standard point-to-point encapsulation scheme. As in Configured tunnels, these tunnels are links between two points, with a separate tunnel for each link. The GRE tunnels are not tied to a specific passenger or transport protocol, but in this case carry IPv6 traffic as the passenger protocol over GRE as the carrier protocol. Similar to the Configured tunnels, the GRE tunnels are used between two points and require configuration of both the source and destination addresses of the tunnel. The edge routers

and end systems used as tunnel end points must be dual stack devices. If GRE
tunnels are to go through an IPv4 firewall this firewall has to be opened for IP
protocol type 47 for IPv4 datagrams coming from or going to the remote tunnel end-point. GRE tunnel end-points are authenticated by a simple key that
is transmitted during the setup of the tunnel. This key is transmitted in clear
text format therefore it does not really add much security. You configure the
IPv4 and IPv6 addresses of the dual-stack router on the GRE tunnel interface,
and identify the entry and exit (or source and destination) points of the tunnel,
using IPv4 addresses. Because each GRE tunnel is independently managed, the
more tunnel end points you have, the more tunnels you need, and the greater is
the management overhead.

Table 1. Comparison of Tunnel-based Mechanisms

Tunneling Mechanism	Advantages	Limitations	Deployment Applications
Configured	Stable and secure links for regular communication. Simple to deploy. Allows transport of IPv6 packets over an IPv4 network. Available on most platforms	Management overhead. Must be manually configured	Site-to-site tunneling mechanism. Used for stable and secure connections
6to4	Its a site-to-multisite mechanism. Easy for IPv6 "Islands" located in IPv4 networks	Security threats and vulnerabilities. Supports only BGP and static routing. complexity of IPv4 and IPv6 in the routing table	Site-to-multisite tunneling.
GRE	Can be used with routing protocols	Firewall challeges (IP protocol type 47 for IPv4 datagrams for inbound and outbound must be opened. Simple key authentication between the tunnel end-points. Key transmitted in clear text.	For Site-to-site tunneling only.
ISATAP	Low maintenance, Easy incremental deployment of IPv6 to disparate nodes within AS (intra-site), Supported on many platforms	Monitoring of traffic is difficult; Works only over the intranet; Can require more setup than other methods, Some security issues; Designed for use within a local network only	Designed for Intra-site use Additional CPU load for encapsulation/decapsulation

Table 1 above is a summarised analysis of the different site-to-site tunneling
mechanisms under this study. From a theoretical review of the transition mech-
nisms, two points are clear when implementing IPv6 for enterprise networks.
Firstly, for single site networks which may not need end-to-end semantics and
where scalability may not be the leading determining factor, translation is appropriate. Secondly, for multi site networks which need end-to-end semantics
tunneling is appropriate.

In the next section, we describe the experimental testbed setup to evaluate
the performance of different tunneling mechanisms.

3   Experimental Testbed

3.1   Experimental Design

We set out to evaluate the performance of three tunneling mechanisms (configured, 6to4 and GRE) in comparison with native IPv6 and native IPv4 network

environments. Thus five different experiments representing each of the mechanisms were used. For each mechanism the experiment was repeated thrice and the average value reported.

3.2   Hardware and Software Specifications

In this research study, all hardware required to have identical specification in order to provide consistency between each mechanism. The experiment made use of two router nodes acting as tunneling end nodes and two computers acting as generator and receiver of the test traffic. The two computers were standard desktop computers with 250GB hardisk space, 2GB memory and Intel Pentium 2.0 Ghz processor speed, each with a single Intel(R) 10/100 ethernet network connection. Each of the computers had windows XP service pack 3 operating system. The tunnel edge nodes for the two IPv6 networks were Cisco 2811 Routers with 256 MB DRAM, Cisco IOS Software image (C2800NMADVENTERPRISEK9-M), Version 12.4(12)T and two 10/100 Onboard Fast Ethernet Ports.

The IPv4 cloud was emulated using 1841 Routers with 128 MB DRAM, IOS Software image (C1841-ADVENTERPRISEK9-M), Version 12.4(12)T, and two 10/100 Onboard Fast Ethernet Ports.

3.3   Network Design

The Figure 1 shows the topological design used for emulating tunneling mechanisms. The topology consists of two IPv6 networks, each connected to an IPv4 internet cloud using router nodes. Each of the two IPv6 networks has two end hosts described above.

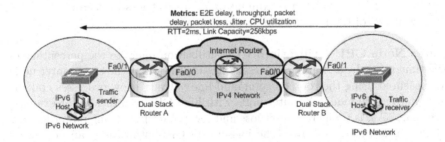

Fig. 1. Tunneling mechanisms design topology

3.4   Measurement Procedures

The D-ITG tool[11] mentioned above is used for traffic generation. The D-ITG tool was used instead of live internet because the researchers did not have access to an enterprise network for experimental purposes. TCP and UDP traffic is generated for each packet size (64, 256, 512, 768, 1024 and 1500 bytes) for each of the five transition mechanism. Both TCP and UDP traffic were tested in the experiment since each of their traffics has unique behaviour and one would not represent the other fairly. We use the exponential model for packet inter-departure with an average rate of 30 packets per second for TCP traffic and a constant packet inter-departure of 30 packets per second for UDP (typical for Voice over IP) to generate the traffic. When the receiver client receives the packet, the whole process is completed. The process is repeated three times for each packet size per transition mechanism. Three traffic flows each of 5 minutes is generated, one flow at a time and the decoded log file at the receiver is analysed for throughput, Jitter, end-to-end delay, packet loss recorded.

End-to-End Packet Delay: In this experiment, one-way transmission latency is measured. Typically, the average transmission latency is the amount of time it takes for a packet to traverse from source to destination. Latency is measured for each traffic of the different packet sizes; 64, 256, 512, 768, 1024 and 1500 bytes, from a sender to a receiver. Most of the delay sensitive traffic are real time applications such as voice over IP, among others and according to the G.114 ITU-T standard, value for one-way delay for such traffic like voice over IP is considered to be 150msec. Delay values upto 200ms is acceptable for other business purposes [10].

Throughput Analysis: Throughput is the amount of packet data that is transmitted over the entire path per time unit.

Packet loss: Packet loss is the amount of packets sent from the sender node which do not reach the destination node. The packets are lost unexpectedly. It is usually an important factor to consider when dealing with real time applications like voice over IP in which a maximum of 1% packet loss is tolerated without substantial loss of the information or signal quality.

Router Node CPU Utilization: CPU utilization refers to the percentage of CPU time taken by a running process. CPU utilization at the edge router node was measured using the router's command line output "show processes cpu" at the router enable mode. A router node with high CPU utilization, for example more than 75%, is prone to packet loss and low packet processing power leading to high packet delay and loss. The increase in CPU utilization can be caused by high number of IPv6 tunnels especially automatic tunneling, encryption and decryption, large size of data traffic probably from high link capacity which may lead to high processor load.

Jitter: Jitter can be defined as the variations in delay of packet delivery. For the end user, large delays are burdensome and can cause bad echoes. It's hard to have a working conversation with too large delay variations.

4   Experimental Results

4.1   End-to-End Packet Delay

The Figure 2 and Figure 3 shows the comparative latency of the Testbed for both TCP and UDP traffic as the packet size was varied from 64 bytes to 1500 bytes. As observed in Figure 2, the TCP end-to-end delay increased with increase in

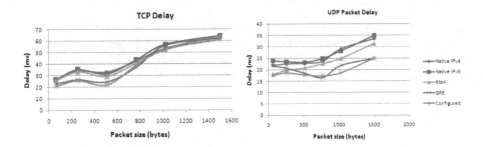

Fig. 2. TCP Packet Delay   **Fig. 3.** UDP Packet Delay

packet size across all the transition mechanisms, native IPv4 and native IPv6. This meant that the higher the packet size the higher the delay. Among the transition mechanisms, Configured tunnels showed the least average delay while the 6to4 tunneling transition mechanism, native IPv4 and native IPv6 had the highest average delay. In UDP traffic, according to Figure 3, just like in TCP traffic, the end-to-end delay increased with increase in packet size, with config-ured mechanism showing the lowest average delay among all the IPv6 transition mechanisms. This was followed by GRE and 6to4. Native IPv6 has slightly higher end-to-end delay than Native IPv4. In summary, it is observed that the TCP traffic had higher average delay than UDP under the same conditions for the same packet size.

4.2   Throughput Analysis

In throughput, it was observed that both TCP and UDP throughput increases exponentially with increase in packet size, with the maximum throughput be-ing achieved at 1500 bytes. The IPv6 transition mechanisms record negligible difference in throughput for the same amount and type of traffic hence was insignificant to plot.

4.3   Packet Loss

In the experiment, we generated traffic just enough for maximum load on the bottleneck link hence there was no congestion. The TCP traffic did not record any packet loss hence it is insignificant to plot. In UDP, Configured tunneling has the least average percentage packet loss while native IPv4 has the highest percentage packet loss. The packet losses were experienced for packet size 768 bytes and above. From 768 bytes, the packet loss increased with increase in packet size with native IPv4 with highest packet loss of 0.1%, GRE tunneling with 0.06%, 6to4 tunneling with 0.05%, configured tunneling and native IPv6 with 0.02% packet loss at the highest packet size of 1500 bytes..

4.4 Router Node CPU Utilization

Figure 4 and Figure 5 plots the TCP and UDP traffic router node CPU utilization respectively, with different packet size range from 64 bytes to 1500 bytes for the transition mechanisms, native IPv4 and native IPv6. CPU utilization is captured from the edge router that functions as the sender. In TCP, native IPv4

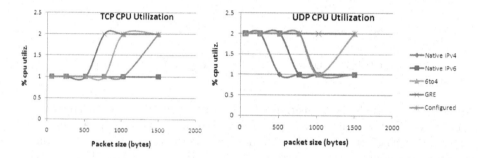

Fig. 4. TCP CPU Utilization   **Fig. 5.** UDP CPU Utilization

and native IPv6 did not record any change in the nodes CPU utilization while all the mechanisms recorded an increase in the CPU utilization for packet size from 768 bytes with Configured tunneling having the least average CPU Utilization across all the packet sizes with utilization only reported from 1024 bytes packet size. UDP recorded a high average CPU utilization at lower packet sizes while decreasing with increase in packet size. Configured tunneling recorded the least average CPU utilization while GRE the highest among the tunneling mechanisms. From the above results, all the transition mechanisms shows a maximum average CPU utilization of 2% when the bottleneck link is at its maximum load. Configured tunneling shows the better average performance when compared to other transition mechanisms. Native IPv4 and native IPv6 did not provide any significant CPU utilization under similar traffic load.

4.5 Jitter

Figures Figure 6 and Figure 7 shows TCP and UDP jitter respectively, for the IPv6 transition mechanisms and native IPv4 with packet sizes range from 64 bytes to 1500 bytes. In jitter sensitive traffic like voice over IP, jitter between

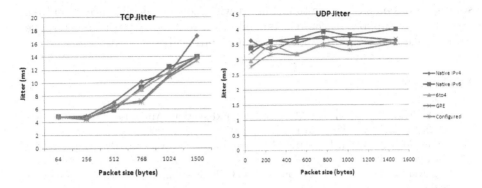

Fig. 6. TCP Jitter   **Fig. 7.** UDP Jitter

the starting and final point of the communication should be less than 30ms. In TCP, the jitter increases with increase in packet size across all transition mechanisms. Configured tunneling shows the least average performance while native IPv4 showing the highest average jitter. The UDP packets show lower jitter compared to TCP with Configured tunneling having the lowest average delay than the rest of the transition mechanisms.

5   Conclusion and Future Work

The results of this experimental study indicated that the Configured tunneling transition mechanism performs better on most of the network performance metrics (end-to-end delay, jitter, throughput, packet loss and CPU utilization) used than the other tunneling mechanisms. We therefore recommend it as the most appropriate tunneling mechanism for site-to-site tunneling on the basis of network performance measurement. In addition, in any migration plan, for either small or large enterprise network, we recommend that a comprehensive analysis be carried out to evaluate all the affected parts of the network, both hardware and software so as to foster the best approach to the migration. For example; Identify the highest priority IPv6-critical areas in your network, Perform IPv6 Assessment on high priority areas to determine scope, Develop a design that enables IPv6 without disrupting your IPv4 network, Test and implement in pilot mode, then extend over time into production. This study is of importance to those enterprise networks which want to implement IPv6 and are concerned about which transition mechanisms to embrace depending on the network performance requirements. This research study focused on IPv4 to IPv6 transition mechanisms for site-to-site enterprise networks in lightly congested networks. The future work would be to evaluate the performance of the same mechanisms in a heavily congested environment. More study need to be done to evaluate the performance and applicability of the different host IPv6 tunneling mechanisms through IPv4 environmnet. More research work will also be done to evaluate the security issues on site-to-site tunneling. It will also be of importance to address how 6to4 can support the most commonly used routing protocols in enterprise network like EIGRP, OSPF and RIP routing protocols.

References

1. Next Generation Internet: IPv4 Address Exhaustion, Mitigation Strategies and Implications for the U.S. An IEEE-USA White Paper (2009)
2. Sailan, M.K., Hassan, R., Patel, A.: A comparative review of IPv4 and IPv6 for research test-bed. In: Proceedings of the International Conference on Electrical Engineering and Informatics, pp. 427–433. IEEE Computer Society, Washington (2009)
3. Govil, J., Kaur, N., Kaur, H.: An examination of IPv4 and IPv6 Networks: Constraints and Various Transition Mechanisms. In: Proceedings of the 2008IEEE Southeastcon, pp. 178–185. IEEE Computer Society, Washington (2008)
4. Waddington, D., Chang, F.: Realising the transition to IPv6. IEEE Computer Magazine 40(2), 138–147 (2002)
5. Internet Systems Consortium. Number of Internet hosts (retrieved July 18, 2012), https://www.isc.org/solutions/survey/history
6. Deering, S., Hinden, R.: Internet Protocol, Version 6 (IPv6) Specification: RFC 2460 (December 1998)
7. Cisco Systems: Next Generation Transition (ngtrans) working group (retrieved July 18, 2012), http://www.ietf.org/wg/concluded/ngtrans.html
8. Odinma, A.C., Butakov, S., Grakhov, E., Bollou, F.: Planning, designing and implementing an enterprise network in a developing nation. Int. J. Enterprise Network Management 2(3) (2008)
9. Hagen, S.: IPv6 Essentials. O'Reilly, ISBN: 0-596-00125-8
10. Vlaovic, B., Brezocnik, Z.: Packet Based Telephony. In: EUROCON 2001, Trends in Communications, vol. 1 (2001)
11. Dainotti, A., Botta, A., Pescapè, A.: A tool for the generation of realistic network workload for emerging networking scenarios. Computer Networks 56(15), 3531–3547 (2012)

SolarMesh - Deployment Aspects for Wireless Mesh Networks in Developing Countries

Christian Mannweiler, Pratip Chakraborty, Andreas Klein,
and Hans D. Schotten

Chair for Wireless Communications and Navigation
University of Kaiserslautern, Germany
{mannweiler,chakraborty,aklein,schotten}@eit.uni-kl.de
http://www.eit.uni-kl.de/wicon

Abstract. This paper presents the latest research activities within the project "**SolarMesh** - Energy-Efficient, Autonomous, Wide-Area Wireless Voice and Data Network". The project is specifically dedicated to develop reliable wireless communications infrastructure for rural areas in developing countries, such as in sub-Saharan Africa. Wireless mesh networks based on IEEE 802.11 Wireless LAN technology combined with intelligent functions for self-configuration and self-adaptation can provide affordable ICT infrastructure for access and backhaul operation while at the same time offering carrier-grade QoS for voice and data services. Specifically, the paper outlines how a coordinated wireless mesh network has to be dimensioned in order to fulfill user requirements in terms of bandwidth and delay. Based on comprehensive simulations, recommendations for node density, backhaul capacity, and number of gateways to fixed line backbone networks are presented.

Keywords: coordinated wireless mesh networks, communications infrastructure for rural areas, network dimensioning, node density.

1 Motivation and Objectives

The SolarMesh project is motivated by a lack of affordable connectivity that at least supplies basic bandwidth and QoS levels for rural areas in both developing and developed countries. Due to financial restrictions, an operator has to carefully consider the deployment requirements of a community, particularly requested services and according bandwidth demands as well as required base station densities. Starting from these basic issues, the project is motivated by four key aspects:

(1) **Opening Up for New Markets** - Billions of people in rural areas and developing regions do not have satisfactory access to the Internet or other telecommunication services. Tapping this demand offers a significant market and business potential.

(2) **Technological Challenges** - The lack of reliable energy supply, large coverage areas in thinly populated regions, scarce availability of technically

K. Jonas, I.A. Rai, and M. Tchuente (Eds.): AFRICOMM 2012, LNICST 119, pp. 105–114, 2013.
ⓒ Institute for Computer Sciences, Social Informatics and Telecommunications Engineering 2013

trained personnel, as well as extremely harsh climate conditions are some of the difficulties faced when deploying and operating a large-scale wireless mesh network. Hardware and software have to be designed accordingly:

(3) Proof of Concept - Due to very heterogeneous demand in rural areas of developing countries, there is no general deployment guideline for wireless mesh networks, e.g., how many base stations or relay stations to install, how many radio interfaces to equip a station with, or how many gateways (i.e., connections to the wired network) to include. Moreover, the determining quantities (such as terminal density, user traffic), despite being identified, have not been incorporated into a precise quantitative mapping to the listed dependent deployment variables.

(4) Economic Cooperation and Development Issues - In many developing countries, communication networks are the only means for accessing information. Hence, investments into these infrastructures will have direct consequences on the quality of medical services, education, interaction with governmental agencies, and diversity of opinion.

Based on the motivation outlined above, the project has identified key objectives that will guide the development of the wireless mesh network:

(1) High-performing, Adaptive and Extensible System Architecture - The overall architecture will be developed in a way that technologies beyond those considered in the project (WLAN IEEE 802.11 and GSM) can be integrated easily. This holds particularly true for the selected radio technologies that reduce costs, energy consumption, and access barriers.

(2) Mesh Network Based on Autarkic Energy Supply - Energy supply of the mesh nodes is based on regenerative sources (solar power). Hence, all components (hardware, software, backbone and air interface) and mechanisms (routing, scheduling, handover, radio transmission) have to be optimized taking into account fluctuating power availability and limited energy storage capacities.

(3) Advanced Auto-Configuration and Self-Adaptation Capabilities - Deployment, start up, network management, and load balancing will not necessarily require technically trained personnel. Individual nodes as well as the network as a whole will configure mostly autonomously and operate with time-variant topology and dynamically changing traffic load. The system has to autonomously cope with mesh nodes shutting down due to low energy supply or with difficult environmental conditions (e.g., heavy rain, sandstorms, etc.).

The objective in this paper is to provide some quantitative answers to a relevant subset of these objectives, particularly to the question of properly dimensioning a coordinated wireless mesh network to be deployed in a rural area of a developing country.

The remainder of the paper is structured as follows: Section 2 provides an overview of the relevant quantities when modeling a coordinated wireless mesh network, Section 3 presents simulation methodology and results. The paper concludes with a short summary and description of future work in Section 4.

2   Modeling a Coordinated Wireless Mesh Network

The following section describes the system model used to evaluate the selection of deployment parameters. It depicts a summary of the overall system architecture and the models used for simulation are presented.

2.1   System Architecture

Several SolarMesh nodes create a wireless, autonomous meshed backhaul network based on IEEE 802.11 wireless technology, as depicted in Fig. 1. The mesh network has three tasks: Providing connectivity to the external core network, offering heterogeneous wireless access to user terminals and, most importantly, serving as a wireless backhaul network within a particular area, thus replacing wired infrastructure. The first one is realized by several gateway connections to the core network and the Internet, whereas the second one is provided by utilizing commonly used Wide Area Network (WAN) technologies, e.g. GSM (in order to take advantage of the cheap off-the-shelf user devices) or Wireless LAN (thus exploiting its affordable network components). Backhaul connectivity is solely based on IEEE 802.11, incorporating mechanisms for carrier-grade QoS; i.e. different services and the accordingly required QoS classes are supported by the overall SolarMesh architecture, namely best-effort and delay-sensitive VoIP services.

Fig. 1. Overview of System Concept

2.2   Node Deployment Model

In accordance with capacity and planning techniques for cellular communications systems (e.g. principles of cellular approach [10], sectorization [5,2], frequency hopping and discontinuous transmissions (DTX) [6], frequency planning [8], or interference cancellation [3]), the design of a SolarMesh network considers environmental topology (landscape, city topology), expected user density, traffic load and requirements, restrictions for SMAP and SMN locations, reuse distances, cell shapes, etc. In the this paper, we have designed a random network layout which employs random node locations being subject to some restrictions, such as minimum number of SMGWs $N_{min,SMGW}$ and SMAPs $N_{min,SMAP}$ as well as minimum SMN density $\frac{N_{SMN}}{A_{tot}}$. Moreover, minimum distance d_{min} between any two nodes, minimum number of neighboring SMNs in coverage area of any SMN (assuring sufficient centrality of each SMN), minimum coverage ratio $a_{cov} = \frac{A_{cov}}{A_{tot}}$ (percentage of total area covered), as well as some rules assuring the formation of a spanning tree mesh network are further restrictions. Table 1 depicts the restrictions and some numerical example values for the random network layout.

Table 1. Network Topology Restrictions

Parameter	Symbol	Example Value
minimum SMN density	$\frac{N_{SMN}}{A_{tot}}$	$4\,\frac{1}{m^2}$
minimum number of SMGWs	$N_{min,SMGW}$	$\frac{N_{SMN}}{10}$
minimum number of SMAPs	$N_{min,SMAP}$	$0.9 N_{SMN}$
minimum coverage ratio	$a_{cov} = \frac{A_{cov}}{A_{tot}}$	0.95
minimum distance between any two nodes	d_{min}	100 m
minimum number of neighboring SMNs in coverage area of given SMN	$N_{nb,min}$	1

A_{tot}: total area
A_{cov}: area in coverage of at least one SMAP

2.3 Traffic Models

In order to account for both a delay-sensitive as well as a best-effort traffic, the system model incorporates two different traffic classes: voice over IP (VoIP) and file transfer protocol (FTP) traffic. This section briefly outlines the used modeling approaches.

VoIP traffic modeling is done using finite state machines on a per user level. For each user in the system, a state machine is introduced that disposes of two states indicating the user's VoIP activity, "active" or "inactive". For each state, transition probabilities $p_i(j)$ are given, where i is the current state and j the possible user state for the next update. The model is evaluated for each user at rate $1/T$, T being the speech encoder frame duration (e.g. G.72x). Figure 2 visualizes the finite state machine [14]. Table 2 depicts the numerical values for the transition probabilities.

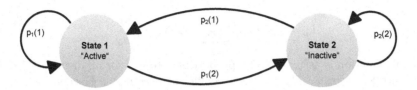

Fig. 2. State Machine for Modeling User VoIP Activity

Table 2. VoIP State Transition Probabilities

Current State \ Target State	Active	Inactive
Active	0.95	0.05
Inactive	0.01	0.99

File transfer protocol (FTP, [13]) traffic represents the class of uploading/downloading services in system simulation. User behavior is grouped in two phases [4,9]: downloading (uploading) time and reading time. Downloading time depends on the file size as well as on the QoS parameters (particularly bandwidth and PER), reading time mainly is a function of two variables: time for processing the downloaded data (e.g. reading a text file, watching a video) and time until the next FTP request is sent. Derived from empirical data, file size S_{file} is modeled according to a truncated lognormal function $p_{FS}(x)$ [14]:

$$p_{FS}(x) = \frac{1}{\sqrt{2\pi}\sigma x} e^{\frac{-(\ln x - \mu)^2}{2\sigma^2}} \tag{1}$$

where $x \geq 0$, $\mu = 14.45$, $\sigma = 0.35$, translating into a mean file size of 2 MB, a standard deviation of 0.722 MB and maximum file size is chosen to be $S_{file,max} = 5$ MB.

Reading time is modeled according to interarrival times of a queueing process. Consequently, an exponential distribution with PDF $p_{RT}(x)$ is employed for drawing random reading times [14]:

$$p_{RT}(x) = \lambda e^{-\lambda x} \tag{2}$$

with $\lambda = 0.006$, i.e. mean reading time $\frac{1}{\lambda} = 180s$.

2.4   Path Loss, Signal-to-Noise Ratio, and Capacity of Links

Path loss for communication over the backhaul links is modeled according to common path loss models, e.g. [1]. Since we assume the IEEE 802.11n backhaul links to operate in the 5 GHz band with sufficient channel separation among neighboring SMNs and no interference resulting from 2.4 GHz access links, mesh links obey the following path loss L_p law [15]:

$$L_p = -20 \log_{10} \frac{\lambda}{4\pi d_0} + 10\alpha \log_{10} \frac{d}{d_0} \tag{3}$$

Signal attenuation is assumed to be proportional to d^{-2} for all distances $d \leq d_0$ (free space loss), for $d \geq d_0$, path loss coefficient becomes α. For simplification, interference is not considered on the mesh link level for the following reasons: channels in the 5 GHz band are well separated from each other, frequency reuse is low, and interference suppression mechanism of the MAC layer is available [11]. $SINR_{Rx,mesh}$ at the receiving node is derived by a link budget calculation [12] which, in a last step, is mapped to channel capacity C_{mesh} (in Mbit/s) according to [7]

$$C_{mesh} = \sum_{i=1}^{N_{MCS}} C_i u(SINR_{Rx,mesh} - SINR_{i,MCS}) \tag{4}$$

where $u(\cdot)$ – unit step function

N_{MCS} – number of modulation and coding schemes

C_i – additional capacity of MCS i compared to MCS $i-1$

$SINR_{i,MCS}$ – required SINR for MCS i

The mapping of experienced $SINR_{Rx,mesh}$ to the according modulation and coding scheme (MCS) and respective (grand) data rate assumes the usage of $N_{ss} = 2$ spatial streams. Access links are modeled in an according way, assuming $N_{ss} = 1$ spatial stream in the 2.4 GHz band and accounting for interference as well as medium access overhead.

2.5   User Mobility

User mobility is an inherent feature in any wireless communications system. Common mobility models include *Random Walk, Gauss-Markov Mobility, Random Waypoint Mobility, Metropolitan Mobility*, and group mobility models. For the scope of this paper, we employ an adapted version of the *Gauss-Markov Mobility* model. The mobility model facilitates the application of customized degrees of randomness by introducing the tunable parameter λ. The usage of a simple finite state machine (FSM) with memory span of 1 for both speed s and direction α helps implementing the correlation of current velocity with that from the previous time step:

$$s(t) = \lambda s(t-1) + (1-\lambda)\mu_s + \sigma_s \sqrt{1-\lambda^2} w_{s,t} \tag{5}$$

$$\alpha(t) = \lambda\alpha(t-1) + (1-\lambda)\mu_\alpha + \sigma_\alpha \sqrt{1-\lambda^2} w_{\lambda,t} \tag{6}$$

where σ_s, σ_α – standard deviation of s and α, respectively

μ_s, μ_α – mean of s and α, respectively

ω_t – realization of standard normal distribution at time t

Initial speed s_0 and direction α_0 are drawn from Gaussian distributions $\mathcal{N}\left(\mu_s, \sigma_s\right)$ and $\mathcal{N}\left(\mu_\alpha, \sigma_{alpha}\right)$, respectively.

3   Simulation Methodology and Results

In order to obtain quantitative results with regard to selected network deployment parameters, a simulation environment implementing the models depicted in the previous section has been set up, featuring a 2.5 km x 2.5 km reference area. It allows for parametrized inputs as well as for monitoring of various performance metrics over arbitrary simulation durations. For the purpose of this work, input variables included (1) number N_{SMN} of mesh nodes, (2) share $\frac{N_{SMGW}}{N_{SMN}}$ of gateways (to fixed line network) in total mesh nodes, and (3) number N_{UT} of moving user terminals. Other input variables, such as coverage area, user mobility settings, data traffic parameters, or number of backhaul and access radio interfaces per node have remained fixed. For performance measurements, average data throughput d_{avg} per user per time interval has been chosen. The objective has been to identify optimum node and gateway densities for differently sized user populations and troughput demands. Simulation time for each input combination has been chosen to be 200 s, which is sufficiently long to account

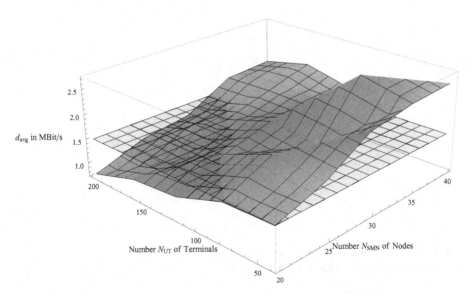

Fig. 3. Average Data Throughput per User with $\frac{N_{SMGW}}{N_{SMN}} = 0.2$

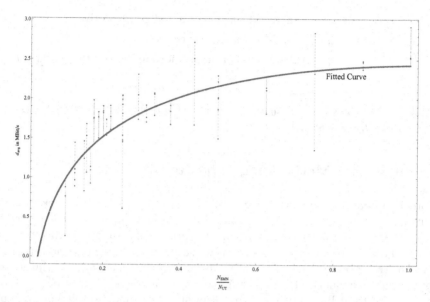

Fig. 4. Average Data Throughput as Function of Mesh Node Density $\frac{N_{SMN}}{N_{UT}}$ (red points: simulation data, blue: fitted curve)

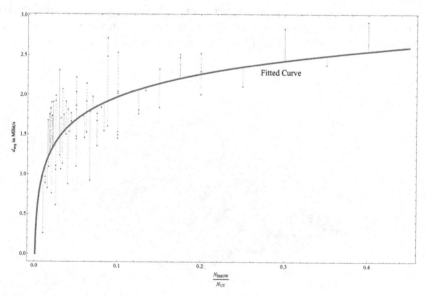

Fig. 5. Average Data Throughput as Function of Gateway $\frac{N_{SMGW}}{N_{UT}}$ (red points: simulation data, blue: fitted curve)

for initialization effects as well as to assure the occurrence of relevant events. Figures 3, 4, and 5 illustrate selected simulation results.

Figure 3 indicates some typical characteristics of a mesh network. For a fixed number of users, an increasing number of nodes improves the average data rate per user. In case of a fixed number of nodes, an increasing number of user dramatically reduces the average data rate since more users have to share a common route to a gateway. These defining characteristics can hold true over the entire analyzed range of input variables. Moreover, it can be observed that, in order to preserve a minimum average data rate of about 1.5 MBit/s for each user, the number ratio $\frac{N_{SMN}}{N_{UT}}$ of mesh nodes to users should not fall below a threshold of approximately 15 to 20%. On the other hand, Fig. 4 clearly indicates that the incremental benefit of additional mesh nodes saturates when crossing a percentage of $\frac{N_{SMN}}{N_{UT}} \approx 0.6$. Similar considerations hold true for the number of gateways to deployed, as depicted in Fig. 5. An initial increase of gateway density dramatically improves user throughput. However, when reaching a value of $\frac{N_{SMGW}}{N_{UT}} \approx 0.3$, saturation settles in.

4   Conclusion

The paper has outlined the motivation, objectives, and system model for the simulation of a coordinated, carrier-grade wireless mesh backhaul network for rural regions in developing countries. Particularly, we have analyzed the dimensioning of a mesh network for different deployment scenarios. Specifically, the decision space including terminal population size, mesh node density, and number of gateway nodes has been evaluated with regards to the impact on throughput per user in order to design a viable guideline for network deployment. Depending on the number N_{UT} of terminals in the system, reasonable dimensioning ranges have been identified for important network design variables (number N_{SMN} of mesh nodes and number N_{SMGW} of gateways). In summary, mesh node density should be in a range of $0.15\,N_{UT} \leq N_{SMN} \leq 0.6\,N_{UT}$, gateway node density in arange of $0.1\,N_{UT} \leq N_{SMGW} \leq 0.3\,N_{UT}$ in order to preserve an average data rate of 1.5 MBit/s for each user on the one hand and to avoid saturation on the other.

Upcoming research challenges lie in the area of multi-objective network optimization, where restrictions stemming from autarkic energy supply and limited energy efficiency of network nodes on the one hand have to be balanced with throughput and delay requirements of the user. The exploration of the resulting solution space includes heterogeneous optimization techniques, among them, e.g., genetic algorithms.

Acknowledgment. This work has been funded by the Federal Ministry of Education and Research of the Federal Republic of Germany (Förderkennzeichen 01 BU 1116, SolarMesh - Energieeffizientes, autonomes großflächiges Sprach- und Datenfunknetz mit flacher IP- Architektur). The authors alone are responsible for the content of the paper.

References

1. 3GPP, and ETSI. Universal Mobile Telecommunications System (UMTS) - Spacial Channel Model for Multiple Input Multiple Output (MIMO) Simulations (January 27, 2004)
2. Babich, F., Vatta, F.: Effects of Sectorization on Cellular Radio Systems Capacity with Different Traffic Loads. Wireless Personal Communications 21(3), 269–288 (2002)
3. Boudreau, G., Panicker, J., Guo, N., Chang, R., Wang, N., Vrzic, S.: Interference Coordination and Cancellation for 4G Networks. IEEE Communications Magazine 47(4), 74–81 (2009)
4. Cao, J., Cleveland, W.S., Lin, D., Sun, D.X.: On the Nonstationarity of Internet Traffic. In: Proceedings of the ACM International Conference on Measurement and Modeling of Computer Systems, SIGMETRICS 2001, pp. 102–112. ACM (2001)
5. Chan, G.K.: Effects of Sectorization on the Spectrum Efficiency of Cellular Radio Systems. IEEE Transactions on Vehicular Technology 41(3) (1992)
6. Frullone, M., Riva, G., Grazioso, P., Falciasecca, G.: Advanced Planning Criteria for Cellular Systems. IEEE Personal Communications 3(6), 10–15 (1996)
7. IEEE. IEEE Standard for Information Technology - Telecommunications and Information Exchange between systems - Local and metropolitan area networks - Specific requirements: Part 11: Wireless LAN Medium Access Control (MAC) and Physical Layer (PHY) - Specifications Amendment 5: Enhancements for Higher Throughput (2009)
8. Katzela, I., Naghshineh, M.: Channel Assignment Schemes for Cellular Mobile Telecommunication Systems - A Comprehensive Survey. IEEE Communications Surveys Tutorials 3(2), 10–31 (2000)
9. Claffy, K.C., McCreary, S.: Internet Measurement and Data Analysis: Passive and Active Measurement (1999)
10. Lee, W.C.Y.: Mobile Cellular Telecommunications Systems: Analog and Digital Systems, 2nd edn. McGraw Hill, New York (1995)
11. Lei, J., Yates, R., Greenstein, L., Liu, H.: Wireless Link SNR Mapping onto an Indoor Testbed. In: Proceedings of the First International Conference on Testbeds and Research Infrastructures for the Development of Networks and Communities (Tridentcom), pp. 130–135 (2005)
12. Molisch, A.F.: Wireless Communications, 2nd edn. Wiley, Weinheim (2011)
13. Postel, J., Reynolds, J.: File Transfer Protocol. RFC 959 (Standard) (October 1985); Updated by RFCs 2228, 2640, 2773, 3659
14. Srinivasan, R., Zhuang, J., Jalloul, L., Novak, R., Park, J.: IEEE 802.16m Evaluation Methodology Document, EMD (2008)
15. Tse, D., Viswanath, P.: Fundamentals of Wireless Communication. Cambridge University Press, Cambridge (2005)

Analysis of Open Source Enterprise Service Buses toward Supporting Integration in Dynamic Service Oriented Environments

Themba Shezi, Edgar Jembere, Mathew O. Adigun, and Mandla T. Nene

Department of Computer Science and Mobile e-Services
University of Zululand, Private Bag X1001,
KwaDlangezwa 3886, South Africa
{mrtshezi,mandlatnene}@gmail.com,
{ejembere,madigun}@pan.uzulu.ac.za

Abstract. Enterprise Service Bus technology is now acknowledged as a central paradigm for today's information systems integration due to its implementation of Service Oriented Architecture. ESBs provide a set of capabilities which include message routing, transformation and service orchestration needed by end-users, business processes or other services. However, there exist different approaches toward achieving these capabilities. This paper provides comparative analysis of Mule, ServiceMix and JBoss ESB in support of application integration in open and dynamic service oriented environment. In particular we used a Multi- Criteria Decision Analysis method known as Analytical Hierarchy Process to deal with the issues of conflicting selection criteria. Results showed that no single ESB is the best solution for all criteria and indicated where each one is best suited. However Mule was found to be a preferable ESB in this context.

Keywords: Enterprise Service Bus, Service Oriented Architecture, Multi-Criteria Decision Analysis, Analytical Hierarchy Process and GUISET.

1 Introduction

In recent years, Service Oriented Architecture (SOA) has become a paradigm for enabling more efficient and flexible business processes in a service-based economy. The significance of this paradigm results in many organizations moving their businesses and making them available as online services so that they can be accessed ubiquitously by anyone connected on the network [1]. The idea is to increase level of resource sharing and collaboration among geographical dispersed individuals/ organizations. However, this shift has partially reached Small, Medium and Micro Enterprises (SMMEs) especially in African countries [2] [3] [4], mainly due to costs associated with the underlying infrastructure that realize this new way of doing business. Therefore to address this issue and others, an open and dynamic Service Oriented environment called Grid-based Utility Infrastructure for SMME Enabling Technology (GUISET) was proposed in [4]. GUISET aims to provide affordable technology to SMME through utility approach to service delivery. The idea is to

K. Jonas, I.A. Rai, and M. Tchuente (Eds.): AFRICOMM 2012, LNICST 119, pp. 115–125, 2013.
© Institute for Computer Sciences, Social Informatics and Telecommunications Engineering 2013

provide a platform that would allow SMMEs to share information and products thereby helping them market and sell their products online without spending much on technology. GUISET intends to manage and deliver wide variety of services to its targeted customers (SMMEs). With a number of services possibly from different sources that may need to interact and exchange information possibly at runtime to provide a specific GUISET function, compatibility of the underlying technologies cannot be assumed in general. Therefore an integration solution is strongly required.

Enterprise Service Bus (ESB) has drawn attention in today's systems integration due to its implementation of SOA [5]. The industrial success of ESB technology resulted in many products being implemented and offered as both open source and commercial ESB products. These product implementations provide different approaches towards realizing ESB capabilities [6]. So the problem of how to select the most suitable ESB product for a given business solution is critical. Not only because there are many factors to consider in this selection, but also owing the relationships between these factors and the requirements of a particular integration scenario. Previous works that assist in ESB selection focus on evaluating ESB capabilities and they have not adequately addressed the issue of conflicting selection criteria.

As an attempt to fill this gab in the GUISET context, this work uses Analytical Hierarchy Process (AHP), a Multi Criteria Decision Analysis (MCDA) technique, to determine which ESB would be most situated for GUISET environment. We analyzed three open source ESB products namely Mule, ServiceMix (SMX) and JBoss (JB) on the basis of GUISET integration requirements.

The paper is structured as follows: GUISET concept and integration requirements, ESB concept and technologies, related works, ESB selection methodology and results, and conclusion

2   GUISET Concept

Grid-based Utility Infrastructure for SMME Enabling Technology (GUISET) aims to address barriers experienced by SMME due to affordability challenges of Information, Communication and Technology (ICT). This is believed to be one of the impediments to growth in SMME enterprises [4]. GUISET leverages on the existing computing paradigms, namely on Grid, Service-Oriented and Utility Computing to allow its services to be shared in a most consistent manner throughout SMME. Grid computing enables GUISET components to be distributed and shared across physically distanced geographic domains. Service Oriented Computing allows everything from an infrastructure to applications to be offered as services to easy usability. Utility Computing allows GUISET services to be offered in a pay as you use model. Regarding service access and focusing on the underlying middleware aspect, uniformity of employed SOA technology cannot be ignored. Therefore an integration solution at the middleware level is required.

Fig. 1 depicts GUISET architecture. The architecture has three layers, namely the Multi-Modal interfaces which define SMME Enablers, Middleware layer which contains Utility Broker(s) and lastly Grid Infrastructure Layer which define Resource Repository. This study focuses more on Middleware Layer where integration capabilities should be supported. There is a great need to ensure the infrastructure employed at this layer is most suitable to guarantee all necessary interaction take place effectively.

2.1   GUISET Integration Requirements

To ascertain GUISET integration requirement, we consider a Stock purchasing application offered by GUISET to its customers. This application is composed of validating purchasing request through validation service. Checking and reserving items purchased can be done through stock control service. In addition, shipping purchased items can be supported using shipping services. From this GUISET usage scenario the following integration requirements were gathered;

1. An integration middleware is required through which all GUISET components and services can have reliable message exchange. Minimizing downtime of services
2. A facility for mapping data format from source application to the one required by destination application to avoid incompatibilities between interacting applications.
3. Intelligent routing of messages between services. GUISET will offer Quality of Service (QoS) aware services. Services with similar functionalities will be selected based on their QoS.
4. Support for service composition to allow service reusability by forming new application from existing. For example Stock purchasing application is formed by existing services which can be used for other functions as well.
5. Support for dynamic service discovery. For example whenever the requested service is unavailable it should be possible to substitute this service without affecting the client application.

The above integration requirements were found to be served with functionality provided by almost all the ESB products as defined by ESB concept in [6]. High Availability (HA) of services can be supported by messaging feature of ESB which provides uniform platform for exchanging messages reliably through persistent mechanisms. Mapping data from one format to another gets fulfilled by Data Transformation (DT) feature of an ESB.

Intelligent routing can be met by Content-Based Routing (CBR) in ESBs. With CBR a pre-defined message field is used to make routing decision.

ESBs support service composition using Service Orchestration (SO) mechanisms where Business Process Execution Language (BPEL) engines act as orchestras. Although not all ESBs support this feature out of the box, however add-ons are available. Dynamic Service Discovery (DSD) is externally offered through support of Universal Description, Discovery and Integration (UDDI) which allow services to be published and discovered by interested parties which make calls via ESB.

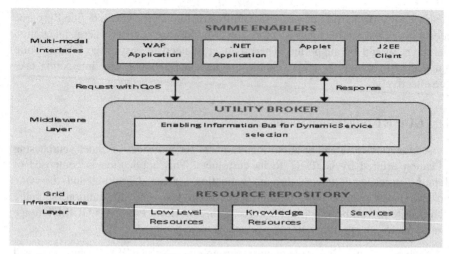

Fig. 1. GUISET Architecture

3   ESB Concept and Technologies

According to Schmidt [5] "an ESB refers to the infrastructure which underpins a fully integrated and flexible end-to-end SOA". In this sense, ESB provides full implementation of SOA. As a standard integration technology, an ESB provides a set of capabilities for data transformation, mediation and routing messages. Data transformation allows interacting services to exchange messages with little or no information about the data format expected on the other end. This is usually achieved using EXtensible Stylesheet Language Transformation (XSLT), XQuery, Smooks and other mechanisms as implemented by ESB products. ESB Mediation capability enables virtualization of services by allowing ESB to be a proxy between service provider and consumer. Another important capability of an ESB is to route incoming message to the appropriate service or application.   This is achieved through support of Enterprise Integration Pattern (EIP). For messaging, most ESBs use Java Messaging System (JMS) to route messages to different components. ESBs also use JMS to support high availability of both stateless and non-stateless services [11]. Wide range of transport methods are supported by ESBs including but not limited to HTTP, FTP, TCP, UDP, E-mail, JDBC, REST and CXF. ESBs exploit different standards including Web Service standards (WS-*) and Java Business Integration (JBI) [7] [8] [9].

A complete analysis is provided in Table 1, which outline the efforts in terms of technologies made by each ESB (Mule, ServiceMix and JBoss ESB) in support of GUISET integration capabilities. We have noted that all ESBs use different approaches in providing each capability. However some technologies are widely used and they keep appearing like transformation using XSLT and content based routing using XPath expressions. As highlighted earlier selecting the most suitable ESB is rather a difficult task. Our evaluation will motivate decision makers to adopt the best ESB suite for their middleware architectures in a GUISET like environment.

Table 1. ESB technologies towards supporting GUISET integration requirements

ESB(s)	ESB products effort towards support of GUISET integration requirements
Mule ESB	**High Availability** Mule support clustered ESB instances, which uses state event driven architecture (SEDA) service event and in-memory message queues. High availability of services on transactional transports like JMS, WebSphere MQ, and JDBC. However for non-transactional transport like HTTP (including CXF web services), File and FTP Mule uses reliable patterns called reliable requisition flow [8]. **Message and data transformation** Messages exchanged in mule can be any format, Mule support JSON, Scripting, Encryption and XML based transformation using XSLT, XStream, JAXB binding framework, XQuery, XmlToDom, XPath expression using JAXP and JXPath. Custom transformers are offered via Apache velocity Engine. **Intelligent routing (Content-based Routing)** For content-based routing Mule use filters, which leverages Mule expression to all configuration of XPath, Groovy and OGNL based filters. XPath filters are implemented with Apache Commons JXPath Library. Payload type, Regular expression and wild card filter is used to determine endpoint service. Mule's ChoiceRouter choose one and only on endpoint route that matches those in the filter. **Service Orchestration** Mule support JPBM process engine and JPDL suite distribution. Mule support invocation of services hosted in any BPEL engine like Oracle SOA BPEL engine using standard SOAP endpoint (web services) and JMS. **Dynamic Service Discovery** Galaxy service registry is used to store and discover service related metadata. Among features provided by searching capabilities using SQL like queries and support for Atom Publishing Protocol (APP). For view, publish, and subscriber Galaxy use Queues, web interface/HTTP, open search, custom query language, XQuery, XPath and Groovy.
ServiceMix ESB	**High Availability** Support WS-Reliable Message standard for CXF binding component which are non-transactional. Non-persistent messages in-memory SEDA flow is used. Alternatively, persistent message on a transactional transport Active MQ can be used including JDBC clustering [9]. Active and standby clustering ensures high availability. **Message and data transformation** Since all messages exchanged in NMR are XML, so Saxon service engine is used for transformation, Saxon is based on XSLT style sheet. XQuery based transformation is also supported. Additional message can be transformed via script, Java class and BPEL. **Intelligent routing (Content-based routing)** This feature is supported using XPath expression on a normalized XML content. Also EIP and Camel service engine. Rules-driven routing using drools and script-driven routing using servicemix-script service engine. **Service Orchestration** Strong support for BPEL specification using Apache ODE as an external service engine. Engine provides a drop-in JBI to execute composite services inside ServiceMix. Alternatively Routing and transformation mechanisms can be used with support of EIP (for individual service connection) and Script or Java beans **Dynamic Service Discovery** JBI provides a very basic registry which map services to WSDL and can be accessed via JBI API (with a provided componentContext) or remotely via JMX. Apache jUDDI can be used as an external service to provide more sophisticated service discovery capabilities.
JBoss ESB	**High Availability** High availability is supported via JBoss MQ (Re-delivery queue), JBoss massaging and JBoss Messaging Core for transactional, reliable transport system [10]. **Message and data transformation** Smooks is the default transformation engine, but XML-based transformation engine XSLT is also supported. Custom transformation is supported using ActionProcessor data transformation. **Intelligent routing (Content-based routing)** Provide support for JBoss Drools rule engine which is a complete enterprise platform for rule based application development, alternatively simpler approach include XPath custom rule and Regex Content based routing **Service Orchestration** Strong support for jBPM which is a default BPM engine for orchestrating services. Alternative from jBPM, ActiveBPEL and Riftsaw BPEL engine can be used. Also support for WS-BPEL via Web service component. **Dynamic Service Discovery** By default JBoss ESB uses JAX-R implementation (Scout) and UDDI (jUDDI) for service registry and discovery. Registry stores EndPoint References (ERPs) for services deployed and its automatically updated when new service start

4   Related Works

In recent years, studies have shown that ESB evaluation according to the integration requirements needed is rather a difficult task. This is because there are many acceptable criteria that lead close to fulfill integration requirements. Studies have been done and they impose evaluating certain ESB capabilities. Kruessmann et al. compared Mule, ServiceMix, and Open ESB on the basis of high availability [11]. Strong support for JMS gave ServiceMix an advantage. Performance evaluation of transformation, content-based routing, and virtualization was presented in [13] [14] [15]. In this evaluation WSO$_2$ performed well followed by Mule and ServiceMix respectively. Analysis of Mule, Fuse, Open ESB and Oracle ESB appear in [12] [16]. Authors used Information security, interoperability and high availability as their criteria to rate ESBs. Another comparison of ESBs based on features and integrating existing services appeared in [10], where secured external BPEL service was invoked through the bus to determine the performance of each ESB. Kusak provided another analysis where JBoss and Mule was compared against multiple criteria and JBoss was rated the first [17].   From these works, most Authors focus on evaluating ESBs against a certain criteria and they have not adequately addressed the issue of conflicting selection criteria. In this work we attempt to fill this gap by applying AHP to analyze ESBs on the basis of GUISET integration needs.

5   ESB Analysis Methodology

Making decisions on competing ideas/solution/artifacts that have multiple conflicting criteria is a challenging task that has drawn attention in the literature from multiple disciplines. From these literatures, methods have emerged that assist decision makers to make the most adequate decisions and they are defined under an umbrella term of Multi Criteria Decision Analysis (MCDA). MCDA methods include Analytical Hierarchy Process (AHP), Bayesian Analysis (BA), and Multi-attribute Utility Theory (MAUT) method [18]. However, AHP since its invention has been the most widely used MCDA method by decision makers and researchers. Outstanding works have been published on AHP application in different fields including software engineering [20], agriculture [21], and project management [19]. AHP allows a decision to be made using either qualitative or quantitative data. AHP use pair-wise comparison to determine trade-offs among criteria and the ability to calculate the degree of consistency (or inconsistency) of judgments in each step. The possibility of applying AHP to evaluate some ESB capabilities is presented in [12]. The authors used Interoperability, Information Security and High Availability as their criteria.   Under this inspiration, this work use AHP method to deal with conflicting ESB selection criteria. Selection process is organized in a number of steps as depicted in Fig. 2.

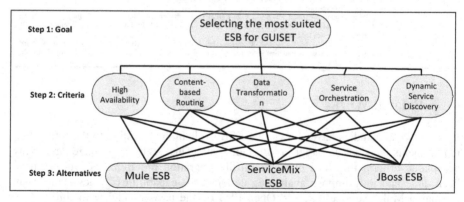

Fig. 2. AHP Steps for Selecting ESB to support GUISET integration needs

5.1   AHP Pairwise Computation and Priority Vector

In this section, pairwise comparisons are used to determine the relative importance of each alternative ESB in terms of each criterion. Our comparisons are based on the nine-point scale proposed by Saaty in [22], as described in Table 2.

Table 2. Intensity Scale and Definition

Intensity importance	Definition
1	Identical
3	Considerable in favor
5	Strongly in favor
7	Very strongly in favor
9	Acute favor
2, 4, 6, and 8	Intermediate values between judgments, used when compromise is needed

We assigned weights on the basis of two evidences. At first we looked at the documentation of each ESB products as published by vendors [7] [8] [9]. With this information as background knowledge we then looked at the published and publicly available articles on ESB evaluations with an aim of verifying the claims made by vendors on the product documentations. We selected the articles on the basis that they provide either empirical or qualitative analysis of the ESB products that are under review. Table 3 to Table 5 represents 3 X 3 matrix for the corresponding judgments in each decision criteria (GUISET integration needs). Alternatives listed on the left are one-by-one compared with each alternative listed on top as to which one is more preferred than the other.

Table 3. Pairwise comparison matrix for High Availability

High Availability	Mule	Service Mix	JBoss
Mule	1	1/3	3
SMX	3	1	5
JB	1/3	1/5	1

A normalized pairwise comparison matrix can be obtained by dividing each element of the matrix by its column total. For example, value 0.2308 in Table 4 was obtained by dividing 1 (from Table 3) with the sum of a column items in Table 3 (1 +3 +1/3). Priority vector (Eigenvector) in Table 4 was obtained by finding the rows averages. For example, the priority vector of Mule with respect to the criterion 'High Availability' in Table 4 was calculated by dividing sum of the rows (0.2308 + 0.2174 + 0.3333) with number of columns (alternative ESBs), i.e. 3 to obtain 0.2605.

Table 4. Normalized table for High availability

High Availability	Mule	Service Mix	JBoss	Priority Vector
Mule	0.2308	0.2174	0.3333	0.2605
SMX	0.6923	0.6522	0.5556	0.6333
JB	0.0769	0.0222	0.1111	0.1062

λ_{max} = 3.0387, CI = 0.0194, RI = 0.58, CR = 0.0334 < 0.1 OK

Now having the pairwise comparisons as given in Table 4, the consistency is determined by using the eigenvalue λ_{max}, to calculate the consistency index (CI) as C1 = $(\lambda_{max}$ - n)/ (n – 1), where n is the matrix size. Judgment consistency can be checked by taking the consistency ratio (CR) of CI with Average random consistency (RI) given in [20]. The CR is acceptable if it does not exceed 0.10, if it does there is a need to review and improve judgments.

For example CR for criterion 'High Availability' can be obtained as follows;

$$0.2605 \begin{bmatrix} 1 \\ 3 \\ 1/3 \end{bmatrix} + 0.6333 \begin{bmatrix} 1/3 \\ 1 \\ 1/5 \end{bmatrix} + 0.1062 \begin{bmatrix} 3 \\ 5 \\ 1 \end{bmatrix} = \begin{pmatrix} 0.7902 \\ 1.9458 \\ 0.3197 \end{pmatrix} \quad \begin{array}{l} \text{weighted} \\ \text{sum} \\ \text{Matrix} \end{array}$$

(1)

$$\lambda_{max} = \frac{[(0.7902/\ 0.2605) + (1.9458/\ 0.6333) + (0.3197/\ 0.1062)]}{3}$$

$$= 3.0387 \tag{2}$$

$$\text{CI} = (\lambda_{max} - n) / (n-1) = (3.0387 - 3) / (3 - 1) = 0.0194 \tag{3}$$

$$\text{CR} = \text{CI/RI} = 0.0194/0.58 = 0.0334 \tag{4}$$

Table 5. Pairwise Comparison matrix for the remaining criteria

Data Transformation (DT) Priority Vector		Content-based Routing Priority Vector	
Mule $\begin{pmatrix} 1 & 5 & 7 \\ 1/5 & 1 & 3 \\ 1/7 & 1/3 & 1 \end{pmatrix}$ SMX JB $\begin{matrix} 0.7235 \\ 0.1932 \\ 0.0833 \end{matrix}$		Mule $\begin{pmatrix} 1 & 5 & 7 \\ 1/5 & 1 & 3 \\ 1/7 & 1/3 & 1 \end{pmatrix}$ SMX JB $\begin{matrix} 0.7235 \\ 0.1932 \\ 0.0833 \end{matrix}$	
λ_{max} = 3.0623, CI = 0.0312, RI = 0.58, CR = 0.053 < 0.1 OK		λ_{max} = 3.0623, CI = 0.0312, RI = 0.58, CR = 0.053 < 0.1 OK	
Service Orchestration (SO) Priority Vector		Dynamic Service Discovery (DSD) Priority Vector	
Mule $\begin{pmatrix} 1 & 1/5 & 1/3 \\ 5 & 1 & 3 \\ 3 & 1/3 & 1 \end{pmatrix}$ SMX JB $\begin{matrix} 0.1062 \\ 0.2605 \\ 0.6333 \end{matrix}$		Mule $\begin{pmatrix} 1 & 1/3 & 1/7 \\ 3 & 1 & 1/3 \\ 7 & 3 & 1 \end{pmatrix}$ SMX JB $\begin{matrix} 0.0882 \\ 0.2431 \\ 0.6687 \end{matrix}$	
λ_{max} = 3.0387, CI = 0.01935, RI =.58, CR = 0.0334 < 0.1 OK		λ_{max} = 3.0072, CI = 0.036, RI = 0.58, CR = 0.0621 < 0.1 OK	

Priority vector computed in Table 4 and Table 5 represent the scores of each ESB when considering GUISET integration requirements. Mule was rated as most preferable in supporting Data Transformation and Content-based Routing because Mule's architecture is based on Enterprise Integration Patterns (EIP) which allows flexible routing message between Mule components and services. In addition Mule allows transformation to be available as part of the enterprise services bus rather that keeping it inside the service components. This approach makes transformation to be more effective [14]. ServiceMix on the other hand has strong support for JMS and its architecture is based on ActiveMQ, to enable better availability for services [11]. Moreover ServiceMix is shipped with Apache Orchestration Director Engine (Apache ODE) to support execution of BPEL processes. JBoss ESBs comes integrated with jUDDI registry to provide UDDI capabilities including publishing and discovering of services via an ESB. Once a service is requested by the consumer, ESB dynamically gets its address to jUDDI. Therefore service management becomes easier [9].

In addition to the pairwise-wise comparison for the decision alternatives, we also used the same procedure to set the priorities for all our five criteria so as to find the importance of each criteria in contributing to the overall goal. Table 6 shows pairwise comparison matrix for the five criteria. Fig. 3 graphically represents criteria rankings, with High Availability and Content-based Routing being the most important criteria, followed by Data Transformation, and Dynamic Service Discovery and Service Orchestration respectively

Table 6. Pairwise comparison matrix for all five criteria

Criteria	HA	DT	CBR	SO	DSD	Priority Vector
HA	1	3	1	5	3	0.3290
DT	1/3	1	1/3	5	1/5	0.2053
CBR	1	3	1	5	3	0.3290
SO	1/5	1/5	1/5	1	1/3	0.0461
DSD	1/3	5	1/3	3	1	0.0906

λ_{max} = 7.1511, CI = 0.5378, RI = 1.12, CR = 0.4802 < 0.1 OK

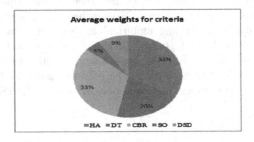

Fig. 3. Average weights for all criteria

5.2   Overall ESB Ratings and Final Decision

Table 7 shows the overall priorities for all ESBs were obtained. For example 0.4852 for Mule was calculated as follows;

$$= 0.3290 (0.2605) + 0.2053(0.7235) + 0.3290(0.7235) + 0.0461(0.1063) + 0.0906(0.0882)$$

$$= \mathbf{0.4852} \tag{5}$$

Table 7. Overall Priority Vector Matrix

Criterion Alternatives	HA (0.3290)	DT (0.2053)	CBR (0.3290)	SO (0.0461)	DSD (0.0906)	Overall Priority
Mule	0.2605	0.7235	0.7235	0.1063	0.0882	0.4852
MX	0.6333	0.1932	0.1932	0.6333	0.2431	0.3628
JB	0.1062	0.0833	0.0833	0.2603	0.6687	0.1520

Results derived from AHP above are shown in Table 7 and graphically represented in Fig. 4 below. Total weights for Mule, ServiceMix and JBoss are 0.4852 or 48.52 %, 0.3628 or 36.28%, and 0.1520 or 15.2 % respectively. Therefore Mule is more preferable for an environment like GUISET followed by ServiceMix and JBoss ESB.

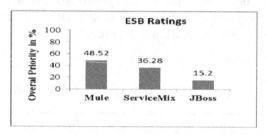

Fig. 4. ESB overall Ratings

6   Conclusion and Future Work

This study presented the use of AHP in the ESB analysis towards supporting GUISET integration requirements. The results presented showed that no single ESB perform best in all criteria. For example, JBoss performed well in dynamic service discovery and comparably worse when considering the other criteria. However, according to further analysis, Mule is more preferred ESB for the criteria used. The future lines of this work will include performing empirical analysis of these ESBs and further determining a strategy for integrating all these ESBs in a form of Federation. Federated ESB allow multiple ESB domains to work together to form a single logical ESB. This strategy will allow each ESB to be used for functions that it best supports. Thereby building an environment that will optimally support GUISET integration.

References

[1]   Serhani, M.: Enterprise services (business) collaboration using portal and SOA-based semantics. In: 4th IEEE International Conference on Digital Ecosystems and Technologies (DEST), pp. 450–455 (2010)

[2]   Bauler, P., Feltz, F., Biri, N., Pinheiro, P.: Implementing a Service-Oriented Architecture for Small and Medium Organisations. In: EMISA 2006, Germany, pp. 105–118 (2006)

[3]   Zdravković, M., Trajanović, M., Manić, M.: SOA-based approach to the Enterprise resource planning implementation in Small Enterprises. Series: Mechanical Engineering, vol. 5, pp. 97–104 (2007)

[4]   Adigun, M., Emuoyibofarhe, O., Migiro, S.: Challenges to Access and Opportunity to use SMME enabling Technologies in Africa. In: 1st All African Technology Diffusion Conference (2006)

[5]   Schmdt, M., Hutchison, B., Lambros, P., Phippen, R.: The Enterprise Service Bus: Making Service Oriented Real. IBM Systems Journal 44, 781–797 (2005)

[6]   Keen, M., Bond, J., Denman, J., Foster, S., Husek, S., Thompson, B., Wylie, H.: Patterns: Integrating Enterprise Service Buses in a Service-Oriented Architecture. IBM RedBooks (2005)

[7]   Mule ESB community documentation,
        http://www.mulesoft.org/mule-documentation

[8]   Apache Software Foundation: ServiceMix ESB documentation,
        http://servicemix.apache.org/documentation.html

[9]   JBoss Community: JBoss ESB documentation,
        http://www.jboss.org/jbossesb/docs

[10]   Garcia-Jimenez, F., Martinez-Carreras, M.: Gomez-Skarmeta: Evaluating Open Source Enterprise Service Bus. In: IEEE International Conference on E-Business Engineering, ICEBE, pp. 284–291 (2010)

[11]   Kruessmann, T., Koschel, A., Murphy, M., Trenaman, A., Astrova, I.: High Availability: Evaluating Open Source Enterprise Service Buses. In: Proceedings of the ITI 31st Int. Conf. on Information Technology Interfaces, Cavtat, Croatia, pp. 615–620 (2009)

[12]   Siddiqui, Z., Abdullah, A., Khan, M., Alghathbar, K.: Analysis of enterprise service busses based on information security, interoperability, and high availability using AHP method. International Journal of the Physical Sciences 6, 35–42 (2011)

[13]   Ahuja, S., Patel, A.: Enterprise Service Bus: A Performance Evaluation. Science Research in Communications and Network, 133–140 (2011)

[14]   Kumarage, D.: OXYGENTANK WSO2 Enterprise Service Bus (ESB) Performance Testing Round 3, Oxygen tank online at http://wso2.org/library/3740

[15]   AdroitLogic ESB Performance Testing – Round 6 (2012),
        http://esbperformance.org/display/comparison/
        ESB+Performance+Testing+-+Round+6

[16]   Alghamdi, A., Nasir, M., Ahmad, I., Nafjan, K.: An Interoperability Study of ESB for C4I Systems. In: IEEE International Symposium on Information Technology (ITSim), pp. 733–738 (2010)

[17]   Kusak, D.: Comparison of Enterprise Application Integration Platforms. In Charles University in Prague, Department of Software Engineering. Master's Thesis (2010)

[18]   Tae, K.: Multi-Criteria Decision Methods: An attempt to evaluate and unify. Methemetical and Computer Modeling Journal 37, 1099–1119 (2003)

[19]   Al-Subhi Al-Harbi, K.M.: Application of the AHP in project management. International Journal of Project Management 19, 19–27 (2001)

[20]   Triantaphyllou, E., Mann, S.: Using the analytical hierarchy process for decision marking in engineering applications: some challenges. International Journal of Industrial Engineering: Applications and Practice 2, 35–44 (1995)

[21]   Alphonce, C.: Application of the Analytical Hierarchy Process in Agriculture in developing Countries. Elsevier Science Agricultural Systems 53, 97–112 (1996)

[22]   Saaty, T.: A scaling method for priorities in hierarchical structures. Journal of Mathematical Physiology 15, 234–281 (2004)

Emerginov: An Open PHP PaaS to Stimulate and Animate Local Co-innovation

Morgan Richomme, David Blaisonneau, Benoit Herard,
Babacar Ngom, and Geerish Suddul

AFRICOMM 2012
Yaounde, Cameroon, November 12-14, 2012
{morgan.richomme,david.blaisonneau,benoit.herard}@orange.com,
babacar.ngom@ucad.edu.sn,
g.suddul@utm.intnet.mu

Abstract. This paper deals with the description of a simple open platform as a service (Paas) dedicated to open innovation. This platform is based on the smart integration of free software components and promote the massive usage of open technologies. It has been deployed in Africa and used to stimulate open innovation in emerging countries. It allows rapid prototyping of "telco-web" micro-services on over the top of traditional operator networks using open APIs. It aims to build a reference library of business applications under free licenses.

Keywords: Co-innovation, free software, micro-service, SMS, Voice.

1   Introduction

Open APIs are now familiar to lots of developers. It is very easy to create a mobile application and deploy it in an application shop. The majority of the mobile applications are very basic and most of them have few interactions with the network (reformat content of a web site to match the format of the devices). A real back-end architecture (e.g. database) is required when the interactions become more complex, Some companies already identify this market of turn key back-end systems. The open PHP PaaS Emerginov aims to provide such framework under free license. The main goal of this framework is to ease the development of micro services by local people for local people. In fact occidental telecommunication services do not always meet expectations on emerging markets. Most of them, usually designed for countries where network constraints are low, consists in flavoring standard American or European services. Such services are thus complex, do not correspond neither to the need of local people nor to the local usage. However micro-services, bridging Telecommunication world (GSM is widely available in emerging countries) and web worlds (expertise and collective intelligence in the network), could have a real impact on development [1] by providing ad-hoc services for people developed by local innovation partners connected to the reality of the field. Several studies showed how SMS based service [4] could have an impact on development.

K. Jonas, I.A. Rai, and M. Tchuente (Eds.): AFRICOMM 2012, LNICST 119, pp. 126–132, 2013.
© Institute for Computer Sciences, Social Informatics and Telecommunications Engineering 2013

Co-innovating with local partners is indeed a good way to change the traditional telecommunication service paradigm. However such co-innovation requires several conditions; local resources to develop services, a shared, open and low-cost infrastructure and finally a connection to the telecommunication network.

Such framework has also some impacts on the user generated content used for the micro services.

Finally the framework could be used to support communicating objects based on open hardware solution. SMS or GSM based services could be associated with open micro controllers to allow creating intelligent objects at a reasonable cost.

2   A Low-Cost Multimedia IP Infrastructure

The goal of the infrastructure is to provide a bridge between GSM and IP worlds. Additionally the architecture shall be open, shared and sustainable. An open source version is planned for 2012 allowing anyone to deploy this solution anywhere.

2.1   Architecture

The architecture is constituted by 2 elements: a core platform and gateways. The architecture is distributed. The architecture can be displayed as follow:

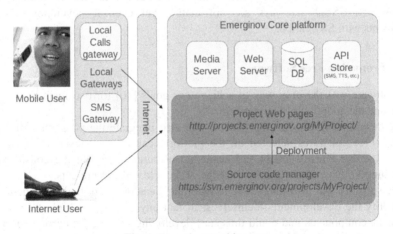

Fig. 1. Emerginov architecture

In the core platform, we distinguish

- **Development framework**: the code is managed using SVN. Deployment scripts allow any developer to deploy the code from the repository to the lived network. The code repository is important because it leads to the creation of a reference library of business applications and encourage massive code reuse.

- **API store** functions: lots of free resources are available through this API shop for the innovation partners: free SMS (inbound and outbound), call control, Text-To-speech, Mobile group management, Device information. This API store is very important because it provides Telecom resources for free, under quota during the incubation of the services. It simplifies greatly the access to the Telecom network for developers. Routable phone numbers, SMS can thus be considered as IT resources. Complex services can be created and immediately tested by any mobile users. The service cycle creation is dramatically reduced.
- **Media Server** functions: these functions may include the management of vocal announcements, voice mail, conference bridge, voice recognition. Vocal services are mandatory assuming that the literacy rate is low. Another consequence is the need of an open vocal framework allowing developments of voice corpus in vernacular languages [11].
- **SQL Database** function: these functions include shared persistence storage

The different gateways have two functions:

- **Vocal gateway**: it allows rapid development of vocal services (kiosk) directly reachable from any mobile phones based on Asterisk
- **SMS gateway**: for inbound and outbound SMS services based on Kannel

It would be interesting to add USSD connectivity but unlike SMS or vocal bearers, open source USSD gateways are not mature yet even if development started (Mobicents with SS7 cards).

2.2   Promoting Free Software

Free software was the only way to achieve our goals [10] for two main reasons: the design and the adoption of the platform.

The design shall be cost-effective. It shall also integrate the possibility of a local support. Free softwares selected on the platform can all be considered as mature. Local expertise already exists and academic resources, that can be considered as future support, have also a high knowledge of the selected components.

Free software was also imperative to facilitate the adoption of the components then to simplify the developments themselves. In fact any student was able to download any of the components and could thus start developing in a local environment before pushing his/her code to the platform. Moreover he/she had access to on-line rich support, usually both in English and French.

Please note that additional developments have been required to lead to a unique all-in-one system. The additional elements are portals (user and administrator) and several scripts to allow smart interaction between the different components (from SVN to web server, from PHP library to Asterisk vocal services, ...). All these portals and scripts will be published in the open source version (see next section).

The main different components can be described in the following table. They all have been selected because they reach a high level of maturity in terms of development, documentation and operational process.

Table 1. Main Free softwares integrated in the innovation platform

Component	Role	Comments
Debian/Xen	OS and virtualization layer	http://www.debian.org/ http://www.xen.org/
OpenSIPS	SIP router (telco part)	http://www.opensips.org/
Squid	HTTP router	http://www.squid-cache.org/
Asterisk	IP/PSTN gateway, Interactive Voice Response and Conference bridge	Asterisk is the media toolbox of the platform. Associated with tools such as audacity, sox, it provides a complete set of media applications http://www.asterisk.org/
Kannel	SMS/WAP gateway	http://www.kannel.org/
LAMP	Linux, Apache, MySQL, PHP	http://www.apache.org/ http://dev.mysql.com/

2.3   Promoting User Generated Content

The platform deals also with content. Some of the services collect data (mainly audio). The content policy is linked to the overall free license policy. Any user may upload and store content on the platform assuming that this content is under public domain or creative commons licenses. Thus as developers can reuse code, they shall be able to reuse also generated content. The global approach simplifies the management of intellectual property on code and on content.

2.4   Towards an Open Library of Business Applications

The goal is to build a shared library of business applications for emerging countries. Any innovation partner joining the consortium could capitalize on previous projects. Thus free software would not be located only into middleware but also in applicative layers. Adullact, OSOR[1] are already referencing free software business applications (400 applications on health, education, associations, administration in adullact).

2.5   Community Version

Emerginov has been used to support FP7 European project Voices. One of the commitments deal with sustainability. It was thus decided to publish a full open source version of the open PHP PaaS. This publication is associated with the creation of a community dealing with this solution. Unlike Cloud solutions (Nimbus, open Nebula, openStack), which are Infrastructure as a Service (IaaS), the Emerginov framework focused on the service delivery in Emerging country.

---

[1] http://www.adullact.org/, http://forge.osor.eu

2 versions are planned:

- ○ Standalone version
- ○ Advanced version

The standalone version shall match university or small NGO needs. It integrates the project management system, the Media and web server. It shall be runnable on a simple PC.

The Telco version is more complete and scalable. This version is based on a XEN virtualized layer.

3   Feedback from the Field

3.1   Codecamp

Two codecamps have been organized in Mauritius in 2011 and 2012. A codecamp is a coding competition. Students have 1 month to design and implement a solution that they show lived to the public during a major commercial events. For the two editions, six teams from the two main universities of the islands participate and submit the result of their development to about 40.000 people.

The first year lead to micro services related to social network and SMS. In 2011 the theme was "Learn" and triggered the development of mobile application for e-education. In both cases, the result was quiet impressive regarding the time frame. The list of the micro services developed during the 2 editions has been summarized in the table hereafter.

Service	Description
Trafficwatch	Road traffic alert system with SMS notificaiton
Conference bridge	Manage conference bridge from mobile only through SMS (book, start confere bridge)
Shopping body	SMS based Voucher system
Call2Play	Control of game through GSM. Your mobile becomes the game controler
Pocket Gazette	Follow Twitter feeds by SMS
Body locator	Foursquare-like with web (GPS) or declarative (SMS) location
Virtual campus	Virtual campus web site (based on Big Blue Button)

Lighter operation involving local students have been performed since 2010 in Egypt, Senegal, Mali and Botswana.

3.2   Hackathlon

Hackathlons consist in one or two day training on the platform. It is a very practical training, the goal is to create a micro service at the end of the training. The audience can be mixed and even non technical. A short introduction on the platform and on free software licence is provided then it is possible to create a web site, a vocal kiosk, SMS based services and mash-up services. Several Hackathlons have been performed in Africa and in Europe. The goal beyond the training and the promotion of free software consists in building a community of users in order to increase the internal community support.

3.3   Research Contracts

Hackathlon and codecamp deal with service creation. Based on the user feedback, we may need to improve the infrastructure in order to provide more APIs, more enablers, more components, a better ergonomy, etc. That is why Orange labs initiated several research contract based on this infrastructure. These contracts are a bilateral agreement between Orange labs and a university.
These contracts deal with:

- Vocal recognition in Wolof (ESMT, Dakar)
- Open source USSD enabler (University of technology of Mauritius)
- Orange Money web API (University of Technology of Mauritius)
- Geolocalization API (UCAD, Dakar)
- Webradio API (University of Botswana)

A new research contract is planned on open Hardware (arduino). It shall start mid 2012.

4   Conclusions

Building a local innovation ecosystem is a key challenge for development in emerging countries. An operator is a key actor of micro-services based on mobile. Telecommunication companies are usually very present on the field. Therefore an operator can bridge the two worlds, connecting end users to the richness of IP worlds. Promoting the creation of services is a good way for an operator to increase the traffic and give an innovative image, especially in multi-SIMS environment. To achieve the stimulation of the eco-system, the operator shall provide an infrastructure, support and associate local actors. That is the goal of the Emerginov solution and community.

References

1. Duflo, E.: Le développement humain, Lutter contre la pauvreté (I). Seuil (2010)
2. Tsietsi, M., Shibeshi, Z., Terzoli, A., Wells, G.: An Asterisk-based framework for E-learning using open protocols and open source software. Rhodes University, Department of Computer Science, Grahamstown, South Africa (2009)

3. Wu, S., Jin, J., Chen, J.: Open innovation strategy in the process of technological capability development: Conceptual framework aspect. In: 16th International Conference on Industrial Engineering and Engineering Management, IE&EM 2009 (2009)
4. Houssian, A., Kilany, M., Korenblum, J.: Mobile phone job services: Linking developing-country youth with employers, via SMS. In: 2009 International Conference on Information and Communication Technologies and Development, ICTD (2009)
5. Davaa, T.: Free and Open Source Software development in Mongolia. Mongolian University of Science and Technology, Ulaanbaatar, Mongolia (2007)
6. Collins, L.: Cutting the cost of computing, Engineering & technology (2007)
7. National Computer Board, Information Society Outlook, ICT Indicator Newsletter 1(1) (April 2010)
8. Google Maps/Google Earth APIs Terms of Service,
   http://code.google.com/apis/maps/terms.html
9. Open Street Map API, http://wiki.openstreetmap.org/wiki/API
10. Ran Reijswoud, V., Toppi, C.: Alternative routes in the digital world, Open Source Software in Africa,
    http://opensource.mit.edu/papers/reijswoudtopi.pdf
11. Tamgno, J.K., Elingui, P.U., Mendo'o, A.T., Richomme, M., Lishou, C., Oyono Obono, S.D.: Voice recognition and text-to-speech solution for vernacular languages, How free software and community approach may help to the development through vocal services. In: ICDT (2011)
12. Ken Banks, Mobile web initiative, The Mobile Web in Developing Countries, Keeping it relevant
    http://kiwanja.net/miscellaneous/W3C_Ken_Banks_kiwanja.pdf

Introducing NikaNOW: A Mobile Platform for Hyperlocal Media in South Africa

Lorenzo Dalvit and Steve Kromberg

MTN Chair of Media and Mobile Communication,
Grocott's Mail
School of Journalism and Media Studies, Rhodes University,
P.O. Box 94. 6140, Grahamstown, South Africa
l.dalvit@ru.ac.za

Abstract. This paper looks at NikaNOW, a turn-key solution for hyperlocal media organisations wishing to enter the online space. The system is optimised for use on mobile phones within the African context. NikaNOW is characterised by a strong focus on locality and immediacy and aims to promote local businesses and civic engagement. The first instance, based in Grahamstown (South Africa), has been operating for two years. Uptake has been good and a number of lessons have been learnt. The project has displayed technological innovation as well as useful content production and service awareness. It has been found that traffic is driven mainly by young and affluent users through a desktop connection which is contrary to original expectations of a mobile site. The core of the project is the presence of advertising initiatives such as competitions and special offers. This has resulted in a sustainable example of thinking locally and acting globally.

Keywords: mobile services, hyperlocal, community media, journalism.

1 Introduction

This paper discusses the NikaNOW platform and its first implementation - 'GrahamstownNOW'. NikaNOW refers to a 'turn-key' solution to support small media organisations in Africa wishing to enter the online space. Such a solution includes a server-based platform that is optimised for access through a mobile phone as well as a content and business model. The solution leverages the two key dimensions of locality and immediacy using context-relevant content to drive 'just-in-time' advertising.

2 Context

2.1 Local vs. Global E-Services: Implications for Africa

The implications of the current process of formation of a global information society and the transition to a knowledge economy are the objects of heated debate.

K. Jonas, I.A. Rai, and M. Tchuente (Eds.): AFRICOMM 2012, LNICST 119, pp. 133–142, 2013.

Following the view exemplified by Negroponte [1], scholars such as Jenkins [2] have highlighted the contribution of new technologies in improving productivity, collaboration and social accountability. Far from subscribing to a simplistic technologically deterministic view, Shirky [3] acknowledges the interrelation of social and technological development and stresses how innovations become socially interesting only once they become technologically boring.

These 'cyberoptimist' views are challenged by scholars such as Morozaw [4] who argues that new technologies can be used as tools of repression and control by authoritarian governments. The potential for Information and Communication Technology (ICT) to reproduce, entrench and exacerbate existing inequalities and social differences has been highlighted and explored[5]. Though such a "Fourth World" cannot be defined along geographical boundaries, the local/global dimension holds center stage in the discussion. Authors such as Castells [5] turn the popular activists' motto "think globally, act locally" on its head. He emphasises the importance of thinking locally and linking to one's interest environment, and subsequently acting globally to challenge global power structures.

The local/global debate is particularly relevant to the development and implementation of e-services in Africa. Moyo [6] notes the danger that the proliferation of ICT on the continent might reproduce patterns of dependency at various levels. At the technological level, infrastructure and services are often produced outside Africa for environments and uses which are not necessarily relevant to the African context. At the economic level, such products tend to benefit businesses outside Africa either directly (through purchase and licensing) or indirectly (through revenue streams). At a cultural level, content and advertising are predominantly developed outside Africa and tend to convey values, world-views, practices and conventions of their original context. Such content and advertising presents a simplistic view of Africa as a homogeneous block and a passive agent on the global scene and would subsequently do little justice to both the complexity of the African context and its productive and innovative potential. Particularly in the area of mobile e-services, Africa has produced several examples of locally responsive solutions, some of which achieved global resonance.

2.2   Mobile Services

Mobile devices have a key role to play in making e-services widely accessible in Africa. Mobile phone penetration on the continent is approximately 70%, vis-a-vis a fixed Internet penetration of less than 10% [7]. Although most mobile phones are feature phones with limited networking capabilities, smartphones are becoming increasingly popular. A number of challenges including the cost of data, poor network coverage and language barriers hamper the progress in uptake of e-services on the continent [8].

Despite these challenges, several innovations in mobile services originated in Africa. Shirky [3] notes the use of mobile phones to monitor elections in Nigeria in 2007, followed by a similar use in the USA's elections in 2008. Ushahidi (meaning "witness" in Kiswahili) is an online portal for the crowdsourcing of information linked to locations on a map. It was implemented in response to outbursts of political violence in Kenya following the 2007 elections and has subsequently been used around the world, particularly for crisis management (e.g. during the earthquake in Haiti in 2010 [9]). A growing number of innovative location-based services, primarily aimed at mobile users, is being developed and implemented in response to local needs [10].

2.3 Hyperlocal Media

'Hyperlocal' media operations are defined as "geographically-based, community-oriented, original-news-reporting organizations indigenous to the web and intended to fill perceived gaps in coverage of an issue or region and to promote civic engagement" [11]. As in the case of other location based services, hyperlocal media focus on interactivity, immediacy and locality. The characteristics of mobile phones (as outlined by Ahonen [12]) make them ideal devices for these types of services. Users can share and access information anytime and from anywhere. Details about location and user preferences can be used to customise content, service and advertising.

Hyperlocal media is a growing and evolving phenomenon. In the US, it constitutes US$36 billion a year business and is responsible for the emergence of several stories of success [13]. The prominent features in such stories include civic engagement (i.e. a commitment towards community development), social cohesion and public accountability. The involvement of citizens as journalists, producers of content or activists is common, but dedicated professionals play a key moderating, editing and coordinating role. The deployment of technological solutions supporting an open and collaborative workflow needs to be complemented by activities such as training and awareness campaigns in the relevant communities. By filling particular niches and through close collaboration with local agencies (e.g. municipal government, NGO's, local businesses, schools and religious organisations etc.) the service can be diversified. This is important for the sustainability of the project.

As such, a "formula" for hyperlocal media in the Western World is slowly emerging and the concept is still in the process of being defined [11]. In South Africa, the hyperlocal online space is largely untapped. The rapid uptake of more focused localised services such as *Gumtree* (http://capetown-westerncape.gumtree.co.za/) and *GroupOn* (http://www.groupon.co.za/) demonstrates the potential thereof. Few of these services are truly hyperlocal and customised for mobile access and few combine journalism with marketing information.

It is in this context that we present the NikaNOW solution and reflect on its first implementation as an instance of hyperlocal media in Africa. In South Africa, where the project was initiated, there are approximately 100 working community radio stations. Many broadcast in African languages and most have no website and no mobile presence. The Association of Independent Publishers has approximately 100 members in South Africa, and many of these constitute the initial target for the solution discussed in this paper. These are generally weekly or monthly publications with a low technology base and an inability to run a continuous broadband internet connection. In South Africa, the ratio between people and active sim cards is close to

1:1 and 80% of phones are expected to be smartphones by 2014 [14]. The number of potential users of mobile e-services, particularly in marginalised communities, is expected to grow.

3   NikaNOW

3.1   Platform

The system features two key components: a workflow management system and a mobisite framework (http://nikanow.com/). The workflow management system is called Nika, which means "to give" in isiXhosa – one of the eleven official languages in South Africa. It is a CMS (content management system) available for free to small media organisations such as community radio stations and newspapers. Stories can be created or imported from other sources and the workflow includes five queues: 1. In Progress; 2. Newsdesk 3. Sub-editing; 4. Layout and 5. On the page. Stories can be dragged and dropped through the five queues and dragged back into previous queues if they need revision or are held over. Within the workflow system it is possible to retrieve earlier versions of a story or receive SMSs from readers.

The mobisite framework component is called NikaNOW to emphasise the characteristic immediacy associated with mobile communication. It is designed for viewing on even the most basic web browser on a cellphone. Instances of NikaNOW for small media organisations can be created (manually for the time being, but soon through an automatic process) on the 'NikaCloud'. A NikaNOW mobisite supports the presentation of location-specific and time-specific information such as: local news and events, competitions, special offers at local businesses, a business directory, maps, live webcam feeds, weather, tweets, SMSs, movie and radio schedules, lift offers/requests and more. The 'maps' section is an example of how different functionalities can be combined to offer a relevant hyperlocal experience. It shows the location of all registered businesses in the area, webcams and other website content that has an associated geo-location. Businesses can thus, for example, offer a special in store or at an event taking place nearby and notify customer accordingly.

NikaNOW supports four different levels of privileges for its users. Visitors can access most content on the site, including special offers and competitions – two distinctive features central to the sustainability model. Registered users can subscribe to e-mail or SMS notifications about business specials, enter sponsored competitions, add a 'lift wanted' or 'lift offered' option to a list of predefined locations or a local event (as moderated by the site administrator). Premium users (e.g. businesses) can create business profiles and associated specials and receive relevant notifications. Administrators (e.g. editors) can perform various tasks on the site. This includes moderation of content such as stories, user feedback, business specials, advertisement banners, information banners pointing to particular sections of the site and events. They can also create competitions and notify the randomly selected winner. Futhermore, administrators can manage news categories, control the SMS gateway, set up Twitter streams with hashtags (#keyword) or handles (@usernames) and configure weather locations and webcams.

The system was realised by combining, adapting and complementing a number of open-source tools. CodeIgniter (http://codeigniter.com/) is a PHP framework characterised by a small footprint, ideal for mobisites running on servers with limited resources. CIMobile is a library for CodeIgniter based on WordPress and optimised for mobisites, The Jquery library (http://jquery.com/) (with UI and JQGrid) handles JavaScript and animations. Datamapper (http://datamapper.org/) is a Ruby objects or relational mapper which uses a single API to interact with different data stores. (This is ideal for use in an integration database). Existing APIs have been used for Twitter locations and Google Maps. As some of these tools are released under the restrictive, copy-left GPL v 2 licence, NikaNOW is released in open source under the same licence. The system can run on a standard LAMP platform with minimal system requirements (500 MB RAM and less than 50MB disk space per instance) and is instrumented to inform research and further development. Administrators can define a Google Analytics account to monitor their site and access system logs stored in a SQL database.

3.2   Service

NikaNOW is a turn-key solution that allows small media organisations to quickly and cost-effectively create and update a monetised mobisite, carrying real-time hyperlocal news, information and advertising. The software is available for download and installation on the media-organisation's server, or can be set up and run in the cloud. In the latter case it provides a service similar to that offered by *Blogger* (http://blogger.com/) or *Yola* (http://yola.com/). It includes an easy-to-use web-based administrative area, enabling publishers to configure their site and manage its content anytime, anywhere. One of the distinctive features of NikaNOW is its ability to 'create its own content' by aggregating locally relevant information from external sources, user generated content and stories. Through simple drag-and-drop interfaces, a basic data-driven mobisite can be rapidly built to offer existing and new audiences real-time localised content, formatted for easy viewing on even the most basic of web-enabled mobile phones.

The target group for NikaNOW mobisites are regular mobile phone users who prefer using their mobile phones (or do not have access to) either traditional newspapers or the Internet via a desktop computer. This definition includes a wide spectrum of people ranging from affluent on-the-go members of the 'thumb generation' to underprivileged individuals for whom the mobile phone is the main, if not the only, medium of communication and access to services. Users in the former group are likely to be interested in up-to-date information on current affairs in their local area or may be able to make use of 'love-a-bargain' (a business model that centers on bargains of the moment). Users closer to the latter end of the continuum can save money by capitalising on short-lived special offers. Providing these users with news and information about upcoming events, or events in progress (e.g. municipal meetings, civic gatherings, school board events etc.) is also a valuable service. This is especially true in a context where there is widespread dissatisfaction about state service delivery and perceived exclusion from the public sphere.

Through its focus on locality and immediacy, the solution can benefit local stakeholders at different levels. Registered users will be able to access news and information, comment ('chirp') in realtime, share via social networks, enter competitions and be aware of time-based specials in their area. For local businesses registered as premium users, NikaNOW mobisites provide an easy entry into the mobile and social media space to stimulate greater consumer awareness of brands, products and services available to both existing and new customers. It is also beneficial for media organisations with regard to site administration. The NikaNOW solution provides a low-cost option to fill a mobisite with time-bound content, automating part of the process by using existing data sources. The platform provides customisable levels of integration with *Facebook*, *Twitter* and other social networks as well as e-mail and SMS integration, reaching audiences 24/7 including those who do not fall under the footprint of traditional media. Small media organisations can access new advertising markets by making use especially of time-based specials. National and multi-national players, such as mobile telecommunicators for instance, could take advantage of NikaNOW to offer compelling value-added services and/or content to their customers locale by locale. By using the leverage made available by hyperlocal media in civic engagement, service provision and advertising, large corporations can promote their social responsibility as well as business agenda at the local level.

Selling advertising is the key revenue stream in the NikaNOW business model. The business model is tightly bound into the content model. Both models stress the notion of instantaneous service and communication and the utility of information. As such, local and national businesses can offer users time and location-bound special deals via the platform. This presents an opportunity to sell advertising nationally for placement on the individual instances for a commission. Each NikaNOW instance could target a strategic selection of consumers. Other potential revenue sources for media-organisations include advanced alerts system for monitoring specific categories of specials (e.g. restaurant specials, supermarket specials). For advertisers the self-service function via SMS, IM and social media notifications are a premium feature of e-commerce. This makes it possible for registered-users to react to advertising and make purchases from within the NikaNOW platform. (e.g. book a movie ticket or bus ticket). QR codes can be generated for items of content and published in other media such as a printed newspaper. The success of both the business and content model depend heavily on deployment within an integrated ecosystem that is responsive to the needs of a specific, real-life community.

4   GrahamstownNOW

4.1   Project History

NikaNOW was designed and developed at Rhodes University in Grahamstown by the School of Journalism and Media Studies and the Computer Science Department. Web Molecole, a Cape Town based company, is also responsible for the development of the platform. The project was made possible by funding provided by the John S. and James L. Knight Foundation through a news challenge grant which ended in 2011.

The first live instance of NikaNOW is called 'GrahamstownNOW' – a mobisite belonging to the local community newspaper, *Grocott's Mail*. Its immediate target group is members of the Grahamstown community including citizen journalists and in terms of audiences with access to mobile phones. Situated in the Eastern Cape, one of the poorest provinces of South Africa, Grahamstown is home to a diverse socio-cultural and socio-economic population of approximately 100 000 people. Grahamstown comprises a continuum ranging from relatively affluent suburbs to informal settlements and can be considered a microcosm of the South African context as well as many other African contexts. It is affected by endemic poverty, high levels of unemployment and alleged corruption and mismanagement of public funds which sometimes spark municipal protests.

The School of Journalism and Media Studies at Rhodes University owns *Grocott's Mail* community newspaper through the David Rabkin Project for Experiential Journalism (DRPEJ). The purpose is for the newspaper to serve as a living laboratory for journalistic research and education whilst simultaneously providing a service to the residents of Grahamstown. *Grocott's Mail* is part of a system which collaborates civil society and academic relations through working relationships with *Radio Grahamstown*, the Unemployed Peoples Movement, Public Service Accountability Monitor, Grahamstown Advice Office, the Legal Resources clinic and others and thus provides diverse opportunities to implement the potential services of GrahamstownNOW.

GrahamstownNOW was piloted in the first half of 2011 and has been successfully used for over a year as a means of disseminating news and other information of value to the community. It builds on a previous initiative called 'Iindaba Ziyafika' meaning 'the news is coming'. This strengthens the news and content supply by working from and already established base. Recent research among marginalised youth in Grahamstown found that youths use the media to express their views, demand better service delivery and mobilise public opinion. However, they find existing media channels expensive to access and difficult to participate in. The language barrier also prevents many from contributing to available media. Over the past three years, Iindaba Ziyafika developed the base of a citizen newsroom to serve *Grocott's Mail* and *Radio Grahamstown*, and trained 90 students and 100 unemployed youth as citizen journalists. Some of them use their mobile phones to capture photos and video for multimedia stories (see: http://www.grocotts.co.za/cjvideos). Contributions to GrahamstownNOW have been minimal and costs, particularly of SMSs, seem to be an obstacle. The technologically deterministic view that a media organisation, through technological innovation and content production, can catalyse change is unrealistic. A key issue is the actual uptake and usage of the information-generated on the user demand and utilisation side.

4.2   Uptake and Usage

In this section we explore the uptake of GrahamstownNOW using Google Analytics and the system logs to answer five questions: how much is the mobisite being used? Where do people access it from? Which devices are used? Who are the users? What do users do on the site? Over the past year (16 August 2011 – 15 August 2012), the GrahamstownNOW mobisite received close to 31,000 visits by 22,500 unique visitors. A substantial portion of the visits (36%) were from users who had visited the site before. The tools do not allow meaningful inferences of one-time visitors, but it is clear that at least 80% of them connected from outside Grahamstown. The 2,500 people who found the site interesting enough to visit it more than once paid a total of more than 7100 visits to it, visiting an average of 3.5 pages per session and spending four minutes on each page. More than half (53%) constituted a one-page visit. These figures are consistent with the quick, on-the-go access envisaged for the site. GrahamstownNOW currently has 794 active registered users and lists more than 300 businesses.

Not surprisingly, the majority (67%) of the returning visits originated from South Africa and an additional 18% from an undisclosed location. However, only 4% of the visits could be traced back to Grahamstown, far behind major South African cities such as nearby Port Elizabeth (28%) and Cape Town (15%). It should be noted that 21% of the visits came from undisclosed locations, which make inferences made on these data unreliable. Of the 539 registered users who disclosed their location, 80% indicated Grahamstown as their permanent address.

Approximately 27% of the visits could reliably be attributed to mobile devices. Most of these were BlackBerry devices (53%), followed by Android smartphones (28%) and Apple mobile devices (13%). Feature phones, mainly Samsung and Nokia, accounted for approximately 5% of the visits. Visits from mobiles were generally shorter and on average less pages were visited compared to visits from desktop computers. Users seemed to prefer access through the flat-rate BlackBerry Internet Service (50%) and wi-fi, with the two major mobile telecommunicators MTN and Vodacom accounting for less than 3% of the traffic. This confirms that, although mobile access is popular, data charges are an obstacle. Among registered users who disclosed their cell phone number, 54% indicated a Vodacom number and 34% an MTN number.

GrahamstownNOW was marketed aggressively among Rhodes students and other young adopters. We promoted GrahamstownNOW through events and at venues frequented by such groups. A substantial portion (31%) of active registered users who listed Grahamstown in their address details lived in the Rhodes University residences. Only a comparatively small portion (8%) of active registered users lived in Grahamstown East – home to a marginalised population that has poor socio-economic conditions. Many users provided only a generic location (e.g. "Grahamstown") making inferences based on this information unreliable. A large portion of the organisations registered as premium users belong to the religious (99), pre-school (55) and health care (42) sectors. Among businesses, retail stores (53), restaurants/ entertainment (33) and transport (20) make up most of the entries. While these figures tell us little about the size and actual engagement of each organisation, they reflect the social as well as business orientation of the service.

Most returning visitors (54%) accessed GrahamstownNOW through a Google search while a comparatively smaller portion (27%) connected to it directly. Social media integration has been crucial to user uptake, as has *Grocott's Mail*'s cross-media channel capability. Direct referrals from the *Grocott's Mail* website and from *Facebook* and *Twitter* combined accounted for 6% of the returning visits each. Visits originating from these sites seemed to be longer (5 minutes) compared to visits from other sources, possibly indicating a more engaged use.

The homepage (http://ghtnow.co.za/) accounted for 19% of the page views. In general, features providing exclusive services or information were the most popular. News stories (available from other platforms) accounted for less than 6% while webcams pointed at various locations in Grahamstown (e.g. to monitor traffic and parking spaces) were the most often viewed (11%). Pages exploiting the locality dimension, such as weather and maps, accounted for less than 1% of the hits while information linked to the immediacy dimension, such as events, exceeded 5%. Services at the core of the NikaNOW business model, i.e. competitions and specials, attracted 6.5% of views each. Pages related to businesses made up 12% of the page views. Admin pages took up 6.5% of the total.

5   Conclusions

This paper discusses NikaNOW, a hyperlocal media solution developed in South Africa and designed to leverage the immediate and local character of mobile communication in Africa. The software and service model intend to serve the social and economic imperatives of diverse communities at a local level. The first implementation as GrahamstownNOW was accompanied by a range of initiatives to support production of content and use and uptake by local users and businesses/organisations has been fruitful. Although the platform is primarily intended as a mobisite, most access is through a desktop computer. University students form a sizeable portion of the registered users, but there is evidence of involvement by members of the Grahamstown community from all walks of life. Registered organisations use the platform for business as well as public interest services. Sustainability is supported by healthy consumption of the services at the core of the business model. In summary, in our experience NikaNOW is a robust service in which immediacy is the key factor in driving social and economic activation at a local level with comparatively little administrative overload.

References

1. Negroponte, N.: Being digital. Vintage Books, New York (1996)
2. Jenkins, H.: Convergence Culture: Where Old and New Media Collide. New York University Press, New York (2006)
3. Shirky, C.: Here comes everybody: How change happens when people come together. Penguin Books, London (2009); Shirky, C.: Cognitive surplus: Creativity and generosity in a connected age. Penguin books (2010)
4. Morozaw, E.: The Net Delusion: How not to liberate the world. Penguin (2012)
5. Castells, M.: The Power of Identity. The Information Age: Economy, Society and Culture, vol. 2. Blackwell, Oxford (1997)

6. Moyo, L.: The digital divide: scarcity, inequality and conflict. In: Creeber, G., Martin, R. (eds.) Digital Cultures: Understanding New Media. Open University Press (2009)
7. International Telecommunication Union (ITU), http://www.itu.int/
8. Pimenidis, E., Sideridis, A., Antonopoulou, E.: Mobile devices and services: bridging the digital divide in rural areas. International Journal of Electronic Security and Digital Forensics 2(4), 424–434 (2009)
9. Nathan, M., Mock, N., Papendieck, A., Kocmich, N.: Independent Evaluation of the Ushahidi Haiti Project. DISI – Development Information Systems International (2011)
10. Hellström, J., Tröften, P.: The innovative use of mobile applications in East Africa. Sida (2010)
11. Metzgar, E., Kurpius, D., Rowley, K.: Defining hyperlocal media: Proposing a framework for discussion. New Media and Society 13(5), 772–787 (2011)
12. Ahonen, T.T.: Mobile as the 7th of the Mass Media, London, Future Text (2008)
13. Gruskin, B., Seave, A., Graves, L.: The Story So Far - What We Know About the Business of Digital Journalism, Columbia Journalism School, Tow center for Digital Journalism (2012)
14. Abrahams, L., Goldstuck, A.: A Decade of e-Development in South Africa: Sufficient for a "Services (R)evolution"? In: Hanna, N., Knight, P. (eds.) National Strategies to Harness Information Technology, pp. 107–152. Springer, New York (2012)

Analysis and Design of Mobile Payment Platform in African Context

Rodrigue Carlos Nana Mbinkeu

National Advanced School of Engineering,
University of Yaounde I, 8390 Yaounde, Cameroon
DBGroupLab – University of Modena, Italy
nanambinkeu@gmail.com

Abstract. This article shows the impact of the growing adoption of mobile phones in the field of money transfer in Africa but also their uses in the field of retail payments or micropayments that is financial transaction from person to person (P2P) for small amounts. We show how these innovations will continue to improve the quality of life of Africans especially those in rural areas. We present M-Pesa as a mobile payment system which has had great success in Kenya. We identify the fundamental principles of success thus this enabled us to create an ECOPAY platform which is an innovative mobile payment system.

Keywords: ECOPAY, payment, transfer, money, m-wallet, mobile phone.

1 Introduction

During the last few decades, the ICT sector in Africa has been rapidly evolving. In some countries, information technology is emerging to boost economies. This evolution is due to the widespread adoption of information technology on the continent. The number of mobile subscriptions in use worldwide, both pre-paid and post-paid, has grown from fewer than 1 billion in 2000 to over 6 billion now, of which nearly 5 billion are in developing countries [1]. In this context, African banks and telecom operators have started to integrate their development strategies in achieving the technological infrastructure including: mobile payment, also called the M-Payment. This technology offers new perspectives in Africa in the field of trade in goods and services. Mobile payments, i.e. payments made from your mobile phone, will continue to take their share of cashless payments for various reasons in Africa.

The aim of this paper is to propose an analysis of this new technology in the African context and to understand what the principles behind the success of these M-payment projects are. Secondly, we present our mobile payment solution.

The paper starts with a brief discussion about M-payment in Africa and opportunities. We study the successful case of the mobile payment system called M-Pesa and consequently we derive the basic principles of m-payment projects. Section 3 presents the general ECOPAY platform and its innovations in terms of user services, followed by conclusions.

K. Jonas, I.A. Rai, and M. Tchuente (Eds.): AFRICOMM 2012, LNICST 119, pp. 143–152, 2013.

2   Mobile Payment in Africa

The main components of the mobile payment system are the money transfer applications and network infrastructure (internet and gsm). Banks, mobile operators, trusted third parties are the main players in mobile payment systems [1]. People will probably be more likely to make financial transactions through M-Payment solutions without opening a bank account. Therefore this technology resolves a problem of low banking penetration in Africa [3]. The development of this new electronic payment method is closely related to the evolution of new information technologies, telecommunications and high mobile phone penetration in the daily lives of Africans. It eases the adoption of M-payment in Africa and encourages banks to create new services for users directly accessible on mobile phones. It is M-Banking.

With the M-Banking, the user accesses several services including account balances, viewing account history and makes financial transactions. One of the features of M-Banking is the ability to rapidly deal with suspicious transactions (credit card stolen) even when they are miles away from their nearest branch.

As for the M-Payment, it offers several services such as, telephone recharges, bill payments, retail payments and more. The advantage of M-Payment is the fact that several functions work with both traditional mobile phones and smartphones.

The basic premise is that mobile payments offer a way for people with low incomes or the unbanked to make financial transactions without getting involved with a traditional financial institution [1, 8].The M-Payment is more advantageous to rural populations [3]. This technology will create competition with older money transfer companies and this will continue to reduce the transfer rates between cities and rural areas in Africa. Africans will benefit from local services with relatively low transaction costs, easier accessibility to financial services. The time savings are immeasurable by reducing the movement of people especially those located in inaccessible areas. M-payment offers several advantages including simplicity and accessibility to the service at any time. This will lead to poverty reduction [3].

2.1   Analysis of the Kenyan Experience: M-Pesa

Mobile financial services are among the most promising mobile applications in the developing world [1, 11]. Mobile money could become a general platform that transforms entire economies, as it is adopted across commerce, health care, agriculture, and other sectors. To date, at least 110 money mobile systems have been deployed, with more than 40 million users [1, 7]. The most well-known system, M-PESA, started in Kenya and is now operational in six countries; it has 20 million users who transferred $500 million a month during 2011and are served by more than 28,000 agents [1, 4, 8].

M-Pesa users can deposit money into their own account, and then make transfers to a contact or withdraw money at a number of bank branches or agents in the country. The amount transferred is cheaper than transfers made in traditional networks. For recipients, several options are available like withdrawing the total sum from an agent. The registered users are managed directly by the M-Pesa system on dedicated accounts also called m-wallet accounts, thus it is not necessary for the user to have a bank account. The subscription service is provided free of charge. Studies showed that the majority of consumers use the service for transferring money to families or close friends [8]. Among the criticisms, consumers mention frequent cases of offices or agents who are short of cash, some cases of attempted fraud and occasional complications on the network. However, the general opinion of consumers about M-Pesa is remarkably positive. M-Pesa has had a significant impact on the domestic transfer market. M-Pesa services have expanded to include bill payments, bundled payments of wages and payment of school fees. M-Pesa is a service offered to subscribers by the first mobile operator called Safaricom in Kenya [4]. According to the International Monetary Fund (IMF) in 2011, M-Pesa has handled more transactions in Kenya as Western Union worldwide [5].

Taking into account the Kenyan experience, it is important to note that the launch of an m-payment service should respect three basic principles [6]:

- A large volume of transactions must be able to compensate for lower rates;
- A higher speed acquisition of new customers and agents to reach a critical mass of registered users enabling the service to be operating. As a reminder, money transfer for example, requires that the sender, the receiver of the money transfer and agents have access to m-payment services.
- A Geographic coverage is important to make the service available anywhere at any time.

In response, five conditions require special analysis to confirm the launch of a mobile payment [6]:

1. The latent demand for transactions;
2. The quality of existing services;
3. The legislations;
4. The mobile services market;
5. The network of agents and partners.

There are also other operators such as Orange money, Airtel money, and MTN money, which are very active in Africa and have also developed their mobile payment solutions.

3   The General Architecture of ECOPAY Platform

The ECOPAY Platform marks our efforts to help bring financial services to consumers in all corners of Cameroon via mobile money services and ECOPAY Network Partners such as banks, microfinance institutions and agents. The ECOPAY platform will be open to all mobile users, regardless of their network, and will allow the daily to any Cameroonian mobile phone number.

Our platform takes into consideration that mobile phones are multifunctional devices which allow for a variety of communication methods. These range from ubiquitous voice and SMS applications to more sophisticated solutions such as software applications or web browsers. To be a viable solution for mobile money, the applications should ideally be universally available (including the cheapest mobile phones) and must be secure. For these reasons, the ECOPAY client applications will be compatible with a range of smartphone, while those without a smartphone can use a simple client built with Java Micro-edition to access our services (figure 1). ECOPAY Client on the phone is controlled by a five-digit PIN.

Users can also access their m-wallet by connecting with computers (web browsers) and they can access a variety of services. The general architecture of our platform ensures that banks of all shapes and sizes can use it. The important aspect of our platform is the fact that it allows more banks and microfinance institutions to interact with each other through our transaction services, clearing and compensation engine (figure 1).Therefore, ECOPAY users can deposit or withdraw money even in other institutions or agents where their m-wallets are not affiliated. Our partner network helps to make the service available everywhere at anytime. All partners of our network can communicate with each other by using our built-in chat or messenger module (figure 1).

During the registration process, users have the choice between two types of m-wallet: simple m-wallet or business m-wallet. A business m-wallet is the account which allows user to receive payments from customers in their shops or websites.

Payment in the shops can be made by using the mobile phone of merchant (section 3.1), while the payment on websites are made by using web services. The objective of the proposed architecture is to replace legacy systems used in the retail industry with mobile technologies.

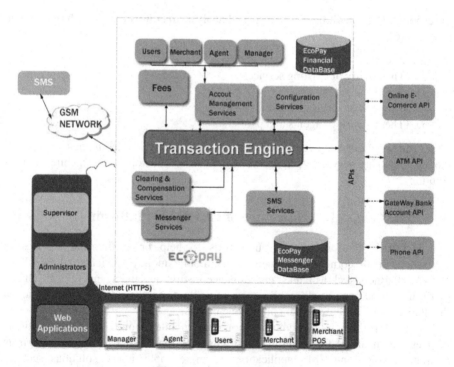

Fig. 1. EcoPay Architecture

We use a robust set of PHP and Java frameworks and SDKs to develop our platform that are light weight and ideal for programmers who need a simple and elegant toolkit to create full-featured web applications with exceptional performance. The ECOPAY Platform has more technical elements defined in [9, 12] and it is built to work only with one currency at this time.

3.1   The Payment Process with ECOPAY

The mobile payment is considered by many people as the new killer-application that will boost e-/m-commerce; according to Wireless World Forum report [13, 14]. To subscribe to the ECOPAY services, consumers have to fill out a form. Once the application is approved, the consumer can use ECOPAY for a range of transactions:

- Person-to-merchant (P2M i.e. for bill payments in markets, shops, website);
- Person-to-Person (P2P i.e. the user can send money to another individual in any bank or Microfinance Finance Institution (MFI) of the EcoPay Network Partners, receiver can be nonusers ecopay;
- Business-to-Business (B2B i.e. for bill payments between companies or merchants)

The typical payment transaction using ECOPAY would go like this (see figure 2):

1. The customer gives his mobile phone number to the merchant;
2. The merchant inserts into the ECOPAY mobile application (client), the phone number of customer and the amount to be paid. He then presses the button to validate;
3. ECOPAY mobile client requests the PIN of customer to perform transaction;
4. The customer verifies the amount of debit and inserts his PIN;
5. The merchant confirms the transaction with the ECOPAY mobile Client;
6. ECOPAY mobile Client interacts with the Platform by using Json's call to settle the payment (direct debit);
7. The transaction is performed by updating accounts involved in the payment process and the clearing engine informs the compensation services;
8. The platform sends the result of transaction (sms) to customer by using GSM network;
9. The platform sends the result of transaction (Json's result) to the ECOPAY mobile client;
10. ECOPAY mobile client shows the result of transaction on the screen of mobile (smart) phone.

Through the ECOPAY mobile client, the merchant can view the receipts of the day and view all transactions validated on the screen of the mobile (smart) phone. In general, the payment is made by using mobile phone or smartphone or accessing the account on a computer (see figure 3 for more technical details of transaction).

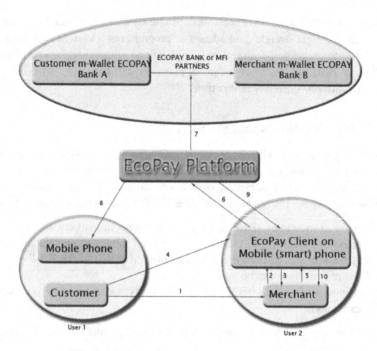

Fig. 2. Payment scenario with ECOPAY Platform

3.2   How to Withdraw Money from an ATM with ECOPAY

Most of the technologies, without integrating with security mechanism originally, have to be redesigned to provide some security services. ATM (Automated teller machines) is one of those technologies [10]. ATM is used by financial institutions to allow their customers to withdraw money even when the bank is closed. We summarize the three major ATM threats:

- Physical, or stealing the cash from an ATM;
- Logical, or the installation of malicious software, and;
- Fraud, or using fake cards and stealing card details in skimming scams.

The threat of getting your card skimmed is the greatest one and continues to increase [10]. Therefore, for our ecopay project, we designed the new way to withdraw money from ATMs by using the mobile phone (see figure 2). The typical scenario using ECOPAY application on mobile phone would go like this:

1. User launches the ECOPAY application on his mobile phone linked with his m-wallet;
2. User must define a random number with six-digit and the amount to be withdrawn;
3. When user validates the withdraw operation on his mobile, he/she has five minutes to withdraw money from ATM;

4. User inserts the random number defined in the ATM and validates the operation;

5. ATM gives user the exact amount defined before on mobile phone.

With this process, we ensure that ECOPAY users can withdraw money out of their m-wallet from ATM more securely. The other advantage of this approach is the possibility to send money to friends by asking them to go to stay in front the ATM and wait our instructions (we send the random number defined to friends or call to give it).

3.3   How to Use Our Online e-Commerce API

For merchants, charities and organizations, Ecopay e-commerce API is an affordable way to accept payments online. Ecopay e-Commerce API is a programming interface, which allows merchants to automate the process of online payments on their websites. API setup is required in order to use Ecopay as a payment option on websites. Currently Ecopay provides JSON functions. The sequence of pages browsed when using online payment is shown in the figure 3.

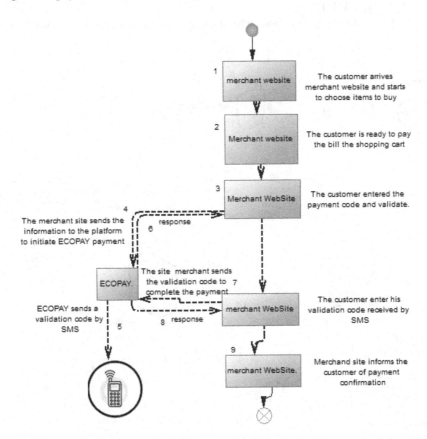

Fig. 3. Online Payment scenario on Merchant Websites

Conditions to Make Shopping on Websites

- The maximum amount spendable will be set by the users in their accounts;
- After validation of the amount spendable, the user gets a payment code;
- During the purchase, the total amount payable by the users must be less than or equal to the amount associated with the payment code.

3.4 Security Features of Transaction

While security features do not guarantee a secure system, they are necessary to build a secure system. Our platform includes the following security features:

- Each type of Transaction requires entering a PIN or validation code;
- All Transactions are encrypted and sent to the ECOPAY Platform;
- ECOPAY Platform receives the transaction order and decrypts it before processing;
- Access to the online account with browser requires two authentication mechanisms (username, password + code session received by sms);
- Internet connections between Users and the ECOPAY Platform are encrypted (HTTPS);
- Users receive notifications when their m-wallets are involved in transactions;

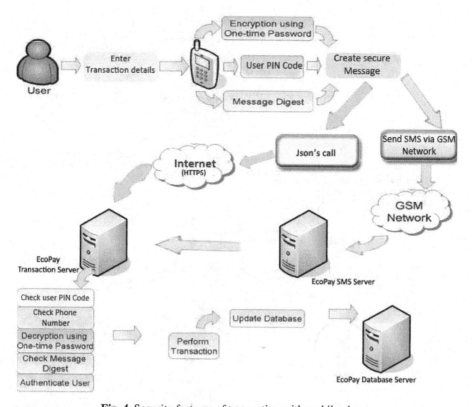

Fig. 4. Security features of transaction with mobile phone

4   Conclusions

The potential of m-payment in financial inclusion is huge because it allows us to offer a large number of people with low income and the unbanked a range of affordable products that meet their financial needs. Today, m-payment must integrate new services such as online payment. It is for these reasons that we decided to implement a mobile payment solution which proposes new features for users. With the online payment feature, ECOPAY users can purchase products or pay for services in local currency on websites by using their m-wallet accounts.

ECOPAY aims at developing a national mobile payment system. Its innovative business model is based on two key concepts:

- Cooperation of Banks and microfinance institution and
- Social trust relationships since each actor transacts only with his trusted bank or microfinance institution.

It is worth noting that ECOPAY features a distributed approach where banks or microfinance institutions can dynamically join the system with their customer base, something which will allow ECOPAY to grow fast and reach a the critical mass that may establish it as a national payment service.

ECOPAY's project is financed by the Community Investment Corporation limited, an investment and business development company established in Cameroon for the purpose of investing in people, ideas and businesses that represent good long term and beneficial growth opportunities for Cameroon and the African continent.

References

1. Donovan, K.: Mobile Money for Financial Inclusion. Information and Communications for Development (2012)
2. Agunloye, O.: Progress on Nigeria's eGovernment and ePayment Projects. A Presentation at the AITEC Banking and Mobile Money Conference (May 2010)
3. Taddesse, W., Kidan, T.G.: ePayment: Challenges and Opportunities in Ethiopia
4. Jack, W., Suri, T.: The Economic of M-Pesa (August 2010)
5. International Monetary Fund. Regional Economic outlook: Sub-Saharan Africa. World Economic and Financial Surveys (October 2011)
6. Salmon, K., et al.: Mobile paiement: Enjeux et perspective du développement du m-paiement (2011)
7. CGAP. CGAP Mobile-money Expectation Survey (September 2010)
8. Alliance For Financial Inclusion. Faciliter les transferts d'argent par téléphone mobile, Le traitement de M-Pesa par la Banque centrale du Kenya, Février (2010)
9. Männle, M.: Interoperable Mobile Payment – A Requirements-Based Architecture. Encorus Technologies GmbH; product management Payment Platform
10. Rasiah, D.: ATM Risk Management and Controls. European Journal of Economics, Finance and Administrative Sciences (2010)

11. Baumüller, H.: Facilitating agricultural technology adoption among the poor: The role of service delivery through mobile phones. ZEF Working Paper Series (2012)
12. Ondrus, J., Pigneur, Y.: Architecture for Mobile Payments and Couponing in the Retail Industry. In: 17th Bled eCommerce Conference Global (2004)
13. Shen, S.: Mobile Payment, Worldwide, 2009-2016, Gartner Research (2012)
14. Mobile Payments 2002 - making mobile services pay. Wireless World Forum (2002)

A Mobile Commerce Solution for Sub-Saharan Countries Such as Cameroon

Paul Dayang and Rebecca Siafaka

Universität Bremen, Dpt. of Mathematics/Computer Science
P.O. Box 33 04 40, D-28334 Bremen, Germany
{pdayang,rsiafaka}@informatik.uni-bremen.de

Abstract. The use of mobile phones as means of communication has exceeded the use of land-lines or that of the Internet in Cameroon and in many African Countries. Therefore the exploitation of the capabilities that mobile phones has to offer seems promising for the development of the everyday life of the Cameroonian population. The aim of this paper is to stress the need of introducing mobile solutions in the everyday activities of Sub-Saharan countries such as Cameroon. Accordingly we suggest a m-commerce solution, called *bayasella*, that will boost the so called Bayam Sellam trading activity and will take advantage of the popularity that the use of mobile phones is gaining nowadays.

Keywords: mobile communications, mobile commerce, mobile web, Bayam Sellam trade, mobile advertising, Sub-Saharan countries, hybrid applications.

1 Introduction

In Cameroon as well as in Sub-Saharan African countries, the use of technology in communication lies more on mobile phones. Mobile phones seem to become more and more popular among their populations and have indeed exceeded the use of land-line or that of the Internet. This popularity led the stakeholders to develop the mobile network more than the Internet network with the former being today the most reliable network in Cameroon. At the end of 2010 the International Telecommunication Union (ITU) estimated the mobile user penetration in Africa at 41%, while the Internet penetration rate reached 9.6% [4]. Realising the importance of mobile phones in Cameroon we researched on the potential that this medium has to improve the everyday life of such populations. We found that electronic commerce has already gained popularity and with the popularity that mobile phones have in the area, mobile commerce should be the next way of performing business activities using the existing mobile infrastructure in Sub-Saharan countries [5]. To that extent we chose to combine the idea of Bayam Sellam, an old trading activity of the underprivileged communities in Cameroon, with the modern trend of mobile commerce which exploits the potential of mobile phones.

K. Jonas, I.A. Rai, and M. Tchuente (Eds.): AFRICOMM 2012, LNICST 119, pp. 153–162, 2013.

The aim of this paper is to draw the attention of the stakeholders to the importance of introducing the use of advanced mobile solutions in the everyday activities of the Sub-Saharan population. In order to do so we suggest "bayasella" a mobile commerce application that supports the Bayam Sellam activity with the use of mobile phones.

What follows in this article is a description of the state of mobile communications in Cameroon as well as details for the Bayam Sellam activity. Later on we describe the technology on which our solution is based, as well as details on the data flow and the benefits that the African populations may have by its use.

2   Mobile Communications in Cameroon

The rural population in Cameroon is estimated to cover more than 80% of the total population and the mobile network similarly covers up to 80% of the country. Considering the importance of telecommunication, now the government has started the implementation of a community program for telecentres in the major cities of the ten regions with the objective of 2,000 telecentres by 2015 [11]. The aim is to increase the Internet penetration rate, which is presently 11% far behind the computer penetration rate, which is 20%. Mobiles however, present undeniable potential for the local population.

2.1   Potential of Mobiles in Cameroon

In Cameroon mobile devices are being used everywhere. Since mobile phones made their appearance in the Cameroonian market at the beginning of 2000, a new era of telecommunication began. Owning a mobile phone was a sign of a higher social status. Nowadays the mobile phone revolution is sweeping through Cameroon like a bushfire. The potential for using mobile phones as a tool for economic development and business has not gone unnoticed. Currently, new job opportunities arise, among which we can enumerate charging services, mobile call boxes, money transfer services, dealing correspondent number for illiterate people, etc.

Nothing seems to be able to stop the triggered booming process of the mobile phone market in the near future. Therefore more effort has been done to improve the mobile network, making it the most reliable network in Cameroon and in many Sub-Saharan countries. Mobile operators have enormously invested in infrastructural facilities. Over 80% of the land area is covered by mobile network. According to the Telecommunications Regulatory Board (TRB), the structure for regulating telecommunications in Cameroon, mobile phone subscribers (not included the random users who buy and use SIM cards without registration) increased from 0.66% (103279 subscribers) to 44.07% (9,6 millions subscribers) from 2000 to 2010 [9].

Mobile services, such as mobile banking, gained popularity in Cameroon because of the extended use of mobile phones. Petipe, a mobile money subscriber and micro finance expert in Yaounde, points out the tendency towards mobile solutions:

Cameroonian banks [...] are forming partnerships with mobile phone op-
erators to provide mobile financial services [...] as mobile phone operators
have a wider reach than banks because more people have cell phones than
bank accounts [12].

An important step in favor of mobile communications in Cameroon and in Sub-
Saharan countries, was the establishment of the first Mobile Virtual Network
Operator (MVNO), "Set'mobile", in July 2012. The operator started its activities with an offer for 50,000 subscribers, a number which outlines the spread rate
of mobile users in the area. Set'mobile operates as a traffic reseller, which means
it buys traffic from other mobile operators and resells its to the subscribers. Also,
the government has tendered for a third mobile operator.

The current state of mobile in Cameroon proves that this field has a great
potential for development. Moreover, the statistical details which shows the increasing number of subscribers proves that mobiles as well as related services are
well received from the Cameroonian populations. Therefore, we believe that more
effort should be done in the offered mobile solutions, as for example, through
the improvement of the m-commerce field with the help of adapted mobile applications.

2.2 Challenges of Mobile Communications in Cameroon

Despite the potential for development in mobile communications in Cameroon,
important challenges are still present and reduce the progress in the field. Existing services such as mobile money, which are very appreciated by the users,
are SIM-dependent and therefore limited. If such ones exist, they present important restrictions that hinder or limit the utility of the existing infrastructure for
mobile communication. If users decide for SIM-apps, the subscribers are immediately committed to official and costly contracts with the corresponding mobile
operator. In regard to SIM-apps, we may understand the restrictions as security
measure from the respective mobile operators. For example, mobile operators
shall ensure the liability of services like mobile money.

Third party apps that support daily activities efficiently, are rare. The Cameroonian apps market, as many other Sub-Saharan application markets, is poor and
consequently the existing infrastructure is used below its capacity employment. It
suffers from under operation. Typical example of the challenges that occur in the
existing mobile solutions is the testimonial of Ndi, a mobile subscriber working
as taxi driver who affirms with regard to the ever long waiting queue at Applied
Energy Services, the electricity service provider, to pay the electricity bill:

I have paid my bills through Orange once [...] The second time I tried it,
the transaction did not go through, and I lost some of my credit money
[12].

Challenging factors can influence the satisfactory and profitable development
of mobile technology in Sub-Saharan countries. Those factors may easily turn
into restrictions and weaknesses of the existing mobile technology. Some of the
factors we can identify are the following:

- Absence of adaptive and tailored apps
- Limited SIM-apps
- Laxness and slowness of services
- High demand of services
- Customer reticence
- Customer dissatisfaction

In order to limit the effect of those factors, it is important to improve the provided solutions and follow a more task-oriented and user-centered approach.

3   The Bayam Sellam Activity

In Cameroon, the Bayam Sellam is an increasing informal economic activity. It is a business activity born out of the struggle to improve individual or family livelihood. Principal actors are the underprivileged populations, comprising mostly women and youths. In many underprivileged African societies, women are those who provide everyday needs in terms of food and healthcare to the family. Therefore, this activity plays an important role by affording to those people the opportunity to run businesses. The term Bayam Sellam is a typical word from the Cameroonian pidgin language which is classified in the category of lingua franca. It comes from the English words "buy and sell". A person who undertakes such an activity is also called Bayam Sellam.

How Do They Operate?
This activity consists in buying products at the lowest possible price from various rural trading areas like markets in hinterland, plantations, road junctions, etc. and retailing them with profit in urban areas. Bayam Sellam are regularly on the move between the rural areas to buy and the urban areas to sell. They operate individually and usually get together only in delicate business ventures where the risk is high.

4   The Bayasella m-Commerce Approach

Having evaluated all the aforementioned information concerning the current state of mobile in Cameroon as well as the challenges found to influence the development in the field, we believe that mobile solutions tailored to the everyday needs of the local population should be the focus of the stakeholders in order to support the everyday activities of the population and boost at the same time the mobile development. Therefore we suggest a mobile commerce solution called bayasella.

4.1   Vision of Bayasella

Bayasella is a mobile facilitated advertising and product information retrieving application in the field of m-commerce. It is classified as an ad app that provides facilities to sellers suggesting products for sale and to buyers finding products for purchase. The bayasella system will store product details offline, i.e locally on the mobile device, and synchronise them with the online database, whenever the Internet in available. The online database shall act as an interface between buyers and sellers. Unlike the advertisement such as sending SMS message, calling friends or shouting at a street corner, bayasella is innovatively designed to support and increase the utility of existing mobile infrastructures and to fulfil the demands of underprivileged mobile phone consumers and the Bayam Sellam in particular. The bayasella model has four entities, which are:

1. **Product**, which represents the products to be sold. The attributes of the products are: *id, name, description* and *price*.
2. **Status**, which represents the state of the product. Its attributes are: *open, sold*, and *sychronised*.
3. **Place**, which represents the place where the product is sold. Its contains geo-location data composed of *latitude* and *longitude*. This is an optional entity in the data set.
4. **Owner** is the seller who provides products. He/she is characterised by *name* and *phone*.

4.2   Data Flow

To depict and visualise the input-process-output of the application, we use the data flow diagram (DFD) shown in Figure   1. The system is represented by the circle. The online bayasella database represents the database for exchanging products information between sellers and buyers. Using a synchronisation process, sellers push their products into the online database and buyers pull the products from it. Sellers (sella) and buyers (baya) manage their products locally.

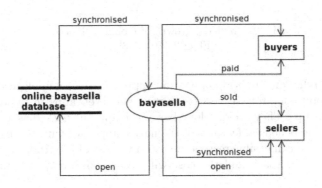

Fig. 1. Data flow

4.3 Technology and Interface

The factors that influenced our choice of the technology to be used are determined by the environment in which bayasella operates, as well as by the current trends in mobile development. From the perspective of the environment, the influence factors can be summarised in low and expensive Internet connection and limited user experience in the m-commerce field. Concerning the trends in mobile development, Fling [6] declares that the mobile web is the only platform that is available in all mobile devices and its growth is rapid and significant (Figure 2). Furthermore, web apps are gaining popularity due to technological innovations, business and user demands. Therefore bayasella exploits the advantages of mobile Web using HTML5 (including technologies such as Web Storage, Web SQL Database, etc.) and CSS3, technologies that play a determining role in the growth of new generation mobile Web and hybrid apps.

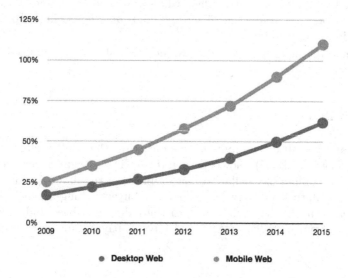

Fig. 2. Predicted growth of mobile web access
[Fling 2009, p. 33]

Bayasella relies on a hybrid application approach. *Hybrid* applications or apps provide a good compromise between native and Web apps to build platform-independent apps. They are developed as a web app but packed as a native app. It combines the beneficial features of the native approach with those of the web. For example, we can easily create a bayasella version of the Android app for the iOS using this approach and the cost will be less than re-developing a native version.

Concerning *native apps*, they are designed to run in a specific OS environment. Coded with a specific programming language (Java, C#, C++ etc.), they are fast, reliable, and powerful but are tied to a specific mobile platform. With regard to the diversified existing mobile platforms, migrating a native app to another mobile platform means to duplicate it using the appropriate programming language. Depending on the app, the migration may be very costly. The cost is dispensed with the hybrid approach.

Bayasella uses a relational database created in MySQL. The database is hosted on a server where also the synchronisation script is located. During the synchronisation process the combination of seller's *phone number* and product *id* is the identifier of the product dataset to be synchronised. Since the products are being managed locally on the corresponding mobile devices, if two sellers set the same mobile numbers in the bayasella application, dataset conflicts may occur during the synchronisation process because the product datasets may have the same id. In this case, the seller receives a warning message in order to correct or change the phone number, if necessary, or to withdraw the conflicted product.

Developing bayasella is supported and facilitated by means of development frameworks like Sencha, PhoneGap, The-M-Project etc. Such frameworks provide JavaScript libraries which help to implement interactive features. Those technological facilities provide the following advantages:

- We use modern technologies (e.g. HTML5) that demand low resources (e.g. memory speed).
- We run the app on different platforms without rewriting it from the beginning.
- We are able to submitt the app to the Cameroonian app market and beyond.

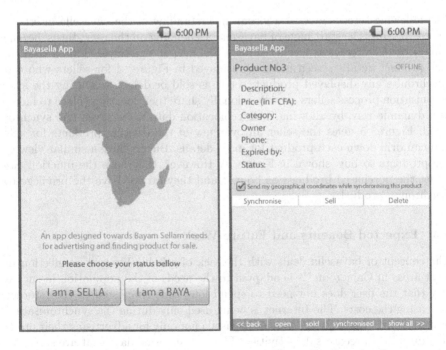

Fig. 3. Start page   **Fig. 4.** Product details

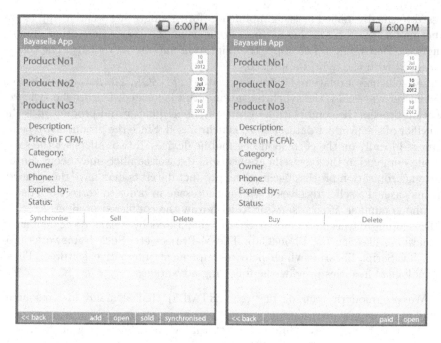

Fig. 5. Product list for sella   **Fig. 6.** Product list for baya

The following screens give us a visual understanding of the bayasella interface. Figure 3 shows the start page of bayasella. Depending on the user status, he/she can choose to interact as a seller (I am a SELLA) or as a buyer (I am a BAYA). The product details screen is being displayed in Figure 4 for sellers who can synchronise any displayed product, set it as sold or delete it. During the synchronisation process sellers can intentionally share their location (place to meet) in a dynamic way, by allowing their geolocation data to be saved and synchronised. Figure 5 gives the seller an overview of the existing products for sale and can drill down each product for more details. Buyers have a similar view of the products to buy, shown in Figure 6. However, they have the function *buy* to set the purchased products as bought and they do not have the privilege to synchronise products.

4.4 Expected Benefits and Future Work

The concept of bayasella deals with the lack of reliable Internet connection in most areas in Cameroon. It is adapted to the needs of the population in such a way that the user does not need to spend long time connected to the Internet increasing the costs. The Internet is being used only during the synchronisation process. Furthermore, users can use bayasella not only for advertising their products but also to record sale activities. The recorded sale data that are stored in a database may become available to other stakeholders, such as for example the government of Cameroon, in order to better control and define the price of the purchased products.

Since the Bayam Sellam populations are also dealing with perishable food, selling them through adapted and cost-effective processes which enable fast purchase, plays an important role. Moreover, the bayasella application may help to establish faster and cost-effective communication between those who sell the products and the customers.

Our next steps forward to the proposed solution is to evaluate the use of our application to the local population. Through user evaluation and interviews we shall collect important information to improve and adjust our solution application.

4.5   Conclusion

Cameroon, as a sub-Saharan country, faces a similar situation as many other Sub-Saharan countries. Since many of them shared colonial and post-colonial history, the countries tend to have similar, although not the same, political and economical status [2]. Showcasing Cameroon highlights similar challenges that African countries in Sub-Sahara are facing. Thus, the bayasella solution approach will support the everyday activities of Bayam Sellam not only in Cameroon but also in other Sub-Saharan communities and help them become familiar with more advanced mobile solutions that may bring further development.

References

1. Rao, M.: Mobile Africa Report 2011: Regional Hubs of Excellence and Innovation. Extensia (2011)
2. Mugoya, A.: African Apps in a Global Marketplace: ideas, observations, tips and some gripes about the African app industry. Asilia (2011)
3. Anderson, J.G.: Professional Flash R Lite R Mobile Development. Wiley Publishing, Inc., Indianapolis (2010)
4. International Telecommunication Union: The world in 2010. ITU World Telecommunication/ICT Indicators database (2010)
5. Mensah, A.O., Bahta, A., Mhlanga S.: E-commerce challenges in Africa: issues, constraints, opportunities. United Nations Economic Commission for Africa 2006 (October 2012), http://www.uneca.org/aisi/docs/PolicyBriefs/E-commerce%20challenges%20in%20Africa.pdf
6. Fling, B.: Mobile Design and Development, 1st edn. O'Reilly Media, Inc., Sebastopol (2009)
7. Sommerville, I.: Software Engineering, 9th rev. ed. Pearson, Amsterdam (2011)
8. Tedonkeng Pamo, E.: Country Pasture/Forage Resource Profiles. FAO, Dschang (2008)
9. Telecommunication Regulatory Board. Informations statistiques sur le marché de la téléphonie (premier et deuxème trimestre 2011) (2011)
10. Eto'o Telecom: C'est finalement ce 21 juillet 2012 (June 2012), http://cameroon-info.net/stories/0,36134,@, eto-o-telecom-c-est-finalement-ce-21-juillet-2012.html

11. Cameroun : 4% de taux de pénétration d'Internet et 9 millions d'abonnés à la téléphonie mobile (June 2012), http://www.nextafrique.com/sciencestech/technologie/1192-cameroun-4-de-taux-de-penetration-dinternet-et-9-millions-d-abonnes-a-la-telephonie-mobile
12. CameroonOnline.org: Mobile Banking in Cameroon Increases Access to Financial Service (June 2012), http://www.cameroononline.org/2012/03/15/mobile-banking-in-cameroon-increases-access-to-financial-services/

Leveraging the Cultural Model for Opportunistic Networking in Sub-Saharan Africa

Jonathan Ouoba[1,2] and Tegawendé F. Bissyandé[1,2]

[1] The FasoLabs Project, Burkina Faso
[2] LaBRI, University of Bordeaux, France
{jonathan.ouoba,tegawende.bissyande}@fasolabs.org

Abstract. The immense potential of ICT for improving users' livelihood has been discussed in a large body of literature and many instantiations in our daily life demonstrate this reality. In developing areas, such as Sub-Saharan Africa, ICT for development has become the frontrunner initiative that decision makers are pushing to bring millions of people out of poverty. Unfortunately, the majority of Africans, who live in rural areas, fail to identify with the existing various solutions.

We propose the *Toolé* approach, which aims at vulgarizing new technologies for facilitating and automating the collection and synthesis of agricultural information. The originality of *Toolé* lies in the fact that it attempts to build on the cultural values of peasants. The architecture on top of which *Toolé* was built relies on cheap, yet powerful, devices and on readily available peer-to-peer protocols to deliver services whose inherent costs make sense for low income areas.

Keywords: Toolé, ICT4D, sub-Saharan Africa, remote areas, e-agriculture, opportunistic networking, cultural phenomenon.

1 Introduction

Despite a steady progress in the last decade, sub-Saharan Africa still lags behind the rest of the world in terms of access to the information society. According to a 2011 report of the International Telecommunication Union, the average Internet penetration rates in the area are less than 12% while the world average is 30% with a 80% rate in developed areas [7]. In last ranked countries such as Burkina Faso, where the Internet penetration rate is as low as 1%, only around 0.2% of households have Internet access. Furthermore, in rural regions, the phenomenon is even more noticeable because of the limited infrastructure. This situation is not expected to evolve, at least not in the foreseeable future, as the priorities of the central government as well as of the local populations lie elsewhere. Actually, investing in telecommunication infrastructure will bring out social inconsistencies since the lack of health care centers, schools, and practicable roads has more damaging impacts on the communities.

Nevertheless, in Burkina Faso for example, about 85% of the workforce live on agricultural activities in rural areas. While communities have been mostly

K. Jonas, I.A. Rai, and M. Tchuente (Eds.): AFRICOMM 2012, LNICST 119, pp. 163–173, 2013.

engaged in subsistence farming, the revenues generated by commercial agriculture, with internationally demanded crops such as sugarcane and cotton, have incentivised peasants to produce for regional, national and international markets. Unfortunately, sub-Saharan farmers have limited means and must regroup in cooperatives that often require logistic support from central and local government officials. One example of such support is communication capabilities for disseminating strategic information to all members of the cooperative. These capabilities mostly consist of on-road transportations of cooperative representatives through scattered camps, villages and agricultural fields, to hold informative meetings. This schema, however, raises numerous issues, the most salient of which are : ❶ the regularity of the information in a world where e.g., feedstock prices fluctuate daily, if not hourly; ❷ the autonomy of cooperatives when financial and natural constraints, such as a bridge collapse during the rainy season, prevent the holding of a meeting; ❸ the possibility for a horizontal cooperation between cooperative members outside planned meetings; and ❹ the complexity/pertinence of the information transmitted when illiteracy is commonplace.

An alternate communication scheme could rely on the local peer-to-peer networking opportunities that arise when cooperative members carrying mobile devices meet and go their ways. This scheme allows to harness the potential of their many devices which can be interconnected in a P2P system for spreading information. Such a system is furthermore self-scalable and naturally balanced, since members can forward as well as retrieve information data [16], and is more suited to the context of rural areas, where farmers are mobile through agricultural fields, and through markets across neighboring villages.

This Paper. In this paper we propose to leverage the cultural model in sub-Saharan Africa to build a collaborative system for exchanging complex data among cooperative members scattered in different villages. In our approach, hereafter referred to as *Toolé*,[1] an opportunistic networking strategy allows to seamlessly propagate a piece of information while sidestepping the difficulties encountered in existing scenarios.

The main contributions of this paper are as follows:

✓ We propose an approach to cooperative-level communication of strategic information data based on opportunistic networking scenarios.
✓ We discuss the opportunity for our approach by revisiting the challenges in collecting, computing and conveying strategic information to and within remote rural areas.
✓ We demonstrate the suitability of opportunistic networking solutions in sub-Saharan Africa through an assessment based on different criteria established in existing literature.

---

[1] *Toolé* refers to an object or/and a message that a given person is asked to deliver to a third party on behalf of someone else. The word is borrowed from mòoré, a major native language of Burkina Faso, and is part of a culture where people by solidarity assist each other in forwarding one's news to his distant relatives or conveying commissions of goods.

✓ We also propose a network architecture based on affordable technologies such as Bluetooth for local P2P communications and NFC for configuring and automating these communications.

The rest of this paper is organized as follows: Section 2 discusses the relevance of ICT in the process of disseminating information in rural areas and the associated challenges. Section 3 presents the context of sub-Saharan Africa with its challenges as well as the cultural facts that are leveraged in this work. Section 4 presents our approach through a real-world application scenario and details the network entities involved as well as a snapshot overview of the algorithms. Section 5 discusses related work and Section 6 concludes.

2   Using ICT in Sub-Saharan Rural Areas

In recent years the focus has shifted on the fight against rural poverty as a sound strategy for hastening development in third-world countries. ICT has then been relied upon to support governments as well as NGOs' initiatives that were directed at finding ways to improve peasants' incomes. In this context, researchers and practitioners alike have shown a keen interest to e-agriculture, which involves the use of ICT for rural development, with a primary focus on sustainable agriculture. One of the main questions in the field is how to *effectively* provide *useful* and *reliable* information to farmers in remote areas. While many projects have proposed various innovations with relative success, we believe that the situation is still unfavorable in many parts of Sub-Saharan Africa because general-purpose off-the-shelf solutions attempt to make users accommodate with the products instead of exploiting properties of the deployment context. Before diving into the description of the different facets of our approach, we revisit in this section the challenges that arise when attempting to build and disseminate "meaningful" information within rural areas.

Useful Information : From What and for Whom? A basic research question that arises in the implementation of ICT solutions for rural areas is : *what types of complex information do farmers need for the prosperity of their activities?* Unfortunately, there appears to be no clear vision of how the agricultural sector should develop in terms of ICT adoption in maximizing benefits for the farmer community [6]. Besides, collecting and disseminating information to improve agricultural steps is a tedious endeavor as service providers must be able to determine *real user needs*. Finally, because coordination of professionals is improbable in sub-Saharan Africa [18], e-agriculture, which requires a *tight coordination* between the agribusiness and professionals, including farm engineers, ICT service providers, soil analysts and e-government agencies, can hardly be implemented successfully.

As a starting point of our approach, we believe that the priority should remain on creating communication channels between farmers, allowing them to benefit from their own experience. Information from external partners need only be advertised at *one end of one communication channel*, the system being responsible for routing it to all participating farmers.

Effective Information : What and How? The actual synthesis of the information is another challenge : *is information directed to rural populations easily extractable and readily accessible to them?* These issues are indeed often overlooked in the process of designing ICT for rural areas, leaving solutions incomplete or unsuitable to the deployment context. Rural radio stations as a mass information dissemination medium is not necessarily suitable for detailing e.g. usage protocols of soil entrants, and for an on-the-need information. Nevertheless, one-to-one communication with cellular phones are still expensive resource-wise.

We believe that establishing communication channels between farmers should improve load balancing by reducing the number of communication sessions with outside support teams while leaving the possibilities for pushing relevant information for specific groups.

Reliable Dissemination: How? Finally, we raise the question of *how information is conveyed into and within rural areas?* In the past decade, the trend has been to take advantage of the vulgarization of mobile phones as a way in the information society. This solution however has its limits: (1) cost of voice is still relatively high; (2) mobile phones, because of their "personal" aspect, do not really integrate the idea of community; (3) text messages, while a global phenomenon, are useless because of high rates of illiteracy. With the recent advances in electronics, cheap, yet powerful, devices have emerged, which can be used as handheld dashboards by farmers. These devices have capabilities for (a) one-to-one and free-of-charge connections with (b) various display modes for representing data in illiterate-friendly formats such as graphs.

We propose to rely on these devices in rural areas to seamlessly build opportunistic, delay-tolerant, networks that reflect the culture of Sub-Saharan populations and provide the means to disseminate strategic information. We discuss in the following the suitability of opportunistic networks to sub-Saharan Africa, to provide the basis for encouraging such networking solutions.

3   Opportunity of Opportunistic Networking in Africa

Opportunistic networks have lately emerged as a viable alternative networking solution for environments where the communication can afford to be challenged by sporadic and intermittent contacts as well as frequent disconnections and reconnections. In this setting, the assumption of the existence of an end-to-end path between the source and the destination is relinquished. We thus find this type of Delay Tolerant Networks to be suitable to the realities of sub-Saharan rural areas. Nonetheless, the deployment of communication systems based on such networks often face fierce criticism from skeptics who question the benefits and long-term value-added of these types of networks [8]. In this section, we revisit the targeted environment to highlight the practical issues that constitute the main barriers to the development of conventional ICT infrastructures. Subsequently we discuss various aspects of the society in this environment that can be explored for proposing a new networking scheme.

In most rural areas of sub-Saharan Africa, there is almost no ICT infrastructure [2]. Information is usually carried by travellers from the city to villages and across villages. Unfortunately, existing roadways accommodate only rural inhabitants who, somehow, can manage with unreliable road transportations during rainy seasons and through zones where bandits are running wild. Immediate networking solutions such as extending the operators' networks into these areas are simply economically infeasible and politically unjustifiable. In rural areas where there is some partial coverage of cellular networks, due to the limited infrastructure, it is impossible to exchange complex data requiring processing steps which may be costly in terms of bandwidth resources for conveying rich information, and computation power for displaying them. There is thus a need for exploring different networking models.

Opportunistic networks, however, present challenges, inherent to the deployment context, that must be carefully dealt with to ensure the success of the application scenarios. We discuss such challenges in the following to demonstrate how cultural models in Sub-Saharan Africa make the case for opportunistic networks. To this end we refer to the conclusions of Lindgren and Hui when they discussed the quest for a *killer app* for opportunistic and delay tolerant networks [8].

Technology Constraints. Opportunistic networks usually rely on short range radios whose characteristics, however, also form the constraints in the design of applications scenarios. The Bluetooth technology, which is widespread in mobile devices and consumes relatively few resources, is limited in terms of the number of simultaneous paired devices. The length of discovery and setup times also constitute important limitations that can hinder the success of a solution where data transfer must remain transparent to the users' regular activities.

The impact of the first limitation is manageable since sub-Saharan rural population density is low [5]. In regular places where the studied scenario is likely to benefit from interconnection opportunities, peasants often regroup in small committees following some criteria of a culturally-defined hierarchy. Furthermore, in sub-Saharan context, members of communities regularly cross paths, leading to a reduction of discovery and connection times as their devices store information about each other.

Human Dynamics. Understanding the target environment and the behavior of potential actors in an opportunistic network is vital to establish the concreteness of the opportunity for interconnecting users in a regular and efficient basis. Daily life of sub-Saharan farmers evolve around agricultural activities in remote fields and trades during market days [19]. Market places, which are generally located at the intersection of all roads leading to the village, constitute the point of arrival/departure for travellers. They also serve various purposes including village meetings [11], and can thus host a central hub for a community network.

For most rural villages in Burkina Faso, market days occur every 3 days without break and provide the opportunities to meet the other people who walk or bike from closest villages. During these days, farmers spend their time, in small groups, conversing and drinking the local beer with their acquaintances, thus creating the opportunities for exchanging data.

Participation Incentives. An application scenario for delivering communication channels through opportunistic networking is only feasible if there are incentives for users to sustain the network. Boot-strapping the adoption of an opportunistic application is thus the first challenge for its success. Another challenge consists in devising an application scenario that users can identify with.

The success of the *microcredit* phenomenon in recent years in developing regions has proved that people feel more familiar and comfortable with concepts that borrow from their own tradition [17]. In sub-Saharan Africa, people trust each other with their verbal messages or letters to forward to a recipient with the possibility for these letters to be handed over to intermediate people who may have no relationship with the initial sender nor the final addressee. Opportunistic networking will therefore fit in such a context.

Business Models. An important challenge with opportunistic solutions is to ensure that they build atop a business model where it makes sense for a service provider to support them. Infrastructure costs and operating expenses can indeed constitute important barriers for the adoption of different applications.

As developed by Brewer *et al.*, when designing solutions for developing regions, the focus must remain on shared technology, such as community kiosks, and even shared devices [4]. Sub-Saharan rural areas indeed have a history of shared technology including tractors and other hardware that are part of a cooperative's resources. The deployment and maintenance of a system for an efficient communication within the community can then also be considered as part of the services that cooperatives provide to their subscribing members.

4   The Toolé Approach

We discuss in this section our approach of opportunistic networking for rural areas. Rather than detailing the algorithms required for ensuring efficiency in the establishment and the management of the network, we focus on the high-level strategies. For more information on the algorithms, we refer the reader to our previous work on the propagation of software updates in high-cost and/or low-bandwidth connectivity areas [3]. To illustrate the approach we rely on a use-case with common rural cooperatives.

4.1   Empowering Rural Cooperative Members

Farmer Adama is a member of an agricultural cooperative which has members in several villages of a rural area. Regularly, whilst engaging in his daily work, Adama gathers information data on his agricultural activities (weight of harvest, local sale prices, quality assessment of products, growth of plants, etc.) and stores them in his *Toolé*-compliant mobile device, using a dedicated application that is illiterate-friendly. The data thus saved by Adama could benefit to other members of his cooperative for their immediate needs such as comparison of strategies, prediction of harvest, inference of best market prices. It can also be recovered and merged with data from other participants to track the evolution of the agricultural situation in a given area. Thus, a synthesis of all information must be performed consistently and transferred among cooperative members within Adama's village and into nearby villages. Because of the complexity of the data, available communication lines are unfit to properly convey the information.

Sharing Locally. As in most villages, at the end of a day of labor, Adama and his farmer friends regroup in one of the establishments that serve the traditional millet beer to discuss, thus providing the opportunities for their devices to synchronize their data through crossed communications that remain seamless and transparent to the farmers. By duplicating all data into every other farmer's device, the approach brings all farmers' devices to the same level of information, thus allowing any of them to forward the message from this village to another.

Storing Reliably. Since local sharing may not enable an effective dissemination of local information into nearby villages, we resort to the widely used strategy of a *black box* located at the center of the village, namely the market. After the meeting where local synchronization was performed, one of the participants heads towards the marker and taps - by approaching very near - his device to the black box. This initiates a rapid transfer of all *Toolé* data into the box. This box, which serves as the community high-capacity database, is a "central hub" that enables a coherent merging of all distributively collected data for multiple cooperatives. It also includes a computation module for synthesizing agricultural information statistics into illiterate-friendly diagrams.

Algorithm 1. Given a commuter C and a set of "unforwarded" information P_k from villages $V_k \cdot k \in \{a, ..., z\}$, select the best pieces of information for commissioning C

Input: $\{V_a, ..., V_z\}$, $\{P_j, ..., P_m\}$
$\{V_i^{urd}, ..., V_{i+n}^{urd}\} \leftarrow$ usual_itinerary(C)
$\{V_j^{prd}, ..., V_{j+m}^{prd}\} \leftarrow$ predictItinerary($\{V_i^{urd}, V_{i+1}^{urd}, ..., V_{i+n}^{urd}\}$)
commissions $\leftarrow \emptyset$
foreach $V_k \in \{V_j^{prd}, V_{j+1}^{prd}, ..., V_{j+m}^{prd}\}$ **do**
   if $\exists P_c \in \{P_j, ..., P_m\} \wedge c = k$ **then**
      commissions $\leftarrow \{$commissions, $P_c\}$

return commissions

Disseminating Globally. Synthesized data stored in the black box needs to be conveyed to neighboring villages to implement an epidemic propagation of cooperative data. In our approach, any farmer commuting to another village, e.g. to attend a market day, can willingly tap his phone on the black box, automatically triggering the transfer of data that the farmer will deliver to his destination black box or to someone else who will, following the culturally-established system of "commissions" in sub-Saharan Africa. It is to be noted that the black box encompasses some intelligence that allows it to track the routes of information across villages and the identities of farmers who transported the data. These traces allow for more efficiency in the select of the best traveller and the best portion of transfer data to match for commissioning. Algorithm 1 provides an overview of the strategy used by the black box to automatically choose the best data to commission a known traveller. With its perpetual learning model which allows it to reconsider evolving information, e.g., as after a bridge collapse (see Fig. 1), that redefines the paths between villages, the Toolé approach ensures that information from a given village will be widely advertised and that no village will remain isolated from the rest.

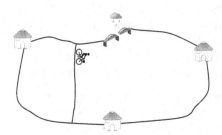

A villager B is biking regularly from village V_i to village V_j for his trade needs. The black box in village V_i has kept track of this travel pattern. After a change in the routines of other commuters, the algorithm "learns" that the road to Village V_j now passes through Village V_k (e.g., a bridge has collapsed). The black boxes forwards, into B's Toolé device, all pieces of information for Villages V_j and V_k as both now belong to the traveler's *predicted* path (cf. Algorithm 1).

Fig. 1. The Black box is an intelligent entity : Inference from environmental events

4.2   Architecture

We briefly highlight aspects of the architecture that we have devised to support our opportunistic scheme. It is a question of defining a system that takes advantage of the local connectivity capabilities of mobile phones to spread, in an efficient way, complex agricultural information in places where they are needed. The architecture is thus built to sustain the operation of three main processes as illustrated in Fig. 2: (1) a seamless local exchange of personal agricultural data among farmers devices; (2) an efficient and automated provision of data into the black box; and (3) a fast and reliable retrieval from the black boxes in neighboring villages.

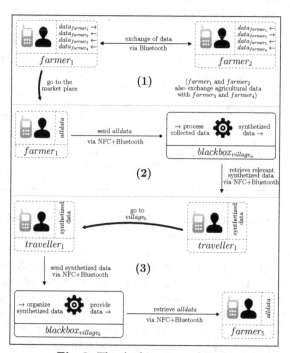

Fig. 2. The Architecture of Toolé

Bluetooth and Data Exchange. We resort to the Bluetooth technology for enabling a free, reliable and opportune communication between devices carried by the farmers and between devices and the black boxes. In previous sections, we have already noted the flaws of Bluetooth, especially its pairing latency and the limitations in simultaneous connections. We have discussed however, how these issues remain irrelevant because of the characteristics of rural areas.

NFC and Transfer Automation. The Near Field Communication technology is gaining ground as a promising technology for simplifying the triggering of radio communications [1]. We rely on the NFC standards which are increasingly implemented in cheap feature-devices, such as the Sagem Cosy Phone [2], to automate the synchronization between Toolé devices and the black box by enabling a seamless and transparent initialization of Bluetooth connections.

5   Related Work

In our work effort to setup bridges between rural areas in Sub-Sahara n Africa and the Information society, we have focused on the organization of cooperatives as they presented an immediate need to access global information. Based on experiences of other researchers that attempted to improve ICT coverage in developing regions, we have taken a backwards approach and reviewed the cultural model of rural societies to establish the suitability of opportunistic networks. Related work therefore span different domains from both technical and social categories.

Cooperatives in Africa. The International Labour Office 2008 report entitled "Cooperating out of poverty" sets the tone on the omnipresence of cooperatives in Africa [13], where they represent a significant part of the private sector in most countries. Such regroupments have show an extraordinary effectiveness in improving peasants' livelihood through initiatives that are born of and reflect their own culture [15]. Nevertheless, in today's global economy, cooperative are now required to integrate themselves to the information society, a step that is complicated by the lack of ICT infrastructure.

ICT in Developing Regions. With the Dot-com bubble, many have seen ICT as the long-waited tool to help close the gap between industrialized countries and the developing world by allowing the latter to leapfrog into the Information economy [10]. Nevertheless the global indicators of ICT development in Sub-Sahara n Africa are still low. Following the Internet bubble, community Internet kiosks as well as public telecenters had boomed in sub-Saharan, but have rapidly declined as interest from under-equipped users has faded [2]. The mobile phone appears today as the new archetypal application allowing users to be producers and encouraging innovations as opposed to simply consuming information. In our work, we propose a step forward to improve this innovation

---

[2] http://www.nfcworld.com/2010/09/10/34448/
hands-on-sagem-wireless-new-nfc-enabled-cosyphone/

process by relying on more efficient networking, and by exploiting more link opportunities.

Opportunistic Networking. Opportunistic networking has been successful in recent years as researchers attempt to leverage the strong patterns of encounters and movements that are involved in human daily activities. Leveraging the notion of *familiar stranger* [14] in big cities, Papadopouli and Schulzrinne [12] and McNamara *et al.* [9] have proposed content dissemination through opportunistic contacts, e.g. in urban transports. In previous work, we have proposed the Typhoon Middleware for epidemic propagation on mobile software updates based on opportunistic networking [3].

These works however remain targeted at demonstrating research state-of-the-art without realistic purposes of impacting real-world scenarios. In this paper, Toolé, is directed at rural areas where peasants can actually benefit from opportunistic networking as a viable road towards integrating the information society.

6   Conclusion

ICT for development has been for the past decade a prolific research field shared by technology enthusiasts, social studies scholars, and NGO members. Despite the proliferation of ideas and solutions proposed, the usage of ICT is still sparse in sub-Sahara n Africa. In this paper we have introduced the Toolé approach for leveraging the cultural model and traditions of sub-Saharans to build opportunistic networks. We have discussed the challenges in today's architectures and presented our approach, using a scenario with rural cooperatives. Another contribution of this paper is the discussion provided on the opportunity of opportunistic networking in Africa, to encourage the exploration of such solutions.

References

1. Near field communication in the real world - turning the nfc promise into profitable, everyday applications. Technical report, Innovision Research and Technology (2007)
2. Alemneh, D.G., Hastings, S.K.: Developing the ICT infrastructure for Africa: overview of barriers to harnessing the full power of the internet. Journal of Education for Library and Information Science 41(1), 4–16 (2006)
3. Bissyandé, T.F., Réveillère, L., Bromberg, Y.-D., Falleri, J.-R.: Typhoon: A middleware for opportunistic propagation of software updates. In: M-MPAC (2011)
4. Brewer, E., Demmer, M., Du, B., Ho, M., Kam, M., Nedevschi, S., Pal, J., Patra, R., Surana, S., Fall, K.: The case for technology in developing regions (May 2005)
5. Dorosh, P., Wang, H.G., You, L., Schmidt, E.: Road connectivity, population, and crop production in sub-saharan africa. Agricultural Economics 43(1) (2012)
6. Harkin, M.: ICT Adoption as an Agricultural Information Dissemination Tool - An Historical Perspective
7. International Telecommunication Union. Measuring the information society (2011)

8. Lindgren, A., Hui, P.: The quest for a killer app for opportunistic and delay tolerant networks (invited paper). In: CHANTS, pp. 59–66 (2009)
9. McNamara, L., Mascolo, C., Capra, L.: Media sharing based on colocation prediction in urban transport. In: MobiCom, pp. 58–69 (2008)
10. Negroponte, N.: The third shall be first. Wired Magazine 6(1) (1998)
11. Obiechina, E.N.: Culture, tradition and society in the West African novel. Syndics of the Cambridge University Press (1975)
12. Papadopouli, M., Schulzrinne, H.: Effects of power conservation, wireless coverage and cooperation on data dissemination among mobile devices. In: MobiHoc 2011 (2011)
13. Patrick Develtere, I.P., Wanyama, F.: Cooperating out of poverty: The renaissance of the African cooperative movement. International Labour Office (2009)
14. Paulos, E., Goodman, E.: The familiar stranger: anxiety, comfort, and play in public places. In: CHI, pp. 223–230 (2004)
15. Pradervand, P.: Listening to Africa: developing Africa from the grassroots. Greenwood Pub. Group Inc. (1989)
16. Shakkottai, S., Srikant, R.: Peer to peer networks for defense against internet worms. In: Interperf, p. 5 (2006)
17. United Nations. Microfinance in africa: Combining the best practices of traditional and modern microfinance approaches towards poverty eradication (2000)
18. Weszkalnysa, G.: The governance of daily life in africa: ethnographic explorations of public and collective services. Review of African Political Eco. 38(128) (2011)
19. Wood, L.J.: The functional structure of a rural market system. Geografiska Annaler. Series B, Human Geography 57(2), 109–118 (1975)

Analysis of Mobile Phone e-Waste Management for Developing Countries: A Case of Uganda

Julianne S. Sansa-Otim, Philip Lutaaya, Tom Kamya,
and Stephen Mutaawe Lubega

Department of Networks,
School of Computing & Informatics Technology,
Makerere University, Kampala, Uganda
sansa@cit.mak.ac.ug, lutaphilo@gmail.com,
k_k762001@yahoo.com, smutaawe@yahoo.co.uk

Abstract. Although considerable efforts are being made by many Governments and other entities in tackling waste-related problems, there are still major gaps to be filled in this area. The current practices of e-waste management in Uganda suffer from a number of problems such as informal recycling, inadequate legislation, lack of awareness from the stakeholders and limited government efforts. In addition to these e-waste management challenges, this paper also discusses the strategies to address this emerging problem in Uganda, considering related efforts in some regions such as Asia-Pacific, Europe and elsewhere in Africa. The paper mainly focuses on Mobile phone e-waste, with emphasis on safe disposal and recycling strategies.

Keywords: mobile phone e-waste, mobile phone e-waste management strategy.

1 Introduction

Electronic Waste (e-waste) comprises of waste electronics/electrical goods that are not fit for their originally intended use or have reached their end of life. Such products include computers and mobile phones. The fast growing application of Information and Communication Technology (ICT) means there is a rapid increase in number of computers, mobile phones and related accessories. This has led to a proportional increase in the e-waste stream not only in industrialized nations but also in developing countries like Uganda.

The challenge of managing e-waste is of greater concern in developing countries than elsewhere because they lack the capacity to handle and recycle the hazardous materials contained in e-waste. Furthermore, disposal of e-waste in dumpsites pollutes the environment, creating health hazards to the nearby community. Additionally, e-waste contains toxic materials that can pose danger to the human respiratory system, reproductive system, circulatory system and nervous system. Improper disposal of e-waste creates evironmental impacts such as global warming, depletion of resources, air and water pollution [1].

K. Jonas, I.A. Rai, and M. Tchuente (Eds.): AFRICOMM 2012, LNICST 119, pp. 174–183, 2013.

More applications are being developed for the mobile phone platform and the future focuses on evolving this device into a hand-held computer [2]. This implies that more mobile devices will be in circulation due to diversity of applications. Therefore, there is an urgent need for strategies to manage and control hazardous mobile phone e-waste.

In Uganda, the ministry of ICT under NITA-U has a draft policy on Electronic waste [3]. The main aim of the policy is to enable a sustainable e-waste management for a safe environment and a healthy nation. As a measure to minimize e-waste in Uganda, the government in 2009 imposed a ban on used electronics such computers and fridges [4]. However, this did not control the number of used mobile phones penetrating the Ugandan market. The United Nations Development Organization (UNIDO) also commissioned a research on e-waste in Uganda [5]. Its report shows that government has the highest number of ICT infrastructure followed by NGOs and large enterprises. The report indicates that there are few resources to manage this e-waste. Given the limited data available on used mobile phones, little attention has been subjected to this category of e-waste.

Therefore, this paper presents the challenges of managing mobile phone e-waste and proposes strategies to address these challenges. The rest of the paper is organized as follows: Section 2 discusses related work, while Section 3 describes the research approach used. Sections 4 discusses the challenges of mobile phone e-waste management in Uganda and the strategies to address these challenges. Section 5 discusses a comparison of proposed e-waste flow with existing strategies. Finally Section 6 contains the concluding remarks and the future work.

2   Related Work

E-waste is an increasing concern in the world and many countries in Europe have started to strictly regulate it. Developed countries like New Zealand have gone further to implement policies and establish regulatory mechanisms for controlling e-waste [6]. Murali [6], highlights that for developing countries, a dedicated policy should be put in place to offer clear guidlines on handling e-waste. Mobile phones like many other modern electronic items contain toxic metals such as Arsenic, Beryllium, Cadmium, Copper and Nickel, which should not be disposed of in ordinary trash. Almost 90% of toxic metals and other materials found in mobile phones can be recovered to make new products. It is good practice for countries to establish collection centers that collect all materials from disposed mobile phones. On the other hand, ICT (computers and mobile phones) has been on the increase all over the world. Table 1 shows the level of ICT (mobile phone and PCs) in East Africa.

From Table 1, there is an increase in mobile phone users from 1.59% in 2003 to 27.02% by the year 2010 for Uganda in particular. This shows an increase in number of mobile phone users. Therefore, it is important to keep track of the life end of these rapidly increasing mobile phones in the country. A few studies about the E-waste management exist in different countries like India, China,

Table 1. ICT Use in EAC year 2010 and 2003 (Source: Edgar Napoleon, [7])

COUNTRY	ESTIMATED INTERNET USERS (%)		MOBILE PHONE USERS (%)		PERSONAL COMPUTERS (%)	
Year	2010	2003	2010	2003	2010	2003
Uganda	7.9	0.2518	27.02	1.59	1.69	0.29
Kenya	8.67	1.5978	47.88	4.15	1.37	0.56
Tanzania	1.22	0.2977	30.62	1.27	0.91	0.36
Rwanda	3.09	0.2516	13.61	1.7	0.30	0
Burundi	0.81	0.0875	5.95	0.45	0.85	0

New Zealand [8] and United States among others. In New Zealand, emphasis is on establishing an integrated and comprehensive national hazardous waste policy to cover reduction, transport, treatment and proper disposal of hazardous waste [8]. The recycling programme in New Zealand is available to all customers via telecom retail stores where partners receive all phones and accessories either for refurbishment or recycling. This ensures that old mobile phones and other consumer generated e-waste do not end up in landfills, potentially causing environmental damage.

The recent quantity of e-waste for most African countries including South Africa, Kenya, Uganda and Senegal were presented by Muller in [9] and Mathias in [10] for Tanzania. Other country reports on e-waste generated from mobile phones were also presented, including Asia and the Pacific [11]. These reports show an increasingly large amount of mobile phone e-waste such as batteries, Liquid Crystal Displays (LCDs), headsets and chargers. This suggests an urgent need for these countries to control mobile phone e-waste. B. Twanza in [4] summarized some of the challenges of e-waste practices in Uganda and later suggested the new trends and action plans to tackle e-waste in general. In her report, most of the strategies suggested lack clarity on how they should be established and who should monitor such implementations. The roles of most stakeholders including mobile phone companies, NEMA and UNBS were not highlighted. Our study focuses on mobile phone e-waste since the mobile phone usage in Uganda is continuously growing. In addition, our study also specifies the relevant organisations/institutions and their roles in handling mobile phone e-waste.

3   Study Approach

This section discusses the methods and approaches taken to identify challenges and strategies to manage mobile phone e-waste in Uganda. These include the following;

- Reading and analyzing the existing e-waste management strategies in other countries.
- Identifying any existing strategies in Uganda as regards the e-waste management problem.

- Suggesting any possible improvements to combat the e-waste problem.
- Understanding and assessing the lifecycle of mobile phones.
- Reviewing e-waste disposal mechanisms including conducting field visits to dump sites and interviews.
- Identifying potential barriers and possible interventions in support of a successful e-waste management program.

4 Mobile Phone e-Waste Management Challenges and Strategies

4.1 Challenges

Mobile phone e-waste management suffers challenges faced by general e-waste management which includes informal recycling, inadequate legislation, lack of awarenesss from stakeholders and limited government efforts [4]. In addition, more challenges facing mobile phone e-waste management in Uganda are identified in this study including the following: (i) Exportation of e-waste material which cannot be treated locally is complicated, since Uganda is a landlocked country. There is insufficient funding for transportation of this waste to recycling plants located in other countries. (ii) For dumpsites in particular, field studies were conducted to assess the challenges while dumping e-waste. After conducting field studies at Kampala City Council Authority (KCCA) dumping site at Namere in Mpererwe, we found out that there are no qualified personnel and infrastructure to manage the ever increasing volumes of mobile phone electronic waste. As a result, many obsolete products are still in use and others improperly disposed of.

4.2 Strategies

Here we discuss the strategies to address challenges mentioned above. The strategies aim at clear mechanism for reduction, recycle, recovery and reuse of hazardous mobile phone e-waste in Uganda. They will also ensure that this e-waste is treated and disposed of properly. These strategies will assist different stakeholders to create awareness among mobile phones users in the country, hence learning the effects of improper disposal of mobile phones to the environment. The strategies are mentioned below:

Establishment of Mobile Phone e-Waste Facilities to Customers (A)

Mobile service providers (or telecom companies) and manufacturers can establish facilities such as collection centers, to accept mobile phone e-waste from consumers. Using their retail shops which are managed by reknown retailers and distributors, manufacturer and service providers can use the same centers to collect obsolete mobile phones. This will ensure that manufacturers and service providers collect and recycle a significant fraction of products they sell every year or after a specific period of time, from each region of the country. All service providers and manufacturers who fail to meet these requirements can be requested to pay an additional recycling fee as a penalty.

Establish and Maintain a Mobile Phone e-Waste Fee (B)

This strategy aims at imposing an annual tax on all registered importers of used mobile phones and mobile phone accessories by the government. This will assist government in regulating the number of used mobile phones that enter the Ugandan market by controlling the percentage imports done by each taxed company. Taxes on used mobile phones should be high enough to discourage consumers from buying used mobile phones. In addition, consumers should pay a fee at purchase of new mobile phone products. This fee will be used to fund recycling and safe disposal of mobile phone e-waste. The government's duty will be monitoring the proper use of this fee.

Restrict or Completely Ban Mobile Phones Containing Higher Volumes of Hazardous Material (C)

Uganda National Bureau of Standards (UNBS) can identify mobile phone types that have higher content of hazardous material, as well as setting acceptable standards for this content. This will ensure that all mobile devices that enter into the Ugandan market constitute of materials that are less harmless to the environment. Bans and restrictions on certain substances can be imposed such that harmful substances do not get into the Ugandan Market.

Mobile Phone Life Cycle Assessment (D)

Mobile phone lifecycle assessment involves carrying out an evaluation of effects of a mobile phone to the environment from manufacturing to end of life. National Environmental Management Authority (NEMA) should assess the impacts of a mobile phone to the environment. Information about the generation of hazardous wastes and their lifecycle, tracking them through to safe disposal, recovery or recycling should be freely accessible by the public. This will ensure that all stakeholders have the necessary information about the mobile phone products and their dangers to the environment at their end of life. The academia should also play an important role by conducting research about mobile phone e-waste, assess the dangers and impact on the environment. In Korea, the recycling practices emphasized an extended producer responsibility program which involves electronic producers taking more responsibility for managing environmental impacts of their products throughout their lifecycle [12]. We propose a mobile phone e-waste flow for a developing country, a case of Uganda as illustrated in Figure 1. This will ensure safe disposal and recycle of mobile phone e-waste. In urban areas, mobile phone repair centers and retailers are the central points for collecting mobile phone e-waste from consumers. For rural areas specifically, e-waste will be collected by the local governments and repair centers. A small fee is given as an incentive to consumers by retailers, mobile phone repair centers or local governments to encourage them dispose of these obsolete products. When received from consumers, the mobile phone e-waste is sorted to identify recyclable and non-recyclable components. Local governments, retailers and repair

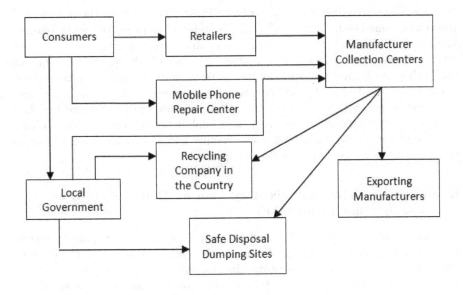

Fig. 1. Proposed e-waste flow for Uganda

centers forward this mobile phone e-waste for recycling, safe disposal or alternatively to the manufacturer collection centers. The manufacturers collect the e-waste from their collection centers and thereafter, forward it to safe disposal dumping sites or to a local recycling company. Mobile phone e-waste components that cannot be recycled in Uganda can be exported to other countries by the exporting manufacturers.

The most cost effective and less administrative way of collecting mobile phone e-waste is by using repair centers and retailers since they deal with the consumers directly. This way, the consumers will get incentives thus encouraging them to dispose of obsolete mobile phones. This cost is recovered when the retailers and repair centers forward this mobile phone e-waste to the manufacturer collection centers. This practice has been successful in Uganda with products such as computers, paper and recyclable plastic bottles. Using the local government is administrative, but this option can be used in rural areas to reach the remote population where very few mobile phone retailers exist.

Creating Public Awareness (E)

All stakeholders will be involved in creating public awareness by educating and informing the entire population about dangers of mobile phone e-waste to the environment. This will provide more information to the consumers and other stakeholders about the dangers of mobile phones. This can extensively be implemented through media houses with the aim of educating different target groups. Public awareness in rural areas can be done through local authorities in local languages that they understand best. This will assist even the uneducated group to acquire the necessary information about the dangers of mobile phones. Manufacturers and mobile service providers should play a great role above all other stakeholders. For example, manufacturers should label parts of the mobile phone that are hazardous (such as the battery) and educate consumers about improper disposal of such components to the environment. Additionally, mobile phone manufacturers can create a separate code that can reveal the date of expiry of a mobile phone. Furthermore, mobile service providers can create automated text message alerts that can remind users to return obsolete mobile phones and the dangers of improper disposal.

Establish and Maintain a Recovery Plan for Collection of Obsolete Products by Manufacturers (F)

Manufacturers and distributors need to implement a recovery plan to enable collection, recycling and reuse of end of life mobile phones and their accessories. Such plans include financing the collection of mobile phone e-waste. Manufacturer financed programs for collection of obsolete products should be freely available to all stakeholders. Little emphasis has been made in Uganda about the establishment of collection centers for used mobile phones. For example, it is only Midcom Uganda that has established such a center. However, this is specific to only Nokia phones. Other industry players should also join and establish user friendly mechanisms for collecting their obsolete mobile phone products.

Fig. 2. Mobile phone e-waste strategy implementation plan

Monitor and Control Entry of Mobile Phones at Border Points and Airports (G)

Regulatory bodies such as the Uganda Revenue Authority (URA) and Uganda National Bureau of Standards (UNBS) need to monitor and control the number of mobile phones penetrating the Ugandan market through border points and airports. This can be done through implementing an integrated customs enforcement system which gets personal information and details of importers and manufacturers. This can be used to track and control the number of mobile phones imported by individuals, importers and different manufacturers. For smuggled mobile phones, innovative methods to detect smuggled phones at border points and airports should be adopted.

From the strategies A to G, we designed a mobile phone e-waste management framework as illustrated in Figure 2. It summarizes the roles of different stakeholders including consumers, manufacturers, government (revenue, environment and standards agencies), mobile service providers and academia, among others.

5   Comparison of Proposed E-Waste Flow with Existing Strategies

In this section, we compare the proposed mobile phone e-waste flow with the existing strategies in other countries. German's approach is by separating e-waste using bins in homes [13]. This practice heavily relies on the willingness of the people to accept and separate this waste. This has cost implications since the bins where waste is disposed are costly. Secondly, there are privacy issues since garbage is collected from individual homes. For India and Switzerland, there are collection centers for e-waste [14]. Collection centers have cost and managerial implications. It is relatively cheaper to use existing mobile phone repair centers for collecting mobile phone e-waste than creating collection centers. It is only manufacturers who can make huge investments to create collection centers which are few in number but cover wider regions. Incentives should backup voluntary initiatives by consumers to dispose of obsolete mobile phones.

6   Conclusion and Future Work

Since mobile phones are on the increase all over the world and especially in the developing countries, it is important that their safe disposal is ensured. This paper has highlighted several challenges faced in mobile phone e-waste management in Uganda which are common to other developing countries. In addition, this paper had discussed strategies which, if embraced will reduce the challenges currently faced. Our contributions are; (i) a mobile phone e-waste flow as illustrated in Figure 1, which if properly controlled by the local government will ensure safe disposal, recycling and refurbishing of mobile phone e-waste. (ii) a mobile phone e-waste management framework as illustrated in Figure 2.

This framework is a multi-stakeholder partnership involving consumers, manufacturers, government (revenue, environment and standards agencies), mobile service providers and academia, among others. The roles of each stakeholder in tackling refurbishment, recycling and disposal of mobile phone e-waste are discussed.

The future includes setting up a database for all mobile phones from different manufacturers to keep track of the manufacture dates, details of importers and end of life period. This will ensure that manufacturers and importers are held responsible for collecting and recycling the obsolete products. Secondly, there are weak methods currently employed to detect smuggled mobile phones. While aiming at tracking smuggled mobile phones, innovative approaches such as using mobile phone detectors and scanners can be employed at border points and airports.

References

1. Pranshu, S., Salla, A., Gareth, R., Markus, S., Markus, T., van der Hans, W.: Key environmental performance indicators (kepis): A new approach to environmental assessment. In: International Congress and Exhibition on Electronics Goes Green 2004+, pp. 697–702 (2004)
2. Wobbrock, J.O.: The future of mobile device research in hci. In: CHI 2006 Workshop (2006)
3. ICT/NITA-U: Electronic Management Policy for Uganda (2010), www.ict.go.ug/index.php?option=com_docman&task=doc_download&gid=28&Item%id=61 (accessed: November 14, 2011)
4. Twanza, B.N.: Uganda (2010), http://www.giswatch.org/country-report/2010-icts-and-environmental-sustainability/uganda (accessed: March 10, 2012)
5. John, W., Mathias, S.: E-waste assessment in uganda (2008), http://ewasteguide.info/files/Wasswa_2008_UCPC-Empa.pdf (accessed: November 14, 2011)
6. Murali, S.: Tackling e-waste (2010), http://www.giswatch.org/sites/default/files/gisw2010thematictacklingewa%steen.pdf (accessed: June 10, 2011)
7. Edgar, A., Napoleon: E-waste management in east african community (2009), http://www.spidercenter.org/sites/default/files/master_theses/sponsored%/Edgar_Napoleon.pdf (accessed: April 4, 2010)
8. R. D: Policy framework to reduce and safely manage hazardous wastes in new zealand (2006), http://www.mfe.govt.nz/issues/waste/hazardous/policyframework/hazwaste-policy-framework.pdf (accessed: November 15, 2011)
9. Mathias, S., Christian, H., Ruediger, K., Federico, M., Claudia, M., Christina, M., Esther, M., Feng, W.: Recycling from e-waste to resources (2009), http://www.unep.org/PDF/PressReleases/E-Waste_publication_screen_FINALV%ERSION-sml.pdf (accessed: November 11, 2011)

10. Anne, M., Mathias, S.: E-waste assessment in Tanzania (2011),
    http://ewasteguide.info/files/Magashi_2011_CPCT-Empa.pdf
    (accessed: April 4, 2012)
11. Satyabrata, S., Nanjundappa, S.: Mobile phone waste. current initiatives in asia
    and the pacific (2008),
    www.techmonitor.net/tm/images/2/24/08julaugsf3.pdf (accessed: November 4,
    2011)
12. Hyunmyung, Y., Yong-Chul, J.: The practice and challenges of electronic waste re-
    cycling in korea with emphasis on Extended Producer Responsibility (EPR) (2009),
    http://www.revive-ewaste.com/casestudies/EPRinKorea.pdf
    (accessed: April 4, 2012)
13. Andreas, J., Rothkirch, G., Schulz, J.: Waste Management in Germany. A driving
    force for jobs and innovation (2006),
    http://wpage.unina.it/vsodano/germanialagestionedeirifiuti.pdf
    (accessed: October 12, 2012)
14. Sinha, D.: The management of electroninc waste: A comparative study in India
    and SwitZerland (2004),
    http://www.empa.ch/plugin/template/empa/*/59241/---/l=2
    (accessed: October 12, 2012)

Open Source in Africa: An Opportunity Wasted?
Why and How FLOSS Should Make Sense for Africa

Hadja Ouattara[1], Jonathan Ouoba[2,3], and Tegawendé F. Bissyandé[2,3]

[1] IST, Burkina Faso
[2] FasoLabs, Burkina Faso
[3] LaBRI, France
{hadja.sanon,jonathan.ouoba,tegawende.bissyande}@fasolabs.org

Abstract. We discuss the topic of a Master's thesis which aims at providing resources for an effective exploration of FLOSS opportunities in Africa. Indeed, in view of the potential of FLOSS, we believe that Africa's developing nations have much to gain from an increased involvement in free software. However, because vulgarization of FLOSS requires a new model of *need assessment*, we propose a road-map for making open-source a new strategic growth platform for Africa. To this end, we introduce in this paper the FLAIR pilot project.

Keywords: FLOSS, ICT4D, open source, Africa, development, FLAIR.

1 Introduction

Building on the potential of the digital economy is essential to countries across the world for a sustainable recovery from the current economic crisis. This *new economy* has, indeed, progressively become the most dynamic sector of the world economy, with a highly paced growth rate, among the few that were not durably affected by the crisis. In emerging countries where it was relied upon as a sustainable pillar of development, the new economy has allowed for the creation of millions of jobs. In developing nations, such as African countries, endless innovation opportunities are brought by the IT sector.

Based on rich services that are built atop software engineering projects, the digital economy has long been dominated by big ICT players such as Microsoft™ or IBM™ which have flooded the market with proprietary solutions whose substantial costs cannot be matched by the financial conditions of African populations, businesses and even governments. Recently, however, the paradigm of Free/Libre/Open Source Software(FLOSS) has brought openness in software engineering and has seen an increasing momentum, leading to the production of competitive software that often shadow their proprietary alternatives.

Unfortunately, even though FLOSS has shaped a new and ever-growing economy that is now supported by many governments around the world and that has steered the interest of prominent IT companies, such as Google™, significant adoption in many areas of Sub-saharan Africa is still lagging. Despite a few successful implementations of Open Source initiatives, such as software localization[1], most

---

[1] See. http://www.africanlocalisation.net

K. Jonas, I.A. Rai, and M. Tchuente (Eds.): AFRICOMM 2012, LNICST 119, pp. 184–188, 2013.

sub-Saharans involved with the information society ignore the reality of FLOSS [2]. At the same time, a large body of literature has been pointing out the numerous advantages of FLOSS to deliver development paths for developing countries [1]. What is at stake in such an unprecedented opportunity? What can be done?

This Paper. This paper summarises the work developed during a master thesis to produce an assessment model for allowing decision makers in businesses, education institutions, and governments, to objectively consider the opportunity of FLOSS.

Due to the limited space, we provide, in Section 2, a quick overview on the nature of FLOSS. Then, in Section 3, we concisely enumerate some benefits for adopting FLOSS in the context of Africa's developing nations. We subsequently explore, in Section 4, a roadmap for promoting FLOSS in Africa building on a community repository of shared insights: FLAIR. Section 5 describes the first steps and the current status of our project.

2   Disambiguating and Demystifying FLOSS

The concept of "free software" is often misunderstood in the user community. The GNU Free Software Foundation provides a regularly-updated definition where pioneers state how free software refers to software that users have the freedom to run, copy, distribute, study, change and improve. They emphasize in the definition of free software philosophy that it is not about the price of the software[2]. Rather, one should think of "free" as in "free speech", not as in "free beer". The word FLOSS was then coined at the beginning of the Dot-com bubble to regroup different terminologies that were, and still are, used interchangeably, to refer to free software.

FLOSS is pervasive in today's computing environments: Linux, the 10-year old operating system kernel, is one prominent success of open source development that is increasingly run in millions of personal computers as well as in mainframes and embedded systems. Free software is also strongly represented in web environments: the Apache HTTP server is omnipresent server-side while, client-side, the Firefox browser has rapidly recovered a large market share despite the fact that its main competitor comes preinstalled in the Windows commodity operating system. Open source development toolkits such as the Eclipse IDE have irreversibly penetrated most software engineering tasks. Finally, the vlc open source media player is reported on SourceForge[3] to be downloaded millions of times every week. There is thus a wide range of opportunities for alternative FLOSS software in all application areas, for every purpose and with different level of features and implementation complexity. Previous studies have however shown that Africa is the last-ranked region in terms of involvement with Opensource [3]. What can Africa gain from a gradual adoption of FLOSS in education, business, government, and at home?

---

[2] http://www.gnu.org/philosophy
[3] sourceforge.net

3   Seven Opportunities and Counting

FLOSS has been reported to provide huge opportunities to countries worldwide. Governments in emerging nations support FLOSS to mitigate costs, to ensure security by limiting dependence to foreign industries, to boost local economies, etc. The ongoing process of computerization that is sweeping through most african countries have lead to a surge of the demand for computer-related products, in particular software. Africa being the fastest growing markets for PC[4], what is at stake with the adoption of FLOSS? In the context of Africa's developing nations we focus on an incomplete list of 7 great opportunities for:

1. Cutting costs. Free software drastically reduces initial costs of software acquisition by waiving license fees. Furthermore, open source products often have limited hardware requirements, reducing the need for extra costs. These benefits are essential for managing cost-conscious budgets in african countries.

2. Enhancing education. An immense learning potential lies in FLOSS. African IT educations systems can leverage open source software for teaching good programming practices learned from the code, and thus contribute to mitigate the numerous insufficiencies in the prevailing inadequate curricula.

3. Fostering home grown companies. Promoting FLOSS would encourage young graduates to build start-ups that could seek and re-provide expertise in FLOSS products. Rather than calling upon foreign companies for proprietary solutions, adoption of FLOSS can empower local economies.

4. Building communities. One of the important upside of FLOSS is its tendency to bring people around a unique project. Building on the philosophy of open source development, african developers can pull together to investigate and address African needs in ICT4D.

5. Fighting piracy habits. Embracing open source software will undoubtedly contribute to the fight against piracy. Furthermore, due to flexible *use and reuse terms*, free software can be re-adapted to fit the context of Africa, its requirements, its needs and its facilities.

6. Strengthening independence. Because the philosophy of FLOSS does not permit any vendor lock-in, the use of free software will empower countries to be autonomous in their IT infrastructures, avoid the need for resorting to specific foreign companies, and estrange us from western "ways of doing IT".

7. Catching up with developed nations. Finally, FLOSS could be the best opportunity for Africa to leapfrog development stages in the area of IT. Indeed, with the possibility of code reuse, Africa does not have to start from scratch as it is the case for many other areas of science.

The above-mentioned opportunities have been seized in recently under-developed countries, such as India, allowing them to gracefully sustain their emergence. Then, why is FLOSS not leveraged in sub-Saharan Africa? What are the missing pieces to realize this?

---

[4] http://www.adzeevents.com/et/html/the_market_africa.html

4   FLAIR: FLoss Alternative Insights Repository

Two main reasons explain why sub-saharan Africa has not yet succeeded in fully leveraging the potentials of FLOSS: (1) First, managers and policy makers lack knowledge about the possibilities of open source and/or they do not trust the reliability of such software. Unfortunately, marketing has never been a priority for FLOSS developers. (2) Second, there are relatively few software engineers that have expertise in FLOSS solutions due to out-dated education curricula; companies willing to use FLOSS may also face the scarcity of local IT businesses that can offer good support. While we do not advocate for a global and immediate switch to FLOSS, we note that the research community can actually help to add the missing pieces in the exploration of FLOSS opportunities as depicted in Fig. 1. This master thesis aims at yielding two contributions in the roadmap for FLOSS in Africa:

Guidelines. First, an assessment model should be established with guidelines for helping developers, education institutions and businesses explore the possibilities of embracing open source. Similar to the concept behind ITIL[5], we wish to devise a library of best practices for first adoption or migration to FLOSS.

Repository. Second, we plan to setup an online repository to collect experiences of practitioners as well as expertise of developers about FLOSS. With the FLAIR repository we aim at providing insights in existing open-source alternatives, by identifying them, discussing their strengths and weaknesses, and allowing users to contribute with remarks on their hands-on experiences.

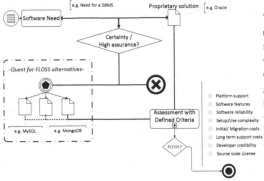

We highlight the example of a business seeking to setup a Database Management System. The proprietary DBMS that the management knows about is Oracle[TM]. Thanks to the extensive guidelines that we propose, they can first raise the question of a need to investigate other, less costly but as efficient, alternatives. To find those alternatives, the FLAIR repository is accessed and used to assess reported FLOSS instances based on criteria proposed by users.

Fig. 1. Work-flow for exploring the opportunity of FLOSS and discovering alternatives

5   Current Status

In the course of this project, we have already investigated the best practices in information systems and business intelligence for producing the guidelines.

---

[5] Information Technology Infrastructure Library –
http://www.itil-officialsite.com

To setup the prototype of FLAIR, we have undertaken to identify proprietary solutions and explore potential alternatives. To this end, we have sent forms to Universities of Burkina Faso to list all software that are used both by the staff and for teaching purposes. Based on this corpus, we hope to design a pilot portal for evaluating the first return-on-experience of FLAIR.

References

1. Ellis, J., Van Belle, J.-P.: Open source software adoption by south african mses: barriers and enablers. In: SACLA (2009)
2. Mtsweni, J., Biermann, E.: An investigation into the implementation of open source software within the sa government: an emerging expansion model. In: SAICSIT (2008)
3. Robles, G., Gonzalez-Barahona, J.M.: Geographic location of developers at source-forge. In: MSR (2006)

Social Accountability for Mozambique:
An Experience Report from the Moamba District

Aaron Ciaghi, Birhanu Eshete, Pietro Molini, and Adolfo Villafiorita

Fondazione Bruno Kessler,
via Sommarive 18,
38123 Trento, Italy
{ciaghi,eshete,pbmolini,adolfo.villafiorita}@fbk.eu
http://ict4g.fbk.eu

Abstract. Empowering citizens in making Governments more accountable and transparent in the services they provide has gained more attention in the last few years both in the developing and in the developed world. At the basis of any such exercise, information and data collection activities play an important role. In this paper we report on a pilot we conducted in collaboration with the Ministry of Education of Mozambique, the World Bank and the Maputo Living Lab to collect data about various procurement indicators of primary schools in the Moamba district of Mozambique. For this purpose we developed a data collection platform and a mobile application to conduct field work.

1 Introduction

Citizen involvement is critical for enhancing democratic governance, improving service delivery, and fostering empowerment. For these reasons many actors, among which the World Bank (see, e.g., [1]), have started or are starting initiatives to empower citizens in making their Governments more accountable and transparent.

Such empowerment, however, can be exercised if an adequate level of awareness and know-how are shared with and by the citizens. This includes not only information about a specific situation or the current status of things in a specific sector (like, e.g., the status of schools in a rural area), but also know-how about the chain of responsibility and accountability.

This paper reports on a pilot we conducted in the region of Moamba (Mozambique) in June 2012 about primary schools in the region. The pilot, sponsored by the World Bank and aided by a platform – called SAMo, Social Accountability for Mozambique – we developed for the project, involved 677 citizens who commented on various procurement indicators meant to measure the efficacy of specific interventions in the region. Our contribution includes an updated report on the status of various schools in the region, some technical consideration about platforms for crowdsourcing data, and some initial steps to better understand the process of social accountability.

K. Jonas, I.A. Rai, and M. Tchuente (Eds.): AFRICOMM 2012, LNICST 119, pp. 189–198, 2013.
© Institute for Computer Sciences, Social Informatics and Telecommunications Engineering 2013

This paper is organized as follows. In Section 2, we describe similar tools to collect data and promote social accountability. Section 3 describes physical and logical architecture of our solution. The pilot design and methodology used in the assessment are presented in Section 4. Section 5 discusses the major findings of the pilot study. Finally, Section 6 concludes the paper by highlighting future directions.

2   Related Work

Several ICT tools for collecting data in resource constrained regions and for social accountability have been developed in the recent years. Different organizations tackled the challenge of collecting data using mobile devices, including low-end mobile phones with only SMS and phone capabilities, in order to manage emergency situations. In this section we review the most relevant ones with respect to our platform.

The most popular technological tools to collect and deliver information in developing regions are doubtlessly SMS and PDA/smartphone based applications. We excluded voice-based solutions from our review because we rely on volunteers who interview directly the members of the target community. We evaluated existing tools starting from the requirements of direct interaction and openness of the data collects.

Among SMS based solutions, FrontlineSMS and RapidSMS [2] are the most complete and customizable solutions for our usage scenario. They are both free and open source frameworks for dynamic data collection, logistics coordination and communication via SMS. They have been adopted in a wide variety of scenarios such as remote health diagnostics, nutrition surveillance, supply chain tracking, registering children in public health campaigns, and community discussion. By being designed to work over an existing infrastructure, these SMS based solution present no particular cost for new equipment and have very limited bandwidth costs. However, in order to conduct the interview designed for our case study, the volunteers would have had to send structured data in a very compact and error prone fashion.

As low cost smartphones and tablets have become more widely available, PDA based data collection in developing regions has been replaced by smartphones and tablet based data collection. An early solution of information collection toolkit based on Java enabled phones – called CAM – was proposed by Parikh et al. [3]. CAM relies on a paper based form that was augmented by an application running on a mobile phone.

A more recent and more complete toolkit based on Android – Open Data Kit (ODK) [4,5] – has been developed and applied in a number of domains. ODK is a free and open-source set of tools to help organizations working in developing regions to collect data to make quick decisions. ODK has three major components. The first component is a mobile component that runs on Android phones. The second is a data storage component which runs in the cloud. The third is a web-based form builder to digitize paper forms for simple data collection or more complex surveys. ODK is limited to collecting survey responses and elaborating results. Social accountability is not an explicit goal of the project, although it is one of its use cases. Furthermore, SAMo is not designed to support generic data collections and it supports a strictly defined workflow, thus requiring a much simpler software stack than ODK.

When discussing social accountability, Ushahidi [6] is the most popular and widely deployed application that best fits in the domain. Ushahidi is an open-source platform to easily crowd-source incident reporting using multiple channels, including SMS, email, Twitter and the Web. It allows users to submit eyewitness reports during a conflict or disaster, which are displayed on a map in real time. In cases where ordinary sources of news and public information are missing, it gives users a way to share information and shape political opinion, guide rescuers, or pool resources. It has been used to monitor elections in Sudan, document violence in Gaza, track the BP oil spill, and assist earthquake recovery efforts in Haiti. Although Ushahidi is a solid tool for empowering citizens, it did not fit our needs as it requires a baseline to be known and it does not support any particular process. SAMo is designed with a more systematic approach in mind by presenting the users with structured interview forms for predefined targets as opposed to allowing users to send free form reports at arbitrary locations.

3   The SAMo Platform

In order to conduct our pilot study in Moamba, we developed a platform called SAMo (Social Accountability for Mozambique) to collect procurement indices defined by a set of indicators to evaluate management and procurement of structures funded by the World Bank and local governments, located primarily in rural areas. The platform allows authorized assessors to collect data through interviews and it allows citizens to freely access all the results of the interviews. The data collection is performed during a *Campaign* within a fixed time frame and on a fixed set of target services.

Figure 1 displays the high level components of SAMo. The platform is composed of a Ruby on Rails web application and a mobile application running on Android tablets. The web application takes care of collecting data from the field and of displaying the results, while the Android application is used on the field by assessors to collect data in areas with no Internet connectivity and later upload it to the server. The responses collected during interviews are temporarily stored in a SQLite database on the mobile device used for the assessment and they can be uploaded to the server as soon as data access is available.

3.1   Roles

SAMo is designed to be used by 3 types of users: Managers, Assessors and Citizens.

Managers can be officials of an organization (e.g., the World Bank) that need to measure the quality of procurement and management of a category of government or donor funded buildings. They can create new assessment campaigns,

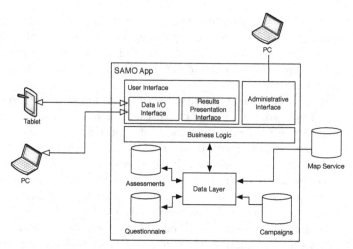

Fig. 1. Architecture of the SAMo platform

fix the goals of the evaluation, determine the indicators for the evaluation and enlist assessors to perform the interviews.

Assessors are responsible for collecting data about one or more targets during a campaign. An assessor acts as an intermediary between the Citizen and the SAMo platform.

Citizens are the ultimate beneficiaries of SAMo. They interact with Assessors by participating to interviews and they have access to the results and to aggregated reports on the SAMo website. Citizens have the actual ownership of the data and, in the long term, they will be provided with the technology for collecting data and generating reports themselves.

Different actors can take the roles mentioned above, depending on the actual campaign being conducted. For instance, an NGO active in the Education sector could use the application to conduct their evaluation campaigns having some of its personnel working as Assessors and some others working as Managers.

3.2   Data Model

Figure 2 depicts the core concepts of the data model on which SAMo is based.

The workflow of SAMo is centered on *Campaigns* conducted to assess a set of targets against a given set of indicators. A campaign contains a structured description of its goal, its data collection procedure, a time period during which data has to be collected, a set of *Targets* (services about which data is collected) and the *Indicators* to be collected for each target. One or more *Assessors* responsible for data collection is identified and assigned to the campaign. The assessors are tasked with the compilation of one *assessment* for each interview that they conduct. Assessors are independent from the people responsible for the implementation of the policies influencing the campaign targets to ensure a fairer evaluation.

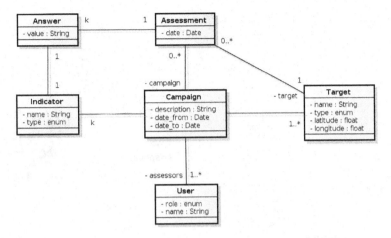

Fig. 2. SAMo Data Model

An indicator represents the specification of a measurement to be collected during an assessment for the targets of a campaign. An indicator is represented as a question during an assessment and is characterized by a type that constrains the type of value it can take (e.g., "Yes/No", "1-5 Likert scale", etc.). Indicators are reusable and are not strictly tied to a specific campaign.

Assessments are the unit of a SAMo campaign. They contain the responses collected during an interview related to one of the targets of the campaign. More specifically, they contain a reference to the assessor who conducted the interview, a reference to the target and the responses collected.

3.3 Workflow

SAMo aims at collecting and publishing the opinions of the end users of public services. Therefore, the typical usage workflow of the platform requires assessors to visit the target locations of a campaign and interview groups of beneficiaries, as shown in Figure 3. More specifically, the approach that we adopted is composed of the following steps:

1. A manager creates a new campaign. The relevant actors (citizens and assessors) are identified. The assessors are invited to register into the system and they are provided with access credentials.
2. The manager opens the campaign. A page containing the information about the campaign is published on the website of the application and the assessors are enabled to upload assessments.
3. During the time frame of the campaign, the assessors collect data about the targets using mobile devices running SAMo's Android client. The data can be inserted more than once and only the last entered value is the one that is saved. The output of this activity are the assessments.

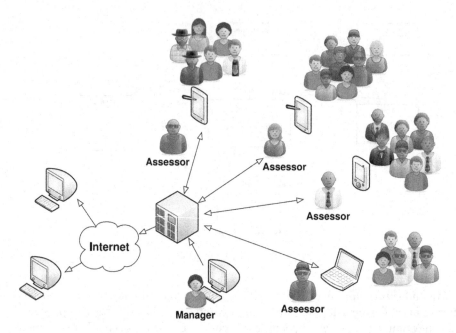

Fig. 3. Communication flow using the SAMo platform

4. At the end of a campaign the system marks it as closed and assessments cannot be accepted anymore. At this point, the final aggregated results of the campaign can be published.

The results collected are made available via the web interface as soon as they are uploaded by assessors. We rely on the APIs provided by Google Maps to display the location of the targets and to obtain satellite imagery of the buildings assessed (subject to availability). The web interface allows citizens to browse through the collected data in aggregated form at different levels of granularity (e.g., by campaign, by target) and to view the answers to individual assessments.

4   Pilot Study

We used SAMo in a pilot study promoted by the World Bank to collect procurement indicators about schools in the rural district of Moamba, Mozambique.

4.1   Overview of the District of Moamba

The district of Moamba is located in the northern part of the Province of Maputo, 75 km from the capital of the country. The estimated population in 2005 was of about 62,392 inhabitants, living in a territory of 4,628 km^2.

The District of Moamba is connected to South Africa through the border of Ressano Garcia and to Maputo by highway no. 4. Most of the roads of the district are made of packed dirt, resulting in significant transit problems, especially during the rainy season.

Electricity covers less than 1% of the population and water supply is available at household level in most of the administrative seats. Other villages use rivers, wells and boreholes for water supply, which are insufficient with respect to the needs of the population.

The district has 77 schools, 55 of which are level 1 primary schools, with a total of about 13,000 students and 330 teachers. Despite this, 55% of the population is illiterate and only 19.8% of the students attend school for at least five years.

Complete statistical data about the district of Moamba is available in Portuguese on the online portal of the Government of Mozambique[1].

4.2   Organization of the Pilot Study

The Moamba region and the targets were chosen not only for their general interest but also for the logistical and technical challenges they pose. To collect data, we equipped 12 volunteers with tablets and two jeeps and we embedded a sociologist within the interviewers to collect the reactions and attitude of the participants to the pilot.

Fieldwork started after a preparatory activity during which the local community was involved and prepared with the help of the district administrators and through the community radio. The interviewers collected assessments from teachers and parents of kids enrolled in the target schools for a period of six days, during which the volunteers visited the target schools, conducting the interviews with the aid of the tablets. The responses from the participants were uploaded to the SAMo server when an Internet connection was available (often in the evening whey the interviewers returned to Maputo).

The interest shown by the population in the initiative was higher than expected. A total of 677 interviews were collected out of an initial target of 500. The citizens participating to the pilot were particularly active in highlighting issues, proposing solutions, and in general participating to the iniative. Although such interest can be expected from people voluntarily showing up to be interviewed, it still provides some hints about the possible large-scale involvement of citizens.

A side result of the data collection activity is the geolocation of schools. Most of the schools in Moamba do not have a formal address and are not close to main roads. The data available to us was limited to the distance in kilometers from the closest administrative center and finding them in many cases represented a challenge volunteers had to tackle by embeeding volunteers living in the region to take them to the schools. The work of the volunteers and the usage of

---

[1] http://www.portaldogoverno.gov.mz/Informacao/
distritos/p_maputo/Moamba.pdf

GPS-enabled tablets allowed us to precisely geolocate all schools: the data is now publicly available on the SAMo platform website[2].

5   The Results

The 21 indicators collected during the assessment can be roughly classified in four types:

- 4 indicators measured general information about the school, namely the age of the building, the number of classrooms, availability of toilets and electricity.
- 8 indicators were meant to qualitatively assess the characteristics of some elements of the building, such as water-tightness of the roof, windows, doors, and floor.
- 9 indicators were related to the facilities and services, such as the presence of a cabinet to securely store books, cleaning of classrooms and toilets.
- Finally, one indicator ("The school has classrooms built by the community with local material?") could be used to measure the level of active participation and involvement of the citizenship.

To simplify data collection, most of the questions required a "yes/no" answer. For each target we collected a minimum of two interviews (in two cases) up to a maximum of 65 interviews (with an average of 13.54 interviews per target). The data is then made available at three levels of granularity: individual anonymous assessments, aggregated data about a target, aggregated data about all targets.

Although we expected a bit of variance to the answers given by different people to the same question about the same target, in some cases the ratio of "yes" and "no" resulted close to 50%. We thus aggregated data in three classes: "yes" ("no") if the percentage of positive (negative) answers is equal or above 80% of the assessments, "do not know" in any other case.

From an analysis of the results, it appears that most of the schools are lacking water and electricity supply (which is expected considering the data outlined in section 4.1) and security walls or lockable closets (in spite of material being regularly stolen, as reported by various citizens). The situation with various other indicators is mixed, with roughly half of the schools satisfying the procurement indicators we measured. We also need to remark that 45% of the data points (where a data point is the aggregated value of an indicator for one target) fall in the "do not know" category. Lowering the classification threshold decreases the number of data points we do not classify (see Figure 4 to see how "uncertainty" drops).

To conclude, it is worth mentioning that one of the parameters was meant to measure how active citizens are in tackling these issues. The question, in particular, was concerned on whether the school had classrooms built by the community with local material. The data shows that citizens took action in

---

[2] http://www.ict4sa.org/samo

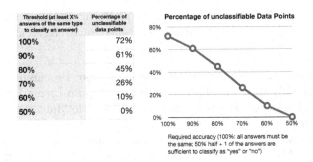

Threshold (at least X% answers of the same type to classify an answer)	Percentage of unclassifiable data points
100%	72%
90%	61%
80%	45%
70%	26%
60%	10%
50%	0%

Percentage of unclassifiable Data Points

Required accuracy (100%: all answers must be the same; 50% half + 1 of the answers are sufficient to classify as "yes" or "no")

Fig. 4. Classification threshold and accuracy

about one fifth of the schools, at a first glance independent of the status of the other indicators. Possibly a hint of the involvement that can be obtained without any specific action targeted to improve active citizenship.

6   Conclusion and Future Work

The last few years have seen a fast evolution of system to crowdsource data. Systems like Ushahidi [6] are extremely effective in involving people in the collection of data about variations over known situations and/or emergencies. Think, for instance, about signaling issues and frauds during an election. However, when the baseline situation is not known, a more systematic approach to data collection is required. This is the purpose of SAMo, a tool we built to systematically collect (procurement) data about targets, through campaigns conducted by volunteers. SAMO is composed of a web application and of a mobile client to collect data on the field.

We experimented SAMo in a campaign to measure procurement indicators about Primary Schools in the Moamba region in Mozambique. During the campaign we conducted 677 interviews. The results have given us the opportunity of experimenting the efficacy of the tool, while, at the same time, having a glance at the current status of buildings and basic services provided by schools in a rural area neighbouring Maputo. The result highlighted various critical situations, which, in some cases, surprised the interviewers themselves, used to the urban setting of Maputo.

The ultimate goal of the platform is fostering forms of empowerment of citizens, to make Governments more accountable (through measurement campaigns), but also by helping citizens understand what they can do to improving local services. This is a topic which, for us, started from a project in a developing country, but which is extremely relevant in both the developing and developed world.

A deeper understanding of how to deal with data quality and the definition of sustainability models for the data collection campaigns are some of the technical issues we need to address. From the project point of view, a return of the results to those citizens who do not have access to the SAMo website, empowering the

Maputo Living Lab [7] in the evolution of the platform, and experimenting with geographically ditributed, crowdsourced data collection exercises are some of the next steps.

Acknowledgments. We thank Dirk Bronselaer (Senior Procurement Specialist at the World Bank), Marco Battisti (Director of Maputo Living Lab), the staff members of MLL who participated to the study, Eduardo Muhamad Ali and Mohammad Tassin Sidi, and the assessors of the pilot campaign: Laura Chilundzo, Sansao Chambala, Danilo Jo, Manuel Lumbela, Alina Ivone Francisco, Carlos Pitagoras Cossa, Manuel Gerson, Estenio Manhica, Fernando Orlando Matsinhe and Mario Moreira.

Copyright Notice

References

1. Chase, R., Anjum, A.: Demand for good governance stocktaking report. Initiatives supporting demand for good governance (dfgg) across world bank group sectors and regions. World Bank, Washington, DC (2008)
2. Surhone, L., Timpledon, M., Marseken, S.: RapidSMS. VDM Verlag Dr. Mueller e.K. (2010)
3. Parikh, T., Lazowska, E.: Designing an architecture for delivering mobile information services to the rural developing world. In: Proceedings of the 15th International Conference on World Wide Web, pp. 791–800. ACM (2006)
4. Hartung, C., Anokwa, Y., Brunette, W., Lerer, A., Tseng, C., Borriello, G.: Open data kit: Tools to build information services for developing regions. In: Proceedings of the International Conference on Information and Communication Technologies and Development, pp. 1–11 (2010)
5. Chaudhri, R., Brunette, W., Goel, M., Sodt, R., VanOrden, J., Falcone, M., Borriello, G.: Open data kit sensors: mobile data collection with wired and wireless sensors. In: Proceedings of the 2nd ACM Symposium on Computing for Development, ACM-DEV 2012, pp. 9:1–9:10 (2012)
6. Okolloh, O.: Ushahidi, or'testimony': Web 2.0 tools for crowdsourcing crisis information. Participatory Learning and Action 59(1), 65–70 (2009)
7. Ciaghi, A., Villafiorita, A., Chemane, L., Macueve, G.: Stimulating development through transnational living labs: The italo-mozambican vision. In: IST-Africa Conference Proceedings, pp. 1–8. IEEE (2011)

Electronic Communication: Stay Connected

Jacques Fouché and Rossouw von Solms

Institute for ICT Advancement, Nelson Mandela Metropolitan University
P.O. Box 77000, NMMU, 6031, Port Elizabeth
s207006274@live.nmmu.ac.za, rossouw.vonsolms@nmmu.ac.za

Abstract. Electronic communication technology offers many services; hence providing the individual with utility. The utility obtained may enable individuals economically, from an organisational or personal point of view, or the utility may lie in safety or morale, a more personal matter. There are many reasons for using electronic communication technology; however, once it has been incorporated into individuals' lives, they may come to rely on it heavily. It is for this reason, that individuals should identify their level of dependency on electronic communication services. Then, a continuity strategy can be established to address the level of dependency. This paper seeks to provide individuals with a framework for establishing a personal ICT continuity strategy to prolong electronic communication service.

Keywords: personal ICT continuity strategy, communication technology.

1   Introduction

The electronic communication services individuals use have become important to them. However, such services cannot operate without supporting devices and the required infrastructure. The availability of these devices and the infrastructure that underpins them should be of equal importance to the services they provide.

The South African president, Jacob Zuma, stated that infrastructure remains critical to South Africa's development goals, underlining its importance in service delivery. Among the infrastructure mentioned in this regard was communications infrastructure [1]. However, South Africa, like the other countries on the African continent, is a developing country and such infrastructure is not always available. An example of unavailable infrastructure would be where a mobile signal becomes unavailable or degraded. Furthermore, the power source a communication device relies on may become unavailable.

Against this backdrop, the objective of this paper is to provide a framework to improve communication technology availability for the individual. To achieve this objective, guidelines for information communication technology (ICT) continuity have been adopted from the SANS 25777:2010 standard. Following these guidelines, individuals could then use the framework to identify the services they require and the dependencies they experience. These dependencies and services have been arranged in logical layers, and will each be discussed in more detail below.

K. Jonas, I.A. Rai, and M. Tchuente (Eds.): AFRICOMM 2012, LNICST 119, pp. 199–210, 2013.
© Institute for Computer Sciences, Social Informatics and Telecommunications Engineering 2013

The rest of the paper is structured as follows: In the next section, the current electronic communication usage trends will be discussed. This will be followed by an account of the importance of communication technology to the individual. The following section contains the focus of this paper, that is, the protection of personal communication technology.

2   Trends in Current Electronic Communication Usage

In a modern society, electronic communication is integrated to a large extent with many aspects of an individual's daily activities. One example of such electronic communication is electronic mail, or email as it has become generally known. Currently, it is estimated that there are 3,1 billion email accounts worldwide; and an average annual growth of 7% can be expected [2]. Another popular communication method is instant messaging (IM), with 2,6 billion accounts worldwide and an expected average annual growth of 11% [2].

A second example of the critical role played by electronic communications is in modern social networking. In the past few years, social media have undergone enormous growth. Social websites like Twitter, Facebook, Google+ and LinkedIn have experienced various levels of growth. Facebook had a 37% growth in 2011 from its 585 million users at the beginning of 2011 to 800+ million users towards the end of 2011. This represents an average growth of seven users per second [3]. Other social networks, such as Twitter, had 100 million followers [4]. Furthermore, in September 2011, the social networking site Google+ entered the arena and reached 50 million users in about 88 days. This is according to Paul Allen, who is well known for his methodology used to count Google+ users [5].

Both of these services, email and social networking, are extensively utilised today by means of electronic communication. In fact, modern mobile phones have lately become the preferred platform for these services. The mobile and smartphone market is prospering. For this reason, most companies now provide a mobile implementation, or even a mobile application to access their services. First National Bank (FNB), one of the largest banking service providers in South Africa, offers Android, Apple, Blackberry and Nokia Symbian applications for accessing online banking via a smartphone [6]. Popular communication applications, such as Windows Live Messenger, Google Talk Skype and many of the social networking sites, all have mobile implementations.

Nevertheless, in South Africa, the leading social network contender remains MXit with approximately 10 million active users [7]. This mobile instant messaging (MIM) platform can attribute its success to the fact that it is capable of functioning on as many as 3 000 different mobile handsets, ranging from the most basic mobile phones to smartphones [8]. However, smartphone users' numbers are growing and they have many more social network options than MXit.

The information above demonstrates how extensively electronic communication is used today, especially when using a mobile platform. Accordingly, the question arises as to how dependent users have grown on these important electronic communications and, consequently, how important this has become to them.

3   The Importance of Communication Technology to the Individual

It may well be said that for something to be important to an individual, it must make a significant difference in his/her life. Furthermore, to be significant, the difference that is makes must be important and be seen by the individual as being an improvement. Therefore, something is important to an individual if it makes a significant difference to him/her and their life [9].

The world is home to seven billion people and there are currently almost six billion mobile cellular subscriptions [10]. Having access to a mobile phone has made a significant different to the way individuals communicate, as well as to how they live and act in general. Since the majority of individuals now have access to mobile phones, these phones provide a certain sense of security. This sense of security stems from being able to call for help, and of being connected, or being part of some group. Thus, the mobile phone, as a communication technology, is a fundamental agent of one of man's basic needs, namely, that of safety [11].

The individual self exists in relation to social conversations. Furthermore, it has been suggested that individuals are the sum of their social interactions [12, p58]. Therefore, if the social media are frequently used for the purpose of social interactions, it may be said that the social media shape the self which is constantly changing through these interactions. Thus, the social media become an important social tool to the individual, which assist in creating a sense of belonging, despite the fact that this may be accomplished electronically. Again, communication technology is of fundamental importance to the mobile phone.

A study by Ericson found that 40% of Android and iPhone smartphone users use their phones in bed before going to sleep at night. Furthermore, 35% of these smartphone users check their email or Facebook account in the mornings before getting out of bed [13].

It can thus be seen that electronic communication technology plays an important part in an individual's personal life. Moreover, it also most certainly plays a major role in a professional context.

Organisations that require a high level of communication with their employees will require them to stay connected. This could be in the work environment only, where ICT continuity strategies are in place, but it could also be away from the workplace, where a personal continuity strategy needs to be in place.

It is thus clear that communication technology is becoming more and more important as well as an integral part of the individual's everyday wellbeing; it also plays an important role in creating a sense of security and belonging and even of being in control, if seen from a business perspective. For this reason, the mobile phone has become a valued possession for most individuals; and such a possession needs to be protected for the future.

4   Protection of Personal Communication Technology

To protect and ensure the continued availability of some infrastructure or service is a well-known function in the business world. SANS 25777:2010 is a South African standard that provides definitive guidelines in this regard. In accordance with the SANS 25777:2010 standard, there are four main steps required in any ICT continuity strategy. These steps are as follows:

1) understand ICT continuity requirements
2) determine an ICT continuity strategy
3) develop and implementing ICT continuity strategies
4) exercise, test, maintain, review and improve [14]

A brief description of these steps follows. Firstly, understanding ICT continuity requirements involves understanding what ICT configuration is generally required. These requirements need to be categorised according to certain priorities. Furthermore, it involves determining the gap between current ICT continuity capabilities and the continuity requirements for each critical ICT service [14].

Secondly, an ICT continuity strategy should define an approach to implementing the required resilience, protection and recovery processes. At this stage, the risk appetite, the costs and the benefits should be considered. The continuity strategy should cater for any likely risk, as well as the effects of possible disruptions [14].

Thirdly, developing and implementing ICT continuity strategies includes putting into place the chosen ICT strategies, along with the steps required to support the implementation. Such implementation may include training to ensure that skills/knowledge gaps are minimised and may also include selecting the technologies required by the chosen strategy [14].

The fourth step in the continuity plan is exercise, testing, maintaining, reviewing and improving. This step aims to ensure that the chosen strategies work as expected and when required. The recovery and resilience implementations should also be tested and documented. Furthermore, maintaining, reviewing and improving are carried out in order to deal with any changes. As the individual's requirements may change, the ICT requirements will therefore change as well. This means that the ICT continuity plan needs to be updated to match these new requirements. Furthermore, the documented tests should be reviewed and improvements implemented where required [14].

It is important to note that the ICT continuity process should be treated as an ongoing lifecycle. The individual will need to determine what ICT requirements he/she has. This is particularly important as the continuity plan has cost implications. Therefore, the continuity strategy that is implemented should reflect the requirements. Once the requirements are known, the individual can use Figure 1 to determine a continuity strategy. The details on how to develop and implement the ICT strategy will be discussed in the following section and figures. After an ICT plan has been developed, it should be carried out, tested, maintained and reviewed.

In order to meet an individual's communication requirements, the following communication technology continuity framework has been developed. Figure 1 can be used to determine an ICT continuity strategy in accordance with the four main steps of SANS 25777:2010, as described above.

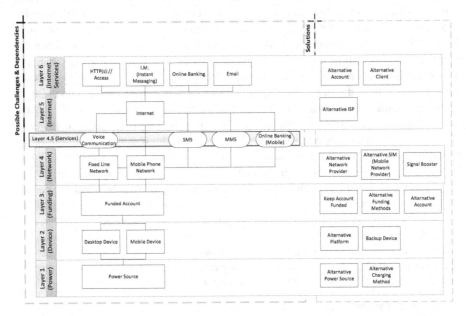

Fig. 1. Continuity framework

Figure 1 represents an example of a typical continuity planning framework. The continuity framework has six layers, which are arranged in order of their dependency.

Layer 1: The base requirement for communication can be found in this layer. All devices are dependent on a power source; in turn, however, a power source may be dependent on either a power outlet or a battery. Once this dependency is identified, it becomes necessary to address the challenges one might face in this layer.

To increase power source availability, individuals might need to find an alternative power outlet. This could include a generator of some sort, such as a solar-powered generator, a wind turbine, or a fuel-powered generator. Further, these generators could be linked up to a battery bank, which could subsequently be charged in order to provide power through an inverter.

A battery is another power source and may be a device's primary power source. However, batteries have to be charged, which is done mainly through a power outlet. It is handy to keep a spare charger in case it is required. One should also have an alternative charging station. Many devices use USB chargers, which are small enough to carry around and can be used to charge by means of a PC or a laptop. A laptop is also capable of charging a device – even while it is using its own battery to power itself. There are many types of charger available today – miniature solar chargers and car chargers. Car chargers usually plug into the cigarette lighter of the car. These car outlet chargers can support USB devices and they can therefore supply power to any such device.

In addition, the operating temperature can improve battery performance. There are many different battery compositions; however, general rules apply to most compositions used in mobile electronic communication devices. Some of these rules will now be discussed. The ideal operating temperature for most battery types is at 20 °C (80 °F). Cold temperature increases the internal resistance and slows down the chemical reaction. Moreover, at certain lower temperatures, batteries will discharge at a reduced rate. Therefore, storing an unused battery at colder temperatures could allow longer battery discharge time, resulting in longer use when warmed up to 20 °C again. In contrast, when warming a battery to temperatures higher than 20 °C, the internal chemical reaction will be speeded up, and the internal resistance lowered. This effect provides improved battery performance, but shortens the service life of the battery if continued for long periods [15], [16]. It should be noted that this should only be done in emergencies, as prolonged use can shorten the lifespan of the battery and the device. Battery life can be extended by changing settings or installing certain applications on a device. For example, a battery-saver application could be installed that automatically configures a device to consume less power. Alternatively, one could change the settings on the device manually so that it consumes less power.

There are several settings that will allow lower power consumption by a device. These settings include turning off unnecessary or unneeded functions, or changing the device operation. Examples of these are the following:

- Dim the display brightness.
- Set the background image and themes to black.
- Turn the device sounds down or off.
- Turn off any vibrating function.
- Turn off the wireless.
- Turn off the Bluetooth.
- Turn off the internet synchronisation.
- Switch to 2G or 3G.

These examples will now be discussed in a little more detail. If email and other internet synchronisation services are used, such as a weather application, turning the synchronisation to manual, or setting the synchronisation time to less often would result in lower power consumption. Another setting on a mobile phone that may allow more talking time, but less standby time, is setting a device to 2G. One example of this is the Nokia Lumia 800. Nokia claims that this device is capable of achieving 13 hours of talk time on a 2G network, but only 9,5 hours on a 3G network. However, the standby time on a 3G network is considerably longer than that of 2G, with 3G achieving 335 hours and 2G only 265 hours [17].

Therefore, a mobile phone user who predominantly makes and receives mobile phone calls is advised to use a 2G network. However, a mobile phone user who prefers to have prolonged availability is advised to make use of a 3G network. The following is a graphic representation of layer 1, as described above.

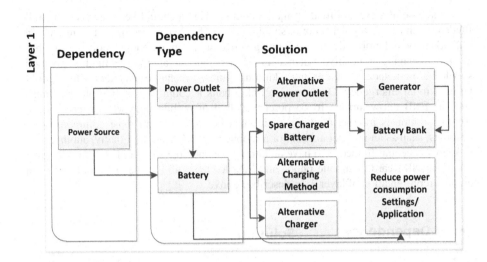

Fig. 2. Layer 1

Layer 2: In this layer, the physical device used to communicate is identified. Such a device can be either a desktop device or a mobile device. In the case of both a desktop and a mobile device, if it becomes unavailable or faulty, the first option is to use a back-up or alternative device, such as another desktop or mobile device. For example, one could keep a spare mobile phone handy for when the current one fails to operate properly.

If, however, a back-up device is not available, one could make use of an alternative platform, such as another device capable of achieving the same goals. For example, if a desktop device were to fail and an individual is waiting for an important email, the email could be retrieved via a smartphone. The following is a graphic representation of layer 2, as described above.

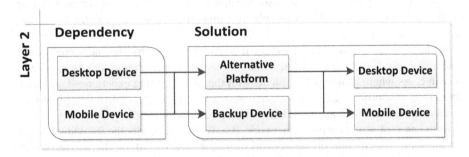

Fig. 3. Layer 2

Layer 3: This layer focuses on a funded account. In this layer, the service provider will provide access to its network and services. However, such access will only be granted to a funded account. There are several steps an individual can take to avoid possible account-funding issues. These steps will now be discussed.

In the case of a prepaid funding method, an individual should keep the account well funded. Such a well-funded account should consist of at least three times the amount an individual would normally use on any given day. If an individual consistently has trouble managing a positive balance in an account, an alternative funding method should be used, such as purchasing additional, unused recharge vouchers, which could be used in an emergency. One can also link a bank account to a mobile phone. Banks such as FNB allow airtime to be purchased free of mobile network carrier charges. Another option is internet banking, which can be used to fund most communication accounts, such as an internet account or a mobile network account. Finally, another way to keep an account funded is to have an alternative back-up account. For example, have a back-up SIM card or mobile phone and SIM loaded with airtime. The following is a graphic representation of layer 3, as described above.

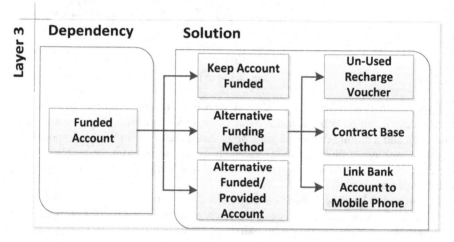

Fig. 4. Layer 3

Layer 4: The network providers are located in this layer. A network provider of some sort is required in order to be able to communicate and can be either fixed-line or mobile phone network.

In the case of a fixed-line network, if a disruption occurs the individual could potentially install an additional fixed line on the premises, although this is suggested only in cases where prolonged problems with the line are being experienced. Another alternative would be to use an alternative network type; for example a fixed-line user could make use of a mobile phone network as a back-up network.

In the case of a mobile phone network, if a disruption occurs the individual could use an alternative mobile phone network provider. The use of an alternative mobile phone network could be to have an additional mobile phone with SIM, 3G USB modem with SIM or just a SIM card. Furthermore, an individual could make use of an alternative network, such as a fixed-line network.

Finally, in the case of a mobile phone network, a network signal is required. Since receiving a signal from a mobile phone network could be a challenge in some areas, an individual should take steps to enhance the current signal strength. This could be done by using an alternative network provider, as some providers have extended coverage. Alternatively, an individual could make use of a signal booster, which could be either a purchased version or a crude manmade device. A simple device can be made by wrapping a piece of cardboard with foil. The foil needs to cover the entire area of the cardboard facing the device. The dimensions of the cardboard should be larger than the device; in our experiment, a 40 x 40 centimetre signal booster was used. The results of the test were an average gain of –2db with a gain of up to –4db. Finally, to implement the booster, place a 3G USB modem or phone in the middle of the signal booster. This booster works much like as a satellite would; it uses signal reflection and concentrates that signal to enhance the signal reception of a device. For this reason, the signal booster should also face the nearest signal transmitter or mobile base station. The following is a graphic representation of a simple manmade signal booster like the one mentioned above.

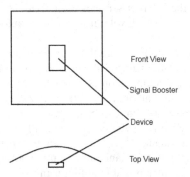

Fig. 5. Signal Booster

The manmade device works by consolidating the signal, very like a satellite dish. The following is a graphic representation of layer 4, as described above.

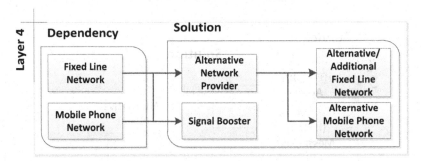

Fig. 6. Layer 4

Layer 5: In this layer, the internet as a service is located. The internet allows for many services; however, in order to use these services, a functioning connection to the internet is required.

In the case of a disruption, an individual could make use of an alternative ISP (internet service provider). This alternative provider should ideally be on a different network and make use of different fibre infrastructures, local and international. The following is a graphic representation of layer 5, as described above.

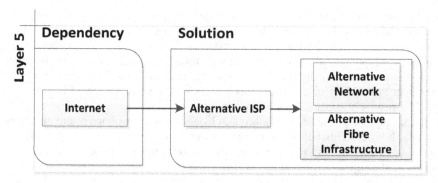

Fig. 7. Layer 5

Layer 6: In this layer, the internet services an individual could use are located. To address potential disruption at this level, an individual could use alternative accounts or an alternative client.

An alternative account would be where the user signs up for an alternative account with an alternative provider. An example of this would be to have an alternative email account. Then, if the email account becomes unreachable, a secondary email could be used. In the case of online banking, an alternative bank account can be used. However, an alternative bank account can be expensive, although there are banks that offer "free" accounts in certain situations. One example of a free bank account is a student account at Standard Bank. Having an alternative bank account could help in some situations; for example when a bank has communication disruptions.

As mentioned earlier, another possible solution in layer 6 is to use an alternative client. The reason for doing this is because a client could become faulty. For example, one could use an alternative browser, such as Google Chrome or Mozilla Firefox. Another alternative client is an interoperable IM client, such as Pidgin or Trillian. The following is a graphic representation of layer 6, as described above.

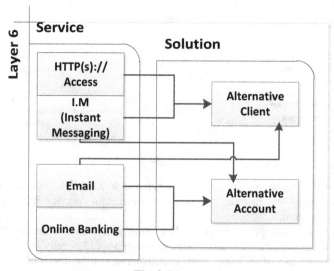

Fig. 8. Layer 6

The above figures serve to help individuals create personal ICT continuity strategies. It should be noted that the details of each layer should be read in conjunction with the corresponding figure describing that layer.

5   Conclusion

It can be seen that communication technology, specifically the mobile phone and the internet, has become integrated and is a very important component of people's daily lives. Although this integration is generally advantageous, it could also hinder daily functioning if it becomes unavailable. For this reason, a personal communication technology continuity plan should be developed. Such a continuity plan would help to determine what is important and how services may be extended when required. To develop a continuity plan, the individual determines his/her personal communication needs – if the requirements are known the continuity framework can also be used. This framework should be used together with the corresponding layers, descriptions and figures. In applying this framework, individuals should trace the service they need down to layer 1, and then implement the suggested solutions. This would provide an ongoing communication technology experience.

References

1. BuaNews: Infrastructure essential to service delivery – Zuma (April 24, 2012), from SA news: http://www.buanews.gov.za/rss/12/12042416251002 (retrieved August 05, 2012)
2. The Radicati group, Inc.: Email Statistics Report. The Radicati group, Inc., Palo Alto (2011)
3. Socialbakers: Facebook grew 7 users per second all of 2011 [Special Infographic] (February 13, 2012), from Socialbakers: http://www.socialbakers.com/blog/361-facebook-grew-7-users-per-second-all-of-2011-special-infographic/ (retrieved February 13, 2012)
4. Twitter: One hundred million voices (September 2011), from blog.twitter.com: http://blog.twitter.com/2011/09/one-hundred-million-voices.html (retrieved February 13, 2012)
5. Allen, P.: Paul Allen (September 26, 2011), from Google Plus: https://plus.google.com/117388252776312694644/posts/EwpnUpTkJ5W (retrieved February 13, 2012)
6. First National Bank: FNB App. (2012), from First National Bank: https://www.fnb.co.za/fnbapp/index.html (retrieved February 16, 2012)
7. World Wide Worx: Social media goes mainstream in SA (October 26, 2011), from World Wide Worx: http://www.worldwideworx.com/?p=322 (retrieved February 15, 2012)
8. Mxit: What is Mxit (2012), from Mxit: http://mxit.com/ (retrieved February 15, 2012)
9. Frankfurt, H.: The importance of what we care about. Synthese, 257–272 (1982)

10. ITU Telecom World: The world in 2011: ICT Facts and Figures (2012), from ITU:
    `http://www.itu.int/ITU-D/ict/facts/2011/material/`
    `ICTFactsFigures2011.pdf` (retrieved January 11, 2012)
11. Maslow, A.H.: A theory of human motivation. Psychological Review, 370–396 (1943)
12. Stinger, P.: Confronting social issues: Applications of social psychology. Academic Press,
    London (1982)
13. Greengard, S.: Living in a digital world. Communications of the ACM, 17–19 (2012)
14. SANS: Information and communications technology continuity management: Code of
    practice. SANS 25777:2010. SABS, Pretoria, South Africa (May 2010)
15. Buchmann, I.: Discharging at high and low temperature (2012), from Battery University:
    `http://batteryuniversity.com/learn/article/`
    `discharging_at_high_and_low_temperatures` (retrieved May 15, 2012)
16. Energizer Battery Manufacturing Inc.: Alkaline manganese dioxide: Handbook and
    application manual. Energizer Battery Manufacturing Inc. (2008)
17. Nokia: Detailed specifications for the Nokia Lumia 800 (2012), from Nokia:
    `http://www.nokia.com/za-en/products/phone/`
    `lumia800/specifications/` (retrieved May 08, 2012)

Modeling and Practise of Integral Development in Rural Zambia: Case Macha

Jasper Bets[1], Gertjan van Stam[2], and Anne-Marie Voorhoeve[1]

[1] Center for Human Emergence, Netherlands
jasper.bets@wise-insights.com,
anne-marie@humanemergence.nl
[2] Nelson Mandela Metropolitan University, Port Elizabeth, South Africa
gertjan.vanstam@worksgroup.org

Abstract. During the last years, the small, rural community of Macha, Zambia transformed from a closed community with fixed thinking paradigms to a community open to change. As a result, the community embraces the implementation and use of information and communication technologies (ICT). Further, interventions result in a significant reduction of malaria. This paper presents how an integral approach to development does undergird the outcomes in Macha. Based upon an ethnographic study of the Macha community, the study indicates components of social innovation through an integral approach. Such approach views activities in a holistic, instead of particularized, manner. Simultaneous investments in education, leadership, and community vitalize and sustain progress. Development practitioners act as mentors that 'hold the space' for change to come. The study indicates the life conditions and interactions that overcome barriers to change, and how a 3rd culture perspective stimulates local initiatives to address local needs and inspires the local community.

Keywords: integral development, change, community, Macha, Zambia.

1 Introduction

This paper reflects the findings of a case study research on aspects of an integral approach to change in Macha, rural Zambia. The document describes the rural environment in which the study took place. The literature base, together with the systematic, qualitative and longitudinal methodology is presented. The outcome of the process results in an integral development model.

The model is corroborated by field observations and disciplinary publications from the community.

2 Environment

The case study focuses on the change in the community of Macha, a small rural community located in the Southern Province of Zambia. Since mid twentieth

K. Jonas, I.A. Rai, and M. Tchuente (Eds.): AFRICOMM 2012, LNICST 119, pp. 211–220, 2013.

century a central area in the community, it contains health and education institutes that retain a small establishment of medical and education professionals. Since 2003 Macha has grown from being a small rural village with limited facilities and accommodations for health and education only, to a rural community with, among others: Internet access, an innovative education campus, a community center, a radio station, entrepreneurial activities and an airstrip. These developments, driven by local talent and local initiative, have proven to be inspirational and enabling and were accompanied by tangible progress in the form of growth of socio-economic activities, agency, and a higher standard of living, as well as intangible progress bringing hope to the local community making them believe they themselves can be the change.

Next to socio-economic growth, Macha has seen important results in the fight against malaria and growth of community-driven projects. The Macha Research Trust, an institute conducting state-of-the-art malaria research, has shown a dramatic reduction of malaria cases in under 5 years olds in Macha of 90%, a significant result in rural Africa. Although the results are clear the etiology for the change remained unclear [1]. The cooperative community venture, Macha Works, acts as the vehicle for social progress, involved with implementation of infrastructures and programs in the Macha community. This entity emerged from a respectful vision informed by the dreams of so-called local talents gathered since 2003. Activities are implemented according to the Macha Works! model [2] and span interventions in education, communications, transport, and energy. Thus Macha Works is also involved in collaborative Internet through its entity LinkNet [3], and innovative primary education through Macha Innovative Community School (MICS).

The case study examined the events in Macha using an integral perspective. The integral perspective builds on the human development theory of Spiral Dynamics [4] and the Integral Model [5]. It recognizes human consciousness as a developmental model in which each stage becomes more complex and inclusive. Next to exterior, tangible aspects (behavior and structures) it recognizes interior, intangible aspects (intentions/culture) at both an individual and collective level and emphasizes their interdependence.

Looking from an integral perspective, an intervention in a changing setting cannot be viewed in isolation. The approach used must be holistic (transdiciplinary) instead of particular (disciplinary), taking different factors into account. These factors show their affect in intangibles like empowerment, self-esteem, and sense of self-worth at the individual level, and social cohesion and strengthening of social fabric at the collective level.

3   Goal, Purpose, and Methodology

The goal and purpose of the case study research is two-fold. Firstly, the research tries to answer the missing etiology for the successful results of malaria reduction in Macha using an integral perspective. Secondly, the research with the integral approach answers the global call for new effective approaches within development, taking the case of Macha Works into account.

The case study uses Macha as a proof-of-concept of implementing an integral approach within development. The case study examines the underlying success factors by using valuable on-ground-knowledge and insights to provide input for reproducing the successful approach used in Macha to other sites in rural Zambia and Africa.

The case study used models as provided through Spiral Dynamics (SDi) [4] and practical interactions to conduct integral research, incorporating tools like the CultureSCAN - a test assessing and plotting value systems, change dynamics and culture - and looked through an integral lens in a five phases approach. Researchers and mentors were trained in SDi, with its five distinct phases:

Phase 1 emperical study at Macha, Zambia;
Phase 2 structuring information;
Phase 3 theory review;
Phase 4 analysis and develop prototype roadmap;
Phase 5 continuous review and development of Integral Development Model.

Phase 1 consisted of an empirical, ethnographic study performed at Macha, Zambia for a period of 10 weeks in 2008. During the period information was gathered using the following method:

1. *Literature/documentation.* Documents and reports only available in Macha were collected and reviewed on important information.
2. *Observation.* Observations were made throughout the ten weeks period that determined the research path that was being followed.
3. *Participation/experience.* By participating within the community, working in local organizations and with local people (LinkNet and MICS) and attending activities (meetings, classes, welcoming visitors, sports, openings, medical research, birthdays, and church) relationships with the local people were built and information was gathered.
4. *Interviews.* Documented (recorded) interviews with local people were held, as well as undocumented interviews and conversations.
5. *Photo/film.* Through use of photo and film, important information was documented.

There were no pre-structured interviews, no queries and there was no schedule of activities. The only part of the research that followed some schedule was the first week in which an introduction was given on Macha and the different activities that took place. The choice of not using a prior set structure was made in order to start the research as blank as possible, being objective and taking everything into account. The only purpose of the empirical study was to understand the community. What is happening, where, how and why? The path followed for the empirical study was determined by the observations, participation and experience of the researcher who used his training in SDi in order to be able do so. By participating within the local community, relationships with the local people were built. These relationships contributed to the acceptance of the researcher and the mutual openness between the local community and the researcher. During the empirical study important actors (organizations, persons and local leaders) were identified and examined for further research.

Although not using a prior set structure in order to be objective, having the research path be determined on the observations and experience of the researcher is sensitive to subjectivity. In order to diminish this subjectivity the researcher at all times followed the principle of 'seeing that what you see is not everything that is what you see', constantly keeping on asking the question *why?* in order to get a deeper understanding of the situation.

Being knowledgeable in theories of human development brought understanding in identifying different mindsets and value systems and helped to make a distinction between the subjective and inter-subjective, thereby contributing to the researcher's objectivity.

Phase 2 of the methodology focused on structuring the information gained from the empirical study. The information was structured for: the actors (organizations, persons and local leaders) within Macha that were identified as important and for which detailed information was available; Macha Works' documentation and extant like Sachs [6], different fields of focus within a holistic approach (water, power, health, education, infrastructure, communication and leadership); and other relevant and important information that could not be assigned to one of the actors or fields of focus. The purpose of phase 2 was to bring structure in the information gathered during the empirical study without relating it to theory in order to give a description of what has and is happening in Macha.

Phase 3 of the study involved the theory review. The following theories were reviewed in order to provide a theoretical background and explanation on integral thinking and interior human development: Spiral Dynamics [4], Wilber's Integral model [5], Barretts four forms of alignment [7] and Merry's evolutionary leadership [8]. Looking at interior human development, different developmental lines can be defined (cognitive, moral, emotional, interpersonal etc. [9]). This case study focused on the value line. Appearing as the most calibrated line, the value line provided the best way to examine the developments that have and are taking place in Macha and gave valuable insights for the study. Leading from the theoretical background, a review was done on using an integral approach within development incorporating a conceptual model for operating on a relational instead of rational basis in order to align with local values. Furthemore, using the theory review, explanation is derived on the basic stages of interior human development from both an individualistic and collectivistic perspective. The purpose of this phase was to provide the theoretical background upon which further analysis could be made.

Phase 4 of the methodology focused on putting the practice to theory. Here the information structured in phase 2 was linked to the theoretical background provided in phase 3 in order to analyze what has and is happening in Macha and explain why and how. The analysis followed the structure as presented in phase 2 (actors, fields, others) and looked at their correlations and interdependence. Here the purpose was to provide an analysis that from the theoretical background:

explains the approach being used in Macha; identifies and captures the success factors; and give insight on the possible degree of re-production.

Phase 5 in this phase a continuous review on the findings of the study took place over the period 2008 - 2012. Being sensitized to the framework, findings were continously reviewed and looped back. When faced with an unknown or remarkable happening, it was approached with the attitudes 'it is not wrong, it is just different', and 'it does not matter why, it only matters that', 'never assume', and 'always look for alternate interpretations'.

4   Integral Development Model

The conceptual model derived from the work provides a road map for integral development. It encompasses three distinct areas of attention, which are *Thinking*, *Practice*, and *Progress*.

4.1   Thinking

This area of attention aggregates the body of thoughts. These thoughts consist of two focus points: interior human development, and holistic approach.

Human Development. People develop through different identifiable stages, or value systems, that become more complex and inclusive. Human consciousness consists of a developmental model in the form of a growth hierarchy, in which each stage influences the entire sequence as people transcend and include the former. In order to recognize and be able to level and interact with different stages, mentors play an important role. They uphold an open view. They operate from a 3rd culture perspective. Next to their personal value system that includes beliefs and intentions, mentors are open to the local value systems, which are likely to be at a different level of human consciousness, in order to provide solutions that fit the local needs and enshrine the local culture in a healthy manner.

Holistic Approach. Mentors operate from an integral perspective, with projects set-up horizontally instead of vertically and with simultaneous investments in different disciplines such as education, leadership, and community, thereby vitalizing and enforcing each other. The intentions and behavior of individuals and collectives, and the existing structures and systems, are seen as interdependent. It is recognized that no challenge or intervention can be addressed in isolation. Different factors as socio-economics and agency, including unquantifiable impacts should be taken into account.

Within a holistic approach, both the exterior, (the structures and behavior), and the interior, (the intentions and values), are taken into account. These are intangible and can only be revealed by speaking with and listening to people, and necessitate the presence of trust. Trust requires an open view, respecting and understanding the local value system(s), and being sensitive to the local community, especially to the interior (intentions and values) of people. Trust diminishes the distance between a mentor and the local community and thereby enables feedback and the ability to reveal and utilize valuable decentralized information.

Aspects of human consciousness, and the practice of a holistic approach, can appear either *folk-informed* in response to the reality on the ground and independent of theory, or transdiciplinarily *integrally-informed*, explicitly drawn on theories providing theoretical background, so long as it enables one to hold an open view. Many interdependent denominators must be taken into account, (for instance all four quadrants - intentions, behavior, culture and structure of the Integral model). Change must address all denominators in order to realize integral and sustainable progress.

4.2   Practice

Building on the body of thought provided by the Thinking phase, *Practice* focuses on the life conditions. This is the environment in which an individual or collective resides. By holding an open view, operating from a 3rd culture perspective and understanding the interior of the local community, activities are aligned to the local intentions and culture. So that Changes needed to be made in structure and systems alter the life conditions to stimulate healthy and sustainable progress. Such is realized by 'holding the space' for change to come.

Transformational change involves the local community to evolve from being reluctant to change, to willing to change, to being capable of change. Or in other words from being a *closed community*, with its thinking frozen in its own value system and seeing no (external) need for change, to an *arrested community*, willing to change but still with barriers to overcome, to an *open community*, capable of change.

With today's growing globalization, even rural areas in Africa are experiencing influence from urban areas and the West, and therefore get exposed to a different set of value systems. This exposure causes the local life conditions to change, possibly sensitizing the community to evolve from being frozen in its own value system, to slowly starting to become willing to change, but still with barriers to overcome. Therefore mentors must 'hold the space' for change to come. At such times focus is on creating the life conditions that break down barriers for change and that transcend and include conventional thinking into breakthrough action. In other words: everything needed for change is already there, it only needs to be given the space to emerge. Focus points for holding the space are:

- *long-term vision*, as change in general, and especially change in intentions and values, involves a long-term process;
- *guide instead of lead*, to assure holding an open view and operating from a 3rd culture perspective the mentor should position him/herself as a *guider* instead of a *leader*, acting from the background providing time and space for local initiative and talent to emerge;

- *local initiative*, providing time and space, acting from a guiding role, allowing for local initiative and talent to emerge;
- *the part and the whole*, to act on behalf of the entire organism for both the greater good and for the individual gain, bringing alignment towards the higher purpose. (Note: holding space, taking a guiding role and operating from the background, does not mean the mentor is not allowed at times to take a leading position. In fact, when healthy development of the local community is jeopardized the mentor should stand up and act accordingly in order to secure the higher purpose).
- *eehee-feeling*, being passionate about the work contributes to the quality of performance. This includes authentic behaviour, being accepted by the local culture, and supported within existing local structures.

4.3 Progress

The *Thinking* and *Practice* results in *Progress* as such progress is defined in the local value system. In a rural African environment like Macha such progress can be witnessed through acceptance, agency and local ownership, and being able to celebrate the contributions.

Living the Life. To be part of the community, the mentor must align to the local life conditions, and *live the life* in order to gain acceptance within the local community. Focus points for living the life in rural Macha are:

- *value relationship*, as the culture is one of collectivism and centers on the relationship, efficiency is approached from a relational perspective which needs time to build and maintain;
- *show commitment*, since to strengthen relationships within the local community a mentor must be able and willing to recognize and value physical presence at important community events;
- *here and now*, since rural life focuses on activities in the here and now, with traditions providing for valuable guidance for todays activities;
- *paucity*, as in a resource-limited environment abundance cannot be shown without having been allowed to do so. All resources are shared with the community. By showing abundance, acceptance and existence within the local community is jeopardized;
- *suffering and sacrifice*, is perceived by the local community as normal and commonplace;
- *recognizing (local) authority* to follow the decision as announced by Chiefs and Government, as having their support will contribute to the impact of the mentor's activities and acceptance within the local community;
- *believes and practices*, as religious life plays an important role in Macha. In order to align activities to the local life conditions, local (Christian) values should be respected and incorporated.

Ownership and Empowerment. For change to be sustainable and embraced by the local community, people must feel they have invested. Activities therefore must be locally owned and operated. Holding the space for local talent and initiative to emerge, not telling people what to do, contributes significantly to local ownership and empowerment with activities better aligned to the local life conditions and use of de-centralized local knowledge.

Celebrate Contributions. In order to get support, whether financial, political or in the form of positive energy, it is important to make contributions known. People at different levels should be aware of what is happening in order for them to provide support. Of course, at an international and national level, making the contributions known can lead to financial, material and/or strategic support. Whereas at a regional and local level, making the contributions known contributes to the acceptance of the activities within in the local community as well as getting support from important local stakeholders. Also following the seeing-is-believing principle, making the contributions transparant and visible to the local community, will contribute to breaking down the barrier to change and enable breakthrough development for the community at large.

5   Field Observations

Being of holistic nature, the integral approach recognized in Macha bases itself on the recognition of human agency as a part of a developmental model, and its effect of changing life conditions. In order for the local community of Macha to develop, *space was held* for change to come. By the mentor taking a *guiding* instead of *leading role*, working from a higher purpose with different horizontal projects simultaneously taking place in the fields: health; education; infrastructure; communication and community, and not telling people what to do, local talent and initiatives did emerge. Macha transformed from being a community frozen in its own old thinking paradigm and beliefs to a community that has opened up to change and that today incorporates new technologies (like the Internet) and exhibits significant agency. Due to the change in the life conditions, caused by exposure to the West, the willingness for change slowly emerged, but still with barriers to overcome. Holding the space and following the seeing-is-believing principle, local change agents in the community stood up and overcame these barriers to change, which enabled breakthrough sustainable progress for the community at large.

When viewed from a knowledge perspective, Macha as a living laboratory provides insights and on-ground knowledge for integral development in general and rural Africa specifically. Progress emphasizes the importance of aligning to, and adapting life conditions in order to stimulate upward development, keeping the water instead of the fish, as well as stimulating local talent and initiatives in order for activities to meet the local needs and assure a sustainable approach. Rather than holding a closed view, providing solutions from their own value system, mentors in the community were effectively holding an open view making them able to level with the local community and act on behalf of the entire organism for both the greater good and individual gain, recognizing the part as well as the whole. They did focus on creating the life conditions that break down barriers for change and that transcend and include conventional thinking into breakthrough action. And although holding space does not give exact direction, it gives the advantage of not knowing and seeing things emerge chaordically that are really needed.

Aligning the activities in Macha Works according to this model for integral development provided base for further growth of mentorship and local talent in the Macha Works model [2]. Over a period of eight years (2003-2011), around forty local individuals in the direct sphere of influence were recognized to have emerged and were able to contribute significantly to strengthen community driven solutions. The three phases of the model were looped together repeatedly, informing the thinking phase by previous progress recognized. By holding the time and space, and purposefully not telling people what to do, the local talents have been stimulated to themselves find what it is they should be doing and how they can contribute to the higher purpose. A high level of local knowledge is thus utilized and initiatives emerge that fit the local needs and that are vested in the community, thereby contributing to a sustainable approach.

The local talent function as a trigger, inspiring the local community with belief that they themselves can bring change and development. It is expected that each of the local talents will have influenced numerous people in their own sphere of influence. The increase in agency and capacity in Macha has been widely recognized. Various elements of the work provided for new viewpoints, of which a number were conceptualized and explained in a book 'Placemark' [10], and inspired contributions to the body of knowledge through essays, numerous publications, and national and international presentations. Such presence has supported understanding and awareness and opportunities for growth and recognition of local and national leadership.

6 Conclusions

The approach in Macha is recognized to be holistic (transdiciplinary) instead of particular (disciplinary). It takes into account a complex array of conceptual, interdisciplinary and qualitative factors. The significant reduction of malaria in Macha is not only realized due to improvements in healthcare, but synchronized with improvements in education, communication, housing, and economic welfare, which have raised the standard of living. Further, the emergence of community-driven projects, including the set up and operation of a large community internet network, coined and guided by local talent was greatly aided by mentors 'holding space' for the local talent to gain grounding and develop.

This case study research presents a model for an integral approach, with three distinct phases: Thinking, Practice, and Progress, that can be an effective approach for social innovation that addresses local needs in rural Africa.

References

1. Moss, W.J., Norris, D.E., Mharakurwa, S., Scott, A., Mulenga, M., Mason, P.R., Chipeta, J., Thuma, P.E.: Challenges and prospects for malaria elimination in the Southern Africa region. Acta Tropica, 33–36 (2011)
2. van Stam, G., van Oortmerssen, G.: Macha Works! In: Frontiers of Society On-Line, Raleigh (2010)
3. Matthee, K., Mweemba, G., Pais, A., van Stam, G., Rijken, M.: Bringing Internet connectivity to rural Zambia using a collaborative approach. In: ICTD 2007. IEEE (2007)
4. Beck, D.E., Cowan, C.: Spiral Dynamics: Mastering Values, Leadership and Change. Wiley-Blackwell (2005)
5. Wilber, K.: Integral Psychology: Consciousness, Spirit, Psychology, Therapy. Shambhala (2000)
6. Sachs, J.: The End of Poverty: Economic Possibilities for Our Time. Penguin (2006)
7. Barrett, R.: Building a Values-Driven Organization: A Whole System Approach to Cultural Transformation. Butterworth-Heinemann (2006)
8. Merry, P.: Evolutionary Leadership. Integral Publishers (2009)
9. Wilber, K.: Integral Spirituality: A Startling New Role for Religion in the Modern and Postmodern World. Shambhala (2006)
10. van Stam, G.: Placemark. Gertjan van Stam, Macha (2011)

Constraints for Information and Communications Technologies Implementation in Rural Zambia

Gertjan van Stam[1], David Johnson[2], Veljko Pejovic[3], Consider Mudenda[4], Austin Sinzala[4], and Darelle van Greunen[1]

[1] Nelson Mandela Metropolitan University, Port Elizabeth, South Africa
gertjan.vanstam@worksgroup.org,
darelle.vangreunen@nmmu.ac.za
[2] Council for Scientific and Industrial Research, Pretoria, South Africa
david.lloyd.johnson@gmail.com
[3] University of Birmingham, Birmingham, United Kingdom
v.pejovic@cs.bham.ac.uk
[4] Macha Works, Choma, Zambia
{consider.mudenda,austin.sinzala}@machaworks.org

Abstract. Introduction and use of Information and Communication Technologies in rural sub-Saharan Africa face a particular array of challenges. Often, challenges interrelate with context, tradition and culture. This poster presentation identifies constraints during sensitisation, introduction and operations of ICT in rural Zambia. Although quantitative engineering aspects play a role, a multitude of qualitative constraints feature prominently. These involve environmental, skills, and cultural ingredients. Research, planning and evaluation has to be sensitive to these challenges if all rural areas are to receive proper inclusion and benefit from the growing penetration of the Internet worldwide.

Keywords: ICT for development, Rural area wireless networks, Technology and Society, Research methodology, Internet adoption constraints.

1 Introduction

The role of Information and Communication Technologies (ICT) in advancing economic growth in the least developed countries is a growing topic of research and debate [1][2][1][3][4][5][6]. Attention focuses on the plight of the least connected. Institutes and nations urge collaboration on addressing the needs in rural areas. Most ICT research approaches from a quantitative, technological perspective, using conventional wisdom [7]. Work often lacks long term contextual evidence [8]. This poster presents an array of challenges that surface during the process of local adoption of ICT, based upon observations and experience with ICT at a rural African community level in seven rural communities in Zambia. These challenges are:

K. Jonas, I.A. Rai, and M. Tchuente (Eds.): AFRICOMM 2012, LNICST 119, pp. 221–227, 2013.
© Institute for Computer Sciences, Social Informatics and Telecommunications Engineering 2013

1. **environmental constraints** determined by environmental challenges specific to rural areas such as unreliable electricity or supply chain logistics. Rural inhabitants have little control over these challenges.
2. **skills constraints** caused by the lack of availability of trained ICT practitioners as well as the process of training and equipping these practitioners in ICT.
3. **cultural constraints** that deal with the complexity of using, installing, and maintaining ICTs in the context of African culture. Examples: perceptions of time and resources, roles and authority and the role of oral tradition versus written tradition.

2   Background

In Zambia, a typical rural community pivots around health and/or education institutions. Traditional leadership structures govern daily activities. In several locations, church-administered mission stations provide the nucleus of activities. The co-operative organisation, Macha Works, is a rural social enterprise. It resides in the rural community of Macha, Zambia. It operates with a holistic approach, aiming for holistic development of services and facilities at a village level. Macha Works strives to inspire people in rural communities to reach their collective and individual potential and operates according to the Macha Works model [9]. It teams up with national institutes like University of Zambia, and international organisations in a collaborative approach [10].

3   Methodology

The approach to this investigation uses mixed methods of research to address multi-disciplinary research questions, within a single-case study methodology. The method of data collection is one of critical ethnography over a period of nine years. Embedded studies involved positive analysis of quantitative, longitudinal usage data derived from the ICT network in Macha, based upon:

1. a network traffic monitoring system on the village network gateway capturing 14 days of traffic from midnight, Sunday 31 January to midnight Sunday 14 February in 2010, two months of network traffic in February, March and April 2011, involving approximately 450 GB of packets to assess the use and locality of traffic [11][12]
2. survey of Internet usage and attitudes towards ICT, private, one-on-one, on-site interviews in Macha in July/August 2010 (23 interviews)
3. follow up through 44 online interviews of Internet users in Macha, June/July 2011, investigating the use of Web 2.0 applications and services [12].

3.1   Environmental Constraints in Macha

Geographical Constraints. Distances between towns are far, with the surface of Zambia (752,600 km) equalling the size of Turkey (783,600 km) or Texas (696,200 km). Oneway travel typically spans a number of days. Sensitive ICT equipment can easily be broken in transport. *Dust* is common in Zambia year around. Further there are periods of *extreme heat* and periods of rain, *lightening and strong winds*.

Infrastructural Constraints. *Electricity* is a vital constraint in rural areas. National electricity supply is either unavailable or unreliable, with power failures and voltage surges or brown-outs being common (dirty power). In practice, there are many *standards* of equipment arriving in rural areas. Standard Uninterrupted Power Supplies (UPS), meant to protect equipment from energy disruptions get easily damaged as first line of defence. In practice, *solar* equipment proves difficult to source. Battery replacement require specialist efforts.

The constraints on providing for *housing or offices* in rural areas are severe. Sources of funding for building activities are sparse.

Most Zambians conduct their activities in accordance with customary law. Customary tenure of *land* and the position of traditional chiefs are respected [13].

Political and Legal Constraints. The regulatory frameworks for ICT are not necessarily conducive to widespread scale up of ICT in rural areas. Universal Service Fund (USF) collection is part of the work of regulators in many African countries [14]. Processes take several years and require many regular visits to monitor and encourage progress, without assurance of success. Property issues and access to physical infrastructure create significant constraints. Different perceptions of time, power distance between all participants, or mundane issues of transport, all serve to compound the challenges in practice.

Deterministic Constraints. Windows users in Macha were experiencing poorer performance in the Linknet network than their Linux or Mac OS counterparts. There was a perception that LinkNet unfairly disadvantages Windows users.

Thorough network analysis of satellite Internet traffic captured over 2 months in early 2011 revealed a large disparity in performance between Windows and Linux/Mac users. Aggregate traffic was broken into hourly bins and then normalized to throughput per IP address per hour. Windows users were separated from Linux/Mac users using the Time to Live (TTL) field in the TCP header. Windows uses a TTL of 64 and Linux/MAC uses a TTL of 128. Table 1 shows the results.

During this measurement period, there were almost double the number of Windows users compared to Linux/Mac users logged in on average. However, Windows outgoing normalized aggregate traffic was three times worse than Linux/Mac during the phase of slow satellite connectivity. Incoming Windows normalized traffic was only marginally worse than Linux.

Table 1. Windows vs Linux/Mac normalized incoming and outgoing throughput

Satellite connectivity phase 2011/01/28 to 2011/04/09	
Linux/Mac avg MB/IP/hour in	5.53
Linux/Mac avg MB/IP/hour out	1.55
Linux/Mac avg IPs/hour	9.75
Windows avg MB/IP/hour in	4.19
Windows avg MB/IP/hour out	0.55
Windows avg IPs/hour	19.24
E1 2Mbps line connectivity phase 2011/04/09 to 2011/05/19	
Linux/Mac avg MB/IP/hour in	6.33
Linux/Mac avg MB/IP/hour out	1.50
Linux/Mac avg IPs/hour	10.07
Windows avg MB/IP/hour in	7.93
Windows avg MB/IP/hour out	1.00
Windows avg IPs/hour	17.12

Further, to confirm that this scenario could be replicated in a lab environment, a Linux and Windows 7 machine were connected to a Linux server over a 1Mbps line and an artificial delay of between 10ms and 1s was introduced to see the effect of increasing the delay on these operating systems. Table 1 shows the results of this simulation. The simulation confirms the significant negative effect of delay on Windows machines. It also confirms that Windows is unfairly disadvantaged when there is a mix of Windows and Linux flows present. Although there was a sound technical reason for the difference in performance between Windows and Linux, it is challenging to share these findings with frustrated users. Users remained convinced that the performance issue was due to a poorly designed network or, worse, that Windows users are being deliberately disadvantaged.

Economic Constraints. With the majority of the Zambian economy being in the informal, unregulated sector [15], publicly available, quantitative data needs appropriate interpretation. Most data describes realities in urban areas exclusively.

Providing ICT in landlocked Zambia is costly due to the high monthly *connectivity costs*, plus the costs involved in the procurement of equipment and its installation. Prices for satellite connectivity have changed little since 2004, depending on one's assumptions, satellite pricing have gone up 55% [16].

3.2   Skill Constraints

300 People possessed graduate qualification in ICTs in Zambia in 2008 [17]. Uneven distribution of the workforce compounds the shortage of engineers. Although the majority of the population lives in rural areas, most engineers live in urban areas. The shortage is particularly acute for ICT as computers enter rural areas, especially in health and education, while all support staff reside in urban areas [18][19].

In contrast with efforts in health and education, there are no national programmes, nor public private partnerships, specifically designed for training of engineers for rural areas. Except for Macha Works' LITA [20], there are no vocational training centres located in rural areas, and training is mostly left to the unregulated, commercial markets in major towns.

3.3 Cultural Constraints

In Southern Africa, Ubuntu culture centres on diversity and sharing. It values trust and lays a moral foundation for interactions and empowerment. Its outward presentation involves the decentralisation of power and spread of decision-making authority to lower-level leaders [21]. Indigenous cultural heritage expresses itself through *oral tradition* and presentations [22][23]. Most researchers are ignorant of the *indigenous system* that help hold the rural community together [24]. Ubuntu culture and Western cultural expressions differ as antonyms [25].

The understanding of the economic choice in rural areas involves broader conceptions of its constitution, restraints and motivations [26]. African systems work well in doing what they are designed to do. However, when coming from other systems, and other historical conditions, outsiders find interactions often incomprehensible [27][28].

When young persons have a professional connection, or link with expatriate persons, they are expected to fend for themselves. This includes: providing for their own shelter, providing for their own essentials of life (food and soap), contributing to the upkeep of parents, and contributing to or providing for the school fees and upkeep for extended family members.

Contextual ingredients define and influence sustainability. The rural communities judge activities 'sustainable' when they are welcomed by all, are comprehended and can be vocalised by all members of the community, and when all persons are included and have a sense of partaking in the development. As such, the strength of 'rhythm', the tuning into the local culture, sustains the balance an African community strives for [29].

4 Conclusion

Based upon findings during nine years of longitudinal activity in implementing ICT in rural Zambia, this poster shows practical constraints to the ICT inclusion in rural Zambia. These constraints are broken down into environmental constraints, skill constraints, and cultural constraints. They are part of a large picture of ethical, conceptual and pragmatic issues. Constraints heavily influence practice and effect all efforts and activities in rural Zambia.

References

1. ITU: The Role of ICT in Advancing Growth in Least Developed Countries. International Telecommunications Union, Geneva (2011)
2. Unwin, T.: ICT4D: Information and Communication Technology for Development (Cambridge Learning). Cambridge University Press, Cambridge (2009)

3. Toyama, K.: Myths about ICT for the Other Billions. In: Picot, A., Lorenz, J. (eds.) ICT for the Next Five Billion People. Springer (2010)
4. IEG (Independent Evaluation Group): Capturing Technology for Development (An Evaluation of World Bank Group Activities in ICTs). Independent Evaluation Group, The World Bank Group, Washington, DC (2011)
5. Frediksson, T., Barayre, C., Gil, S.F., Korka, D., Lang, R., Nigmatov, A., Schaus, M., Hamdi, M., Miroux, A.: Information Economy Report 2010: ICTs, Enterprises and Poverty Alleviation. United Nations Publication, New York and Geneva (2010)
6. World Bank: Information and Communications for Development 2012: Maximizing Mobile. World Bank, Washington, DC (2012)
7. Gomez, R., Pather, S.: ICT Evaluation: Are We Asking The Right Questions? EJISDC 50(5), 1–14 (2012)
8. Lee, P.: Putting Problems Before Solutions in Development (2011)
9. van Stam, G., van Oortmerssen, G.: Macha Works! In: Frontiers of Society On-Line, Raleigh (2010)
10. Matthee, K., Mweemba, G., Pais, A., van Stam, G., Rijken, M.: Bringing Internet connectivity to rural Zambia using a collaborative approach. In: ICTD 2007. IEEE (2007)
11. Johnson, D.L., Pejovic, V., Belding, E.M., van Stam, G.: VillageShare: Facilitating content generation and sharing in rural networks. In: ACM DEV 2012 (2012)
12. Johnson, D.L., Belding, E.M., van Stam, G.: Network traffic locality in a rural African village. In: ICTD (2012)
13. Adams, M.: Land tenure policy and practice in Zambia: issues relating to the development of the agricultural sector. Mokoro Ltd., Oxford (2003)
14. Calandro, E., Moyo, M.: Is the Universal Access Fund in Africa creating an enabling environment for ICT infrastructure investment in rural and perceived uneconomic areas? In: 5th Communication Policy Research Conference, Xi'an, China (2011)
15. Gewald, J.-B., Hinfelaar, M., Macola, G.: One Zambia, Many Histories. Towards a History of Post-colonial Zambia. The Lembani Trust, Leiden (2008)
16. van Stam, G.: Is Technology the Solution to the World's Major Social Challenges? In: 2012 IEEE Global Humanitarian Technology Conference, Seattle, USA. IEEE (2012)
17. Habeenzu, S.: Zambia ICT Sector Performance Review 2009/2010, vol. 2. Research ICT Africa (2010)
18. Karsenti, T., Collin, S., Harper-Merrett, T.: Successes and Challenges from 87 African Schools Pedagogical Integration of ICT. IRDC, Ottawa (2011)
19. Reddy, M., Purao, S., Kelly, M.: Developing IT Infrastructure for Rural Hospitals: A Case Study of Benefits and Challenges of Hospital-to-Hospital Partnerships. Journal of the American Medical Informatics Association, 554–559 (2008)
20. Mudenda, C., van Stam, G.: ICT Training in Rural Zambia. Case Study: LinkNet Information Technology Academy. In: Jonas, K., Rai, I.A., Tchuente, M. (eds.) AFRICOMM 2012. LNICST, vol. 119, pp. 228–238. Springer, Heidelberg (2013)
21. Khoza, R.: Let Africa Lead: African Transformational Leadership for 21st century Business. VezuBuntu, South Africa (2005)
22. van Stam, G., Mweetwa, F.: Community Radio Provides Elderly a Platform to Have Their Voices Heard in rural Macha, Zambia. The Journal of Community Informatics 8(1) (2012)
23. van Stam, G.: Information and Knowledge Transfer in the rural community of Macha, Zambia. The Journal of Community Informatics (in press)
24. Harden, B.: Africa: Dispatches From a Fragile Continent. Mariner Books (1991)

25. van Stam, G.: Observations from rural Africa: An engineer involved in ICTs and critical ethnography in Macha, Zambia. In: UCSB Center for Information Technology and Society Lecture Series, Santa Barbara, CA, USA (2012)
26. Sheneberger, K., van Stam, G.: Relatio: An Examination of the Relational Dimension of Resource Allocation. Economics and Finance Review 1(4), 26–33 (2011)
27. Maranz, D.: African Friends and Money Matters: Observations from Africa. SIL International (2001)
28. Platteau, J.-P.: The Evolutionary Theory of Land Rights as Applied to Sub-Saharan Africa: A Critical Assessment. Development and Change 27(1), 29–86 (1996)
29. Ulimwengu, J.: What we learn, How we learn it, and for What? In: eLearning Africa, Dar Es Salaam (2011)

ICT Training in Rural Zambia, the Case of LinkNet Information Technology Academy

Consider Mudenda[1] and Gertjan van Stam[2]

[1] Macha Works, Choma, Zambia
consider.mudenda@machaworks.org
[2] Nelson Mandela Metropolitan University, Port Elizabeth, South Africa
gertjan.vanstam@worksgroup.org

Abstract. LinkNet Information Technology Academy (LITA) is a rural based ICT training centre in Zambia. Since its inception in 2004, LITA has endeavored to provide vocational training to facilitate the creation of ICT engineers in rural areas. Following the expansion of its sister unit LinkNet, within the co-operative Macha Works, LITA expanded with training in two other rural communities. The institute provided training for 588 persons in rural Zambia up to 2012.

This case study of LinkNet Information Technology Academy (LITA), in rural Macha, Zambia, provides analysis and review of the positioning, activities and constraints of LITA. It shows that, when training is properly aligned with rural practice, ICT training in rural Zambia is a feasible and beneficial activity.

Keywords: ICT training, rural Africa, Macha Works, vocational training, LITA.

1   Introduction

In developing countries, there is a shortage of properly trained engineering professionals, with few engineers (most being technicians) and few training institutes. For equipment to perform optimally and have a long service life in rural areas, engineering staff are indispensable in the same way as, for instance, the medical staff in the delivery of healthcare. Skilled staff must have appropriate training so that they can carry out the work effectively [1]. The shortage of skilled staff is particularly acute for ICT as computers are invading rural areas, especially in education and health, while skilled persons live mainly in urban areas [2][3].

Lack of skilled human resource or challenges to its formation hamper the growth in ICT in least Developed Countries [4][5][6][7][8][9][10][11][12]. However, apart from policy announcements and program announcements, there are scant reports on how practical trials in rural areas have ventured.

Zambia recognised a shortfall in critical ICT skills required for developing its information and knowledge economy at managerial, professional and technician levels for the development, deployment and application of ICT in both the private and the public sector [13][14]. The national ICT policy calls for the creation of

K. Jonas, I.A. Rai, and M. Tchuente (Eds.): AFRICOMM 2012, LNICST 119, pp. 228–238, 2013.
© Institute for Computer Sciences, Social Informatics and Telecommunications Engineering 2013

Centres of Excellence for the research, manufacturing, and assembly of ICT products, as well as training of ICT professionals. Zambia faces challenges in producing skilled personnel that can meet the needs of industry, especially in technical functions. This is particularly evident in science education, which can provide a strong platform for technical training. As a result, there is a general shortage of technical (and especially engineering) skills [15]. However, in contrast with efforts in health and education, in Zambia there are no national programmes that specifically aim to train engineers in rural areas. Training is mostly left to the unregulated, commercial markets.

2   Environment and History

Macha Works is a rural cooperative organisation that aims to operate services for its rural community in Macha, Zambia. The Macha Works unit LinkNet has been providing internet access in the rural community, using a collaborative approach since 2004 [16]. Its interactions take place according to the Macha Works model [17] and its implementation is in line with its international development model [18]. The LinkNet effort scaled up with implementations in 7 rural communities throughout Zambia.

To assure availability of qualified staff, Macha Works operates the *LinkNet Information Technology Academy* (LITA). LITA aims to provide vocational training focused on rural areas, for jobs in rural areas. It provides local people in the rural community with the opportunity to acquire internationally acknowledged certificates on computer literacy and ICT engineering. This facility is an indispensable component of the overall capacity building objective of the co-operative. LITA is the only rural training centre in Information and Communications Technologies in Zambia. Its main operation is in rural Macha, Zambia.

LITA started its activities in 2004 in a fablab setup in an existing building of the local Macha Research Trust. Formal training started in 2005, utilising a store room in the local Vision Community Centre. Upon renting a room at the local hospital, LITA moved to a more formal set up from 2007 to 2009. In 2009, upon completion of dedicated facilities, LITA moved operations to Macha Works' Ubuntu Campus. The LITA-Centre at Ubuntu Campus operates three class rooms.

With the roll-out of LinkNet sites throughout Zambia, LITA also commenced training activities in other rural areas. In 2010, LITA expanded with a training centre in rural Chikanta. Following years of on-site training, a LITA site started operations in Mukinge in 2012. LITA registered with Zambia's Technical Education, Vocational and Entrepreneurship Training Authority (TEVETA) in 2009.

3   Methodology

This case study is based upon review of documentation, in-depth interviews, and in-person observations. The study performed semi-structured interviews with

LITA and Macha Works' leadership, intended to capture information in line with the local traditions in knowledge and information transfer [19]. 50 LITA graduates have been followed up in person or by telephone to assess what they ended up doing after finishing their studies at LITA. Lastly, international training experts' observations were solicited in an effort to assess LITA's effectiveness and adaption to local cultures.

4   LinkNet Information Technology Academy (LITA)

LITA attracts students from throughout Zambia. Some students come from abroad. Most students came to LITA through personal recommendations by word of mouth. Some responded to advertisements, e.g. via Vision Community Radio Macha or newspaper advertisements and computer-printed flyers. Four people came to LITA from other African countries: 1 from Ghana, 3 from Zimbabwe. Backgrounds of most trainees were Grade 12 school leavers, farmers, nurses and teachers. Intake was 90% from rural areas, and 10% from urban areas. The number of females was greater than males.

A LITA school term typically spans 5 months, with training Monday to Friday. Training consists of 2 hours in class with a teacher and 2 hours of self study. Most students stay longer than the prescribed periods. They mention that they are not able to pass the international exams within such a time frame.

Although not simple in a rural area where housing is constraining, when in Macha, students find their own lodging, stay with relatives or find other means of staying in the area.

The training needs can be categorised as follows:

1. LinkNet associates that need to be sensitised and exposed to tools and technologies. Students typically participate in existing or anticipated LinkNet implementations throughout Zambia,
2. studies upon requests by Non Governmental Organisations, for instance for training in operations of the Smart Care electronic health register systems,
3. students who want to seize an opportunity for education, for their own purposes.

The curriculum of LITA consists of:

1. International Computer Drivers Licence (ICDL),
2. CompTIA A+,
3. short computer literacy courses, and
4. on site training.

In 2012, LITA expanded with a course in entrepreneurship. LITA is also the co-ordinator of Research and Development at Macha Works.

a) International Computer Driving Licence (ICDL)

LITA is the first accredited International Computer Driving Licence (ICDL) training and exam centre in a rural area of Zambia. LITA provides training up to *ICDL level-4* certificate. The training centre classifies as *ICDL Grade-2* and is certified for both training and exams.

LITA operates two training rooms and one exam room. Since its existence, LITA trained 292 persons in ICDL in Macha. Of these trainees, 55 persons passed all 7 ICDL modules, and 30 persons passed the exams for 4 ICDL modules (ICDL start).

b) CompTIA A+

LITA's Comptia A+ training aims to instil competency as a computer technician. *A+* is an internationally recognised programme that covers a variety of technologies and operating systems.

At the start of the activities in 2004, access to *A+* curriculum was not available. Therefore, training started unguided by literature. An expat volunteer trained the first technicians upon receiving a donation of *A+* training book.

In Zambia, *A+* examination can only be done in the capital Lusaka. Upon completion of the studies, 7 students travelled the 380 kilometres to Lusaka a number of times. During the first exams, the students found out that the A+ curriculum had changed. Subsequently, all students failed the exam. It took one year to acquire new A+ books. They had to be paid for and imported from oversees. Training continued on receipt of new books. Upon completion of the revised training, students traveled again. At this time, the exam centre computers were inoperable or the internet connection not working. Consequently, the costs of doing exams represent more than half of the costs of the whole training.

LITA trained 20 students in *A+*, out of which 5 passed the Comptia A+ exam. LITA plans to introduce a *Network+* training. However, due to the unavailability of books and the barriers to acquiring them, the course has not started.

c) Short Computer Literacy Courses

Computers are still a rare artefact for most people in rural areas in Zambia. Many health and education staff and volunteers working in peripheral, deep rural centres have never seen a computer. There is a distinct need for sensitisation and arrangements for a first encounter with computers. This provides for a demystifying and often exhilarating experience.

d) On-the-Job Training

LITA trainers do travel to provide training, especially in the initial phase of a new LinkNet implementation in a remote, rural area. At that stage it is usually the key stakeholders and nearby professionals who receive on-the-job training in their own environment. The training includes an introduction to computers and their operations and the use of internet facilities.

Macha Works' introduction of networked computers and LITA to Nurses Training Schools exposed the Nurses Training Schools (NTS) to ICT and the internet [20]. During 2010, 106 nurses partook in LITA courses, on site at the NTS.

Output

The first group of 8 persons to be trained in ICT in Macha started in 2004. During the first year, three left the training before the end. All three acquired formal jobs in the capital, Lusaka. Upon completion, the group was highly successful in facilitating the set-up of the LinkNet network in Macha, using a collaborative approach [16]. For instance, they were able to install a 52 node mixed wireless mesh network, transporting the internet throughout the community [21]. After the first group, LITA trained 396 persons in ICDL, 20 persons in A+, and 10 persons in the Smart Care electronic health records system in Macha. Another 60 followed introduction courses. LITA grew its own 4 trainers, selecting suitable talent from previous LITA trainings.

In remote Chikanta, LITA trained 65 persons in ICDL. In Mukinge 25 have completed ICDL training since 2008 with 14 trainees ongoing during 2012.

LITA trained 588 persons in ICDL, A+, Smart Care and entrepreneurship in rural Zambia up to the year 2012.

During 2011, we traced and contacted 50 persons that studied at LITA in Macha. We asked about their employment outcomes after their LITA studies:

1. 30%, got a formal job at Macha Works, 70% in Macha and 30% elsewhere;
2. 10%, got a formal job outside of the scope of Macha Works;
3. 60% of the trainees did not find a formal job and continued to function in the informal economy.

Outcomes in A+:

1. 12 persons got a job at Macha Works;
2. 3 persons got a job somewhere else;
3. 5 person has not found a formal job.

From the total of 588 students, an estimated 75% had never accessed any form of ICT training before coming to LITA. More than 25 university students passed through Macha; 10 came to Macha on their own initiative, after graduation.

LITA provided for sensitization training for various rural professionals:

1. 25 primary school teachers from the Macha Zone (30% of all teachers in the Zone),
2. 5 secondary school teachers,
3. 106 nurse students in Macha's Nurses Training School, and
4. 25 health professionals in Mukinge hospital.

LITA performed many One Day Sensitization Courses for *rural health professionals*. During 2010 and 2011, a total of 60 rural health workers participated in these courses.

From the rural Macha Works environment, LITA students continued with international training programmes aiming for academic certification or graduation. From 20 persons trained in A+, one person graduated with an international BSc in Computer Science, done through distance education in the United Kingdom. An international course in Italy admitted one LITA A+ graduate, and several other graduates travelled the African continent to interact with peers.

5   Findings

LITA is a rural case, a social enterprise addressing the need of ICT training in Zambia. It takes the position that ICT provides a component that is essential for the development of rural Africa. ICT training in Zambia is an important aspect of capacity building for sustainable progress in a rural area [22]. Respondents in interviews mentioned

1. their increased awareness,
2. increased information and implementation of ICT in promotion of sustainable farming and business practices,
3. better access to training opportunities (for farm activity and enterprise diversification),
4. return to work and business start-ups by women,
5. development of employment guidance by eLearning, and
6. effective delivery of services.

International observers commented on the discursive way of teaching at LITA. The teaching method caters for the rural context as it addresses rural experiences and expectations. Inferences are drawn from both the teaching and the rural practice. With a few words, often in rota-type sequence, the LITA trainer packages the complex message effectively for the rural participants. Apart from the actual training, much time is spend understanding the exam procedure, which appears foreign to rural students. Being able to execute an ICDL exam needs much time and exercise.

Intellectual, non-discursive lectures are not an effective method of vocational training in rural Macha. When LITA connected with the day-to-day practice in the operational LinkNet network, and started research and development, results went up. Therefore, in 2007 LinkNet signed a Memorandum of Understanding with the University of Zambia (UNZA), after which students of UNZA came to Macha to participate in research and development as part of their studies or extra-curricular activity. Also, students from the Copperbelt University (CBU), the second university in Zambia, came to perform research and development internships in Macha.

Macha Work produced proposals for Master's programmes, undergraduate research agenda, programme proposals, input for national research agenda and performed in workshops and published papers. Further, Macha Works provided for a presentation series 'The Evolution Of the Internet' (EVOINT) at UNZA. International research co-operation was established with Fraunhofer, the Global

Research Alliance, UCSB and other research institutes. Unfortunately, none of the international research proposals resulted in funding for the Macha Works side of research. All research activities, publications, student and conference participation took place on a pro-Deo basis.

International Computer Drivers License. ICDL provides attainable training at the right level for rural Africa. However, ICDL curriculum focuses on Windows operating system and programmes. Licensing of Windows computers is difficult to perform in rural areas, and Windows update and upgrades are elaborate and necessitate reliable internet connectivity. Further, Windows computers are prone to viruses especially in a multi-user setup as at LITA, in line with Bhattacharya's findings in India [23]. To overcome the most pressing problems, LITA re-installs the Windows operating system on a frequent basis.

ICDL Zambia resides in Lusaka. LITA visits ICDL frequently to acquire curriculum and certificates, to perform payments, and to discuss innovations. LITA did not succeed implementing ICDL or an equivalent on Free and Open Software (FOSS) platforms.

The necessity of accredited invigilation hampers examination. The process requires two persons: one without computer knowledge for observation, and one to operate the examination system. ICDL demands written exam reports from both the invigilator and the examination co-ordinator to ICDL international to ensure exam transparency. The sheer logistics of such a procedure, and the primacy of orality and apprehension for writing, handicaps this process.

Resource Planning and Allocation. The LITA turnover is about USD 5,000 per year. At the start of LITA, all funding came through from LinkNet. This turned around, and since 2011 most funding comes from student contributions. The cost of TAVETA and ICDL registration and paperwork account for over 50% of LITA's yearly budget.

The local Ubuntu culture does not encourage discursive planning. Resource allocation focusses on *today* and *the past* [24]. LITA's planning consists of lessons learned and utilises the method of oral budgeting [25]. Growth is gradual and depends on experience built up through the history. Without any history or experience of ICT training in rural areas, LITA spent seven years co-operating with communities in collaborative setup. The community scrutinised the national accreditation process before committing to LITA courses. The abilities of local leadership were tested before community members felt LITA suitable to invest in. Trainees waited several months before signing up so as to see what experiences the early adopters had.

It seems ambitious to expect ICT training in rural areas to be commercially viable; if the business case existed, the main stream businesses would have done it by now. There is frequent advice from national, urban-based experts to relocate LITA from rural areas to urban areas. The reasoning is that, in towns, demand is high, and economy of scale can be achieved. Although the advice make sense from a commercial perspective, it introduces an ethical and conceptual tension. The thought undermines the exact purpose of the positioning of LITA in rural areas: to provide ICT training in and for rural areas to engender a technical base in and for rural areas.

LITA experiences the following environmental constraints:

Housing. For the training institute, its trainers, and for students the most pressing issue is lodging. Rural areas do not have many buildings for rent, nor has built accommodation for ICT trainers. There is no ready investment nor capital available to invest in buildings in communal lands. Macha Works is investing considerably in providing for facilities for LITA, while teachers build their own housing in the area.

IT Systems. Computer systems do deteriorate rapidly due to environmental challenges like transport over rough roads, dirty electricity, heat, and dust. Upgrades of hardware is difficult to source, due to the multitude of (donated) computer systems and the distance to commercial centres. Viruses in the Windows environment hampers system performance. No Virtual Learning Environment (VLE) is deployed due to lack of exposure to the benefits and/or how to implement and operate such a system and environment.

Consumables. Training necessitates writing, which needs paper and printing. Printer toner runs out. Toner is not readily available and expensive. It is available in towns only. To align the availability of currency bills with steps in procurement procedures - to assure an audit trail - and travel scheduling are substantial challenges.

Curricula and Trainers. Current training materials invariably refer to circumstances in urban environments where social codes and context are different from rural areas. LITA transposes existing curriculum for rural dissemination. Trainers from urban and/or international environments are not willing to stay in rural areas, and, when persuaded, only commit for short periods of time and/or ask for inflated remuneration. Also, the effectiveness of trainers from outside the community is challenged by cultural differences. LITA has the experience that it takes at least one year of trial and error for an international volunteer to reach a level of effectiveness in rural Zambia.

Transport. Any discussion of LITA development necessitates travel to town. A visit to Lusaka covers at least 800 kilometres and two days of travel. Partners in towns are not available for online meetings nor are willing to travel to rural areas reciprocally.

Copyright and License Fees. LITA is not able to acquire sufficient training material due to their high costs, copyright issues, or complicated and protracted licensing discussions. License fees for ICDL, A+ curriculum and TAVETA registration deplete over 50% of LITA's income.

6   Discussion

Throughout the establishment of LITA, trainers or students reflected on other setups by participating in courses in the commercial markets in ICT training in town. They reported that programs tend to be short and are of varied quality. Pure lecture-based training proved unsustainable, both from views of resource use and outcomes. When LITA combined its training with a pragmatic approach with practicals in the organisation and then introduced research and development components, the yield went up considerably. With hundreds of graduates in rural areas, LITA shows impressive results. However, the effects of ICT training cannot be assessed by quantitative evaluation only. The benefits for rural areas, its socio-economic situation, and the quality of life must be taken into account, as well as the effects on sustainable progress in rural areas.

Benefits of ICT training are not only linked to ICT engineering. The LITA case shows it also influences professionals in health and education, and agriculture and entrepreneurship. It contributes to the betterment of the community as a whole. As such, the embedding of LITA in the setting of Macha Works, a co-operative involved in a broad range of activities in the rural community, is advantageous.

In the predominantly informal setting of Macha Works, technicians at LinkNet acquire ICT skills and grow in stature when developments are in line with the Macha Works Model and the Integral Development model. They appear to slow down and lose drive when going through costly and time consuming formal training classes based on western methodology. Obviously, even acquisition of ICT skills in rural Africa can utilise the often well-honed observation capabilities of people. LITA's introduction of entrepreneurship training increases self-employment and empowers indigenous ICT enterpreneurship in rural areas.

LITA management mentioned that necessary and active inclusion of local organisations and people does influence project development and management. Many views need to be taken into account and an objections from any stakeholder can slow down progress. However, such processes do generate ownership and long term take-up within a community.

The particular way in which training takes place indicates that ICT skills are not necessarily acquired through imparting and absorption of abstract concepts. This contrasts with the construction of western-centric courses in which technological realities are predominantly communicated through writings and deconstruction of various components that build the whole.

The difficulties with passing exams might stem from the fact its analytic questioning stems from a highly developed textuality. Written examination questions came into being after print had worked its way on consciousness, much after the invention of writing [26]. Such a process did not take place in rural Zambia.

7   Conclusions

ICT training in rural Macha is feasible and beneficial. Locally embedded implementation and scaling up of ICT training involves a distinct set of challenges in resource-limited setting. The LITA case shows that, when training is properly aligned with rural practice, significant results are achievable in rural settings.

Capacity building in ICT necessitates a combination of lectures and on-the-job activities. Hundreds of students showed remarkable outputs after going through a combination of classroom and on-the-job training and research and development. The interaction of LITA in the holistic setting of Macha Works provides for a productive setting. The interaction between rural practice and rural training builds capacity that aligns well with the needs in rural areas.

References

1. UNESCO: Engineering: Issues Challenges and Opportunities for Development. UN-ESCO Publishing, Paris (2010)
2. Karsenti, T., Collin, S., Harper-Merrett, T.: Successes and Challenges from 87 African Schools Pedagogical Integration of ICT. IRDC, Ottawa (2011)
3. Reddy, M., Purao, S., Kelly, M.: Developing IT Infrastructure for Rural Hospitals: A Case Study of Benefits and Challenges of Hospital-to-Hospital Partnerships. Journal of the American Medical Informatics Association, 554–559 (2008)
4. ITU: The Role of ICT in Advancing Growth in Least Developed Countries. International Telecommunications Union, Geneva (2011)
5. Schwalje, W.: A Conceptual Model of National Skills Formation for Knowledge-based Economic Development. London School of Economics (2011)
6. Roxburgh, C., Dorr, N., Leke, A., Tazi-Riffi, A., Van Wamelen, A., Lund, S., Chironga, M., Alatovik, T., Atkins, C., Terfous, N., Zeino-Mahmalat, T.: Lions on the move: The progress and potential of African economies. McKinsey Global Institute (2010)
7. Johnson, D.L., Pejovic, V., Belding, E.M., van Stam, G.: Traffic Characterization and Internet Usage in Rural Africa. In: Proceedings of WWW, Hyderabad, India (2011)
8. Heinemann, E., Prato, B., Shepherd, A.: Rural Poverty Report 2011. International Fund for Agricultural Development (IFAD), Rome (2011)
9. United Nations: Trends in Sustainable Development, Africa Report. United Nations Publication, New York (2009)
10. Otty, M., Sita, A.: It's time for Africa. Ernst & Young (2011)
11. Kožul-Wright, Z., et al.: The Least Developed Countries, Report 2010. United Nations (UNCTAD), New York and Geneva (2010)
12. Budde, P.: Broadband: A Platform for Progress. ITU/UNESCO (2011)
13. Government of the Republic of Zambia: ICT Policy Zambia (2005)
14. Habeenzu, S.: Zambia ICT Sector Performance Review 2009/2010, vol. 2. Research ICT Africa (2010)
15. Ministry of Commerce Trade and Industry: Investment Policy Review of Zambia. Advancing investment policy reform. Government of the Republic of Zambia, Lusaka (2011)
16. Matthee, K., Mweemba, G., Pais, A., van Stam, G., Rijken, M.: Bringing Internet connectivity to rural Zambia using a collaborative approach. In: ICTD 2007. IEEE (2007)
17. van Stam, G., van Oortmerssen, G.: Macha Works! In: Frontiers of Society On-Line, Raleigh (2010)

18. Bets, J., van Stam, G., Voorhoeve, A.-M.: Modeling and Practise of Integral Development in Rural Zambia: Case Macha. In: Jonas, K., Rai, I.A., Tchuente, M. (eds.) AFRICOMM 2012. LNICST, vol. 119, pp. 211–220. Springer, Heidelberg (2013)

19. van Stam, G.: Information and Knowledge Transfer in the rural community of Macha, Zambia. The Journal of Community Informatics 9(1) (2013)

20. Vallis, J.M., Mason, A.C., Afari-Dekyi, K., Ansotinge, E., Antwi, J., Chifwaila, L., Fraser, F., Moyo, P., Mudenda, C., Turner, C., Urquhart, G., van Stam, G., Wales, A.: Building Capacity for E-learning for Nurse Training in Zambia and Ghana: Appropriate Computer Technologies? In: Appropriate Healthcare Technologies for Developing Countries, AHT 2012 (2012)

21. Backens, J., Mweemba, G., van Stam, G.: A Rural Implementation of a 52 Node Mixed Wireless Mesh Network in Macha, Zambia. In: Villafiorita, A., Saint-Paul, R., Zorer, A. (eds.) AFRICOM 2009. LNICST, vol. 38, pp. 32–39. Springer, Heidelberg (2010)

22. van Stam, G.: Placemark. Gertjan van Stam, Macha (2011)

23. Bhattacharya, P., Thies, W.: Computer Viruses in Urban Indian Telecenters: Characterizing an Unsolved Problem. In: 5th ACM Workshop on Networked Systems for Developing Regions (2011)

24. Sheneberger, K., van Stam, G.: Relatio: An Examination of the Relational Dimension of Resource Allocation. Economics and Finance Review 1(4), 26–33 (2011)

25. van Stam, G.: Oral Budgeting in rural Macha, Southern Province, Zambia. Anthropological Notebooks 18(3), 41–46 (2012)

26. Ong, W.J.: Orality and Literacy: The Technologizing of the Word. Methuen (1982)

Relevant Computing Curricula in Sub-Saharan Africa

Idris A. Rai, Anthony J. Rodrigues, Isabella M. Venter, Godfrey Mills,
Hussein Suleman, and John Edumadze

Kampala Summit task team, Uganda
rai@cit.mak.ac.ug, tonyaniceto@gmail.com, iventer@uwc.ac.za,
gmills@ug.edu.gh, hussein@cs.uct.ac.za, jedumadze@ucc.edu.gh

Abstract. The principle objective of this research was to establish what computing curricula are required for the Sub-Saharan Africa region. Input from academics, businessmen and the analyses of curricula from several African universities revealed a gap between existing curricula and what is considered to be ideal for this region. Required knowledge clusters were identified: Science and Technology; Soft and Research skills; Society and Development; Environment; Business and Entrepreneurship; Institutional; and Practical Skills. These were used to propose a model for enhancing the computing curricula of the Association of Computing Machinery and the Institute of Electrical and Electronic Engineers' for the SSA region.

Keywords: computing curricula, curriculum development, relevant curricula.

1   Introduction

Computing as a discipline was adopted by some Sub-Saharan African (SSA) universities only in the early 1990s, many years after computing was an established discipline in the United States of America (USA)–in 1993 Odedra et al. noted: "*Only a handful of countries such as Nigeria, Malawi and Zimbabwe have universities that offer computer science degrees.*" [1]. In the USA such programmes emerged in the 1960s [2]. The first (and still the most popular) of the computing disciplines to be adopted in SSA was computer science (CS), which was in most cases initially hosted in the mathematics units of the institutions, with mathematicians delivering most of the modules of these CS programmes. As capacity building for CS trainers became necessary, graduates of mathematics trained at MSc or PhD level in disciplines related to CS. Obviously, those who did not train in CS at the undergraduate level lacked aspects of CS foundation and thus could not competently undertake the research required by higher degrees in CS.

At the time most institutions offered CS as a major with mathematics-related disciplines such as mathematics or statistics as a second major. As CS gained popularity and more CS training capacity became available, institutions established stand-alone departments to host the CS programmes.

K. Jonas, I.A. Rai, and M. Tchuente (Eds.): AFRICOMM 2012, LNICST 119, pp. 239–248, 2013.
© Institute for Computer Sciences, Social Informatics and Telecommunications Engineering 2013

Computing disciplines, defined jointly by the ACM (Association for Computing Machinery) and IEEE (Institute of Electrical and Electronic Engineers) Computer Society are: computer science (CS); information technology (IT); information systems (IS); software engineering (SE); and computer engineering (CE) [2]. In addition to defining core knowledge areas for each discipline, the joint committee of the ACM and IEEE define clear boundaries amongst the different but otherwise overlapping computing disciplines (see Fig. 1). In addition, they provide detailed recommendations of specific modules and the relative importance of each discipline.

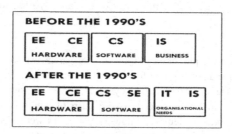

Fig. 1. Focus of the various computing disciplines [2]

Curricula cannot be developed in isolation but must consider *community* challenges so that graduates have the necessary skills to address these community challenges. The needs of a community can be very distinct depending on how the community is defined. At a micro-level, communities can be seen as local groups of people geographically located in a close proximity. The people who share a common culture, and often language, are subject to some form of socio-economic environment that can be uniquely identified and differs from what communities in other geographic areas experience. Consequently curricula recommendations developed by experts from one community may fail to consider the needs of other communities. SSA has unique challenges and needs, and thus relevant knowledge areas (curricula knowledge clusters) need to be considered for SSA institutions.

As citizens of the so-called global village, SSA graduates should have skills that will enable them to work for any global IT company. Additionally they should be equipped with more specific skills to tackle challenges faced by their communities. Related to the need for the development of the region, graduates from SSA (much more than their counterparts in the developed world) should be able to build their own IT businesses—small and medium enterprises (SMEs) have proven to contribute significantly to economic growth in the SSA region [3].

In August 2010, a two-day summit was organised and held in Kampala, Uganda, and computing scholars, from all parts of SSA–West Africa, South Africa and East Africa–attended. The aim of the summit was to determine what graduate attributes are required of SSA graduates other than what is considered to be the "problem space" as defined by the ACM & IEEE (see Fig. 2). Stakeholders from some local IT industries were invited to contribute on what skills (from their experience) they would appreciate in SSA graduates. At the summit, a task force was constituted (and given terms of reference) to design a tool for the quantitative and, to a lesser degree, qualitative, analysis of data collected from various institutions in SSA.

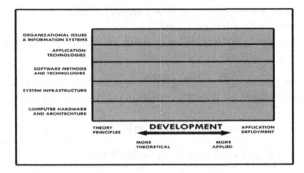

Fig. 2. Problem space of computing as defined by the ACM & IEEE [2]

The remainder of the paper is organized as follows: the outcomes of the summit are presented in Section 2; the collected data and the findings derived from the analysis are presented in Section 3; recommendations are outlined in Section 4; and, finally, conclusions are drawn in Section 5.

2   The Outcomes of Kampala Summit

The two-day summit was attended by 40 educators in computing disciplines from around the continent (15 universities from Sub-Saharan Africa were present), some IT practitioners and some researchers from in- and outside Africa.

Before the summit, all participants completed an online pre-summit questionnaire to gather ideas, which fed into the summit agenda. On the first day of the summit, participants discussed various matters pertaining to their existing programmes (design issues, accreditation, pedagogy, delivery methods, relevance, managing stakeholders' expectations, and supporting resources such as infrastructure, laboratories and software). The first session ended with a plenary session, lead by a panel of four chief executive officers (CEOs) of local IT industries. These industrialists are IT entrepreneurs in Uganda who own and leed IT businesses largely focusing on software development. Their companies employ on average 20 staff each. In addition, they have been interacting with students doing internships or fieldwork. The objective of including IT businessmen in the summit was to get feedback from them on what they felt are the gaps in the skills-base of the graduates they employ.

The following is a summary of the aspects highlighted by the industrialists (detailed feedback can be obtained from the summit website [4]). The industrialists felt that there was:

- A *lack of basic skills and the ability to work independently;*
- *Limited problem solving skills;*
- *Inability to handle practical problems; and*
- *Poor communication skill.*

Furthermore the industrialists observed that:

- *Top students are just naturally smart irrespective of what they were taught;*
- *Content should be real-world based and relevant to the local the industry;*

- *Technology changes very fast – students should acquire the basic skills to allow them to become life-long learners; and*
- *Communication and problem solving skills should be integrated within other modules.*

This feedback shed some light on what skills-base is required, and what needs to be considered when developing a relevant computing curriculum for SSA.

Table 1. Knowledge clusters and corresponding topics

Science and Technology: Theory, Design, Modeling
Soft and Research Skills: Problem solving, Team work, Communication
Society and Development: Community outreach, Ethics, Learner centric teaching
Environment: E-waste, Carbon footprint, Health
Business: Innovation, Commercialisation, Entrepreneurship
Institutional: Management and organisation, Structure, Governance
Practical Skills: Projects, Field work, Internship

During discussions on the second day of the summit, the delegates identified the *knowledge clusters* (building blocks of skills or knowledge areas) they felt should be part of each curriculum. The meeting came up with 7 knowledge clusters, namely: Science and Technology (S&T); Soft and Research skills (S&R); Society and Development (S&D); Environment (ENV); Business and Entrepreneurship (BU); Institutional (INST); and Practical Skills (PR). Each of these knowledge clusters can further be defined by a number of knowledge areas. The detailed definition and examples for each knowledge cluster is shown in Table 1.

Table 2. The current state of programmes

	S&T	S&R	INST	S&D	ENV	BU	PR
CS	4	1	1	1	0	1	4
SE	4	1	1	0	0	1	4
IS	3	1.5	3	1	0	2	4
IT	2	1	3	1	0	2	4
CE	4	1	0	1	1	1	3

Table 2 shows the degree of importance (0 = least- and 5= most-important) of each knowledge cluster in current computing programmes as agreed upon by the delegates during the summit. From the table it can be seen that some of the knowledge clusters (ENV, S&D, S&R and INST) are considered to be very low or non-existent for most of the current computing disciplines. Even for S&T the delegates indicated that the degree of importance was less than optimal.

Table 3. The degree of importance for the ideal computing programme

	S&T	S&R	INST	S&D	ENV	BU	PR
CS	5	4	2	3	2	2	5
SE	5	4	3	3	1	3	5
IS	3	5	5	4	2	4	5
IT	2	5	4	4	3	3	5
CE	5	4	1	3	4	3	5

Table 3, on the other hand, shows the degree of importance delegates believes each of the knowledge clusters should have, in order to constitute the ideal relevant computing curricula for SSA. There is a distinct discrepancy between Table 3 and Table 2. In effect, the summit delegates believed more emphasis should be placed on both the PR (Practical) and the S&T (Science and Technology) knowledge clusters. They felt that S&T should be more emphasized for CS, SE and CE compared to IT and IS. IT and IS, it was felt, should emphasize S&R (soft and research skills), INST (institutional skills), and S&D (society and development). It is clear that some knowledge clusters such as S&R, S&D, ENV and BU currently receive little emphasis. Albeit to a lesser degree, this also applies to the S&T knowledge cluster, which is considered to be a core element of most computing programmes. The outcomes of the Kampala summit are based on the rich integrated experiences of computing academics in SSA and a selected number of experts from industry. It indicates that the largest gaps are in soft and research skills as well as the skills to explore societal developmental needs.

At the end of the summit, a task force was established to develop tools to empirically investigate the existing computing programmes in SSA in order to establish the gap based on realistic data from the programmes. In the next section, the developed tools for the quantitative analysis (excluding the qualitative analysis) of the programmes are presented as well as the findings derived from the data.

3 Data Analysis and Findings

A task force of six academics–two each from East, West and South Africa–was constituted to collect data about the syllabi of the computing programmes currently being taught in their respective regions. The findings of the team were an important step towards validating the gaps between the existing curricula and the identified knowledge clusters. Syllabi from a total of 22 computing programmes were collected and analysed. More than half of the syllabi (13 of the 22) were CS, three were IT, three were CE, two were IS, and only one was SE. It is not surprising that the most popular of the computing programmes in SSA is still CS (the oldest discipline among the computing disciplines). The rest of the programmes are new to SSA. Of the universities considered, most offer CS only, a few offer two computing disciplines and one offers all computing disciplines as defined by the joint IEEE and ACM committee.

Table 4. Analysis of 15 CS programmes in terms of the defined knowledge clusters

CS	S&T	S&R	S&D	ENV	BU	INST	PR	E-PR	Years
CS_1	0.73	0.06	0.06	0	0.04	0.06	0.08	N/A	4
CS_2	0.77	0.025	0.075	0	0	0	0.08	N/A	3
CS_3	0.75	0.16	0	0	0	0	0.09	N/A	4
CS_4	0.82	0.06	0	0	0.036	0	0.14	0.112	3
CS_5	0.85	0.045	0.03	0	0.03	0	0.045	N/A	4
CS_6	0.88	0.064	0.056	0	0	0	0	N/A	3
CS_7	0.95	0.041	0	0	0	0	0	N/A	3
CS_8	1	0	0	0	0	0	0	0.2	3
CS_9	0.82	0.02	0.006	0	0	0	0.09	0.1	3
CS_{10}	0.79	0.045	0.054	0.02	0.02	0	0.073	N/A	3
CS_{13}	0.83	0.055	0	0	0.055	0	0.06	N/A	4
CS_{14}	0.86	0.03	0.03	0	0	0	0.07		3
CS_{15}	0.8	0.02	0.006	0	0.026	0.013	0.14	0.16	4
Max	1	0.16	0.075	0.02	0.055	0.06	0.14		
mean	0.83	0.048	0.024	0.001	0.015	0.005	0.066		
Min	0.73	0	0	0	0	0	0		

It was a challenge to collect the required data: only a few of the computing departments' syllabi are available online and many that were approached through other means did not respond; the representation of the data and the amount of information available differed considerably from one programme to another; and some universities offer programmes not defined by the joint IEEE and ACM committee.

Each module (for each programme) was categorised in terms of the knowledge clusters and whether it is core or an elective. The relative weight for each module (for each knowledge cluster) was computed as a fraction of the total CUs or CHs in the programme. For a few programmes, it was possible to identify the number of practical hours embedded within the knowledge clusters (it is shown as E-PR). Table 4 shows the relative weight of each of the knowledge clusters for the 15 CS programmes collected from selected regions of SSA. It can be observed that in the existing programmes, significant emphasis is placed on the core technical module of all the programmes (S&T) and far less emphasis is placed on the remaining knowledge clusters. S&R (emphasized by the IT professionals) is only considered to be of relative importance and in only one programme constitutes more than 10% of the programme (CS_3).

The most popular S&R course is *Communication Skills*. It was not possible to establish if more skills were embedded within other knowledge clusters. The ENV and INST knowledge clusters are the least emphasized. Only one programme offered a module on ENV and two programmes offered INST modules. Only six programmes provided some modules on BU. Most programmes emphasised PR (Practical skills) either as a separate module or embedded within S&T modules. Where it was possible to determine its "embeddedness", it is provided in the E-PR column in Table 4. Relative weights provided in the table are based on individual modules that focus specifically on offering practical skills; it may include a final year project, field work/internship, or individual projects. In Table 5 the data for other computing disciplines is shown. It can quickly be observed that a similar pattern in terms of emphasis given to the different knowledge clusters (as observed for the CS programmes) exists for the other computing programmes (IT, SE, CE and IS).

Table 5. Analysis of IT, SE, CE and IS computing programmes in terms of the defined knowledge clusters

IT	S&T	S&R	S&D	ENV	BU	INST	PR	E-PR
IT$_1$	0.71	0.114	0	0	0.03	0	0.15	
IT$_2$	0.56	0.036	0.115	0	0.115	0.06	0.06	0.12
IT$_3$	0.66	0.016	0.04	0	0.065	0.1	0.12	
Average	0.635	0.075	0.057	0	0.073	0.03	0.105	
SE								
SE$_1$	0.76	0.02	0	0	0.04	0	0.11	0.18
CE								
CE$_1$	0.82	0.1	0	0	0.02	0	0.1	N/A
CE$_2$	0.82	0.02	0	0.01	0.03	0	0.11	N/A
CE$_3$	0.82	0.02	0.007	0	0.03	0.0013	0.013	0.22
Average	0.82	0.047	0.002	0.003	0.027	0.0004	0.0743	
IS								
IS$_1$	0.64	0.11	0.03	0	0.086	0	0.133	
IS$_2$	0.7	0	0	0	0.27	0	0.023	N/A
Average	0.67	0.055	0.015	0	0.178	0	0.078	

Finally the syllabi of the participating CS computing programmes in SSA were analysed in terms of modules offered in each knowledge cluster. Table 6 shows the number of modules (in each knowledge cluster) for the various CS programmes analysed and should thus not be used to compare the different programmes, since the number of credit units assigned for each module may differ greatly from one programme to another. What can be derived from the table is that there is very little emphasis on all the knowledge clusters, except S&T and PR, which is considered necessary for curricula in SSA. In the next section, recommendations regarding the development of computing curricula in SSA are presented.

Table 6. Number of modules per knowledge clusters for CS programmes

CS	S&T	S&R	S&D	ENV	BU	INST	PR	YRS
CS_1	36	1	3	0	2	3	4	4
CS_2	57	3	2	0	2	0	3	4
CS_3	46	8	0	0	0	0	2	4
CS_4	42	3	0	0	3	0	4	4
CS_5	49	1	1	0	2	1	6	4
CS_6	28	2	0	0	1	0	4	3
CS_7	34	3	2	0	0	0	0	3
CS_8	36	1	3	0	0	0	3	3
CS_9	34	2	3	1	1	0	4	3
CS_{10}	30	3	3	0	0	0	4	3
CS_{11}	36	2	2	0	0	0	3	3

4   Recommendations and Conclusion

Before presenting recommendations, a few assumptions are made about the desired relevant computing curricula and the degree of importance of each of the knowledge clusters (see Table 1). These assumptions are:

- Each module in the programme contains the same number of credit units (CU) (that is 1.5% of the total number of CU in the programme):
- Each skill is provided using a separate module, i.e., skills are not embedded in any module.
- In total, the programme will have 100/1.5=67 modules distributed amongst the seven knowledge clusters in the defined programme.
- The goal is to derive some relative weights for each of the knowledge clusters for all computing programmes.

It is hoped that the process (adopted in this section) can serve as a benchmark for academics to follow when deriving their programmes. In order to get the relative weights for each knowledge cluster (based on the values provided in Table 3), and to determine the fraction of contact hours each knowledge cluster should have in each computing programme, the values in Table 7 were intuitively defined by the authors. Relevant academic units can come up with a different distribution to yield the learning outcomes of the designed curricula.

Take CS for example, the values in the row show that 51% (equivalent to 51/1.5 = 34 modules) of the weight of the programme should be assigned to S&T, S&R covers 18% of the programme (12 modules), S&D, ENV and BU are covered by 2, 2, and 3 modules respectively, and finally the practical knowledge clusters is covered by 12 modules. To get the normalized weights for each knowledge cluster in each programme under the relevance metrics values obtained in Table 3, the corresponding values of knowledge clusters in Table 3 and Table 7 are multiplied for all entries in the tables and finally the resulting values is divided by the sum of values for all knowledge clusters of a given programme (see equation 1).

Table 7. Hypothetical relative weights

	S&T	S&R	S&D	ENV	BU	INST	Pr	Total
CS	0.51	0.18	0.03	0.03	0.04	0.03	0.18	1
IT	0.45	0.24	0.03	0.03	0.04	0.06	0.15	1
IS	0.45	0.24	0.03	0.03	0.04	0.06	0.15	1
SE	0.51	0.15	0.03	0.03	0.04	0.03	0.21	1
CE	0.51	0.15	0.03	0.03	0.04	0.03	0.21	1

Let W(i,j) be the weight assigned for a given knowledge clusters j of programme i in Table 7, and D(i,j) be the degree of importance of the same knowledge clusters of the programme in Table 3. The corresponding normalized relative weight of each knowledge cluster j of programme i is computed as

$$RW(i,j) = \frac{W(i,j)D(i,j)}{\sum_{\forall j} W(i,j)D(i,j)} \qquad (1)$$

The normalized relative weights are shown in Table 8. The table offers some benchmark against which the values derived from the collected data presented in Table 4 can be compared. What needs to be noted is that in Table 8 no skill is embedded within the S&T modules. It nevertheless provides a good comparison for the remaining knowledge clusters. When comparing these two tables (Table 4 and Table 8), it represents the outcomes of the discussions during the summit, and the findings of the collected data of computing syllabi in SSA.

Table 8. Proposed normalized relative weights for relevant computing curricula

	S&T	S&R	S&D	ENV	BU	INST	Pr
CS	0.57	0.16	0.02	0.013	0.020	0.013	0.20
IT	0.26	0.35	0.035	0.026	0.039	0.070	0.22
IS	0.34	0.30	0.030	0.015	0.045	0.076	0.19
SE	0.56	0.13	0.02	0.007	0.030	0.02	0.23
CE	0.56	0.13	0.02	0.026	0.030	0.007	0.23

Based on the initial findings of the workshop and the subsequent survey of institutions, a number of recommendations can be made for the development of future computing programmes in SSA:

- Firstly, and most importantly, curricula need to place greater emphasis on complementary skills to S&T as outlined in Table 1. The degree of importance of each of these areas to the different disciplines was outlined in Table 3. While this does not translate to numerical proportions of contact hours or credits, it does clearly indicate the relative importance of each knowledge cluster across disciplines. For example, S&T is the most important cluster for CS but S&R is the most important cluster for IT.

- Secondly, it is imperative that curricula are in fact assessed and improved on as soon as possible, given the clear distinction between the current and ideal distribution of effort across knowledge clusters in all the disciplines (as shown in Tables 2 and 3). The difficulty in obtaining information on curricula is a further concern that must be addressed by a greater sense of transparency at institutions. Current programmes are delivered differently in every institution and no effort is made to map one programme to another - thus finding and addressing gaps to improve on curricula requires substantial effort. A suitable auditable baseline should be adopted by all institutions as they move forward with curriculum development. This could be derived from ACM/IEEE/British Computer Society, augmented with topics in the non-S&T knowledge clusters identified in this study.

As these processes unfold, the lack of active community engagement in ACM and IEEE curricula must be addressed by appropriate involvement in the respective organisations. This will ensure that the results from this study are ultimately incorporated into future international curricula recommendations.

This outcome dovetails well with a recent study by academics from the Pacific Rim that concluded that CS curricula should be expanded, thus adapted, to suit their needs, which is to include international competitiveness, legal-, social-, and environmental-skills in their curricula: "... *internationalization will move our discipline towards the maturity and recognition it deserves, as more computer scientists move into leadership positions in commerce, education, and government*" [5].

Acknowledgments. We would like to thank Google for the funding of this project and all the Kampala summit participants for their valuable contributions. A special thank you to Belinda Nichols (Project Manager at Google) whose support saw this paper to completion.

References

1. Odedra, M., Lawrie, M., Bennett, M., Goodman, S.: Sub-Saharan Africa: A technological desert. Communications of the ACM 36(2), 25–29 (1993)
2. ACM & IEEE. Computing curricula 2005: An overview report. ACM, AIS and IEEE (CS). ACM & IEEE (2005)
3. Ogbor, J.O.: Entrepreneurship in Sub-Saharan Africa: A strategic management perspective. Authorhouse, Bloomington (2009)
4. International conference on ICT research. Summit on relevant computing in Sub-Saharan Africa (2010),
   https://sites.google.com/site/cs4africanuniversities/
   (retrieved December 03, 2011)
5. Douglas, S., Art, F., Lo, G., Proskurowski, A., Young, M.: Internationalization of Computer Science Education. In: SIGCSE 2010, pp. 411–415. ACM, Milwaukee (2010)

Mobile Phone Technology Acceptance and Usability in the Delivery of Health Services among Health Surveillance Assistants in Rural Areas of Malawi

Clement Khalika Banda and Harry Gombachika

University of Malawi, The Polytechnic
Private Bag 303, Chichiri, Blantyre 3, Malawi
clementkhalika@yahoo.com, hgombachika@poly.ac.mw

Abstract. This paper investigates the relationship between acceptance and usability of mobile phones in the delivery of health services among Health Surveillance Assistants (HSAs) in rural areas of Malawi. A questionnaire was distributed to 44 HSAs, however only 38 were returned correctly completed.

Firstly, the results show that HSAs in the area had a positive attitude towards mobile phones (M=5.02, SD=0.901) on a 6 points Likert Scale. Furthermore, the results show that the HSAs attitude was positive irrespective of gender and age. However, the attitude was moderated by level of education. HSAs with Junior Certificate of Education had lower attitude towards mobile phones than those with Malawi Schools Certificate of Education. Secondly, the results show that HSAs perceived usability of the Mobile Phones in support of health delivery services was positive irrespective of gender, age or level of education. Finally, the results showed that there was no significant relationship between mobile phone acceptance and usability among HSAs.

The study was, however, limited to HSAs who had received mobile phones and were residing in the rural villages under study. Further, the study was based on a convenient sample that was dominated by young, male and relatively educated individuals.

Keywords: Mobile Phone, Technology Acceptance Model, Technology Usability.

1 Introduction

Recent studies indicate a growing adoption rate of ICTs in the developing world. A common proxy for this is the use and ownership of mobile phones. Although, the ownership of mobile phones is generally lower in Malawi than other African countries, the market is growing rapidly. According to the 2010 ITU report, mobile phone subscription in Malawi rose from 7.3 to 12.0 inhabitants per 100 between 2007 and 2008, representing an increase of 64 percent. This has further increased from 12.0 in 2008 to 24.0 inhabitants per 100 towards the end of 2011 [1]. Accordingly, there has been a parallel increase in studies on the use of mobile phones in the healthcare service delivery [2-5] and on how users accept the use of the technology in their daily

K. Jonas, I.A. Rai, and M. Tchuente (Eds.): AFRICOMM 2012, LNICST 119, pp. 249–258, 2013.
© Institute for Computer Sciences, Social Informatics and Telecommunications Engineering 2013

work [6-9]. Additionally, several studies have shown that there is a link between the delivery of health services and information management [2,10,11]. Specifically, the availability of reliable, relevant, comprehensive and timely health information helps in the delivery of health interventions.

In Malawi, there are some projects through Non Governmental Organisations (NGOs) which use mobile phones in the delivery of various healthcare services. Firstly, the Millennium Villages Project (MVP) has implemented a programme where mobile phones are used by health personnel to assist the project in the implementation of healthcare services [12]. Secondly, St Gabriel's Hospital in Namitete uses mobile phones through the FrontlineSMS platform with the help of community health workers (CHW) to deliver various healthcare packages [13]. Thirdly, Baobab Health is also working in the development of mobile phones applications to be used in the delivery of healthcare services. Finally, UNICEF implemented a programme on using mobile phones to improve child nutrition surveillance in Malawi using a RapidSMS platform [14].

Despite these projects, there has not been any empirical study to assess user acceptance and technology usability of the mobile phones in the delivery of healthcare services among HSAs. This study therefore investigates the relationship between acceptance and usability of mobile phones in the delivery of maternal health services among HSAs in rural villages of Malawi.

The remainder of the paper is arranged as follows: Section 2 reviews the available literature while section 3 presents the methodology that was used in this study. Section 4 presents the results of the study while section 5 discusses the results. Finally, section 6 concludes the paper.

2   Literature Review

2.1   The Technology Acceptance Model

Conceptually, Technology Acceptance Model (TAM) is an information systems theory that models how users accept and use a technology. The model is based on the theory of reasoned action (TRA) described by Fishbein and Ajzen [15] and the theory of planned behaviour (TPB) coined by Ajzen [16]. It posits that users are influenced by a number of factors on how and when to use a new technology. Specifically, Davis [6] demonstrated the influence of the perceived ease of use and the perceived usefulness of a technology on the users' attitudes towards technology and its use. Perceived usefulness (PU) is defined as the degree to which a person believes that using a particular system will enhance his/her job performance while perceived ease-of-use (PEOU) is defined as the degree to which a person believes that using a particular system would be free from effort [6]. The main objective of the TAM is to provide a basis for explaining the impact of external variables on internal beliefs, attitudes and intentions [9]. Bagozzi et al. [7] argued that since new technologies are complex and are associated with some level of uncertainty regarding its successful adoption, users form attitudes and intentions towards the new technology and its use even prior to actual use.   Therefore, TAM is considered the most influential and commonly employed theory for describing an individual's acceptance of information systems. There are different version of TAM depending on the circumstances in which it is applied as evidenced by Venkatesh *et al.* [8], who reviewed eight popular models and combined them to the unified theory of acceptance and use of technology (UTAUT) to explain the acceptance of information systems.

There has been some research on the use of the technology acceptance in the context of healthcare which has provided direction and future research [17-19]. Schaper and Pervan [20] predicted that the use of ICT across the health sector will increase and further said that the ability to identify, predict and manage people's acceptance of technology will facilitate implementation efforts, as the acceptance of ICT by users is necessary for its ultimate success.

2.2   Usability of the Mobile Phones

Literature showed that there are various perspectives of the concept of usability. Miller [21] defined usability in terms of measure of ease of use while Nielsen [22] defined usability based on learnability, efficiency, memorability, errors and satisfaction. Furthermore, Bevan [23] defined usability as a set of attributes that bear on the effort needed for use, and on the individual assessment of such use, by a stated or implied set of users. The International Standard Organization (ISO), on the other hand, defined usability as the extent to which a product can be used by specified users to achieve specified goals with effectiveness, efficiency and satisfaction in a specified context of use [24]. In this study, the definition by ISO was used, thus the users are the HSAs, the tasks refer to the maternal healthcare services, the equipment refers to the mobile phones and the environment refers to the complexity of the healthcare services.

Usability evaluations are used in different areas ranging from information technology, medicine [25], agriculture [26], and education [27]. Additionally, there are several mobile phone usability studies based on product testing, environment testing or user testing [28-30] suggesting that usability evaluations in mobile phones and its applications depend on the objective of the evaluation and the methodology.

3   Methodology

A cross- sectional survey study based on quantitative research approach was conducted using a pre-tested questionnaire at the Millennium Villages Project (MVP) in Zomba district, Malawi. The MVP is helping the rural communities towards achieving the Millennium Development Goals (MDGs).

Data were collected through a self-administered questionnaire that was developed based on TAM adapted for mobile technology and usability of the mobile phones. The questionnaire consisted of three parts. Firstly, it comprised items that measured respondents' acceptance of mobile phones based on TAM's six dimensions [6,8]. Secondly, it included items that measured respondents' perspective of the usability of the mobile phones based on the ISO's usability dimensions and metrics [31]. All the items were measured on a six-point Likert Scale (1=strongly disagree to 6=strongly agree). Finally, the questionnaire included items to collect demographic data that included age, academic qualification and gender. A total of 44 questionnaires were distributed, however only 38 questionnaires were correctly completed and returned representing a response rate of 86.4%. Both descriptive and inferential statistical analyses were carried out using SPSS. Descriptive statistical analysis was used to summarize the results while inferential statistics was used to test the relationships between usability and acceptance.

This study ensured that consent was granted from the individual interviewees before participating in the study. Furthermore, permission was granted from relevant authorities before conducting the research to ensure that all ethical issues were taken care of. Specifically, the Millennium Villages Project was requested to provide clearance so that the study could be conducted in the project area and Ministry of Health was requested to provide ethical clearance.

4   Results

4.1   Demographic Characteristics of the Respondents

Table 1 summarises the demographic characteristics of the respondents. Firstly, the results show that out of the 38 respondents who returned accurately completed questionnaires, 65.8% were male. Secondly, the results show that the majority of the respondents (65.8%) belonged to the age group of 20-30 years old, while 12 belonged to the 31-40 age category with only 1 respondent being over 40 years. Finally, the results show that 60.5% of the respondents had Malawi Schools Certificate of Education (MSCE) while 39.5% had Malawi Junior Certificate of education (JCE).

Table 1. Demographic data characteristics of the respondents

Variable	Attribute	Percent (%)
Gender	Female	34.2
	Male	65.8
Age (Years)	20-30	65.8
	31-40	31.6
	Above 40	2.6
Academic qualification	JCE	39.5
	MSCE	60.5

4.2   Acceptance of Mobile Phones by the HSAs

Firstly, the study assessed the HSAs attitude towards mobile phone technology as a tool for delivering healthcare services using TAM based on six dimensions and the results are presented in table 2. The results show that the overall attitude towards mobile phone technology among HSAs was positive ($M=5.02$, $SD=0.901$) on a 6 points Likert Scale. Furthermore, the results show that the HSAs had a positive attitude towards mobile technology acceptance on all the six dimensions: perceived usefulness ($M= 5.58$, $SD= 0.599$), perceived ease of use ($M=4.47$, $SD=0.862$), perceived behavioural change (*M=4.82, SD=0.834*), subjective norm (*M=4.84, SD=0.973*), voluntary (*M=4.78, SD=0.947*) and behavioural intention (*M=5.64, SD=0.639*). Additionally, the study assessed whether the attitude towards mobile technology acceptance was moderated by the demographic characteristics (age, gender and academic qualification) of the HSAs. The results show that there was no statistically significant difference in means of overall attitude towards mobile technology based on gender *t(36)=0.806*, p>0.05 and age *F(37)=2.68, p>0.05*. However, the results revealed that there was a statistically significant difference in the overall acceptance of the mobile phones based on the academic qualification *F(37)=4.31, p<0.05*. HSAs with low education (JCE) qualification had a lower acceptance level *(M=4.60, SD=0.632)* than those with high education (MSCE) qualification *(M=5.09, SD=0.668)*.

Table 2. Mobile phone technology acceptance among HSAs

Acceptance Dimension	Mean	Std. Deviation
Perceived Usefulness (PU)	5.58	0.599
Perceived Ease of Use (PEOU)	4.47	0.862
Perceived Behavioural Change (PBC)	4.82	0.834
Subjective Norm (SN)	4.84	0.973
Voluntary(V)	4.78	0.947
Behavioural Intention (BI)	5.64	0.639
Acceptance of the Mobile Phones	**5.02**	**0.901**

Furthermore, the study assessed the relationships among the six dimensions of mobile phone technology acceptance and the results are presented in table 3. The results show that there were statistically significant relationships between perceived behavioural change and perceived usefulness *r(37)=0.328, p<0.05*; subjective norm and perceived usefulness *r(37)=0.347, p<0.05*; subjective norm and perceived behavioural change *r(37)=0.363, p<0.05*; voluntary and subjective norm *r(37)=0.538, p<0.05*; behavioural intention and perceived ease of use *r(37)=0.567, p<0.05*.

Table 3. Correlation matrix of the acceptance dimensions

Construct	PU	PEOU	PBC	SN	V	BI
PU	1.00					
PEOU	.292	1.00				
PBC	.328[*]	.313	1.00			
SN	.347[*]	.124	.363[*]	1.00		
V	.270	-.112	.306	.538[*]	1.00	
BI	.164	.567[*]	.256	.325	.191	1.00

Note: PU= Perceived Usefulness, PEOU=Perceived Ease of Use, PBC=Perceived Behavioural Change, SN= Subjective Norm, V=Voluntary, BI=Behavioural Intention; *Correlation is significant at the 0.05 level (2-tailed).

4.3   Usability of Mobile Phones

Secondly, the study assessed attitude of HSAs towards usability of mobile phones and table 4 presents the results. The results show that HSAs perceived overall usability of the mobile phones was positive $(M=4.33, SD=0.644)$ on a six point Likert scale. Furthermore, the results show that the HSAs had a positive attitude towards usability of mobile phones on satisfaction $(M=4.80, SD=0.480)$, efficiency $(M=4.26, SD=1.178)$ and effectiveness $(M=3.9, SD=0.273)$. In addition, the study assessed whether the attitude towards mobile technology usability was moderated by the demographic characteristics (age, gender and academic qualification) of the HSAs. The results show that there was no statistically significant difference in means of the overall perceived usability of mobile phones based on gender $t(36)=0.896, p>0.05$, age $F(37)=0.012, p>0.05$ and academic qualification $F(37)=2.72, p>0.05$.

Table 4. Usability of mobile phones

Usability Dimension	Mean	Std. Deviation
Satisfaction	4.80	0.480
Efficiency	4.26	1.178
Effectiveness	3.92	0.273
Overall Usability	**4.33**	**0.644**

Furthermore, the study assessed the relationships among the three dimensions of usability of mobile phones and the results are presented in table 5. The results show that there were statistically significant relationships between efficiency and satisfaction $r(37)=0.644, p<0.05$ and effectiveness and satisfaction $r(37)=0.544, p<0.05$.

Table 5. Correlation matrix of usability constructs

Construct	Satisfaction	Efficiency	Effectiveness
Satisfaction	1.00		
Efficiency	0.644[*]	1.00	
Effectiveness	0.544[*]	0.318	1.00

* Correlation is significant at the 0.05 level (2-tailed).

4.4   Relationship between Acceptance and Usability of Mobile Phones

Finally the study assessed the relationship between usability of the mobile phones and the acceptance by the HSAs through correlation analysis. The results showed that there was a weak negative correlation between usability and acceptance of the mobile phones and that the correlation was not statistically significant $r(37)=-0.127, p>0.05$.

5   Discussion of the Results

A review of literature showed that there is little research on the relationship between technology acceptance and usability of mobile phones in healthcare domain from both the developed and developing countries [32]. Although developing countries such as Malawi have much to gain from application of mobile technologies, they have received little research attention [33]. Additionally, developing countries such as Malawi are culturally different from developed countries. Malawi can be classified a predominantly associative culture [34]. This study therefore contributes towards technology transfer and diffusion discourses [35] in that it demonstrates how mobile technology can be used to deliver healthcare services in rural setup.

Firstly, the findings indicate that there is positive attitude towards mobile phones technology in the delivery of healthcare services among the HSAs in the Mwandama project area in all dimensions of TAM irrespective of gender and age. This suggests that mobile phones can be adopted as one of the means for delivering healthcare. Nevertheless, the attitude was moderated by level of education consistent with results reported in [36]. Individuals with higher education qualifications are more likely to accept mobile phone technology than those with low education qualifications. Further, the findings show that social influence has an effect on the attitude towards acceptance of the mobile phones among the HSAs in the study environment. Specifically, subjective norms (a measure of social influence) is significantly related to behavioural intention consistent with results reported [38] for e-services. However, these results contradict results reported in [18,25,38] for the health sector. The plausible reason is that the use of mobile phones as a tool for delivery of healthcare services was part of the objective of the project in the study area and HSAs were under some external pressure to use the mobile phones.

Secondly, the findings show that there is a positive perception of the usability of mobile phones as a tool for delivery of healthcare services in the three dimensions adopted in the study irrespective of age, gender or level of education. This result contradicts those reported by Hashizume [39] who found that perceived usability of mobile phones depended on age and gender. Further, the results suggest that usability is dominated by satisfaction consistent with the findings by Frokjaer [40] who asserted that usability relies much on the results of one or two of the three dimensions. However, these results are based on a convenient sample that was dominated by young, male and relatively educated individuals.

Finally, the findings show that there is no statistically significant correlation between usability of the mobile phones and acceptance among HSAs contrary to the results reported in [41,42] who found that usability affects acceptance of Technology among clinicians [41] and for small screen information systems [42]. The reason could be because the HSAs were using mobile phones for delivery of health services not out of their volition but by requirements of the project.

6   Conclusions

In this study, we used the technology acceptance model and the usability principles to assess the relationship between attitudes towards acceptance and usability of the mobile phones in the delivery of maternal health services among HSAs in the rural parts of Malawi. Firstly, we demonstrated that HSAs in the rural part of Zomba in Malawi have a positive attitude towards the use of mobile phones in maternal health service delivery irrespective of gender or age. However, the acceptance of mobile phones use amongst the HSAs was moderated by the level of education. Secondly, we showed that HSAs have a positive attitude towards usability of the mobile phones in the context under study irrespective of age, gender and level of education. Finally, the study showed that there is no significant relationship between usability of the mobile phones and acceptance amongst the HSAs in the study context. The study was however limited to HSAs who had received mobile phones and were residing in the rural villages under study. Further, the study was based on a convenient sample that was dominated by young, male and relatively educated individuals.

Acknowledgement. This study was conducted with funding from the National Commission of Science and Technology (NCST). We therefore acknowledge such financial support accordingly.

References

[1]   ITU Measuring the Information Society. International Telecommunication Union, Place des Nations, Geneva (2011)

[2]   Richards, T.B., Croner, C.M., Rushton, G., Brown, C.K., Fowler, L.: Geographic information systems and public health: mapping the future. Public Health Reports (14), 359–373 (1999)

[3]   Voskarides, S., Pattichis, C.S., Istepanian, R., Kyriacou, E., Pattichis, M.S., Schizas, C.N.: Mobile health systems: A brief overview. In: Proc. of SPIE (2008)

[4]   Ramachandran, D.L.: Mobile Persuasive Technologies for Rural Health. A dissertation submitted in partial satisfaction of the requirements for the degree of Doctor of Philosophy in Computer Science in the Graduate Division of the University of California, Berkeley (2010)

[5]   Loo, J.F.: Acceptance of Health Services on Mobile Phones, a Study of Consumer Perceptions. A dissertation submitted to the faculty of the University of North Carolina at Chapel Hill, in partial fulfillment of the requirements for the degree of Doctor of Philosophy in the School of Information and Library (2009)

[6]   Davis, F.D.: Perceived usefulness, perceived ease of use, and user acceptance of information technology. MIS Quart. 13(3), 319–339 (1989)

[7]   Bagozzi, R., Davis, F., Warshaw, P.: Development and test of a theory of technological learning and usage. Human Relations 45(7), 659–686 (1992)

[8]   Venkatesh, V., Morris, M.G., Davis, G.B., Davis, F.D.: User Acceptance of Information Technology: Toward a Unified View. MIS Quarterly 27(3), 425–478 (2003)

[9]   Legris, P., Ingham, J., Collerette, P.: Why do people use information technology? A critical review of the technology acceptance model. Information & Management 40, 191–204 (2003)

[10] Lippeveld, T., Sauerborn, R., Bodart, C.: Design and implementation of health information systems. World Health Organization, Geneva (2000)

[11]   Damtew, A.Z.: Analyzing the role of Health Information Systems for enhancement of child health services: A case study from Ethiopia. In: 10th International Conference on Social Implications of Computers in Developing Countries, Dubai, United Arab Emirates, and Doctoral Colloquium (2009)

[12]   Millennium Villages Project: Millennium Villages Project: Childcount+- A Community Health Events reporting and Alerts System, Earth Institute, Columbia University, New York, USA (2009)

[13]   Mahmud, N., Rodriguez, J., Nesbit, J.: Mobiles in Malawi: A text message-based intervention to bridge the patient-physician gap in the rural developing world, GLOBE PULSE. The American Medical Student Association's International Health Journal 6(1) (2010)

[14]   Blaschke, S., Bokenkamp, K., Cosmaciuc, R., Denby, M., Beza, H., Raymond, S.: Using Mobile Phones to Improve Child Nutrition Surveillance in Malawi: UNICEF Malawi and UNICEF Innovations (2009)

[15]   Fishbein, M., Ajzen, I.: Belief, attitude, intention and behaviour: An introduction to theory and research. Addison-Wesley, Reading (1975)

[16]   Ajzen, I.: The theory of planned behavior. Organizational Behavior and Human Decision Processes 50(2), 179–211 (1991)

[17]   Chau, P.Y.K., Hu, P.J.H.: Investigating healthcare professionals' decisions to accept telemedicine technology: an empirical test of competing theories. Journal of Information Management 39(4), 297–311 (2002)

[18]   Chismar, W.G., Wiley-Patton, S.: Does the extended technology acceptance model apply to physicians? In: 36th Hawaii International Congress on System Sciences, HICSS 2003. IEEE Computer Society, Big Island (2003)

[19]   Kijsanayotin, B., Pannarunothai, S., Speedie, S.M.: Factors influencing health information technology, adoption in Thailand's community health centers: Applying the UTAUT model. International Journal of Medical Informatics (8), 404–416 (2009)

[20]   Schaper, L., Pervan, G.: A Model of Information and Communication Technology Acceptance and Utilisation by Occupational Therapists Decision Support in an Uncertain and Complex World: The IFIP TC8/WG8.3 International Conference 2004 (2004)

[21]   Miller: Human ease of use criteria and their tradeoffs. IBM Report TR00.2185.Poughkeepsie. IBM, NY (1971)

[22]   Nielsen, J.: Usability Engineering. Morgan Kaufman, San Francisco (2004)

[23]   Bevan, J.: International Standards for HCI, Based on chapter in Encyclopedia of Human Computer Interaction. Idea Group Publishing, Serco Usability Services, 22 Hand Court, London WC1V 6JF (2006)

[24]   ISO. ISO 9241-11:1998. Ergonomic requirements for office work with visual display terminals (VDTs) – Part 11: Guidance on usability. International Standardization Organization, Geneva (1998)

[25]   Fairbanks, R.J., Caplan, S.: Poor Interface Design and Lack of Usability Testing Facilitate Medical Error. Joint Commission Journal on Quality and Safety 20(10) (2004)

[26]   Koniuszy, A.: A new method of usability evaluation of agricultural tractors based on optimum working index [OWI], TEKA Kom. Mot. Energ. Roln. – OL PAN, 2008, 8a, pp. 93–99 (2008)

[27]   Sullivan, J.M., Hall, R.H., Hilgers, M.G., Luna, R., Buechler, M.R., Lawrence, W.T.: Iterative Usability Evaluation Methods Applied to Learning Technology Development. In: World Conference on Educational Multimedia, Hypermedia and Telecommunications, EDMEDIA (2005)

[28]   Klockar, T., Carr, D.A., Hedman, A., Johansson, T., Bengtsson, F.: Usability of Mobile Phones. Department of Computer Science and Electrical Engineering, Luleå University of Technology, SE-971 87 Luleå, Sweden (2003)

[29]   User Vision Limited. Focusing on the user experience, Mobile Usability Comparison. Mobile Usability White Paper, 55 North Castle Street, Edinburgh (2008)

[30]   Kaikkonen, A., Kallio, T., Kekäläinen, A., Kankainen, A., Cankar, M.: Usability Testing of Mobile Applications: A Comparison between Laboratory and Field Testing. Journal of Usability Studies 1(1), 4–16 (2005)

[31]   Lewis, J.R.: IBM Computer usability Satisfaction Questionnaires: Psychometric Evaluation and instructions for use. International Journal of Human-Computer Interaction 7(1), 57–78 (1995)

[32]   Han, S.: Understanding User Adoption of Mobile Technology: Focusing on Physicians in Finland, Doctoral dissertation, Åbo Akademi University, Finland (2005)

[33]   Fusilier, M., Durlabhji, S.: An exploration of student internet use in India the technology acceptance model and the theory of planned behavior. Campus-Wide Information Systems 22(4), 233–246 (2005)

[34]   Kedia, B.L., Bhagat, R.S.: Cultural constraints on transfer of technology across nations: implications for research in international and comparative management. Academy of Management Review 13(4), 559–571 (1988)

[35]   Avgero, C.: Information systems in developing countries: a critical research review. Journal of Information Technology 23, 133–146 (2008)

[36]   Luo, N., Koh, W., Ng, W., Yau, J.W., Lim, L., Sim, S.S., Tay, E.: Acceptance of Information and Communication Technologies for Healthcare Delivery, a SingHealth Polyclinics Study. Ann. Acad. Med. Singapore 38(6), 529–536 (2009)

[37]   Igbaria, M., Zinatelli, N., Cragg, P., Cavaye, A.: Personal computing acceptance factors in small firms: a structural equation model. MIS Q 21(3), 279–302 (1997)

[38]   Rigby, M.: Essential prerequisites to the safe and effective widespread roll-out of e-working in healthcare. International Journal of Medical Informatics 75, 138–147 (2006)

[39]   Hashizume, A., Kurosu, M., Yamanaka, T.: Relative importance of design and usability of Cell Phone in terms of age and gender. In: International Conference on Kansei Engineering and Emotion Research, Keers, Paris (2010)

[40]   Frokjaer, E., Hertzum, M., Hornbaek, K.: Measuring Usability: Are effectiveness, Efficiency and Satisfaction Really Correlated? Computer Human Interaction 2(1), 345–352 (2000)

[41]   Croll, J.: The Impact of Usability on Clinician Acceptance of Health Information Systems. PhD Thesis submitted to the Centre for Learning Innovation, Faculty of Education, and Queensland University of Technology, Australia (2009)

[42]   Acton, T., Golden, W., Gudea, S., Scot, M.: Usability and Acceptance in Small-Screen Information Systems. eCollECTeR Conference Proceedings

Implications of Integrating Information Systems in Healthcare at District Level in Malawi: A Case of DHIS and Drug LMIS

Patrick Albert Chikumba[1] and Auxilia Nyaukaya Kaunda[2]

[1] Department of Computing and Information Technology,
University of Malawi-The Polytechnic, Private Bag 303, Blantyre 3, Malawi
[2] Concern Universal, 21 Link Road, Namiwawa, P.O. Box 1535, Blantyre, Malawi
patrick_chikumba@yahoo.com, nyaukaya@yahoo.com

Abstract. While Health Management Information Systems (HMIS) at the national level in Malawi is integrated, separate health information subsystems operate independently at the district level. For instance, computerized Information Systems, such as District Health Information System (DHIS) and Drug Logistics Management Information System (LMIS) operate as separate independent systems at the district level. Findings reveal that integration at district level can be implemented using two possible strategies, namely (1) integration of work practices and (2) integration of databases. Some social implications of work practice integration are enhanced communication, development of personnel skills and experience in integrated reporting, as well as encourage teamwork. The integration of technology can result in interconnectivity and/or interoperability of database software. The paper discusses social and technical implications of integrating information systems in the healthcare at the district level in Malawi with DHIS and Drug LMIS as examples.

Keywords: Drug Logistics MIS, DHIS, Integration, Integration Strategies, Work Practices.

1   Introduction

Health Information System (HIS) is widely recognized as a technology enabler, improving patient care coordination, enhancing provider productivity, as well as facilitating knowledge management activities. A multitude of stand-alone administrative and clinical management systems exist, but their true value is realized when they become an integrated electronic health record solution that can address information requirements across multiple functions and sites.

Subsystems of HIS are common in most countries and are the major cause of fragmentation [1]. Fragmentations are invariably highly complex, developed over time as a result of disease burdens and administrative, economic, legal or donor pressures [1, 18]. The fragmentations are prevalent in developing countries where there are rampant monetary constraints [10].

K. Jonas, I.A. Rai, and M. Tchuente (Eds.): AFRICOMM 2012, LNICST 119, pp. 259–269, 2013.
© Institute for Computer Sciences, Social Informatics and Telecommunications Engineering 2013

While HMIS is integrated at national level in Malawi, at the district level independent subsystems exist. Consequently, HIS is fragmented with multiple and very often overlapping demands of disease-focused and specific service program systems. A result of these fragmented systems is "painfully apparent in the inability of most countries to generate the data needed to monitor progress …" [1, p. 578]. In Malawi health reports are disintegrated and therefore restrict effective services delivery and planning [7]. The reporting standards for fragmented systems might not be consistent to what is required at one point in time by the different health system stakeholders. The main reason for the inconsistence is that the reporting standards for the disparate HMIS in Malawi have not been documented and several existing systems run parallel to the HMIS which even complicates standardization process.

District Health Information System (DHIS) and drug Logistics Management Information System (LMIS) are significant information systems at the district level which are not integrated to each other and other information systems. DHIS manages distributed collection, processing and reporting of routine health data from primary health facilities to district health office (DHO) while drug LMIS collects, processes, and reports drug logistics and medical supplies data. District health programme managers frequently need access to information from both DHIS and drug LMIS from a single point of view for better management in improving health care services effectiveness and efficiency in their districts.

DHIS and drug LMIS are such significant systems which lack effective central coordination to allow for efficient and effective integrated reporting [5, 10]. The fragmentation exists in HIS in Malawi even though commendable efforts had been made by the Ministry of Health to achieve an integrated HIS through the implementation of the HMIS [10]. There is need for integration of drug logistics data with health data for system effectiveness and efficiency [5].

District health level is central to health system planning, implementation, monitoring and evaluation of primary health care interventions [18, 22]. Under decentralization, districts have been given authority and independent management of health facilities in the provision of health care [16].

Integration of DHIS and drug LMIS will provide information that is relevant, reliable, timely, adequate for the purpose of quality reporting to facilitate effectiveness and efficiency in improving health care services delivery. Currently, district health programme managers do not have a single point where they can access reports from both subsystems. Health programme managers are therefore inclined to make uninformed and delayed decisions based on inadequate information that is made available to them at specific times and not necessarily when needed.

2   Challenges of HIS Integration in Developing Countries

Disintegrated systems do not reflect the organization's way of operations considering that there are functional departments which are interdependent and need to exchange information that is crucial to their operations. Information from isolated files does not provide a complete picture of the organisation at any point in time since data cannot be easily gathered in an effective manner. Information from disintegrated systems is therefore not suitable for managerial informed decision-making [17, 23].

It is very difficult for health service organizations to acquire information for use in any of the managerial roles [6]. This is generally due to the fact that successful health information systems have been developed on a small scale, that is, specific health services or programmes without encompassing the entire organizational information requirements to fulfill their set goals and objectives.

'One size fits all' approach to system design does not fit in other settings and that 'the perfect is often an enemy of the good', applying to standardization, functionality, requirements and commercial decisions [11]. Donor-initiated systems designed for developed countries' health sector meet specific donor requirements and are mostly not compatible to existing national HMIS. These cause data duplication and data synchronization problems and thus compromise on performance. Such systems are not appropriate for use in many health care organizations as they do not provide comprehensive solutions to HIS integration in interoperability. Some vendors package stand-alone systems as a solution to integration which ultimately fails to achieve the desired interoperability in the health care organization [15]. Health care organizations need cohesion in inter-operations for an integrated access to health information in a unified view at all levels of management [3].

As heterogeneous systems blossom from different system stakeholders, different platforms are used which are incompatible with subsequent systems that are developed in the same operational environment. Development standards used are different in each system as there is no cohesion in designs. Programs in these systems have defined data structure for processing to take place and hence creates maintenance burden for the organisation whenever there are functional or data changes [11]. The management of such systems poses a great challenge to both the system users and system designers, hence difficult to integrate. Consequently there is lack of uniform infrastructure development and uneven distribution of resources and in most countries, this has been cited as one of the critical and major challenges to achievement of a comprehensive integrated HIS from a single point of access [18].

HIS integration in developing countries is impeded by lack of proper technological communication infrastructures in most health sector organizations. This is due to the fact that health sectors and Information Technology (IT) in developing countries are characterized by inadequate resources, inadequate and/or poorly trained staff and inappropriate incentives for health workers [12] poor infrastructure, lack of an information culture [14] and lack of managerial capacity to work in an integrated manner [21]. Most health sector organizations do not have computers for basic record keeping and therefore data is captured manually from its source of data collection [19, 20]. Registers, forms, pen, pencil and a simple calculator are common data collection tools for capturing patient data at each health facility in most developing countries.

Aggregate data from all health programmes at the health facility is processed manually to produce reports from the local health facility to the next level, contrary to the global trend of computerized data processing. In most health sector organizations where computers are available, the challenge is the existence of disparate systems which operate in isolation of the other systems in different departments. There is normally no network connectivity among various departments to interconnect systems for communication flow to and from across departments. In some areas where required equipment is available, there is lack of adequate skill in using and managing IT infrastructure. Effective IT use, maintenance and implementation in health and social sector requires experienced and skilled personnel to manage and develop use of information for health care services delivery at the local health facility level [11].

Adoption of innovation from developed countries into developing countries involves transfer of technology and practices originally designed and proved useful in those countries' socio-organizational contexts [2]. Adapting such innovation for local socio-organizational conditions and feasibility use, poses a great challenge in developing countries where new information and communication technologies are either not in existence or just emerging [2].

Poor infrastructural conditions and lack of effective transport in many parts pose great challenges in developing countries especially flow of health information between community health facilities and district health facilities [18]. Poor road networks impede effective transmission of collected data between health facility and next reporting level. This is eminent during rainy season when some dirty roads leading to health facilities become impassable due to muddy and slipperiness. It thus becomes difficult for health information documentation to be physically transmitted between such places and next reporting level until end of rainy season. In the process, health information is submitted late for report compilation and consequently delayed decision making by respect management and stakeholders.

On Integrated Health Information System in Tanzania, socio-cultural traditions of health administrators have acted as a serious impediment for enabling decision-making at the local community level [21]. Cited examples are reverence given to traditional authority, the cultural norm of lower-level officials not to disagree openly with their superiors, and the aftermath of colonial behavior. All these created conditions under which local level operating agencies' staff failed to exercise their limited authoritative roles in the community. Under these circumstances, it was difficult to effectively implement foreign assistance programmes as there was need for reformation in public sector and local political and cultural process to support local community level interventions.

There is therefore need for sustainable and nurtured local politics for effective health sector reform, one of which is through implementation of District Health Information System (DHIS) by Health Information Systems Project (HISP) in developing countries. This is partly in an effort to infiltrate informal practices and cultural norms in decentralized health systems and enhance effective performance of systems and structures in the districts. DHIS1.3 is implemented at district level in Malawi.

Politics occurs at various levels of the country's health sector, that is, from the donor community, to the ministries within the country, to the local political environment within which health workers operate [21]. Efforts to implement integrated information systems at the local health facility level have not had any substantial and long-term impact. Many health information systems are politically instead of clinically motivated, consequently health professionals and other health stakeholders tend to be discouraged and lack interest in the implementation thereof [4]. Political decisions override socio-cultural implications of new developments on patterns and organizational processes [4].

While the concept of integration continues to influence the launching of health sector reform initiatives in developing countries, Smith et. al. [4] argue that this approach to reform actually leads to the institutionalization of control mechanisms stifling autonomy of decision-making at the health facility level. Priorities of health workers at grassroots level are very different from the mandate of integration imposed by public sector reform policy prescriptions. For example, in Northeast Brazil it was found that primary objective for the rural clinician is attending to patients and these workers would rather spend as much time and resources as possible on patients rather than on papers and form-filling. This is due to the fact that health workers 'have little autonomy to modify reporting systems and to introduce locally relevant indicators' [21, p. 4].

Integration is not just a reform to be enacted but rather a continuous change process where the local health facility needs to reflect upon and proactively interprets its own way of working. The actual effecting of the standards at the local level often requires flexibility and adaptation, contrary to management perception, which consider standardization as essential to harmonize and integrate information [13]. Avgerou [2, p. 2] asserts that it "entails high risk of misguiding and frustrating local efforts to make sense and appropriate new technology".

3   Methodology

A case study approach was deemed appropriate for bringing out an understanding of DHIS and drug LMIS which use different data collection policies, standards and procedures. The case study approach is appropriate where there are different patterns, design and complexity in the study [8]. The study used qualitative research methods to explore the possibility of integrating DHIS and drug LMIS.

Documents were analyzed with a view to make sense out of texts and images, which helped to get information to supplement other forms of data collection techniques. Written materials can be very effective in trying to understand the organizational philosophy pertinent in case studies. Background information to the study was informed by going through HMIS Training and Reference Manual in order to understand principles and procedures followed in DHIS. Health Commodities Management System Standard Operating Procedures Manual provides information guiding drug LMIS operations. Main documents reviewed for purposes of this study were the HMIS15 form (for data collection in DHIS) and monthly LMIS01A form (for data collection in drug LMIS) with the aim to identify a possible strategy of DHIS and drug LMIS integration.

DHIS1.3 (software) for HIS data management and Supply Chain Manager (software) for drug logistics data management were analyzed as another primary source of data. The intention for DHIS1.3 and SCM software analyses was to identify similarities in the two systems that could be used as a basis for possible integration.

Semi-structured interviews were conducted with District Health Environmental Officer (DEHO), Statisticians and Pharmacy Technicians aiming at identifying challenges in accessing health and drug logistics data at the district level.

4   District Health Information System and Drug LMIS

With reference to Fig. 1, data at health facility is collected, processed and reported by statistical clerks with the assistance of medical staff using out-patients register, HMIS forms, pens and paper on data elements and selected indicators using specific standards. At close of each business day, key data elements are aggregated and analyzed for a general overview of the situation for necessary action and responsiveness in the next day by the health facility-in-charge. In the case where the health facility is a catchments point, it also receives data from other health facilities within its catchments area. Data is then compiled into an aggregate report on a monthly basis. These reports are used by the health facility during their monthly meetings for data management and decision making to improve healthcare services delivery. At the end of each quarter, the health facility personnel compile an aggregate data report using HMIS15 form and sends to the statistician at DHO.

DHO HMIS Unit personnel are responsible for data management, ensuring that data is collected, processed and reported effectively for management use. Aggregate data reports received from all health facilities within the district are captured into computerized DHIS1.3 for processing and analysis of data quality before generating reports which are sent to district health management team (DHMT) for use in management planning, budgeting and decision making. Electronic versions of the same reports are sent to national level.

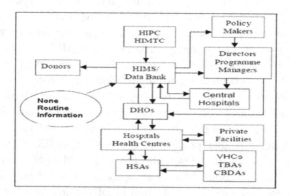

Fig. 1. Information Flow in Health Information System in Malawi (**Source:** Ministry of Health and Population [9])

People are at the core of drug LMIS from health facility up to national level. Every health facility has a health-facility-in-charge who manages and oversees administrative issues and a Drug Store Manager (Nurse, Medical Officer or Clinical Officer) is chosen to manage drug store or pharmacy by issuing out drugs and medical supplies and immediately recording in a register and on a stock card. The stock card is a type of form used to keep records of all transactions of drugs, contraceptives and other medical supplies as well as physical inventory. At the end of each business day a report is compiled on drug data transactions that can be used for planning, budgeting and decision making at health facility. On monthly basis, daily data reports are aggregated into a data report by filling in the monthly LMIS01A form which is sent to district level before the 5th of every month.

Once the district pharmacy technician receives monthly LMIS01A forms, he/she checks data quality, which is, correctness, completeness, consistence and timeliness before capturing data into computerized Supply Chain Manager (SCM). The pharmacy technician uses SCM to process and analyze data reports received from health facilities. Once data reports are processed and analysed, the pharmacy technician generates aggregate district reports for dissemination to the Regional Medical Stores (RMS), Central Medical Stores (CMS) and District Health Management Team (DHMT) for information use in improved health care services delivery through management decision making. Refer to Fig. 2 below.

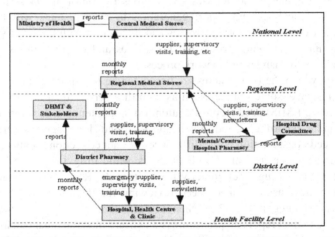

Fig. 2. Information Flow and Feedback between Levels in the Drug LMIS (**Source:** Chikumba [2])

5   Social and Technical Implications on Integration of IS

In both DHIS and drug LMIS, statistician and pharmacy technician receive aggregated quarterly data reports (HMIS15) and monthly data reports (LMIS01A) respectively from health facilities within the district. Work practice integration entails combining statistician's work processes with pharmacy technician's work processes into a single work process in order to produce an integrated district aggregate report for use in management decision making and planning for improved health services delivery.

Integration of these systems would facilitate communication between pharmacy technician and statistician at district level, through information exchange, in order to achieve a common objective. They can work together in collecting data for both DHIS and drug LMIS from health facilities within the district and then process and analyse data for report generation. The most cost effective and efficient data processing techniques need to be identified and applied in order to integrate work practice for optimum benefits.

In accessing two systems to produce an integrated report, added skills can easily be learnt and a norm developed for integrated reporting, moving away from the normal way of processing reports from an independent system. Collaborated efforts can be essential in terms of teamwork between the Pharmacy and HMIS units in generating integrated reports for effective use in planning and decision.

Integration of the two data reports into a single report will require changes in work processes of both pharmacy technician and statistician. The implication could be accumulation of work due to the fact that both health and drug logistics data are submitted. Consequently, this could lead to more time required for effective processing of comprehensive reports and therefore prone to creation of routine work practice. Change in work practice can either lead to job satisfaction or lack of it depending on how the job holder views it. Job description of officer responsible for data processing, analysis and report generation in both systems will need to be modified to allow for extra work processes and interaction with the other system as a result of the integrated work processes. Their roles and responsibilities need to be reviewed to align to changes in the work processes.

Policies on which the two systems are based can be incorporated into a new work policy. For instance, some policies such as reporting period (quarterly for DHIS and monthly for drug LMIS) need a consideration. For consistence, a decision needs to be made on similar reporting periods for health data and drug logistics data. Another policy that need consideration is the differences in data collection points used in both systems, DHIS use catchments health facilities while drug LMIS uses any health facility that receives drug stock directly from either the Regional Medical Stores or DHO. Such policy inconsistencies need reviewing for flexibility in the integration process otherwise integration process cannot be effective.

Consistence in data reporting procedures can ensure integrated data quality through standardisation of work processes throughout the health sector levels, that is, from health facility to district level. Standardisation can set right data collection tools, for appropriate data elements and standards, with a purpose to generate integrated information reports that are accurate, reliable, adequate, timely, complete and suitable for management use in health care services delivery.

With work practice integration, the district health office needs to modify some existing policies and standards in drug LMIS and DHIS system operations in order to come with common policies and standards for coding and naming of health facilities and pharmacies for consistence. Any change in policy, standards and procedure require approval at the national level.

DHIS and drug LMIS can be integrated through technology in use, that is, tools (report forms) and databases. Each system uses specific though similar tools in data processing and report generation. DHIS and Drug LMIS use different types of forms in reporting. Integration of health data and drug logistics data reports means modifying these forms in order to incorporate information from both systems. Modification of the forms can only be done at national level by personnel involved in policy formulation which would require changing reporting procedures and setting new data standards, data elements and indicators for integrated reporting. Current standards, data elements and indicators were designed in compatibility with the computerised software that processes and analyse data. Integration of tools therefore needs modification for consistent and applicable reporting at all health sector levels.

DHIS and drug LMIS can be integrated through interconnection of DHIS1.3 and SCM databases. Both DHIS1.3 and SCM run on Windows Operating system and Microsoft Access database management system. For effective DHIS1.3 and SCM database integration, there is need to identify a common field in the two databases with consistent data standards, for instance, data collection points must be the same in both databases for easy identification.

However, interconnectivity and interoperability of the two systems would require Local Area Network (LAN). There is a cost to implementation of this infrastructure at the district level. Currently, few DHOs have LAN connectivity that can be accessed by all offices and where there is no LAN connectivity, integration of the two systems cannot be easy. Lack of LAN connectivity can be an impediment to effective integration of the two systems which are normally physically positioned away from each other. In the case where there is LAN at DHO, implementation of interconnectivity of DHIS1.3 and SCM systems can mean extension of available infrastructural resources. Information Technology (IT) in developing countries is characterised by inadequate resources [2, 12, 14].

Integration of DHIS and drug LMIS implies extension of existing health personnel's work practices, tools, standards, data elements, indicators, policies, procedures, data management system and equipment, among others. In the case where a new integrated database is required to import and export predefined data sets captured in DHIS1.3 and SCM, designing can require an extension of the existing DHIS1.3 and SCM systems using the same data standards, elements and indicators that were used in designing the current systems.

6   Conclusion

Integration of DHIS and drug LMIS through work practice can turn out to be cost efficient, instead of two reports being generated; only one report can be generated from the two systems. This can ease up the work processes of both pharmacy technician and statistician through sharing of the report generation activity, time gained in integrated report generation activity can be utilised by doing other duties. Consequently leading to pharmacy technician and statistician being more productive and thus enhance their performance in improving health care services delivery to the population. However, work practice integration implies change in work processes of both DHIS and drug LMIS policies, procedures and standards which requires involvement of national policy decision makers, as this decision cannot be undertaken at district level.

References

1. AbouZahr, C., Boerma, T.: Health Information Systems: the foundations of public health. Bulletin of World Health Organisation 83, 578–583 (2005)
2. Avgerou, C.: The significance of context in information systems and organisational change. Information Systems Journal 11(1), 43–63 (2001)
3. Boochever, S.S.: HIS/RIS/PACS Integration to the Gold Standard. Radiology Management 26(3), 16–24 (2004)
4. Catwell, L., Sheikh, A.: Information Technology (IT) system users must be allowed to decide on the future direction of major national IT initiatives. But the task of redistributing power equally amongst stakeholders will not be an easy one. Informatics in Primary Care 17(1), 1–4 (2009)
5. Chikumba, P.A.: Application of GIS in Drug LMIS at District Level in Malawi: Opportunities and Challenges, LAMBERT Academic Publishing (2010)
6. Cibulskis, R., Hiawalyer, G.: Information systems for health sector monitoring in Papua New Guinea. Bulletin of the World Health Organization 80(9), 752–758 (2002)
7. Conticini, A.: Macroeconomics and Health in Malawi:What Way forward. World Health Organisation, Geneva (2004)
8. Creswell, J.: Research Design: Qualitative, quantitative and mixed method approaches. Sage Publications Inc., California (2003)
9. Fumo, T.G.: Health Information Systems Integration: A Data Warehouse Architecture Model for the Ministry of Health in Mozambique. Master Thesis, University of Oslo (2003)
10. Galimoto, M.S.: Integration of Health Information Systems, Case Study from Malawi. Master Thesis, University of Oslo (2007)
11. Hayes, G.: The NHS Information Technology and Social Care Review in 2009: a synopsis. Informatics for Primary Care 18(2), 81–88 (2010)
12. Hill, J., Kazembe, P.: Reaching the Abuja target for intemittent preventive treatment of malaria in pregnancy in African women; a review or progress and operational challenges. Tropical Medicine & International Health 11(4), 409–418 (2006)
13. Jacucci, E., Shaw, V., Braa, J.: Standardisation of Health Information Systems in South Africa: The Challenge of Sustainability. In: Proceedings of the 9th International Conference on Social Implication of Computers in Developing Countries, Abuja, Nigeria (May 2005)
14. Lungo, J.H.: Data Flows in Health, Master Thesis, University of Oslo (2003)
15. Meyer, M., Levine, W.C., Brzezinski, P., Robbins, J., Lai, F., Spitz, G.: Integration of Hospital Information Systems, Operative and Peri-operative Information Systems, and Operative Equipment into a Single Information display. American Medical Informatics Association (2005)
16. Ministry of Health and Population: Health Information System, National Policy and Strategy, Lilongwe (2003)
17. Nishtar, S.: The mixed health systems syndrome. Bulletin of the World Health Organisation 88(1), 74–75 (2010)
18. Nyella, E.: Challenges and Opportunities in the Integration of HIS: A case study of Master Thesis, University of Oslo (2007)
19. Odhiambo-Otieno, G.: Evaluation of existing District Health Management Information Systems: a case study of District Health systems in Kenya. International Journal of Medical Informatics, 734 (2005)

20. Sandvand, J.: Organisational Strategies for Improving Health Information at the district level: a field study of management Implemented support structures in Malawi. Master Thesis, University of Oslo (2007)
21. Smith, M., Madon, S., Anifalaje, A., Lazarro-Malecela, M., Michael, E.: Integrated Health Information System in Tanzania: Experiences and Challenges. Electronic Journal of Information Systems in Developing Countries 33, 1–21 (2008)
22. WHO: Frameworks and Standards for Country Health Information Systems, 2nd edn. Health Metrics Network, Geneva (2008)
23. Yeates, D., Shields, M., Helmy, D.: Systems Analysis and Design. Pitman Publishing, London (1994)

Eb@le-Santé: Networked Electronic Health Records in Academic Hospitals in RDC

Marc Nyssen[1], Frank Verbeke[1], Marcel Remon[2], and Yannik Hallet[3]

[1] Vrije Universiteit Brussel
Laarbeeklaan 103, 1090 Brussels, Belgium
mnyssen@vub.ac.be
[2] FUNDP: Facultés Universitaires Notre Dame de la Paix de, Namur
[3] CUD: Commission universitaire pour le déeveloppement, Bruxelles

Abstract. The Eb@le-Santé EuropAid project (2009-2012) is a partnership between Belgian and Congolese (RDC) institutions. The main aim is to improve health care in RDC via electronic records [4] [5] [7] and educative medical teleconferencing [1]. Therefore we equip four academic hospitals with a server providing medical software, linked workstations in a local area network at the hospital and interconnections to the academic network Eb@le that interconnects seven universities in the country. The project also aims at educating local teams towards both technical and medical autonomy. Currently, the main equipment in the four locations (the university teaching hospitals of Kinshasa, Lubumbashi, Bukavu and Kisangani) is installed and the local teams have started recording medical patient records. The project's methodology aims at solid registration of complete patient records, resulting in high quality data, improving the care of the patient and, enabling swift reporting [10][11] and data-mining for research on anonymous epidemiological data. Moreover, correct and adequate administrative data become available to the hospital management and teleconsulting/tele-education components complete the package.

Keywords: electronic health record, academic network, telemedicine, teleconferencing.

1 Introduction

The Eb@e-Santé project was successfully submitted as an "EUROPAid" project in 2008. The project has run for a period of two and a half years until the end of 2011. The goal of Eb@le-Santé is to link up four major hospitals in the Democratic Republic Congo with the respective nearby universities, to install an operational infrastructure (hard- and software) in order to enable systematic recording of patient records, to evaluate these recordings and to study their impact on the functioning of the hospital and on the quality of care. OpenClinic was chosen as the medical record package [2] with a proven track record in the region [3] [9] but as far as we know, this is the first coordinated deployment over multiple sites in the Democratic Republic of Congo.

Another goal was to connect the partner hospitals to the international RAFT network [1] [6], originally initiated by Geissbuhler and colleagues from Geneva and now spanning over more than 10 African countries.

K. Jonas, I.A. Rai, and M. Tchuente (Eds.): AFRICOMM 2012, LNICST 119, pp. 270–278, 2013.
© Institute for Computer Sciences, Social Informatics and Telecommunications Engineering 2013

RAFT enables international teleconferencing sessions about medical subjects and both on- and off-line multimedia teaching, even when the Internet connection is slow, thanks to the java-based "DUDAL" software.

2   Project Methodology

Teamwork and Links to "Universitic"

Each partner hospital teams up with its neighboring university, to enable virtual private network access via the university's "Universitic" connection. Universitic is the university backbone project, initiated and conducted by the two Belgian university cooperation bodies: VLIR-UOS and CIUF-CUD, together with 8 academic partner institutions.

Universitic aims at deployment of a local institution-wide backbone, with central servers, routers and Internet connections, each suited to the needs of the seven partner universities of VLIR and CIUF in RDC, amongst which the four Eb@le-Santé partners: UNIKIN (Université de Kinshasa), UNILU (Université de Lubumbashi), UCB (Université Catholique de Bukavu) and UNIKIS (Université de Kisangani).

One originality of Eb@le-Santé, is the "piggy-backing" on the deployment of the Universitic project. This enables us to capitalize on the deployment realized with and by the universities, while enriching this development with medical applications. At the start of the project, the general methodology, described below was agreed upon with the four clinical partners, but specific choices were made by the local groups, in agreement with the priorities of the participating hospitals concerning the registration modalities of patients and the selection of the medical departments to be involved from the start.

Via monthly (structured) reporting, the local team leaders kept the project managers informed about progress and all other aspects, so that, where possible, swift action could be taken, for example in case of urgent repairs, connection/current problems or to provide back-up resources to some extent.

The connection to the Internet via the web application "Global Health Barometer" also allows to share data amongst the partners of the project, aiming at future research, once sufficient clinical data will be collected by the partner hospitals.

Start Situation Study

At the start of the project, an "in depth" study was made regarding the existing solutions for electronic patient records at the partners' sites: for each university hospital, the technical and operational needs were evaluated. The main resulting elements were:

- capturing the patients' admission, transfer- and leaving data
- coding the financial and insurance data regarding all patients
- keeping and updating structured and coded electronic clinical patient records (contact motifs, diagnosis, follow-up).
- making use of international standards: ICD-10, CISP-2, LOINC, financial nomenclature...);

- statistical exploitation of the data
- user friendly (French) interface
- full user access control with user profiles available

For each of the partners, specific needs were identified:

- specific prioritized needs for each university hospital
- integration of existing work stations
- internal network needs: wireless or cabled
- power back-up tailored to each institution
- number of end-users to instruct and guide.

Hardware Deployment

The project provides to each partner hospital (via its university) the following hardware components

- no-break installation comprising batteries and no-break group enabling 24 hours autonomy in case of mains interruptions
- a server machine
- 20 laptop workstations (being deployed in the hospital departments) running open source software
- wireless base stations near the workstations in the hospital with maximum security and access restrictions
- router to interconnect wireless stations and server.

For the server machines, special attention was paid to the power consumption (max 250W) of the servers as this has an immediate impact on the sizing of the no-break group and batteries / autonomy in case of power failure. As endpoint workstations, "thin client" machines are most appropriate, but the selection between thin-clients and laptop PC's was left to the local teams, to comply with their vision and previously installed base. On figure 1, this standard set-up is depicted.

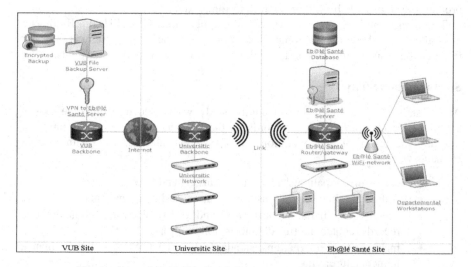

Fig. 1. set-up of an Eb@le Santé site next to an UNIVERSITIC site

Preference was given to a set of wireless stations, linked to a central switch to interconnect the departmental workstations to the OpenClinic server. Thus drastically reducing the number of cables to be installed, allowing more flexibility in the deployment and increasing reliability, as cables only run over ceilings and in cable guides, beyond the normal reach of clinical or logistic personnel and cleaning teams.

The Universitic backbone offers the "off-the-shelf" connectivity to the seven Universitic sites in the major universities and higher education institutes in RDC and allows for specific purpose Internet connections: link to RAFT and support from a distance (Belgium) over a virtual private network. Software and configuration adjustments, requiring otherwise very expensive displacements by experts now can be realized in the evenings from a distance.

Software Deployment

As a basis for the installation, stable Linux distributions (Debian) are recommended for the operating system of the server machines. For client machines, Linux-based (Ubuntu) laptops offer both the strength of being relatively resistant to (short) power interruptions and they are less prone to viruses. Disk-less thin clients are another possibility.

Several hospital information management systems have been evaluated for the purpose of the project and finally the OpenClinic open source software was selected for deployment in the eb@le-santé project. TheOpenClinic standard software package has been customized for the RDC hospital environment and was installed on the server in all 4 sites. MySQL has been chosen as a back-end database server.

For the purpose of the project, it has been decided to limit the scope of implementation to a number of hospital departments:

Table 1. Project overview

Location	Hospital size (#beds)	University	Priority Departments
Kinshasa	CUK 800	UNIKIN	Admin, Statistics, Lab
Lubumbashi	CUL 500	UNILU	Admin, Statistics, Pediatrics
Kisangani	CUKIS 400	UNIKIS	Admin, Statistics, Internal Medicine
Bukavu	HPGRB 350	UCB	Admin, Statistics, Internal Medicine

For any of the selected hospital departments, existing business procedures, reports and documents were collected and analyzed, in order to adapt the OpenClinic software to perfectly match the functional needs of these departments. Based on these analyses, the following OpenClinic modules have been re-engineered:

- Patient administration
- Financial management and care delivery data entry
- Reason for encounter registration
- Patient discharge diagnosis management

- Clinical data entry screens for pediatrics and internal medicine departments
- Work list based lab order entry and results management
- Clinical statistics and activity reporting [10]

Finally, a number of OpenClinic data structures have been adapted to match aspects that are specific to every site (available hospital departments, available lab analyses, care deliveries and their prices, local health insurance contracts...).

Following patient data are recorded:

- administrative data (identity, admissions, discharge, fees)
- medical contacts during the stay (exams, treatments, ...)
- reason for admission and discharge diagnoses
- patients' evolution

OpenClinic accords special attention to unambiguous patient identification, so that on re-admission, the correct patient is recovered along with his history, avoiding multiple recordings for a single person and leading to better care as the history of the patient is immediately available to the treating physician.

Diagnoses are recorded in ICPC and ICD [8], via the three-way thesaurus developed in Belgium. The encoder is presented a hierarchical pick-list, guiding him towards the adequate level of detail and performing both ICD- and ICPC coding at the same time.

When correct patient recording is performed, the hospital's statistics generation and reporting to higher instances becomes straightforward [10][11].

Training

Based on the customized OpenClinic software deployments, several kinds of training were organized:

1. System administrator training was provided on every site to the local ICT staff
2. User training was set up in Kinshasa and Bukavu (an average of 20 attendees has been registered), serving also users from the other sites in Lubumbashi and Kisangani:

    - Administrative user training
    - Clinical encoder training
    - Financial user training
    - Clinical user training

These intensive training programs have proven to be extremely important before putting the hospital information management system into production. In order to offer permanent training possibilities to the already trained users as well as to future hospital staff, an OpenClinic test-environment has also been set up at every site, enabling new users to get acquainted with OpenClinic electronic health records, while not "endangering" real clinical data during their apprenticeship. On the "test site", every page is explicitly marked as such, in order to avoid any confusion.

For each institution, a local responsible has been designated, in accordance with the top management of the hospital; then a number of medical, paramedical and technical persons have been selected and trained.

During the training sessions, attention was given to the "main picture" so that everyone can clearly identify his or her role in the whole process.

Fig. 2. ICT and health informatics training sessions are an essential part of the project! Co-author Frank Verbeke introduces Open OpenClinic in Bukavu

Training was observed as a "bottleneck" for the deployment speed of the project and where we originally aimed at "training the trainers", this objective was not fully reached to the point we had anticipated: too few local "trainers" were brought up to level, most trainees were end-users, lacking both the ambition and the time to become resource persons as trainers themselves.

Teamwork and Information Sharing

To share information on developments in the project among all partners, a blog was updated regularly at www.ebalesante.net . Mailing lists were created for different groups and allowed discussion on various topics related to the project. Finally, a project follow-up procedure was initiated, requiring the local clinical responsibles to report about the progress on their site via standardized forms. By sharing the accomplishements in the participating centers, a project-wide team spirit was created, but also a competitive element that made the team members eager to perform, aware of the progresses made in the other hospitals.

3   Results

At the start of the project, we aimed at registration of 10.000 medical records, which was judged "over-ambitious" by the evaluators. In February 2012, the number of records registered passed above 30.000! Via the Internet based secure application:

Fig. 3. Global Health Barometer "overview table"

"Global Health Barometer", we obtain both "global" and detailed views on the activities in the four participating centers.

Moreover, detailed and even diagnosis-specific views can be produced on-line, based on the recorded data: in Fig. 4, malaria incidence is depicted versus time. Several possibilities for data sharing and data mining across the project's sites are now available to the researchers of the partners. Of course, the more records will be registered, the more interesting this multi-site dataset will be for epdemiological purposes and for comparisons between regions.

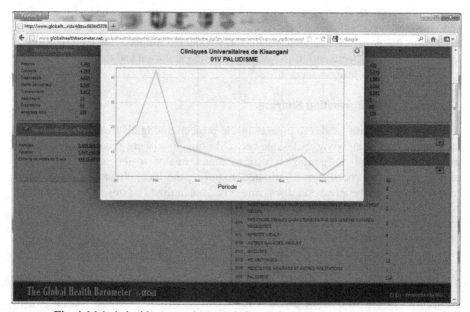

Fig. 4. Malaria incidence vs. time graph, based on data recorded at Kisangani

4   Discussion

The challenges posed by the introduction of electronic health records into academic hospitals in RDC were met by the project method and by the participating teams. Although the "teach the teachers" strategy and the integration into RAFT were lagging behind expectations, the registration of patient's records and the integration into medical practice proved to be successful, far beyond the expectations. The main lessons learned were:

- the human resources and the ambition to introduce electronic health records in RDC exist;
- when providing sufficient motivation and guidance, the hospital teams are quite effective and adequate, but they do not have time to become "teachers" in their own environment;
- follow-up projects can boost themselves by providing full-time teaching and coaching staff locally;
- although the current instability remains a major concern, the chosen solutions: no-break for server and routers and laptops as work-stations proved adequate;
- the reliability of the external network connection should improve to make distance support really feasible on a daily basis;
- sharing of the aggregated project data as via the "Global Health Barometer" web tool, automatically fed on a regular (daily) basis by all partners, boosts the project by introducing a tangible measure of the common accomplishments and an element of competition between the participants.

5   Conclusions

After just two years, the EuropAid project "Eb@le-sante" produced most of its deliverables as expected or beyond expectations.: the hardware is installed on the four sites, the local teams all got their technical, medical and administrative training and data collection has started in the form of patient registrations and patient records.

The security procedures are in place and in operation, distance support is effectively performed from Belgium as well as a nightly secured back-up from the four participating sites in RDC.

During 2011, we were able to make sufficient recordings in order to demonstrate the feasibility and the advantages, both organizational and medical for the project partners. Moreover, this will enable us to perform epidemiological and co-morbidity studies in RDC, for the first time, based on standard electronic clinical records.

Reporting on the hospital level, towards the Ministry of Health will be activated as soon as the number of recordings becomes representative. We hope that by the end of the project's second phase, starting in April 2013, all incoming- and outgoing patients will be recorded in the four sites.

We think the results of this project prove feasibility and effectiveness of this approach and, more than a "proof of concept", it has resulted in an effective operational set-up. Beyond doubt, we still need a continuing effort to enhance the impact in order to reach sustainability: the point where the hospitals themselves generate sufficient income via their ICT, in order to maintain an ICT team and the related infrastructure themselves. Further efforts are needed to reach the point of sustainability (full administrative patient handling) and for the "teach the teachers" goal.

Acknowledgements. We are very grateful to the academic authorities and administrative teams in Europe and in RDC, who made this project possible and thank all team members participating in the Eb@le-santé and Universitic projects for their involvement "beyond the line of duty".

References

1. Geissbuhler, A., Bagayako, C.-O., Ly, O.: The RAFT network: 5 years of distance continuing medical education and tele-consultations over the Internet in French-speaking Africa. Int. J. Med. Inform. 76(5-6), 351–356 (2007)
2. Verbeke, F.: OpenClinic,
   http://sourceforge.net/projects/open-clinic/
3. Verbeke, F., Murekatete, C., Tran Ngoc, C., Karara, G., Gasakure, E., Nyssen, M.: Evaluation of a new method for in-patient co-morbidity analysis based on KHIRI Pathology Group Set codes at the Kigali University Teaching Hospital. Journal of Health Informatics in Developing Countries 3(2) (2009)
4. Samake, K.D., et al.: eHealth in Africa: A Vision for Healthier African
5. Mars, M., Seebregts, C.: Country Case Study for e-Health: South Afrika
6. Geissbuhler, A., et al.: Telemedicine in Western Africa: lessons learned from a pilot project in Mali, perspectives and recommendations. In: AMIA Annu. Symp. Proc., pp. 249–253 (2003)
7. Pierre, B.: Unit ICT for Health, Assessing the opportunities and the pertinence of eHealth in developing countries. European Commission, Information Society and Media (February 2009)
8. Hategekimana, T., Tran Ngoc, C., Porignon, D., De Jonghe, M., Verbeke, F., Van Bastelaere, S.: Monitoring of clinical activities and performances by using international classifications ICD-10 and ICPC-2. Electronic Journal for Health Informatics 5(1) (2010)
9. Three years experience of the Kigali University Teaching Hospital, Rwanda
10. WHO World Health Assembly 58 (2005) Resolution WHA 58.28 on eHealth (2005)
11. WHO Report on e-health Document A58_21, WHA 58 (2005)

A Model for Information Security Governance in Developing Countries

Jacques Coertze and Rossouw von Solms

Institute for ICT Advancement, Nelson Mandela Metropolitan University,
Port Elizabeth, South Africa
jacques.coertze@gmail.com, rossouw.vonsolms@nmmu.ac.za

Abstract. The proliferation of e-business, e-services and e-governance in developing countries has resulted in businesses and governments becoming highly dependent on business information and related information technologies. Such information is, however, constantly exposed to real threats that could result in security breaches. If these are realised, the prevailing economic structure of a developing country, which is often frail and dependent on the success of its businesses, may be significantly affected as a result of monetary losses. It is thus vital for businesses in these countries to implement, manage and govern information security adequately so as to ensure that valuable information resources are effectively protected. Regrettably, many businesses in developing countries lack the expertise to perform these activities owing to a lack of resources or expertise. Accordingly, the aim of this paper is to establish a model for information security governance that can be implemented with little expertise, as well as minimal effort and capital outlay.

Keywords: information security, corporate governance, enterprise security, IT governance, information security governance, managing information security, security policy and procedures, developing countries.

1 Introduction

Information is a critical strategic asset to any business, irrespective of the size [1]. Although businesses continue to reap many benefits from information, in our modern society such benefits cannot be obtained without the help of information technology (IT).

IT is essential to managing the information and knowledge required in the daily operations of a business and thus contributes significantly to its success. Unfortunately, many security threats exist that may compromise information [2]; therefore IT and the information related to it should be adequately protected [3]. This is generally done through a process termed "information security".

Information security pertains to the protection of the confidentiality, integrity and availability of information, which is usually managed by a process called "information security management" [3]. As information and its proper protection are very important to the wellbeing of the modern enterprise, it has become

K. Jonas, I.A. Rai, and M. Tchuente (Eds.): AFRICOMM 2012, LNICST 119, pp. 279–288, 2013.
© Institute for Computer Sciences, Social Informatics and Telecommunications Engineering 2013

imperative that this be well governed. This is done through a process that is referred to as information security governance [4].

Von Solms [5] defines information security governance as

> consisting of the management and leadership commitment of executive-level management towards good information security; the proper organizational structures for enforcing good information security; full user awareness and commitment towards good information security and the necessary policies, procedures, processes, technologies and compliance enforcement mechanisms, all working together to ensure that the confidentiality, integrity and availability of the company's electronic assets, or information, are maintained at all times.

Many guiding documents, in the form of best practices, guidelines and standards, exist to help in the implementation of information security governance [3, 6, 7]. However, in developing countries, businesses and government departments often lack the expertise needed to interpret and use these guiding documents owing to an absence of resources [8]. This is of particular concern, since these businesses and government departments are now becoming heavily dependent on IT as they integrate electronic services into their daily operations. If the security risks related to such electronic services go unnoticed, it could spell disaster for both them and the economy of the country in which they operate.

Developing countries are thus facing a looming information insecurity tsunami which, if not addressed, could cripple businesses and, ultimately, entire economies [8]. Consequently, the objective of this paper is to establish an information security governance model to assist these businesses in governing their information security activities adequately.

This paper follows a design science research methodology, as outlined by Peffers, Tuunanen, Rothenberger and Chatterjee [9]. Following the methodology, this paper will firstly discuss businesses in developing countries in order to provide an overview of the area of study and to clearly identify a business problem. Secondly, a proposed information security governance model that can be used by businesses in developing countries will be presented. The paper will then conclude by discussing the feasibility of the proposed model.

2 The Business Environment in Developing Countries

Small, medium and micro enterprises (SMMEs) constitute an important part of the business environment in developing countries [10]; consequently, they hold significant implications for society and the environment [11]. Furthermore, SMMEs are labour intensive and therefore make a significant contribution to both the generation of income and the reduction of poverty in developing countries [11].

Many developing countries are rapidly introducing computers and information technology to SMMEs in order to facilitate e-commerce and worldwide service delivery [12]. Furthermore, governments are making more frequent use of e-infrastructure, e-governance and e-services. All of this is creating a high dependence on information and information technology [13]. The concern is, thus, that if the security aspects of this technology and information are not adequately addressed, severe security breaches may occur [3]. These, in turn, may contribute to monetary penalties for SMMEs and governments alike, leading to loss of the income on which the frail economic structure of developing countries is dependent [11]. There is, thus, significant evidence that a definite problem currently exists in the area of information security in SMMEs and the governments of developing countries. This needs to be addressed if these countries are to reap the benefits of their IT investments and enjoy continued economic growth.

The literature on information security [6, 14, 15] recommends that information security should be directed and controlled by executive-level management of SMMEs and government departments. Unfortunately, owing to the limited expertise and resources available in developing countries [10, 16], this level of management in such institutions often does not pay much attention to these duties, as it would rather focus on the operational aspects vital to business survival [8]. Consequently, the security concerns that are inherent in the dependence that is being placed on information and IT are often overlooked.

It can therefore be argued that a solution is required to assist executive-level management of businesses, as well as government departments in developing countries, with information security governance. A contribution in the form of a model for effective information security governance will be outlined in the following section.

3   The Information Security Governance Model

3.1   Principles

The proposed information security governance model is based on the assumption that a lack of expertise exists in businesses and government departments and in the implementation of information security governance, specifically in developing countries. Before such a model can be presented, however, the principles that it should exhibit in order for it to be adopted and implemented successfully have to be made known. Based on the literature, five principles have been established.

Firstly, businesses in developing countries often operate with limited funding and human resources [13, 17]. Moreover, they also have many competing needs [18]. For this reason, a model for information security governance should require minimal effort and capital outlay as well as limited human resources in order for it to be usable and effective.

Secondly, such businesses often cannot afford to hire full-time information security professionals or consultants [17, 19]. In some cases such experts may not even be available [8]. It is therefore vital that the model be presented in an easily understandable format.

Thirdly, as the model addresses information security governance, it should exhibit the actions depicted in the direct-control action cycle established by Von Solms et al. for all forms of governance [14].

Fourthly, the interconnectivity between the input and output requirements of each management level in a businesses should be identified. This will allow businesses to select appropriate tools for generating the inputs and outputs.

Fifthly, the model should facilitate both the *direct* and *control* actions over information security on all levels of management [14]. It should especially address strategic-level management, as this is often neglected in other governance models.

In summary, the principles that need to be exhibited by an information security governance model include the following:

1. It should require minimal effort to obtain the required result.
2. It should be easily understandable.
3. It should be based on the direct–control action cycle.
4. It should identify inputs and outputs at each management level.
5. It should depict complete direct and control activity.

These principles were used to design the information security governance model that will be discussed in the next subsection.

3.2   Model

The information security governance model (see Fig. 1) is based on the direct-control action cycle for information security governance, as outlined by Von Solms et al. [14].

Information security governance operates on three levels of management in a business, namely, the strategic, tactical and operational levels. These three levels are clearly indicated in the model as layers. This is because each management level will generally require different aspects of information security to be implemented – or produced – and monitored in order for proper information security governance to be present.

Similarly, the three actions of governance, namely, *direct, execute* and *control*, are also depicted in the composition of the model. These actions provide mutual support and are reinforced by input/output indicators that form the process flow of the model.

The Direct Action. According to international standards and best practices for information security governance, executive-level management must offer direction and exercise control over information security. Directing starts at the strategic level where executive-level management has to indicate clearly the importance it attaches to the information assets and the way in which such assets contribute to the strategic vision of the business. Such evaluations will need to be based on several factors that may originate from both external and internal sources, including risks, regulatory aspects and business requirements [3]. These factors, in turn, offer input to the security directives that executive-level management should establish.

There are various guidelines that can assist executive-level management in deliberating these factors and establishing directives, for example *Information*

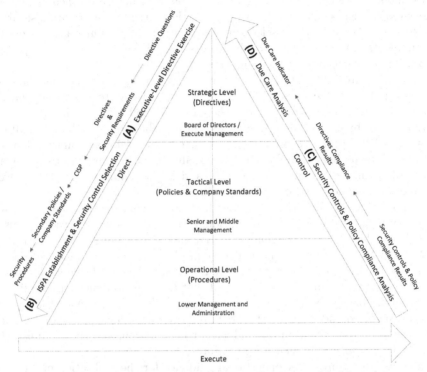

Fig. 1. The Information Security Governance Model

Security Governance: Guidance for Boards of Directors and Executive Management [15]. The model facilitates the use of such aids by suggesting that an executive-level directive exercise should be performed (as indicated by (A) in Fig. 1). The output of this exercise will be a set of clearly defined information security directives. These directives will reflect the expectations of executive-level management in terms of information security in the business and will become input to the policies and procedures that should be produced by the lower levels of management. As a result, these directives will contribute to the business's security requirements and policies.

In any business it is vital to determine the applicability and appropriate levels of security requirements. These may include, but are not limited to, aspects such as availability, integrity, confidentiality, auditability and authentication. An existing framework [20, 21] has been developed that supports an adapted risk analysis process for establishing security requirements by making use of a business-oriented questionnaire. In terms of this framework, management is asked a series of security-related questions.

The model proposed in this paper allows for the integration of the existing framework, but indicates that the defined directives from executive-level management should also have an impact on the security requirements. As a result, the responses to the business-oriented questionnaire, together with the directives, should influence the security requirements that are established. These security requirements will consequently govern the content of information security policies and the subsequent selection of security controls. Once these security requirements are known, the model suggests that the drafting of the corporate information security policy may commence.

The corporate information security policy (CISP) can be seen as the cornerstone policy that defines all the high-level security statements that will be applicable to the business. Typically, the CISP will reiterate the directives that have been set by executive-level management, set the scope for the information security policy, specify security roles and specify the vision for information security within the business. The CISP is usually supported by various company standards, which offer further adherence and implementation details to lower levels of management and operational staff.

Company standards generally detail the security controls that have been selected and that will act as the operational security measures in the organisation. A standard that is commonly used for the selection of security controls is ISO/IEC 27002 [3]. This standard offers multiple controls, which may be considered for selection and implementation in a business. Despite the controls offered by the standard, it must be kept in mind that the selection and applicability of security controls will be directly related to the security requirements, the type of business involved and the current state of information security. Further, security controls do not offer procedural guidance or information, and therefore usually need to be supported by security procedures.

Security procedures offer operational guidance for the realisation of security controls. They contain statements that can be followed during day-to-day operations; therefore operational staff depends heavily on such procedures to ensure that a safe and secure environment is maintained.

The model depicts the process for determining security requirements and drafting the security policies and procedures pertaining to the establishing of an information security policy architecture (as indicated by (B) in Fig 1). As already mentioned, an existing information security management framework [21] allows for this to take place through a semi-automated process based on ISO/IEC 27002 [3].

The model thus demonstrates that the establishing of all the above mentioned components, directives to the information security policy architecture, constitute the *direct* action of information security governance. Unfortunately, adherence to these components per se is not guaranteed, owing to the human nature of employees; therefore, ongoing *control* and *compliance* are vital.

The Control Action. Proper information security governance can be preserved if ongoing compliance evaluation or monitoring is carried out. Firstly, the security controls and procedures selected and implemented should be checked for usage and adherence by operational staff in the business and, secondly, the duties of executive-level management should be constantly evaluated to determine if due care and due diligence are being exercised with regard to information security.

The *control* action starts at the operational level, where a compliance analysis is performed based on the established security controls (as indicated by (C) in Fig. 1). The compliance analysis aids in determining if the established, or selected, security controls are properly implemented, efficient and effective. This subsequently allows for corrections, or improvements, to be made to the implementation of these security controls.

The model suggests that a policy and security control compliance analysis should be performed by operational and tactical-level management when initiating the *control* action (as indicated by (C) in Fig. 1). In the event that an existing information security management framework is used, a compliance questionnaire consisting of multiple audit questions per security control, based on the auditing guidelines of ISO/IEC 27001 [22] may be drawn up and used for this purpose. Once the compliance analysis has been successfully completed, the results should be used to correct ineffective or unimplemented controls by operational and tactical-level management. Further, the results must be aggregated to the upper management levels for decision making, strategizing and reporting.

To facilitate the decisions of executive-level management, they should receive regular aggregated reports on the implementation and effectiveness of security controls. They also need an indication of whether their own security directives are being met. Further, this level of management should be active in determining their own compliance with legislation, regulations and best practices.

In order to do this, executive-level management should perform a frequent due care analysis (as indicated by (D) in Fig. 1), which will indicate whether due care with regard to information security governance is being taken. In order to perform such a due care analysis a checklist may be used, such as the one established by Von Solms et al. [23]. On completion of a due care analysis, executive-level management will be able to ascertain both possible mismanagement and successful information security governance implementation.

The model depicts this process of policy and security control compliance analysis and due care analysis as constituting the *control* action of information security governance.

The established model can be argued to be feasible and can be shown to be practically viable for businesses in developing countries. This will be substantiated in the following subsection.

3.3 Motivation and Demonstration

The model combines numerous concepts, or works, that were established by previous and ongoing research. The aim of the model is therefore to facilitate the grouping of these established ideas. As these ideas are well known and have received great support, it is believed that the model will prove to be feasible and useful. Furthermore, all the concepts portrayed by the model have already been implemented in a prototype software application which may provide additional valuable support for businesses operating in developing countries.

A practical desktop application prototype was developed to demonstrate the feasibility of the model. This prototype is called *The Information Security*

Governance Toolbox (ISGT) and is an enhanced version of the existing *Information Security Management Toolbox (ISMTB)* developed during previous research [20].

This prototype facilitates the requirements of the *direct* and *control* action in all management levels of the established model. These include the establishment of security directives, drafting of information security policies and procedures, checking of compliance with these policies and, finally, executing a due care analysis to ascertain whether due care was taken in the information security governance implemented by executive-level management.

It should be noted that a research project is currently underway to evaluate the established model and to improve the current prototype. The findings of the model evaluation and improvements fall outside the scope of this paper, however, and will be presented in future publications.

4   Conclusion

Information is a business asset and has become vital to the successful existence of nearly all businesses. Accordingly, the protection of information is crucial. This protection of information is referred to as information security.

Information security deals with the protection of the confidentiality, integrity and availability of information. Literature on information security recommends that in order for information security to be successful, it has to be well managed and governed.

As a result of a lack of expertise and resources, many businesses in the developing world find it difficult to address the implementation, management and governance of information security adequately. In order to address this problem, this paper presented an information security governance model. In addition, it illustrated the overall actions and workings involved with the concept of information security governance.

The model exhibits five principles, all of which are deemed necessary for the successful implementation of information security governance by businesses in developing countries. The principles include the following:

1. It required minimal effort to obtain the required result.
2. It was easily understandable.
3. It was based on the direct–control action cycle.
4. It identified the interconnectivity between, inputs and outputs at each management level.
5. It depicted complete direct and control activity.

The objective of establishing an information security governance model that can be used by businesses in developing countries has therefore been met (see Fig 1).

It should be noted that ongoing research is being conducted to evaluate the established model and to improve the prototype based on it. These improvements and evaluation results will be presented in future publications.

The authors of this paper envisage that the information security governance model will prove highly beneficial to businesses operating in developing countries. Furthermore, since these businesses form such an important part of a developing countrys economic structure, information security researchers should remain vigilant in their attempts to assist them.

Acknowledgments. The financial assistance of the National Research Foundation (NRF) for this research is hereby acknowledged. Opinions expressed and conclusions arrived at are those of the authors and are not necessarily to be attributed to the National Research Foundation.

References

[1] Von Solms, R.: Information security management (1): why information security is so important. Information Management & Computer Security 6(4), 174–177 (1998), doi:10.1108/EUM0000000004533

[2] Von Solms, S.H., Von Solms, R.: Information Security Governance. Springer (2008) ISBN 0387799834

[3] Information technology - code of practice for information security management. Number 27002. International Organization for Standardization (ISO) (2005) ISBN 978-0-626-21372-5

[4] Posthumus, S., Von Solms, R., King, M.: The board and IT governance: The what, who and how. South African Journal of Business Management 41(3), 23–32 (2010) ISSN 20785976

[5] Von Solms, S.: Information Security - The Fourth Wave. Computers & Security 25(3), 165–168 (2006), doi:10.1016/j.cose.2006.03.004

[6] Institute of Directors in Southern Africa. King III Report on Corporate Governance. Institute Of Directors in Southern Africa, Parklands (2009) ISBN 2300000012576

[7] IT Governance Institute. Cobit 4.1. ISACA (2007) ISBN 1933284722

[8] Goodman, S., Harris, A.: Emerging markets: The coming african tsunami of information insecurity. Communications of the ACM 53(12), 24–27 (2010), doi:10.1145/1859204.1859215

[9] Peffers, K., Tuunanen, T., Rothenberger, M., Chatterjee, S.: A Design Science Research Methodology for Information Systems Research. Journal of Management Information Systems 24(3), 45–77 (2007), doi:10.2753/MIS0742-1222240302, ISSN 0742-1222

[10] European Multi stakeholder Forum on CSR. Final results & recommendations. Technical report, European Multi-stakeholder Forum on CSR (2004)

[11] Raynard, P., Forstater, M.: Corporate social responsibility: Implications for small and medium enterprises in developing countries. Technical report, United Nations Industrial Development Organization (2002)

[12] Wall, D.: The internet as a conduit for criminal activity. In: Patavina, A. (ed.) Information Technology and the Criminal Justice System. Sage Publications (2005)

[13] Gupta, A., Hammond, R.: Information systems security issues and decisions for small businesses: An empirical examination. Information Management & Computer Security 13(4), 297–310 (2005), doi:10.1108/09685220510614425, ISSN 0968-5227

[14] Von Solms, R., Von Solms, S.: Information Security Governance: A model based on the Direct/Control Cycle. Computers & Security 25(6), 408–412 (2006), doi:10.1016/j.cose.2006.07.005

[15] IT Governance Institute. Information Security Governance: Guidance for Boards of Directors and Executive Management. IT Governance Institute, 2nd edn. (2006) ISBN 1933284293

[16] Perera, O.: How material is iso 26000 to small and medium-sized enterprises (smes). Technical report, International Institute for Sustainable Development (2008)

[17] Upfold, C.T., Sewry, D.A.: An investigation of Information Security in Small and Medium Enterprises (SMEs) in the Eastern Cape. In: Venter, H.S., Eloff, J.H.P., Labuschagne, L., Eloff, M.M. (eds.) Proceedings of the ISSA 2005 New Knowledge Today Conference, pp. 1–17 (2005)

[18] Tawileh, A., Hilton, J., McIntosh, S.: Managing information security in small and medium sized enterprises: a holistic approach. Proceedings of the ISSE/SECURE, pp. 331–339 (2007)

[19] Yildirim, E., Akalp, G., Aytac, S., Bayram, N.: Factors influencing information security management in small- and medium-sized enterprises: A case study from Turkey. International Journal of Information Management (November 2010), doi: 10.1016/j.ijinfomgt.2010.10.006, ISSN 02684012

[20] Hoppe, O.A., Van Niekerk, J., Von Solms, R.: The Effective Implementation of Information Security in Organizations. In: Proceedings of the IFIP TC11 17th International Conference on Information Security: Visions and Perspectives, pp. 1–18. Kluwer, B.V., Deventer, The Netherlands (2002) ISBN 1-4020-7030-6

[21] Vermeulen, C., Von Solms, R.: The information security management toolbox - taking the pain out of security management. Information Management & Computer Security 10(3), 119–125 (2002), doi:10.1108/09685220210431872

[22] Information technology - Security techniques - Information security management systems - Requirements. Number 27001. International Organization for Standardization (ISO) (2005) ISBN 0-626-17724-3

[23] Von Solms, R., Von Solms, S.: Information security governance: Due care. Computers & Security 25(7), 494–497 (2006), doi:10.1016/j.cose.2006.08.013, ISSN 01674048

Cyber Security Education in Developing Countries: A South African Perspective

Noluxolo Kortjan and Rossouw von Solms

P.O. Box 77000, Nelson Mandela Metropolitan University,
Port Elizabeth 6031, South Africa
{Noluxolo.Kortjan,Rossouw.VonSolms}@nmmu.ac.za

Abstract. Cyberspace has become significant to the wellbeing of the individuals, organisations and general economy of a country. It is for this reason that a country should play a leading role in securing cyberspace. However, in the face of the inherent challenges, the awareness of and education on cyber security cannot be overlooked. This paper aims to determine the current situation regarding cyber security in South Africa (SA) as a case of developing countries, specifically from an awareness and educational point of view. This will be achieved by providing a comparative analysis between two well-advanced countries and South Africa in order to abstract key points from a policy and policy implementation point of view to the actual execution of cyber security education initiatives. From the identified key points, some aspects are highlighted that a developing country should perhaps consider in engineering its cyber security education plan.

Keywords: cyberspace, cyber security, cyber security education.

1 Introduction

In modern technology, the internet has become one of the most significant inventions to date [1]. Over the years the internet has developed immensely, providing billions of individuals and enterprises across the globe with digital communication [2]. In the modern way of doing business, enterprises use the internet to meet their aims and to enable business processes [1]. Over and above its communication value, people use the internet for financial and entertainment purposes [3]. As a result, large numbers of enterprises and individuals have become dependent on the technology.

Although the internet offers numerous advantages, it is constantly threatened by many risks. These risks can have serious adverse effects on both enterprises and individuals making use of the internet. One of these risks is online crime [4]. The internet has given criminals a platform on which to grow and proliferate [5]; further, it is easy for criminals to go unpunished because of the abstract nature of the internet and the difficulty involved in tracing the origins of such crime [1]. Core to criminal activities on the internet is the exploitation of personal and corporate information [6]. As a result, every person or enterprise using the internet is at risk of having such information compromised.

K. Jonas, I.A. Rai, and M. Tchuente (Eds.): AFRICOMM 2012, LNICST 119, pp. 289–297, 2013.
© Institute for Computer Sciences, Social Informatics and Telecommunications Engineering 2013

Not only has the internet become critical to the wellbeing of many people and organisations; but it has also become part of several components that are critical to the wellbeing of national economies and society at large [7]. Accordingly, in light of the increasing adoption of the internet, developing countries and Africa, in particular, lack general safety and security measures in terms of this resource. This is due in part to a number of unique factors. However, with the continuous rise in the adoption of the internet measures should be put in place to address the security risks.

Many developed countries, such as the United States of America (USA) and the United Kingdom (UK), have developed and implemented cyber security protocols, standards and implementations for internet security and policing. Education in this regard is critical to cyber security implementation. Realising this, these countries have taken the initiative in educating society at large, including enterprises, on the threats related to the internet and to cyberspace. This includes how to recognise and avoid the threats, as well as how to recover from them.

In contrast with developed countries, many developing countries do not, as yet, have comprehensive cyber security initiatives in place [8]. These countries include Egypt, Libya and Morocco in the northern region of Africa. In addition, in other parts of Africa, such as Central Africa, the concept of cyber security is still vague [8].

Using South Africa as a case, this paper aims to explore the current situation as it pertains to cyber security education in developing countries. It furthermore aims to identify criteria that should be considered when creating a comprehensive cyber security educational plan for a typical developing country. These criteria are an attempt to contribute to education on cyberspace security in developing countries and underline the role education plays in it. This will be achieved by conducting a comparative analysis between South Africa and two advanced countries in terms of cyber security, namely, the UK and the USA.

2 A Snapshot of the United Kingdom's and United States of America's Efforts Regarding Cyber Security

The UK and the USA have taken definitive steps towards securing cyberspace. These entail a complete suite of aspects that need to be addressed and implemented, including drafting policies and implementing cyber security protocols. This section will assess what is currently in place concerning cyber security education. The cyber security efforts of these two countries are studied merely because a great deal of relevant information is available in this regard.

2.1 Cyber Security Education in the United Kingdom

Six and a half million pounds has been has been allocated by the UK government to educate UK citizens on cyber security awareness [9]. An education scheme "Get Safe Online" has been developed to assist organisations and the general population with cyber-related issues [10]. This scheme provides advice on cyber threats and ways in which to recognise and recover from the threats. "Get Safe Online" provides cyber safety tips for teachers, parents and young people. Moreover, its knowledge base comprises information on protecting both individuals and businesses. The UK intends to expand the scope of the scheme to include more innovative ways of disseminating cyber security education. The UK has also launched the Cyber Security Challenge which aims to groom young cyber specialists to fill the skills gap in IT security [11].

Therefore, it would seem that, from a UK perspective, objectives have been set for cyber security education, funds have been set aside, and well-planned, coordinated activities are taking place to educate all levels of cyber users.

2.2   Cyber Security Education in the United States of America

The USA has formed the National Initiative for Cyber Security Education (NICE) [12]. The NICE initiative aims to improve the cyber behaviour, skills, and knowledge of the US population, enabling a safer cyberspace. One of the major goals of NICE is "to strengthen the future cyber security environment by expanding cyber education; coordinating and redirecting research and development efforts across the Federal Government; and working to define and develop strategies to deter hostile or malicious activity in cyberspace" [12].

This initiative is currently active and has awareness campaigns that include the "Stop.Think.Connect" online educational scheme [13]. This scheme underpins the notion that cyber security is the responsibility of everyone who benefits from using cyberspace. Therefore, everyone should take a moment to **stop** and **think** carefully about the risks associated with using cyberspace. Once the risks are considered one can make an informative choice and continue to **connect** and enjoy cyberspace [13]. "Stop.Think.Connect" has also spawned another online education scheme "OnGuardOnline.gov" with a similar intention. Moreover, the USA holds a National Cyber Security Awareness month in October every year, which is intended to remind American citizens that cyber security is a shared responsibility [14].

The NICE cyber security workforce structure consists of the US Federal workforce, the government and the private sector. In addition, the US Department of Homeland Security has formed partnerships with the private and public sector in its quest to mitigate cybercrime against critical infrastructure [12]. The USA also has a Computer Emergency Response Team (CERT) aimed at improving the nation's cyber security. The CERT serves as a point of contact for the US nation to share and communicate directly with the US government about cyber-related threats and incidents [15].

The UK and the USA have positioned cyber security alongside other governmental priorities, consequently taking the initiative in securing cyberspace. Steps have been taken to develop policy and strategy in this regard, as well as with regard to the educational facet of cyber security. However, cybercrime is still an issue and there are calls for more innovative ways to secure cyberspace. Therefore, constantly improving cyber security protocols should also be a concern. The following section will explore cyber security from a South African perspective.

3   South Africa's Efforts towards Cyber Security

Cyber security issues are not unique to the UK and the USA. As South Africa becomes ever more reliant on cyberspace to govern and to conduct business, it is increasingly being affected by threatening cyber issues [16]. As with the previous section, this section will provide a brief summary of the key points addressed in South Africa's Draft National Cyber Security Policy Framework. It will evaluate the vision of this policy together with that way in which its objectives are to be achieved. Further, it will assess what is currently implemented in South Africa in terms of cyber security education.

3.1   South African Cyber Security Policies and Strategies

In the year 2010, the South African government released a draft cyber security policy [17]. This draft policy implied that South Africa is not currently in a position to deal effectively with cyber-related threats. In addition, the draft stated that South Africa lags behind other countries in the development of cyber security protocols and standards, as well as in the implementation of such protocols and standards. The objectives of this policy document include developing structures that would be capable of adequately supporting cyber security, as well as establishing and promoting a cyber security culture, and encouraging compliance with certain security standards. However, this policy remained stagnant for a period of two years.

This draft has, nevertheless, led the way to the recently published National Cyber Security Policy Framework. Articulated in this policy is the intent to secure cyberspace and to ensure that the protection of South Africa's national critical information infrastructure is not hindered. This policy aims to create a knowledgeable society that understands cyber-related threats. Moreover, it intends to provide a cyber security approach that is holistic and, in doing so, it requires the support of all role-players. These role-players include the state, the public and private sector and society at large [17]. This policy addresses the following:

- developing and implementing an integrated approach to cyber security that will be led by the government
- creating a Cyber Security Response Committee dedicated solely to coordinating cyber security measures
- synchronising effective departmental resources in order to ensure uniform cyber security goals
- promoting partnerships with all role-players in cyber security
- creating an environment that has well-coordinated approaches, plans, manpower and infrastructure
- strengthening the legal sphere to incorporate cyber crime prevention
- promoting a cyber security culture that subscribes to minimum cyber security measures
- establishing a comprehensive framework to govern cyberspace
- establishing a partnership with public and private entities to coordinate action plans that correspond with the intents of this policy.

Currently, South Africa merely has a vision; as yet there have been no concrete developments.

3.2   Cyber Security Education in South Africa

The policy at hand says little regarding cyber security education. This is only "hinted" at in terms of the idea of promoting a cyber security culture; a culture that is not elaborated on in detail.

Further, the policy fails to provide a clear vision on how South Africa plans to implement the objectives expressed and no resources have been set aside to fund their implementation. Seemingly, apart from the Electronic Communications and Transactions (ECT) Act, the Draft Cyber Security Policy and the recently published National Cyber Security Policy Framework, South Africa is still in the infancy stages of preparing to secure cyberspace. Moreover, there are no known cyber security awareness initiatives, as would seem to be the case in a number of developing countries. As education plays a core part in introducing any cyber security-related policy or strategy, the next section will propose some aspects that need to be addressed in this regard.

4   Bridging the Gap between South Africa and Its Counterparts in the United Kingdom and the United States of America

Cyber security has become a burning issue worldwide. In the attempt to mitigate this issue, education has been identified as an important tool. As mentioned in the previous section, the UK and the USA have taken definitive steps in implementing cyber security education. However, South Africa is still in the preparation stage in this regard. This section provides a brief summary of what is envisioned and has been implemented in the UK, the USA and South Africa. This summary is intended to highlight what is "missing" from South Africa's national cyber security policy as regards education, and proposes some aspects that South Africa should consider when engineering its cyber security education plan.

4.1   What Has Been Said and Done in the United Kingdom, the United States of America and South Africa

It is important to note that the UK and the USA are improving initiatives that are already in place, while South Africa is still struggling to lay the foundations of cyber security education. This point is expanded on in the summary in Table 1. The information provided in Table 1 is grouped according to four categories. Firstly, **what** each country wants to achieve in terms of cyber security education, namely, its **objective**. Secondly, **when** is the **outcome** pertaining to the objective expected? Thirdly, **who** is **responsible** for certain tasks? Lastly, **the way in which** each country plans to achieve the expected outcome is stated.

Table 1. Cyber security education overview of the United Kingdom, the United States of America and South Africa

WHAT	
UK	Concerning cyber security education, the UK wants to create a knowledgeable society and commercial world that is able to protect itself from cyber-related threats [9].
US	The USA is also working towards educating the general public on cyber-related threats [12].
SA	SA, on the other hand, is set on creating a cyber security culture [17]. As mentioned in the previous section, the policy does not go into detail on what this "culture" entails.
	SA has indeed embarked on securing cyberspace; albeit, years after other countries and therefore with a very big deficit.
WHEN	
UK	In 2015, the UK intends to have achieved what it is set out to do in terms of educating society and enterprises. [9]
US	The outlook is even more promising in the USA, given that it is continually delivering on its intention to educate society at large. The USA has an ongoing awareness programme coordinated by the NICE [12].
SA	The policy does not clarify this aspect.
	At this stage no definite milestones have been set which raises the fear that this policy framework might remain merely good intentions.
WHO	
UK	A number of government departments, alongside the GCHQ, have instigated the Get Safe Online scheme to serve as a focal point for cyber security awareness and education [18].
US	The Department of Homeland Security is routing the implementation of cyber security awareness and education. However, the NICE is fully dedicated to coordinating all that is necessary for cyber security education [14].
SA	According to the final draft cyber security policy, the Department of Communications (DoC) will be responsible for awareness raising. No specific body within the DoC has been established as yet to deal with cyber security education.
	The chances of creating a cyber security culture in SA will most probably remain a dream if no dedicated group is mandated, empowered and resourced to do so.

Table 2. *(Continued)*

HOW	
UK	As mentioned in section 2, funds have been made available for what needs to be done. Furthermore, all levels of education will be addressed to equip people better. The role of Get Safe Online will be strengthened to include more innovative ways of spreading awareness [9].
US	The USA is using NICE, Stop.Think.Connect, the National Cyber Security Month and OnGuardOnline.gov as tools to educate individuals and enterprises [13].
SA	The policy does not set out how it plans to promote a cyber security culture.
	The policy framework is silent on how the way a cyber security culture will be instilled as well as the target audience that is to be made aware and educated in this regard.

4.2   Bridging the Gap

After comparing the criteria from these countries, one can clearly identify the areas in which South Africa lags behind. Using South Africa as a typical example of a developing country, the objective is to address the shortfalls from an awareness and educational point of view. In doing so, we list some of the aspects that should be considered by developing countries in this regard:

- setting an undisputable objective
- identifying definite milestone dates
- creating, empowering and resourcing a responsible group
- defining a reasonable action plan
- allocating resources

It would be a good start for developing countries to have clear-cut **goals** for cyber security education. This would make it easy for such a country to rate its performance in this regard [19]; in addition, it essential that performance be monitored against **targets**. Accordingly, once South Africa knows exactly what it wants to achieve and when, it will be easier to benchmark its progress. As vital as this is, identifying who is responsible for what is just as important. Merely assigning responsibility for awareness and education to the Department of Communication is not enough; if a definite grouping **is made responsible** for awareness and education, delivery will be assured.

It is all very well to abstract that which the UK and the USA have in place; however, it is crucial to be aware that these countries are different to Africa. The difference lies in how technologically advanced the UK and the USA are. Having considered that, the responsible party could coordinate a tailor-made **action plan** that would be suitable for a developing country. Finally, resource allocation is crucial; for example allocating a budget will play a major role in tying the all the aspects together.

Table 1 summarised the areas in which South Africa lags behind in cyber security. In mitigation, some suggestions have been made to ensure that South Africa does indeed embark effectively on the road to "create a cyber security culture" in SA.

5   Conclusion

The reliance on cyberspace to live, to conduct commerce and to govern has placed cyber security alongside other global concerns. Hence, cyber security education should be viewed in the same important light. The UK and the USA are well on their way to educating their citizens to behave in a safe, secure manner when connected to cyberspace. Such safe and secure behaviour will be beneficial to the individual, businesses and, eventually, for the entire country. By contrast, developing countries are barely armed, owing to a number of unique factors. However, as there is a continuous rise in the adoption of the internet globally, every country should be preparing to create a secure virtual environment. With the evidence and arguments that have been provided, one can ask and answer the questions posed below:

1. Are the enterprises and individuals in developing countries as dependent on the internet as their US and UK counterparts?

   Developing countries are becoming increasingly as dependant on the internet, particularly in the areas of governance and economics.

2. Are developing countries equally prepared to educate enterprises and individuals on how to protect themselves in cyberspace?

   No.

The suggestions made are intended to assist developing countries in their endeavours to derive a strategy for solidifying an envisaged cyber security culture. It is acknowledged that the suggestions are only part of the eventual solution.

Acknowledgement. The financial assistance of the National Research Foundation (NRF) in this research is hereby acknowledged. The opinions expressed and the conclusions arrived at are those of the authors and are not necessarily to be attributed to the National Research Foundation.

References

1. Hunton, P.: A rigorous approach to formalising the technical investigation stages of cybercrime and criminality within a UK law enforcement enviroment. Digital Investigation 7, 105–113 (2011)

2. Digital Britain In: Digital Britain the interim report,
    `http://webarchive.nationalarchives.gov.uk/+/http://www.cultu`
    `re.gov.uk/images/publications/digital_britain_interimreportj`
    `an09.pdf` (accessed January 2009)
3. Maignan, I., Lukas, B.: The Nature and Uses of the Internet: A qualitative Investigation.
    Journal of Consumer Affairs 31(2), 346–371 (1997)
4. Reim, A.: Cybercrimes of the 21st Century. Computer Fraud & Security 2001(3), 13–15
    (2001)
5. Selwyn, N.: A Safe Haven for Misbehaving? An Investigation of Online Misbehavior
    Among University Students. Social Science Computer Review 26(4), 446–465 (2008)
6. de Joode, A.: Effective Corporate security and cybercrime. Network Security 2011(3), 16–
    18 (2011)
7. Nickolov, E.: Critical Information Infrastructure Protection: Analysis, Evaluation and
    Expectations. Information & Security 17, 105–119 (2005)
8. Cole, K., Chetty, M., LaRosa, C., Reitta, F., Schmitt, D., Goodman, S.: Cybersecurity in
    Africa: An Assessment, `http://www.cistp.gatech.edu/publications/`
    `files/AnAssessmentofAfricanCybersecurity.pdf`
    (accessed April 25, 2008)
9. Cabinet Office In: Cabinet Office,
    `http://www.cabinetoffice.gov.uk/news/`
    `protecting-and-promoting-uk-digital-world` (accessed Month 2011)
10. Get Safs Online In: Get Safs Online,
    `http://www.getsafeonlineblog.org/get-safe-online-the-rough-`
    `guide-to-online-safety` (accessed April 2012)
11. BBC News: Technology In: BBC News,
    `http://www.bbc.co.uk/news/technology-107425888?print=true`
    (accessed April 2012)
12. NICE In: National Initiative for Cybersecurity Education,
    `http://csrc.nist.gov/nice/` (accessed August 2011)
13. Homeland Security In: Homeland Security,
    `http://www.dhs.gov/files/events/stop-think-connect.shtm`
    (accessed August 2011)
14. Homeland Security In: Homeland Security,
    `http://www.dhs.gov/files/programs/gc_1158611596104.shtm`
    (accessed October 2011)
15. US-CERT In: US-CERT, `http://www.us-cert.gov/` (accessed August 2011)
16. Lamprecht, I.: In: News24, `http://www.news24.com/SciTech/SA-ranks-`
    `high-in-cyber-crime-20110327-2` (accessed March 2011)
17. Department of Communications In: Cloud Front,
    `http://d2zmx6mlqh7g3a.cloudfront.net/cdn/farfuture/mtime:126`
    `6829764/files/docs/100219cybersecurity.pdf` (accessed February 2010)
18. Houses of Parliament: Cyber Security in the UK
19. Locke, E., Shaw, K., Saari, L., Latham, G.: Goal setting and task performance: 1969–1980.
    Psychological Bulletin 90(1), 125–152 (1981)

Intellectual Property (IP) Integration Approach for Data-Flow Parallel Embedded Systems

Anne Marie Chana[1] and Patrice Quinton[2]

[1] National High School Polytechnic, University of Yaounde I, Cameroon
anne_chana@yahoo.fr
[2] ENS Cachan Bretagne, Université européenne de Bretagne Campus de Ker Lann,
35 170 Bruz, France
patrice.quinton@bretagne.ens-cachan.fr

Abstract. The growing complexity of new chips and the time to market constraints require fundamental changes in the systems design approach. Systems on chip (SoC) based on reused components called intellectual property (IP) has become an absolute necessity to the embedded systems companies in order to remain competitive. This paper focuses on the IP reuse to design parallel and multi-frequency applications. The flexible parallel components described by the ALPHA functional language are modelled and assembled using a scheduling method which combines the synchronous data-flow principle of balance equations and, the polyhedral scheduling technique. Our approach allows a flexible component to be modelled and, a full system to be assembled and synthesized by combining the component hardware descriptions with automatically generated wrappers. We discuss the relationship of this approach with stream languages, latency-insensitive design, and multidimensional data-flow systems.

Keywords: IP reused, flexible component, SoC, Polyhedral model, data-flow model, parallelism, multi-frequency system.

1 Introduction

Over the past 20 years, embedded systems have become the supports of the most advanced hardware and software technologies. In this period, the implementation of embedded system technology has evolved from microcontroller to fully integrated systems-on-chip (SoC). SoCs and related technologies are driving embedded systems today and in the foreseeable future. New demanding applications in terms of processing power appeared over the past 20 years, driven by PC boom, Internet and wireless environments. These applications are called systematic and intensive processing and are found both in scientific computing and signal processing (telecommunications, multimedia processing, image processing and video, etc.) for exemple, in short in cyber-physical [1] systems in general. Processing such applications requires systematic and extensive high

K. Jonas, I.A. Rai, and M. Tchuente (Eds.): AFRICOMM 2012, LNICST 119, pp. 298–307, 2013.

capacity data processing often using techniques of parallel and distributed computing. The difficulties to develop those applications are primarily due to the exploitation of data and arithmetic parallelism, time and resources constraints.

Many such systems are designed by re-using existing software or hardware modules often called *flexible blocks* or *Intellectual Property* (IP). These flexible components are available as software or hardware functions and represent specific application elements for signal processing blocks (DCT, FFT, etc.), telecommunications (Viterbi codes, Turbo-codes, etc.), or Multimedia (MPEG2, MPEG4, JPEG, etc.).

In practice, it is not easy to assemble and operate components from different designers. Even if they are tested beforehand, there is no guarantee that, when put together the system will work correctly.

Integrating components together must take into account several aspects. The components must be synchronized to allow a correct overall operation of the system, and to ensure proper data exchange and valid communication protocols. Inputs/outputs must sometimes be stored to meet the synchronization constraints.

We present in our paper a systematic method to automatically generate a hardware architecture for multi-frequency, parallel data-flow (or streaming) systems with flexible generic components. The flexible components that we use are similar to those synthesized using the MMALPHA environment, which allows parallelization and hardware synthesis. They can model parallel architectures operating on multi-dimensional streams of data, in a regular fashion.

Our method consists of specifying such flexible components, their scheduling and synthesis, and then determines their assembly conditions. If the assembly is possible, we produce a hardware architecture by adding a wrapper to each component so that the whole system becomes synthesizable. The wrapper is used to control the frequency utilization of the component and achieve the system control.

Our scheduling technique combines the method used in the *synchronous data-flow model* [5] and the *polyhedral model* method, as described in [6]. This schedule allows one to deduce the different logic sub-clocks that meet the I/O constraints of each component, and the number of additional registers that may be needed between some of the components.

In this paper we present the main ideas of our method; our main contribution is to show how automatic method allows one to synthesize such complex system. We present the steps of the automatical synthesis that starts with the description of the system by ALPHA and ends with the scheduling and automatic generation of synthesizable code.

2   Integration Approach

Our approach to integration consists of several step, namely:

- The system specification: behavioural description of the system as SDF graph and checking the system hardware feasibility. In this step we also select the suitable behavioural flexible components (IPs) to use.

- System description: in this step, one produces a system behavioural description that takes into account the selected IPs. After this phase, the synthesis of the adapter can be done manually or automatically through a synthesis environment such as MMAlpha. in our paper we use the second approach.
- The automatic synthesis: this stage takes as input an ALPHA description of the system. The automatic synthesis is to compute the scheduling, determine logical clocks period and generate the VHDL controller code.
- System and IPs integration: This last phase is to include in the code obtained in the previous step the VHDL code of the various components. The final code can thus be subjected to a physical synthesis tool such as Xilinx ISE or Quartus of Atera.

2.1   System Specification

The system is modelled using the synchronous data flow graph. This model is more suitable for periodic multi-frequency applications. It offers to the designer the possibility to verify the feasibility of the description of the system before starting the synthesis.

Consider the system described by the SDF graph in figure 1, which is an example of the multiplication of two FFT (Fast Fourier Transform) outputs, operation widely used in signal processing. It consists of elementary hardware components (rectangles), synchonization components (circles). The nodes represent the treatments and the arcs are communication (FIFOs) which are bounded and unidirectional memory; the values on the arcs are the amounts of data produced or consumed at each iteration. This system can also be described by a system of balance equations as follows:

$$x_1 - 128x_3 = 0$$
$$x_2 - 128x_4 = 0$$
$$128x_3 - x_5 = 0$$
$$128x_4 - x_5 = 0$$
$$x_5 - x_6 = 0$$

where the $x_i's$ are the frequencies at which the nodes must be invoked.

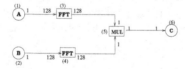

Fig. 1. Two FFT multiplication

A balance equation is based on the following condition: when iterating, the total number of information produced by the source block is equal to the number of data consumed by the target block. Finding a solution to this systems means ensuring that the SDF graph can be executed with a limited amount of memory.

We can write the system in the matrix form $\Gamma x = 0$ or

$$\begin{pmatrix} 1 & 0 & -128 & 0 & 0 & 0 \\ 0 & 1 & 0 & -128 & 0 & 0 \\ 0 & 0 & 128 & 0 & -1 & 0 \\ 0 & 0 & 0 & 128 & -1 & 0 \\ 0 & 0 & 0 & 0 & 1 & -1 \end{pmatrix} \begin{pmatrix} x_1 \\ x_2 \\ x_3 \\ x_4 \\ x_5 \\ x_6 \end{pmatrix} = \begin{pmatrix} 0 \\ 0 \\ 0 \\ 0 \\ 0 \\ 0 \end{pmatrix}$$

Γ is called topological matrix, the columns represent the nodes and the lines the arcs. $\Gamma(i,j)$ represents the amount of data produced or consumed by the node j on arc i each time it is invoked. This quantity is positive or negative depending on whether information is produced or consumed. It is zero if node j is not connected to the arc i.

If the rank of the matrix is $s - 1$ (s is the number of the column), then the dimension of its kernel is 1 and the base is reduced to a single element which is the vector solution of the system $\Gamma x = 0$. This is the necessary condition for the existence of an statical and periodical the system scheduling. The components of this vector give for each node of the graph how often it should be invoked during a period T for the system to remains consistent [6]. For the above example the unique solution is,

$$x = \begin{bmatrix} 128 & 128 & 1 & 1 & 128 & 128 \end{bmatrix}^T \quad .$$

2.2 Automatic Synthesis Using MMALPHA Environment

In this section we present an ALPHA specification of parallel data stream application whose modules run at different frequencies. Those applications called Multirate Parallel Alpha Data Flow Systems (MP&DFS) were introduced by [6]. We summarize the formalism of modelization and scheduling of such systems.

Notice that, an ALPHA structured system is an ALPHA system that uses subsystems or components.

Component Hardware Modelization. The components are *synchronous elements*, and their synchronization is based on a fundamental clock signal denoted by clk. Each component is physically synchronized with a clock validation signal *clock-enable* denoted by ce which is a component of the vector $\hat{x}$ obtained as described in [3]. For the system in fig.1 we have

$$\hat{x} = \begin{bmatrix} 1 & 1 & 128 & 128 & 1 & 1 \end{bmatrix}^T \quad .$$

In other words, all registers of the component are loaded under the control of this ce signal.

So, each elementary hardware component is considered as *combinational element component*, computing a c stream in term of input streams a and b and storing the result c in a register. As illustrated in Fig. 2, this component is synchronized by a clock-enable signal, to operate at a period of 3 clock cycles, and with an initial shift of 2 clock cycles.

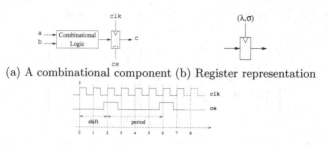

(a) A combinational component (b) Register representation

(c) A clocking with initial shift 2 and period 3

Fig. 2. A combinational component (a) and its synchronization (c) using a clock-enable signal. Here, the period is 3 and the initial shift is 2. (b) shows the representation of a register with period λ and shift σ.

We can see that, by changing the pattern of the `ce` signal, we may use the same component with different periods and different shifts: indeed, all registers of the component operate at a virtual clock whose period and shift are specified by `ce`. The combination of `clk` and `ce` is denote by a pair (λ, σ) where λ represents the period of the signal and σ its initial shift.

ALPHA **Specification.** ALPHA programs are functional (declarative) description that operate on variables which are functions from a polyhedral domain to some type of data. This is best explained by the example of Fig. 3 which presents a sketch of the system describes in fig.1. Line 1 is the declaration of a *system* of ALPHA equations, i.e., an ALPHA program. Line 2 and 3 define the inputs of this system, namely, the A and B variables. Both variables correspond to an semi-infinite sequence of 2-bit signed integers, that we call *streams* for the purpose of this paper. Similarly, lines 6 defines the outputs C. Line 8 and 9 contain the declaration of local variables. Line 11 is a simple assignment of A to the local stream `Amirr`. Line 12 makes use of an ALPHA subsystem, here representing a

```
1   System TwoFFTs
2     (A :{i|0<=i} of integer[S,2];
3      B :{j|0<=j} of integer[S,2])
4   returns
5   –output data and control
6     (C :{i|0<=i} of interger[S,2];
7   var
8     fft1, fft2, fftmul:{i|0<=i} of integer[S,2];
9     Amir, AmirReg, Bmir, BmirReg, Cmir:{i|0<=i} of integer[S,2];
10  let
11  Amir =A;
12  use registerFile[1](Amir) returns(AmirReg);
13  Bmir = B;
14  use registerFile[1](Bmir) returns (BmirReg);
15  use FFT(AmirReg) returns (fft1);
16  use FFT(BmirReg) returns (fft2);
17  use mul(fft1,fft2) returns (fftmul);
18  use registerFile[1](fftmul) returns (Cmir).
19  C=Cmir;
20  tel
```

Fig. 3. The ALPHA Program of two FFT Multiplication presents in fig.1

register file of length 1. Line 15 instantiates a FFT. Each **use** statement allows one to instantiate the definition of another, pre-defined, ALPHA subsystem.

2.3   Scheduling

We have already explained elsewhere [6] how to schedule stream components, but we summarize here our method in order to illustrate its power. The method that we propose has two steps: first, find out the *period* of each subsystem, then compute an overall *affine* schedule for the entire system. Consider a subsystem S with input I and output O (to simplify matters, we assume only one input and one output). Assume that this subsystem admits an integral schedule of the form $T_I(i, ...) = i + \alpha_I$, and $T_O(i, ...) = i + \alpha_O$, where i denotes the index of the input and output streams. (Notice that streams of values are multi-dimensional, and the other dimensions of the streams are represented by dots.) Such schedules are called *data-flow* schedules, since they are monotonic increasing functions of the first index i of the stream.

In other words, we assume that whenever an output $O(i, ...)$ depends on an input $I(j, ...)$ through the equations which define S, then $T_O(i, ...) > T_I(j, ...)$, and moreover, we assume that T is nonnegative.

Notice that, for all positive integer λ, λT_I and λT_O are also a valid schedule for this system. Indeed, if $T_O(i, ...) > T_I(j, ...)$, then $\lambda(T_O(i, ...)) > \lambda(T_I(j, ...))$, since T is nonnegative for all i. We call this a λ-*slow* version of S.

To implement such a system, it suffices to clock the corresponding hardware subsystem with a λ times faster clock, but with the clock enable signal valid every other λ clock tick. Note that, with this implementation, *the number of registers is unchanged* inside the hardware subsystem.

In general, a *data flow* ALPHA *schedule* is a linear function T which assigns to each variable A of an ALPHA data-flow system a schedule of the form $T_A(i, ...) = \lambda_A i + \beta_A$, with the constraints that:

1. if A depends on B through a regular data-flow system, then $\lambda_A = \lambda_B$;
2. if A depends on B through a K-up-sampler, then $\lambda_B = K\lambda_A$;
3. if A depends on B through a K-down-sampler, then $\lambda_B = \frac{\lambda_A}{K}$;
4. $\beta_A = \lambda_A \alpha_A$, for all A.

The λ's are positive integers, and the α's are nonnegative integers. This definition ensures that all elements of the system are scheduled with buffers whose length does not depend on i. The conditions on the λ coefficients give a system of homogeneous integral equations of a special type, since all equations have the form $\lambda_1 = K\lambda_2$, where K is a strictly positive rational number. In [6], it is explained how such a system can be solved in time linear in the number of equations. Once the periods are found, they can be combined with the schedule constraints that correspond to each component (i.e. ALPHA subsystem), and any solution provides a scheduling for the whole system. A structured polyhedral scheduling approach can be taken to solve this problem, as explained in [6].

3   Wrapper Architecture

The method we propose is to add to the hardware description of each component a *wrapper* that allows this component to be executed according to its imposed schedule. Fig. 4 illustrates the model of the wrapper we have developed. Besides its data inputs and outputs, a component has a clock signal (clk), a general clock-enable signal (ce) and a reset signal (rst).

It includes a finite state machine that is initialized by the reset signal, the purpose of which is to generate the various reset signals for the internal components, depending on the result of the scheduler. The wrapper includes also clock-enable generators, one for each period used in the system. These clock-enable signals are used to generate the various delayed clock-enables, by means of delay lines. Clock-enable generators are simply modulo counters, the register of which is triggered by the general clock-enable signal of the wrapper.

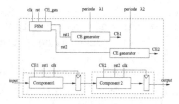

Fig. 4. Wrapper architecture. In this representation we have two components which used clock-enable signals CE1 and CE2 generate with periods λ_1 and λ_2 respectively.

4   Comparizon with Related Work

The interface between our system model and the physical world constitutes a simple model of time, whose characteristics can be summarized as follows:

- Our systems are *synchronized*, in the sense that computations are triggered by a common background clock.
- The time behavior of our components is *affine-periodic*. Each component in the system is supposed to execute at periodic instants of time, after an initial shift. This model does not support exceptional events, as true reactive systems do, unless these events were watched at regular, periodic instants of time.
- Our model of time supports some forms of parallelism. Indeed, each component can be an affine-parameterized assembly of parallel components, either pipeline (or systolic) components, or true parallel systems operating on vectors of data.
- The systems that we consider are *time-delayable*. This means that a component can be scheduled several clock ticks later or earlier, without affecting the semantics of the whole system. In other words, provided the final implementation of the system meets the dependence constraints expressed by the

initial description, we consider that its behavior is correct. This contrasts with the underlying hypothesis of *synchronous languages* such as Signal [8], where the description of the flows of data represent a strict specification of the behavior of the physical constraints put on the system, and therefore, cannot be relaxed.

- Components are *slowable*. This means that they can operate at any sub-clock of their fundamental clock, under the control of the clock-enable signal. This property has some relationship with *delay-insensitivity* where components can be executed even in the presence of some delays in their inputs.
- Time is *stretchable*. A clock is a logical clock, and nothing is said about the actual duration of clock ticks.

The work presented here is related to three separate research topics: multidimensional synchronous dataflow, latency insensitive theory, and stream languages.

4.1 Multidimensionel Synchronous Dataflow Model

The Synchronous Data Flow (SDF) model introduced by Lee and Messerschmitt[5] and its extensions are very popular for the design of digital signal processing systems, especially because of their formal properties, which allow deadlock detection, determinacy, static schedulability and the possibility to model multi-frequency systems. Initially, the SDF model was proposed for single-dimensional signal processing but work has been done to extend it to multidimensional signals, which are found for example in image processing system. Besides having greater expressive power than SDF, multidimensional synchronous dataflow (MDSFD)[5] can reveal data parallelism in a system. This model gives the ability to implement nested resetable loops and facilites data parallelism exploitation.

MDSDF shares a lot of properties with the model presented in this paper. The calculation of the periods of our components appears as a transposition, in the domain of recurrence equations, of the balance equations of SDF. But the expression of ALPHA programs is much more suited to the description of parallel systems, and closer to a loop-like description of calculations.

4.2 Latency Insensitive Design

The theory of latency-insensitive was introduced by Carloni [9] for the design of complex systems by assembling IP (Intellectual Property) components. It is based on the assumption that communications between the components is done by means of channels having *zero delay*. This theory has enabled the development of a new design methodology for large systems on a chip: the *latency-insensitive design* or LID. The main idea for communication is pipelining : the critical interconnections are partitioned into interconnections whose duration meets the time constraints imposed by the clock period by inserting logic blocks called relay stations. The relay stations are responsible for traffic regulation and deadlock management.

Carloni et al [9] proposed an approach where a wrapper provides all signal activations that are necessary for a component. The wrapper here is composed of a combinational logic whose rle is to produce those signal activations. The IP is activated only if all its inputs are valid and if one has enough memory to store the results of its next execution. If these conditions are not satisfied, the input/output process is interrupted and the component is frozen by using a clock enable signal.

Singh and Al proposed[11] an extension of Carloni's approach where it is assumed that components are frozen if no data is available for the next execution. So instead of generating one stall signal for all inputs and outputs, it generates one signal for each port. In addition, instead of the combinatorial logic it uses a finite state machine.

Casu and Macchiarulo [10] show that it is possible to replace the synchronization protocol used in the previous approaches by a periodic scheduling algorithm applied to the module clocks. This approach relies on the hypothesis that there is no irregularity in the data streams: it is never necessary to randomly freeze the IPs.

These models generate a significant additional hardware resource in order to take into account these different control signals.

4.3 Stream Languages

The approach of this paper has a relationship with *stream languages* [12]. Stream languages such as StreamIt have been developed as specialized languages to handle systems computing on streams of data. Thies [12] presents a taxonomy of such languages and relates them to functional or synchronous languages. Clearly, the model we developed here belongs to this category, as our MMALPHA description can be seen as a specialized sublanguage of ALPHA for the representation of stream calculations.

The originality of this work is to introduce a relationship with the polyhedral model, thus enabling the use of very powerful techniques to handle parallelism and to massage the adaption of parallel programs to architectures.

5 Conclusion

We have presented a model for the automatic hardware synthesis of stream systems. A simple model of time was introduced, and its properties were shown to allow a detailed scheduling to be found automatically. A hardware implementation was presented, based on the addition of a simple wrapper.

Our work combines the synchronous data-flow approach and the polyhedral model to achieve a fully automated synthesis for some kinds of streams systems which are often found in cyber physical systems. Our main contribution is to provide a model that combines both stream processing and parallel management. Indeed, the polyhedral model is a very powerful framework to discover and exploit loop parallelism, either for programming parallel architectures of for the high-level synthesis of hardware devices.

Further research will aim at investigating the limits of our simplified model of time, both in term of potential for tractable automatic methods, and in term of interface with complex cyber physical systems, where the interaction with the physical world cannot be represented only as *regular* streams of data.

References

1. Lee, E.A., Seshia, S.A.: Introduction to Embedded Systems - A Cyber-Physical Systems Approach, LeeSeshia.org (2011)
2. Saleh, R., Wilton, S., Mirabbasi, S., Hu, A., Greenstreet, M., Lemieux, G., Pande, P.P., Grecu, C., Ivanov, A.: System-on-chip: Reuse and Integration. Proceedings of IEEE 94 (2006)
3. Chana, A., Quinton, P., Derrien, S.: Conception par composants de systèmes matériels pour des applications de télécommunications. In: Proceeding of the 10th African Conference on Reseach in Computer Science and Applied Mathematics, CARI 2010, pp. 551–558 (October 2010)
4. Nikolov, H., et al.: Automated Integration of Dedicated Hardwired IP Cores in Heterogeneous MPSoCs Designed with ESPAM. EURASIP Journal on Embedded Systems, Article ID 726096, 2008, 15 pages (2008)
5. Murthy, P.K., Lee, E.A.: Multidimensional synchronous dataflow. IEEE Transactions on Signal Processing 50, 2064–2079 (2002)
6. Charot, F., et al.: Modeling and scheduling Parallel Data Flow systems using structured systems of Recurrence Equations. In: Proceedings of the 15th IEEE International Conference on Aplication-Specific System, Architectures and Processors, ASAP 2004 (2004)
7. Quinton, P., Risset, T.: Structured scheduling of recurrence equations: Theory and practice. In: Deprettere, F., Teich, J., Vassiliadis, S. (eds.) SAMOS 2001. LNCS, vol. 2268, pp. 112–134. Springer, Heidelberg (2002)
8. Smarandache, I., Le Guernic, P.: Affine transformations in SIGNAL and their application in the specification and validation of real-time system. In: Rus, T., Bertrán, M. (eds.) ARTS 1997. LNCS, vol. 1231, pp. 233–247. Springer, Heidelberg (1997)
9. Carloni, L.P., McMillan, K.L., Sangiovanni-Vincentelli, A.L.: Theory of Latency-Insensitive Design. IEEE Transactions on Computer-Aided Design of Integrated Circuits ans Systems 20(9) (September 2001)
10. Casu, M.R., Macchiarulo, L.: Adaptive Latency-Insensitive, Globally Asynchronous, Locally Synchronous Design and Test. IEEE Design & Test of Computers (2007)
11. Singh, M., Agiwal, A.: Multi-Clock Latency-Insensitive Architecture and Wrapper synthesis. Electronic Notes in Theoretical Computer Science (2006)
12. Thies, W., Karczmarek, M., Amarasinghe, S.: StreamIt: A language for streaming Applications. In: Nigel Horspool, R. (ed.) CC 2002. LNCS, vol. 2304, pp. 179–196. Springer, Heidelberg (2002)

Wireless Community Network Services: Opportunities and Challenges for DCs: Case of Rural Cameroon

Soulamite Judith Nouho Noutat, Thomas Djotio Ndié, and Claude Tangha

University of Yaounde I, National Advanced School of Engineering,
B.P 8390 Yaoundé, Cameroon
{noutatsoulamite,tdjotio,ctangha}@gmail.com

Abstract. In this paper, we present the evolution of wireless community networks (WCN), opportunities and challenges of implementation of their services. We propose an architecture of proximity phone service based on this type of network for Cameroon rural areas. Wireless technologies used in our proximity architecture are mainly the 802.11 and Bluetooth. In developing countries (DCs) such as Cameroon, a significant disparity in terms of information and communication services exist between the rural and urban communities. Our service aims at bridging the digital divide in terms of mobile telephony in DCs, with a practical case in rural Cameroon. Our approach advantages are low cost and ease of deployment of WCNs which constitute the support of our service.

Keywords: Wireless community networks, Services, Proximity telephony, WiFi, Bluetooth.

1   Introduction

To provide broadband access to citizens, communities, public institutions and enterprises in developing countries has become a strategic objective for governments and international organizations around the world. Many initiatives called community wireless networks (CWNs) have been taken in many countries [1] [2]. WCNs or wireless community projects (WCPs) designate wireless computer networks deployed within communities that develop them. These networks use wireless technologies, taking advantage of the development of standard low cost wireless technologies at (802.11x) to build clusters of networks, with the more and more increasing size at cities scale. Today, the benefits and decreasing costs of wireless networks (WNs) are motivating factors in developing countries (DCs) such as Cameroon. In addition, rural areas of Cameroon have very limited access to information technology and communication (ICT) because of the high deployment cost of operators' infrastructure and the isolation regions. For example, there are areas where it is almost impossible to make a phone call or to access the Internet and often, when possible, it is expensive.

The digital divide is a major problem in DCs. This problem is most noticeable in rural areas where no ICT service is provided, and even when found, the access to such

K. Jonas, I.A. Rai, and M. Tchuente (Eds.): AFRICOMM 2012, LNICST 119, pp. 308–317, 2013.
© Institute for Computer Sciences, Social Informatics and Telecommunications Engineering 2013

services is limited and very expensive; indeed, the installation costs are often higher in rural areas because to the lack of infrastructure such as roads and electricity. The access to these services has a direct and reciprocal correlation with the gross domestic product (GDP) per person of a country [1]. Consequently, access to services offered by ICT strongly influences the financial and social well-being of a population. In DCs, the vast majority of people (about 70 to 85% of the population) live in rural areas [3]. To allow a DC to increase its productivity and the public to enjoy a better quality of life, it would be and essential that rural communities have easy access and low cost ICT services. In this context, these services now deserve consideration because it creates new opportunities to advance health and nutrition, to expand knowledge, to stimulate economic growth and give people means to participate to the life in the community [4]. The access to these services implies on one hand, the existence of adapted networks and ICT services and on second hand, the ability of using these tools to build useful applications for the whole community. Some questions are then raised, what are relevant ICT services to a specific community? How to provide effective services at low cost? What is the operational, technical and economic feasibility development of possible solutions?

WCNs can be an alternative of bridging the digital divide in DCs, because they are based on low-cost technologies, are easy to deploy and allow implementing various specific and beneficial services to community.

The planning, deployment and operation of WCNs are specific to each community. All services and applications deployed on a WCN depend on the needs of the community. In addition, wireless technologies used for the implementation work on the free band (2.4 GHz) and the operation of these types of networks requires no license.

Our goal in this article is to present the evolution of WCNs and its services, its opportunities and its challenges in DCs. We also offer a practical case study: the development of proximity telephony in rural areas of Cameroon. Later in this paper, we are presented in section II, a state of the art on the evolution of WCNs. In section III, we present challenges and opportunities of WCNs services in rural areas. In section IV, we study the implementation feasibility of the proximity telephone service in rural areas of Cameroon and we propose an architecture of this service. We end by a conclusion and future works.

2   State of the Art

Community Networks (CNs) initially based on wired networks have emerged in North America from years 1970s to 1980s with the creation of community health services and education [5]. A community network or community project designates computer networks deployed within communities that develop them. The term community refers to a set of people with common interests. For example, if people do the same work, they are a community of practice, if they work in the same building, they are members of a professional community, if they like the same music, they are a community of musical interests, and if they make purchases on the same website, they are part of an online community [5]. The birth of the Internet in the year 1990s has greatly promoted the development of CNs, because communities could now be able to easily create from web portals. The standard wireless WiFi, born in 1999 revolutionizes Internet, because this standard allows one or more wireless terminals to connect to Internet from radio waves, and therefore, the emergence of this standard gives birth to WCNs [6]. In addition, many services can be developed from this standard however without Internet. Today, the benefits and lowering the cost of wireless networks have fostered the development of WCNs based on technologies and wireless equipment. Wireless networks have become the technology of choice for improving access to telephony and Internet services in DCs [7]. They are not only cheaper, easier and faster to deploy than traditional fixed alternatives, but make possible various business services delivery models and they are better adapted to rural communities, low-income. In addition, the integration of mobile technology in community networks allows the interaction of the user with his community as it moves, because the variety and easy of acquisition of mobile devices today make users more and more mobile [8].

Many services can be developed in WCNs. Among them we can mention: file sharing and Internet services, VoIP, streaming and location services [6] [9] [10]. File-sharing and the Internet services allow community members to send and receive files from the network community for all kinds of information (e.g health or school learning programs) on one hand, and to extend the Internet connection to other members for making online activities (buying and selling goods online, for example) on the other hand. VoIP applications allow making low cost telephone calls by using the IP protocol. Streaming applications allow community members to download streaming videos. Location-based services allow members locating in a given area strategic points such as pharmacies, bakeries, etc.

Services, benefits and lower costs for the development of WCNs are strong motivations in DCs to solve the problem of digital divide in rural areas. Analysis [11] of access to ICT in DCs shows that in addition to the lack of the costly communication infrastructures, environment (humidity, moisture and bad roads) and lack of political will (custom taxes) are not conducive to the development of these technologies However, the characteristics of the WCN show that they are appropriate and adapted to rural areas in DCs. This is what show examples of CNs deployed at Macha in Zambia [1] and at Dwesa in South Africa [2]. Traffic analysis in these two communities [12] shows that the development of these networks has improved the lives of local people, because now farmers can for example use the internet to acquire expertise on crop rotation and sell their products online or obtain telecommunications services at low cost. Furthermore, schools and health institutes have been networks thus promoting the development of telemedicine and e-learning.

3   WCNs Services: Opportunities and Challenges in DCs

A service in WCNs is an application available to members of the community and brings added value to their daily life. These services are limited or absent in rural areas of DCs. We will illustrate our remarks by the example of mobile telephony. While the mobile telephony has experienced a rapid expansion in the DCs, in particular where it is coupled with the use of prepaid cards, network providers often appear to be skeptical of its deployment in rural areas. Attempts to address this demand by developing units or entities providers of community services such as cybercafés and the small shops phones have had success in some areas, particularly in peri-urban areas, but the overall results to date are unequal [13]. Mobile phone service and a few related services (access to Internet, e-mail, computer training, etc.) to meet the development needs of the communities, there are also medical assistance services, distance education services, etc. We present in this section, some community wireless services (CWS) and the opportunities and challenges of their implementation.

3.1   Services and Opportunities

Rural areas whose activities are generally based on agriculture in DCs suffer from a more serious digital divide. For example, the training is still rudimentary and traditional, mobile telephony services are limited or absent, remote medical assistance services are completely absent. WCNs are new approaches to meet the needs of rural development. The introduction WCS in these rural areas could be a technological and economic lever to improve the level of local training and receive the service of distance education, the expertise of trainers of developed areas are the cities. For example, the rural exodus limitation is one of the consequences of the introduction of a platform or distance education service infrastructure in rural areas.

Today, mobile telephony services are limited or absent in rural areas. Because of this, rural communities have difficulty to disseminate or transmit information between them and to other externally. Even nowadays, some communities for cultural and traditional reasons use traditional methods such as drums and special sounds to communicate. The need to communicate is very important in a community and the mobile phone has become an accessible tool, to develop telephony services in rural areas improve their communication's method. Telephony services can enable the community members to make and receive telephone calls, receive emergency alerts, view information and to send and receive messages.

In the field of health, ICT services can play a role to alleviate some problems. They may do so by improving access to healthcare in rural areas, expanding the public education campaigns to promote health behaviors, by transferring diagnostics information to specialized centers, enhancing information for decision-making, by promoting the exchange of information between researchers and students, and promoting the establishment of health [4]. Generally, in rural areas, health centers provide health care basic lack of medical specialists residing mostly in urban areas. Thus, patients are poorly monitored and their life is at stake. However, remote medical assistance services can enable rural patients to benefit from the expertise of specialists in urban areas. These health services can be developed for the prevention and management of disease. Epidemiological studies can be performed and health information about epidemics can be put at the disposal of the community members [1]. These services can also provide distance or remote consultations in the community [8]. In this case, a patient could be assisted in real time by a remote doctor from his home, by using his mobile phone [14]. Although huge are opportunities for these services in the DCs, their development and implementation are facing many challenges.

3.2   Challenges

The implementation challenges community-based services vary from one region to another. However, they can be grouped into 3 categories: technical challenges, environmental challenges and cultural challenges.

a-   Technical challenges
Technical problems typically found in rural areas are: equipment failure, energy and remote information management [11].

- **Equipment problems**
Most of the typical equipment are not adapted to rural areas. The most obvious problems are: moisture, heat, dirt and dust [1] [11]. The equipment must operate in a wide range of temperature due to the lack of widespread climate control. Exposed outdoor equipment must be regularly cleaned and robust water and ultraviolet exposures. In Pailin in Cambodia, for example, a rural center staff should clean the inside of computers once a week using an electric fan [11]. Without this intervention, the machines would become less reliable and will stop functioning over time. The poor state of the roads makes transportation of difficult equipment; they may fall and be damaged.

- **Power problems**
Rural areas are generally subject to power outages. This causes damage both at the equipment level and at the network level. For example, after a power outage, the equipment may be missing and the connection may not normally take back [1]. When UPSs are used, pop-up cuts reduce the duration of battery life because the UPS is turned on and off intermittently. Regularly, the voltage can vary between 1000 and 170 Volts on a network of 220 Volts [11]. To remedy this problem, the rechargeable batteries by solar energy are an interesting alternative.

- **Remote management information problems**
The network monitoring allows technicians and administrators to improve the quality of customer service. However, rural people do not often have the required expertise. Thus, the remote network monitoring is preferred; but most existing tools are based on the Internet. How to get rid of this approach to remotely monitor community networks? One solution is to use SMS (Short Message Service) to remotely manage the network [15].

b-   Environmental Challenges
Environmental issues include: the Customs and the delays and natural disasters. Some equipment can be purchased locally, but others must be shipped. Customs and tax formalities very costly often delay the acquisition of equipment. To avoid this delay,

the equipment must be shipped long in advance [11]. Hardware import taxes are generally declining; they still remain high in many DCs including Cameroon. Life in rural areas is generally very fragile, less prepared and overcrowded. These conditions make these areas prone to natural disasters

c- Cultural Challenges

Cultural issues are one of the main challenges and vary from one region to another. It faces problems of forgery, theft, corruption and illiteracy [11]. Education, training and awareness of rural communities play a central role to solve this [4].

Taking into account these different challenges in implementation and management of WCNs, we suggest in the following section, a feasibility study and an architecture of our proximity phone service in rural areas of Cameroon.

4   Case Study: Proximity Telephony in Rural Areas of Cameroon

Cameroon is a DC located in the heart of Central Africa. It extends over an area of 475,000 km² and approximately 19 million of inhabitants [16]. In Cameroon like in many DCs, urban areas are preferred for the deployment of ICT services, while access to these services in rural areas is limited or absent. The benefits of WCNs coupled with the ease of deployment of the infrastructure and the variety of services offered are favourable for the development of ICT services in disadvantaged areas.

For our case study, we propose a proximity telephony architecture in WCN for rural areas of Cameroon.

4.1   Presentation and Relevance of the Solution

The proximity telephony service in a wireless community network is a voice, video and data service, based on proximity wireless technologies such as WIFI and Bluetooth. The communication is an essential tool in the social and economic development of a country. The availability of free or inexpensive communications services reduces the isolation of communities in rural areas and can improve the delivery of services in the areas of health, education, agriculture, etc. [17]. In his research on the rural telecommunications, Owen [18] shows that when one takes into account the literacy rate of people living in rural areas, demand for voice services is stronger than data in almost all rural communities' services. Many projects of rural telephony in South Africa, Nigeria and Zambia [19] show that the need for communication is real in rural areas and the mobile community telephony is the appropriate and adapted service to implement at a very reasonable price, a network of telephony in rural areas. In Cameroon, there is 1 (one) fixed telephony operator and 2 (two) major mobile operators [20]. They are concentrated in urban areas and provide services to yet expensive prices [20]. To improve access to telephone service in rural areas of Cameroon, we will in the next section suggest a feasibility study of the implementation of proximity telephony service based on WCNs and propose an architecture of this service.

4.2   Feasibility Study

The feasibility study is to conveniently evaluate the implementation feasibility of our service. This study is done following three axes: operational, technical and economic.

a- Operational feasibility

Proximity telephony based on wireless technologies is operationally feasible. Indeed today, many of the PDA manufacturers, such as Nokia, Motorola and BlackBerry etc. in addition to the Bluetooth standard add VoIP and Wi-Fi client applications in their mobile and portable equipment (telephones, Smartphones, PDA, Tablet, etc.). So, by Bluetooth or Wi-Fi, telephony applications can be operational on homogeneous mobile phones and can extend to heterogeneous terminals.

b- Technical feasibility

Voice over Wi-Fi or Bluetooth solutions are proposed in the literature [17] [18] [21]. Some phone manufacturers incorporate into their portable phones wireless technologies-based applications for detecting other phones from the same manufacturer in a low range zone and able to make free calls. We have the example of the T-Mobile [22] company in the United States which has a function of WIFI call in and a free WIFI phone to its subscribers. Today, voice over IP has been widely proven and knows a great success. However, voice over 802.11 uses the same Protocol mechanisms than voice over IP as procedures for H.323 and SIP (Session Initiation Protocol) [23]. This similarity guarantees the technical feasibility of our service. In addition, 802.11e variant offers the quality of service required for traffic vocal [24].

c- Economic feasibility

The development and implementation of our service will be oriented towards software and free tools such as Android and Linux with the publication of sources codes and prototypes (release management) on Sourceforge.net. The Support for deployment, the 802.11 operates in a public range (2.4 GHz) frequency without a license.

4.3   Proposition of Architecture

Our proximity telephony architecture is based on wireless technologies such as 802.11 and Bluetooth. For ensuring the QoS and to avoid collisions, one must ensure himself that there are no other wireless networks in the area sharing the same channel. The implementation architecture of the service consists of the following equipment:

- The wireless mobile, WiFi or Bluetooth compatible devices (phones, PDAs, tablets, etc.) on which the service will be installed.
- A telephony server or telephony gateway to manage telephony connections.
- The wireless terminals (access points) to route calls within the community.
- A switch wireless voice network to control and ensure the quality of service.

To make a call, two terminals must be able to open and maintain a communication session. This function is provided by the SIP (Session Initiation Protocol) [23] and QoS by WIBACK [25] or DiffServ [26] for WIFI calls and protocol TCS (Telephony Control protocol Specification) [27] for Bluetooth calls. Figure 1 below shows our proximity telephony architecture.

Fig. 1. Proximity telephony architecture

The communication's scenario within the architecture is as follows:

- A call is initiated by a terminal;
- The application checks if the maximum number of simultaneous calls is reached;
- If yes, the call is rejected;
- Otherwise, a communication session is open.

4.4   Operation of Our Solution and Its Relevance

The service will be installed on the mobile phones of community members. These phones must support Bluetooth or WIFI technology. Members will be able to make and receive calls anywhere within the community. A value added service will be also provided to enable inter-communities calls (Roaming).

Wireless networks have become the technology of choice for improving access to telephony and Internet services in DCs. Many WCNs projects are described in the literature. These projects focus much more on the deployment of wireless infrastructure [1] [2] and the quality of traffic [12] while our project focuses much more on the implementation of operational services in this type of network.

5   Conclusion and Futures Works

In this article, we have presented the evolution of community networks, from wired on fixed terminals to wireless on mobile equipment. The emergence of wireless technology has revolutionized the WCNs. Indeed, although its implementation raises many technical, environmental and cultural challenges, opportunities for its services and low cost of deployment are factors favorable to the development of ICT services in rural communities of DCs. The architecture of proximity telephony based on WCNs- in rural areas of Cameroon presented in this article is designed on the basis of free tools. We are currently exploring the problems of mobility in the WCN: the handover and roaming.

Our future work is first to study protocols SIP and H.323 for their adaptation in the WIFI, then DifServ and WiBACK protocols for the management of the QoS, then to concretely implement the proximity phone service. We will finally build a prototype to operate in a rural area of Cameroon.

References

1. Matthee, K.W., Mweemba, G., Pais, A.V., van Stam, G., Rijken, M.: Bringing Internet Connectivity to Rural Zambia using a Collaborative Approach. In: ICTD 2007, Bangalore, India (December 2007)
2. Mandioma, M.: Rural Internet Connectivity: A Deployment in Dwesa-Cwebe, Eastern Cape, South Africa. Master's thesis, University of Fort Hare (November 2007)
3. Kozma, R.: Toward and African Knowledge Network: ICT, Rural Development and the Green Revolution. In: Proc. Intl Conf. eLearning Africa 2007, Nairobi, Kenya, May 28-30 (2007)
4. Chaker, S.: Pour une stratégie en faveur des nouvelles technologies d'information et de la communication dans les pays les moins avancés d'Afrique, UIT- Novembre (2002)
5. Carroll, J.M., Rosson, M.B.: Theorizing mobility in community networks. Int. J. Human-Computer Studies 66, 944–962 (2008)
6. Frangoudis, P.A., Polyzos, G.C., Kemerlis, V.P.: Wireless Community Networks: An Alternative Approach for Nomadic Broadband Network Access. IEEE Communications Magazine (May 2011)
7. Hammond, A., Paul, J.: A New Model for Rural Connectivity, world Resources Institute-Development through Enterprise (May 2006)
8. Farooq, U., Carroll, J.M.: Mobilizing Community Networks, Center for Human-Computer Interaction, Department of Computer Science,Virginia Polytechnic Institute and State University (Virginia Tech), umocec (2003)
9. Efstathiou, E.C., Elianos, F.A., Frangoudis, P.A., Kemerlis, V.P., Paraskevaidis, D.C., Polyzos, G.C., Stefanis, E.C.: Building Secure Media Applications over Wireless Community Networks. In: 13th HP Openview University Association (HPOVUA) Workshop, Nice, France (May 2006)
10. Elianos, F.A., Plakia, G., Frangoudis, P.A., Polyzos, G.C.: Structure and Evolution of A Large-Scale Wireless Community Network. In: Proc. 10th IEEE Int'l. Symp. World of Wireless, Mobile and Multimedia Networks (WoWMoM 2009), Kos, Greece (2009)
11. Brewer, E., Demmer, M., Ho, M., Honicky, R.J., Pal, J., Plauche, M., Surana, S.: The challenges of technology research for developing regions. IEEEComputer (June 2005)
12. Johnson, D.L., Pejovic, V., Belding, E.M., van Stam, G.: Traffic Characterization and Internet Usage in Rural Africa. In: WWW 2011 – Web for Emerging Regions Paper, Hyderabad, India, March 28-April 1 (2011)
13. Ó Siochrú, S., Girard, B.: Community-based Networks and Innovative Technologies: New models to serve and empower the poor, A Report for UNDP (2005)

14. Ndié, T.D., Batchakui, B., Tangha, C.: VeSMDiag: a VeSMp-based System for Remote Medical Diagnosis. In: ICEGOV 2010 Proceedings of the 4th International Conference on Theory and Practice of Electronic Governance, pp. 369–370 (2010)

15. Ndie, T.D.: Contribution à l'Administration et à la Sécurité Réseau: Very Short Message Protocol (VeSMp) et Modèle d'Ontologie Centré sur la Gestion d'Intrusions réseaux (MOCGIR), Thèse de Doctorat PhD, Ecole Nationale Supérieure Polytechnique, Université de Yaoundé 1 (2008)

16. 3e Rpgh, La Population du Cameroun En (2010),
    http://www.statistics-cameroon.org/downloads/
    La_population_du_Cameroun_2010.pdf

17. Julius, W.: Voice Over WiFi: On Fabricating an Open Access Neighbourhood Wireless Local Loop for Telecommunication, Degree Master of Science in Computer Scie Makerere University, Option: Computer Science (March 2008)

18. Owen, D.: Community Telecommunications: A new Technical and Business Model. USAID (Janvier 2006)

19. ICT update, Telephonie rurale, Numéro 45 (Octobre 2008),
    http://ictupdate.cta.int

20. Les nouvelles de l'ART « Magazine d'informations et d'analyses de l'ART Cameroun (Janvier 2008)

21. Sahd, C., Thinyane, H.: Community Telephone Networks in Africa Bridging the gap between poverty and technology. International Journal on Advances in Networks and Services 5(1&2) (2012)

22. http://support.t-mobile.com/docs/DOC-1680 (visité le August 03, 2012)

23. Rosenberg, J., Schulzrinne, H., Camarillo, G., Johnston, A., Peterson, J., Sparks, R., Handley, M., Schooler, E.: SIP: Session Initiation Protocol, Request for Comments: 3261 (June 2002)

24. Mangold, S., Choi, S., May, P., Klein, O., Hiertz, G., Stibor, L.: IEEE 802.11e Wireless LAN for Quality of Service

25. Fokus, F.: WiBACK – Wireless Backhaul Technology, An overview about the concepts and the current status (as of July 2011) of our ongoing research & development efforts,
    http://net4dc.fokus.fraunhofer.de/en/projects/wiback.html

26. Francois, S., Renard, A.-L., Rovaris, J.: Etude du service DiffServ (2002-2003)

27. Telephony Control Protocol Specification, BLUETOOTH SPECIFICATION Version 1.1, 22 pp. 443–510 (February 2001)

Implementation of a Function
VoWiFi Communication
on Android-x86

Christian Engelbert Ngono and Thomas Djotio Ndié

UY1, Faculty of Science, Department of Computer Science,
LIRIMA, MASECNESS,
P.O. Box 8390 Yaounde, Cameroon
Ngono.christian@yahoo.fr,
tdjotio@gmail.com

Abstract. In this paper, we present the implementation of a VoWiFi communication function in android-x86- based environment . The goal is to implement a communication program that uses VoIP WiFi to allow making free communication with computers.

Keywords: Android, *Wi-Fi,* VoIP, VoWiFi, *SIP.*

1 Introduction

VoWiFi is a hybrid technology that has qualities of both ascendants that are: Wi-Fi that provides the freedom of wireless with a saving of cabling, VoIP, which provides all the benefits of IP convergence with prior all, an ability to reduce telecom costs. For a user with a computer, VoIP solutions like Skype are numerous. VoWiFi is already supported to allow two Android phones to communicate freely with each other through P2P (Peer-to-Peer) or via an AP (access point) [1]. Android is the open source operating system based on the Linux kernel, dedicated to smartphones, PDAs, tablets and more others. It is possible to use Android on any computer based on the x86 architecture through the open source project Android-x86 [2] with the extension "Buildroid for VirtualBox" [3], the initiative aims to provide "as good as possible" to use Android support in VirtualBox machine. Buildroid VM supports emulation of the WiFi connection. The main objective of this paper is to develop a mechanism for communication on VoWiFi in the environment of Android-x86 without worrying about the cost of communication.

2 Related Concepts

2.1 VoIP

The VoIP is a pure IP communication technology. It is possible for any company to merge network and telecom applications benefit from extensive local (unified

K. Jonas, I.A. Rai, and M. Tchuente (Eds.): AFRICOMM 2012, LNICST 119, pp. 318–322, 2013.

messaging, CTI, ...) and optimize costs by using a common output network, the Internet. These choices are reasoned according to technical criteria, functional, economical ... and must be completed at the level of analysis by a real approach to service level. Figure 1 illustrates the VoIP communication.

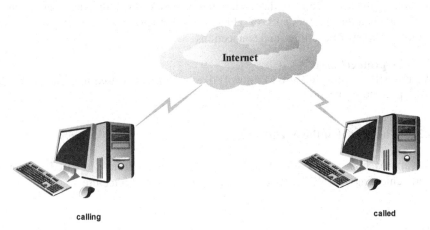

Fig. 1. Example of VoIP communication

2.2   VoWiFi on IP Phones

In VoWiFi, the protocol uses the same mechanisms as VoIP (H.323 and SIP). But it does not benefit to the extent of the allocation procedures Diffserv service classes or booking flow RSVP (Resource Reservation Protocol). This is explained by the very foundations of Wi-Fi technology which grants equal access to resources.

3   Our Solution

3.1   Android-x86 Environments

a)   Advantages
The Android operating system has several advantages: it breaks the boundaries of the application, it is opened, which allows developers to create pertinent mobile applications and it allows easy development of rich applications by providing range of useful tools and libraries.

b)   Structure
Android consists of four layers: the applications layer which contains all third-party applications that developpers create, the applications Framework layer which provides components used for application developers, the native libraries layer that contains the libraries C / C + + used by Android system. These are provided to

developers through the Framework implementation and the linux kernel layer to manage the equipment and providing hardware abstraction to the rest of the software stack.

c) Work with Wi-Fi
Android provides access to the underlying network state, broadcasting intents to notify application components of changes in network connectivity and offering control over network settings and connections

d) The protocol used
We use SIP (Session Initiation Protocol) like in VoIP. It is used to establish, modify and terminate connections.

3.2   The Model of the Architecture

Our approach is based on VoIP technology to allow Android-x86-based computers communicating in a WiFi network. Figure 2 shows our architecture.

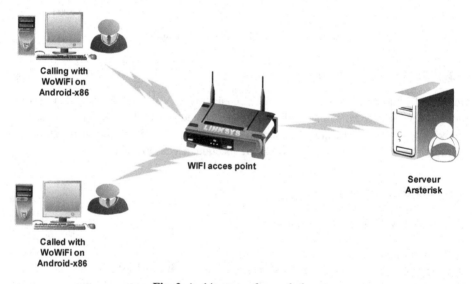

Fig. 2. Architecture of our solution

4   Implementation and Deployment

Our solution is developed with the eclipse IDE. The operating system used is Android-x86 for VirtualBox Buildroid *(http://www.buildroid.org)*. It is deployed as shown in the figure 3.

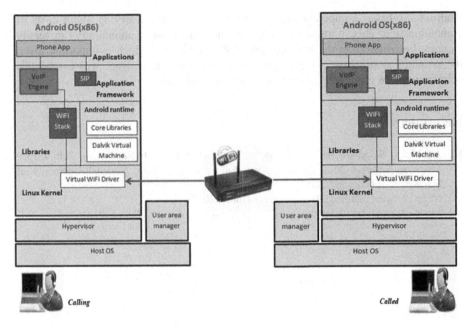

Fig. 3. Deployment of the solution

5   Economic Feasibility of the Solution

Today, many communities use the wireless network for Internet connection, in rural areas this network becomes useless due to lack of internet service provider; without it, we can exploit this solution requires only one access point and computers equipped with the wifi technology. To prove the economic feasibility of our solution here is the price of equipment required[1].

- A PCMCIA Wifi - TEW-421PC to connect laptops in a wireless network costing 17.00€
- The PCI WiFi-N Essential 300Mbps TEW-643PI to connect the PC in a wireless network costing 22.99€
- The Wireless N Access Point TP-LINK TL-W801ND can create or extend a wireless broadband network N or connect to a wireless network costing 32.50€

The implementation of our solution is economically feasible because it is cheaper an adequate for DCs.

6   Conclusion and Future Works

We present in this article the implementation of a communication function VoWiFi on Android-x86-based environments. It allows VoIP communication between

---

[1] http://www.touslesprix.com/comparer/

Android-x86-based computers in a WiFi network without worrying about costs of communication. This solution allows to communicate within a community (university campus, business, short on distances up to 300 or 500 m), which is important given the economical situation of developing countries. Our future work will extend this solution to allow computers to communicate different cells.

References

[1] Ali Malik, S., ulAin Ali, N., Jahan, S.: Android Wi-Fi P2P Networking 26th IEEEP Students' Seminar 2011 Pakistan Navy Engineering College, National University of Sciences & Technology (2011)
[2] http://www.android-x86.org/ (Juillet 2012)
[3] http://www.buildroid.org/blog/?page_id=121 (Juillet 2012)

An Approach of Making Telephony in a Local Wireless Environment: Application to Bluetooth Technology

Nono Louenkam Guy Gaspard and Thomas Djotio Ndié

University of Yaounde I, National Advanced School of Engineering,
B.P 8390 Yaoundé, Cameroon
gnonog@ymail.com, tdjotio@gmail.com

Abstract. In this paper, we study the possibility of making telephony using Bluetooth wireless technology in order to significantly reduce the cost of communication for two or more users within a short or medium range wireless area. For this, we defined an hybrid (semi ad-hoc and semi infrastructure) GSM[1]-based network model with a set of protocols (scatternet building protocol and routing protocol) to manage the exchange of text and voice packets through the network.

Keywords: Bluetooth, protocol, routing, telephony, voice, synchronization, piconet, scatternet.

1 Introduction

Despite the significant evolution in the telecommunications sector over the past 20 years worldwide, the problems of communication costs and network coverage are still a major challenge for developing countries (which is sometimes due to lack of financial resources). Bluetooth was originally designed to connect various wireless devices like printers, wireless headsets, mice, keyboards, cell phones, PDAs, GPS and others [1]. With its evolution over the years since its creation in 1994 by Erickson, many companies (more than 15000) in the areas of telecommunication, computing, networking, and electronics consumer have formed an association call SIG[2] to oversee the specifications development, to manage the programs qualifications, and to protect the trademarks. Because of that association, Bluetooth is seen as a future solution in reducing cost of mobile communication due to its low energy consummation, the low cost of its chip and its expansion over the world.

That said, we question the feasibility of using the various features of Bluetooth technology to deliver to people in developing countries and others a telephony solution of good quality and low cost in a short or medium range wireless area.

---

[1] Global System for Mobile Communication or Groupe Spécial Mobile :
http://en.wikipedia.org/wiki/GSM
[2] Special Interest Group:
http://en.wikipedia.org/wiki/Bluetooth_Special_Interest_Group

K. Jonas, I.A. Rai, and M. Tchuente (Eds.): AFRICOMM 2012, LNICST 119, pp. 323–330, 2013.
© Institute for Computer Sciences, Social Informatics and Telecommunications Engineering 2013

2   Related Works

Several wireless technologies exist nowadays such as: GSM [2], GPRS (General Packet Radio Service)[3], UMTS (universal mobile telecommunication system), Wi-Fi[4], Wi-Fi direct [3], infrared and Bluetooth. Each of these solutions has its advantages and disadvantages when it comes to telephony.

Many works have been done in the domain of Bluetooth communication. We have for example point to point voice chat application, point to point talky–walky application. But all that applications are unusable when the distance is more than 10 meters.

In addition to being a challenge, we opted for the Bluetooth technology because it offers interesting characteristics like low energy consumption, the small size of its chip and its relatively low cost compared to other wireless technologies mentioned above.

3   Applications of Bluetooth Telephony

3.1   Application in the Academic Field

A University campus is constituted of a large mass of people in a small perimeter. The majority of them are students and teachers. Each one has each a Bluetooth-enable phone most of the time. That said, it is a good environment to deploy and experiment our solution to allow people to easily communicate within a short range distance, less more than 100 meters (with the routers nodes). Such a solution would significantly reduce communications costs because two students could for example mutually share their positions in the campus without the need of any third party telephony operator.

3.2   Applications in the Field of Health

Bluetooth telephony could be very useful in hospitals. In generally in some health centers, staff uses "bippers" to contact doctors or specialists in cases of emergencies. But in general, there is not enough "bippers" for all staff including nurses, support staff and patients care. Nevertheless, each of these can easily obtain a Bluetooth-enabled mobile phone to be contacted at any time when it is expected of emergency and if he wants to be located in the hospital. It would also be easy to the visitors who often have difficulty to locate their patients.

3.3   Application in the Administrative Field and Company

The phone by Bluetooth could facilitate interpersonal communications in the administrative institutions such as ministries, delegations, central services and many.

---

[3] http://fr.wikipedia.org/wiki/General_Packet_Radio_Service
[4] http://fr.wikipedia.org/wiki/Wi-Fi

In general, in these structures, internal communications are made via wire line operators networks. With our solution, the staff can communicate freely through only the cost of installing nodes routers necessary for its deployment. It is the same for private organizations (companies) who, instead of spending large sums of money in terms of internal phone calls, could simply deploy our solution in their structure to minimize communication costs.

3.4   Application in the Field of Proximity Security

Some districts to ensure their safety organize groups of self-defense who spend all the night watching the people movements in the neighborhood. But in districts that have multiple entries or that are large enough, it becomes very difficult for a group to ensure the security of all residents or of all buildings in the neighborhood simultaneously. Well with our solution, all residents could contact the self-defense group in case of aggression or any incident even though he did not have enough airtime to make a call via the GSM network.

3.5   Application in the Field of Proximity Advertising

It is commonly called Bluetooth marketing. This is an application for streaming media (sound, image, slideshow and video) to any nearby Bluetooth devices. Similarly, our application can be used to broadcast SMS in a close neighborhood. For example a supermarket in full promotion may advertise its products using our solution to broadcast SMS and even multimedia content to anyone who has a Bluetooth phone and that are within range of the terminal distribution.

4   Our Solution

4.1   Presentation of the Approach

Our approach is simple. A device to communicate will first check if the peer device with which it wishes to communicate is its vicinity. If it is the case, a synchronous communication channel is created to allow voice communication between both devices.

under 10m

Fig. 1. point to point communication

Otherwise, the device initiates a communication request to the access point (AP) (router node) that he has chosen as the master. This request includes among others: its address in the piconet notably its BD_ADDR, its clock, and the address of the recipient node. The AP will therefore be responsible to locate the position of the destination node and to choose the best route to allow communication.

4.2   Model and Architecture of the Solution

Here we will define all the elements involved in the implementation of our solution that the architecture will be presented below in figure 4. Particularly, the router node, the scatternet formation protocol, the routing protocol and the protocol for mobility management.

4.2.1   The Router Node

We define a router node simply as a Class 1[5] Bluetooth device. In our model, a router node can be a set of smart Bluetooth device connected to an USB Bluetooth hub to increase not only the number of simultaneous connection of mobile devices to the router node but also to increase its capacity to support a large flow of data. Figure 2 below depicts an example of a Bluetooth hub:

Fig. 2. Example of Bluetooth hub

The main functions of that node will be:

- The formation and the management of the piconets
- The receipt and relieves of the different signals radio
- The formation and management of the piconets and scatternet
- The reception and relays of different radio signals.
- Creation of communicational channel between the sender and the recipient.
- The encryption and decryption of the data on the network
- Routing of packets between different Bluetooth terminals
- Management of enabling and disabling a link to a Bluetooth mobile station.
- Eventually the management of mobility of mobile nodes i.e. the handover.
- It will also handle the network management, the subscribers (users), services, and other goods.

---

[5] Note that Bluetooth has 3 class classified by maximum permitted power and maximum range.

To ensure wide signal range and good visibility, we will need a pylon which can be located above a two-levels building. The figure 3 below is an example of an installation of the routing node. We have called it the Bluetooth BTS.

Fig. 3. Example of router node called BTS Bluetooth

4.2.2   The Scatternet Formation Protocol

We have defined a protocol for scatternet formation based on the BTCP (Bluetooth Topology Control Protocol) [4]. Like BTCP, our protocol consists of 3 basics' phases:

- Phase1: election of a SUPER MASTER (among different routers nodes) to manage the scatternet formation process. It is the same as electing the coordinator in BTCP protocol. The only difference is that in our case, nodes in competition are only router nodes. To assure this constraint, we will add in the FHS[6] messages [5] a constant to limit the involvement of the other Bluetooth mobile devices.
- Phase2: the definition of roles for each router node. A router node can be a MASTER or a ROUTER-BRIDGE[7] in a piconet. If we have less than seven participants (router nodes) to the scatternet formation, the SUPER MASTER will be the bridge of all router nodes. If we have more than 7 in the scatternet formation, we will have a complex network with many piconets. Having a global view of the network, SUPER MASTER will define a list of router nodes that will have the role of master in a piconet. And for each master of that nodes list, it will define another list of Bridge nodes to interconnect the piconet of that master to other piconets in scatternet formation.
- Phase3: the formation of the piconets for each router node. In this step, the SUPER MASTER gives the order to other router nodes to send connections

---

[6] FHS (Frequency Hopping synchronization) is used to synchronize the slaves during the establishment of the piconet. This package contains: 240 bits of useful data, address BDA from the source, the clock of the source and more.

[7] ROUTER-BRIDGE is a router node which is a BRIDGE in the high level network where all slaves are only router nodes.

requests to every Bluetooth mobiles phone around them. For that, its piconet will be formed by all devices which will accept its request. If a device is in the range of scope of two masters, the one with the strongest transmission signal will be chosen as its master.

4.2.3   The Routing Protocol

We have also defined a hybrid routing protocol based on B.A.T.M.A.N. [6] protocol and ZRP (Zone Routing Protocol) [7] protocol in other to have a good quality of service (i.e. a good fluidity of voice communications), to limit the saturation of the network resources and the consumption of electric energy by mobiles phones and to effectively identify the position of a device in the network. Our routing protocol is divided into two parts.

First, like B.A.T.M.A.N. every node sends regularly in the network a broadcast message to inform its neighbors of its existence and to share with it its routing table. We use this method because we suppose that router nodes which are fixed will be permanently alimented and should not have problems of electric energy.

The second part concerned every piconet. When a node leaves a piconet, its router node update immediately its routing table and sends a broadcast message through the network to all its neighbors. This will ease the mobility management in our network.

We have also thought a way of managing the equipment mobility by setting many parameters in mobile application to choose a good AP based on the strength of the signal received and to update routing tables of nodes during a change of a router node to another one.

The figure 4 below depicts the graphical architecture of our solution.

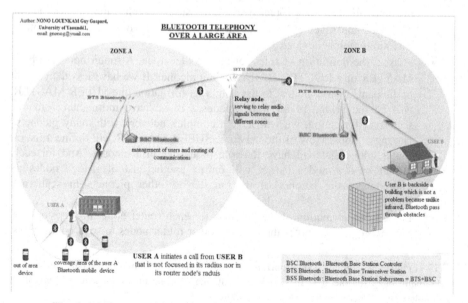

Fig. 4. Architecture with more than 10 meters of distance between two users

This architecture presents a communication between two users who are not in the same router node area. The user B is backward a building which is not a problem because unlike infrared, Bluetooth pass through obstacles

This architecture is based on the functioning of the classical GSM with the BTS[8] and the BSC[9]. But in our case, each Bluetooth BTS is connected to a Bluetooth BSC. The whole form what we call Bluetooth BSS like the BSS[10] in GSM networks. A Bluetooth BTS here is a router node and Bluetooth BSC is a Server which will manage different queries, routing communications and information storage about users.

4.3   Technical and Economic Feasibility of the Solution

Here we outline a technical and economic study with a small cost analysis of our solution. For each router node, we'll need a Bluetooth hub (less than 100 € [7] based on the number of ports) and Bluetooth key (5 minimum less than 20€ * 5 = 100 €). For the tower that we will use, it should be more than 10m in height. To reduce the cost, a tower of only 10m height can be located on a building with more than 2 levels (less than 1000€). For the individual Bluetooth BSC, we'll need a server capable of managing different queries, routing communications and information storage about users. We think about to a server less than 1000€ [8] according to the characteristics. This gives us a total cost of 2200€ for each node router against € 160 000 [9] for a GSM solution. But these prices may be scaled down with the manufacture of a specialized component containing only the features we need.

5   Conclusion and Future Works

In this paper, we have suggested a very interesting model to make the telephony using Bluetooth technology considering the low range of that technology. For this, we have defined several new concepts such as "router nodes", and we have based our architecture on the GSM network model that has proven its effectiveness so far over the world. Since we have not yet finished with the concrete implementation of our model, we propose to make further study of that model to make it operational on a large scale and in the service of larger number of user by management of mobility, handover and moreover.

References

1. SIG, Bluetooth. BLUETOOTH SPECIFICATION. Version 4.0. Europe, Japan, USA, Canada: Bluetooth SIG (2010)
2. De Wulf, M.: Memoire de Master, Un logiciel d'illustration des protocoles GSM et GPRS sur la voie radio. Rue Grandgagnage (2001)

---

[8] http://en.wikipedia.org/wiki/Base_Station_subsystem
[9] http://fr.wikipedia.org/wiki/Base_Station_Controller
[10] http://en.wikipedia.org/wiki/Base_Station_Subsystem

3. Wi-Fi Alliance. Wi-Fi CERTIFIED Wi-Fi Direct™: Connect with the possibilities. s.l. : Wi-Fi Alliance (2010)
4. Theodoros, S., Bhagwat, P., Tassiulas, L., LaMaire, R.: Distributed topology construction of Bluetooth personal area networks. In: Proceedings of the Twentieth Annual Joint Conference of the IEEE Computer and Communications Societies, University of Maryland at College Park, Maryland, p. 10 (2001)
5. ICU, Bluetooth Packets, multimedia Laboratory, Information and Communication University. Korea: special topic on ad-hoc and sensor network (2003)
6. Neumann, A., Aichele, C.E., Lindner, M.: B.A.T.M.A.N Status Report (2007), http://open-mesh.net/batman
7. Twenga. Hub Bluetooth : 8 offres parmi 5 boutiques. reseaux.twenga.fr. (August 14, 2012), http://reseaux.twenga.fr/hub- (cited: August 14, 2012)
8. RueDuCommerce. RueDuCommerce. Serveurs (2012), http://www.rueducommerce.fr/Ordinateurs/17-PC/1947-Serveurs.html (cited: August 14, 2012)
9. Delmas, J.: Les relais GSM, vol. I. Creative Commons, California (2006), http://lesrelaisgsm.juliendelmas.com

Author Index